Comments from Readers

Your book is great! Easy to understand, clear examples - it is already dog-eared!
- Nancy Campbell, HR Mgr
  Mountain View, CA

I wanted to let you know that I received the "secrets" book today and I am already finding it very helpful. We have done our first data export ... I am finding all sorts of helpful information in the book to help me "clean" up our data. Thanks again.
- Kathleen Titano
  HR Manager
  San Francisco, CA

I believe I have already sent you one note about how valuable and what a well-written workbook "Secrets.." is; however, it's worth mentioning again!!
- Diane K. Roper
  HR Manager

The Secrets of Affirmative Action Compliance is a handbook for my activities. Thank you.
- Dottie A. McElyea
  UTMCK

I love the book and could hardly put it down. I haven't finished it but it is a high priority for me. Really really super job.
- Ann J. Willson, SPHR
  Owner, Human Resource Directions - Consulting Services for Employers

Secrets of Affirmative Action Compliance

of

Affirmative
Action
Compliance

William H. Truesdell, SPHR
President
The Management Advantage, Inc.

Ninth Edition
2010

"This publication is designed to provide accurate and authoritative information in regard to the subject matter covered. It is sold with the understanding that the publisher is not engaged in rendering legal, accounting or other professional service. If legal advice or other expert assistance is required, the services of a competent professional person should be sought."

- from a *Declaration of Principles* jointly adopted by a
Committee of the American Bar Association and a
Committee of Publishers and Associations.

First Edition: January, 1996
Second Edition: February, 1997
Third Edition: May, 1998
Fourth Edition: February, 2000
Fifth Edition: January, 2001
Sixth Edition: July, 2003
Seventh Edition: April, 2006
Eighth Edition: March 2008
Ninth Edition: January 2010

Printed in the U.S.A.

Published by: The Management Advantage, Inc., P.O. Box 3708, Walnut Creek, CA 94598-0708.

ISBN: 978-1-879876-51-4

Library of Congress Control Number: 2009940920

<u>DEDICATION</u>

For the better part of my adult life, I have worked with people from the U.S. Department of Labor's Office of Federal Contract Compliance Programs. I have always been on the outside, looking into the federal organization. Over that time, my appreciation for the role they play has increased. They are guardians of the process for Equal Employment Opportunity within the community of federal contractors.

As you can imagine, there is a mix of talent among the compliance officials, just as there is a mix of talent within contractor organizations. Yet, through all these years, compliance officials have become better trained and more properly oriented in their role because of their commitment to better fulfill that role.

It is to those federal employees that this edition of *Secrets of Affirmative Action Compliance* is dedicated.

INTRODUCTION

Since the *Civil Rights Act of 1964* was first enacted calendar pages have been turning for 46 years. In that time, countless numbers of HR professionals (and legal professionals) have come and gone. Many of them have done their very best to abide by the letter, and the spirit, of that law. Equal Employment Opportunity can be found in Title VII of that Act. It has given us a guidepost for everything else, including Affirmative Action and Diversity programs.

When Affirmative Action was invented as a way to implement Equal Employment Opportunity across the nation, it was almost universally misunderstood. I remember being told in employee meetings that introduced the subjects, how affirmative action would give a "leg up" to people who just hadn't had the chance yet. In reality, those early days saw much misuse of the program. Affirmative Action became the shining light for minorities…the beacon of preferential treatment. That perception has been quite tenacious and those of us in the field continue to battle to correct it today.

Over the many years since 1964 our U.S. Supreme Court has helped us understand more about what Congress intended in its original work. And, it has helped us clarify in our thinking what types of applications fit with our Constitution and which do not.

Today, all but the seriously uninformed among us, understand that Affirmative Action Plans are a tool for assuring Equal Employment Opportunity. They force federal contractors to construct outreach and recruiting programs so the representation of qualified minorities and women can be on par with the supply of qualified folks in our self-defined recruiting territory. As days go on, more and more emphasis is being placed on recruiting qualified people with disabilities and veterans into our workforce.

While the system is not perfect, and there remains some misunderstanding (as well as some abuse by contractors and enforcement officials alike) the programs we call "Affirmative Action" in the employment world have given us more equal employment opportunity. That, after all, is what they were supposed to do from the beginning.

Best wishes on your efforts in these important areas of employment management.

Bill Truesdell
January 2010

TABLE OF CONTENTS

<u>TABLE OF CONTENTS</u>

CHAPTER 1

UNDERSTANDING THE BASICS
(Foundation, Basis, Authorization, Reasoning, Politics)

EMPLOYMENT AFFIRMATIVE ACTION DEFINED

Those results-oriented actions that a contractor must take to ensure equal employment opportunity.

In the Beginning – A Business Decision

In the beginning is a business decision: "Do we want to do business with the federal government?" It might be stated in other ways, like: "Do we wish to have revenue from federal government business?"

That is a basic business decision. Any organization can make that decision, opting for or against federal government business and revenues. Once made in favor of conducting business with the federal government, then there is no choice but to comply with existing regulations and laws on affirmative action implementation.

The trick is to make the basic business decision with the knowledge that affirmative action **may** be required in your organization.

In some ways it is like the question of taxes. If we wish to live in this country and earn our living here, we must abide by the laws that say we have to pay income tax. We may not like that, but comply we must. Failure to comply brings stiff penalties in tax evasion cases. The same is true of affirmative action compliance. The penalties are loss of government revenue on existing contracts and prevention (debarment) from participating in future contracting opportunities for up to five years.

Affirmative Action - The Programs We Love to Hate

The term "Affirmative Action" has come to mean many different things. But, where did it originate?

According to Michelle P. Crockett and James B. Thelen, attorneys with Miller, Canfield, Paddock and Stone in Lansing, Michigan, the earliest mention of the term was in an Executive Order (E.O. 10925) issued by President John F. Kennedy on March 6, 1961. It was used in a description of the obligation federal contractors have to avoid employment discrimination in their workplaces. Ms. Crockett and Mr. Thelen wrote about their research in SHRM's *Legal*

Report, July-August 2007.[1]

Presidential Executive Order #10925, March 6, 1961:

"...*The contractor will not discriminate against any employee or applicant for employment because of race, creed, color, or national origin. The **contractor will take <u>affirmative action</u> to ensure that applicants are employed, and that employees are treated during employment, without regard to their race, creed, color, or national origin**. Such action shall include, but not be limited to, the following: employment, upgrading, demotion or transfer; recruitment or recruitment advertising; layoff or termination; rates of pay or other forms of compensation; and selection for training, including apprenticeship...*"

(See the entire Executive Order at: http://www.eeoc.gov/abouteeoc/35th/thelaw/eo-10925.html)

As you are likely aware, the original affirmative action program for federal contractor's employment actions has been expanded by federal, state and local governments to include purchasing programs and college admissions under the heading of affirmative action. Since there has been so much attention paid to the subject of affirmative action by the media in recent years, it might be helpful to sort out what affirmative action really is and how it has changed in recent times.

The term "Affirmative Action" has been used as a blanket to cover several programs originated by federal, state or local governments. Much political fodder has been generated by fostering this obfuscation. Whether one agrees with any of the programs or not is immaterial. What is important is achieving clarity about what has been impacted by court decision recently and what will likely happen in the future with any or all of these programs.

The three major areas of "affirmative action" are: 1) Market place programs; 2) College and university admissions programs; and, 3) Employment programs.

1. Market Place Programs

As recently as 1990, the U.S. Supreme Court held that preference in public contracting is legal. The preference was in favor of minorities in the case of *Metro Broadcasting v. Federal Communications Commission*. That was the practice until 1995 when the Court again addressed the question in *Adarand Constructors, Inc. v. Pena*. In June, 1995 the Court held that **racial preference in public contracting is illegal**. This decision calls into question what have been generally referred to as Minority Business Enterprise Programs and Women Business Enterprise Programs (M/WBE) as well as incentives under federal contracts for hiring "disadvantaged" subcontractors. Federal statute presumed that minority-owned firms, regardless of size, were "disadvantaged." The *Adarand* decision had three recurring themes in Court direction about what can constitute valid preferential procurement programs: 1) They must remedy past discrimination (which must be specifically identified); 2) They must be temporary in nature; and, 3) They must not constitute a quota system.

---

[1] Society for Human Resource Management (SHRM), Legal Report, 1800 Duke Street, Alexandria, VA 22314

Meanwhile, California Governor Wilson signed Executive Order W-124-95 on June 1, 1995, repealing approximately 100 orders he and previous governors had signed regarding preferential treatment of minorities and women in California state programs subject to the control of his office. His Executive Order mandates that individual merit be the new standard for employment and contracting in state government programs controlled by the Governor's office. This Order does nothing to impact programs created by the State Legislature and operated under scrutiny of state agencies such as the Department of Fair Employment and Housing.

For all practical purposes, special treatment for minorities and women in government contracting programs has come to an end. The only such programs from now on will be under court direction or constructed using the Supreme Court's narrow guidelines.

The current shape of program design has moved away from sex- and race-based identification to economic status identification. They are often referred to as "economically disadvantaged" programs. (Small Business, Disadvantaged Business) Anyone can qualify if they meet the economic criteria thresholds established for the programs. And, that seems to reflect the general emotional positioning of the American populous.

2. College and University Admissions Programs

The 1978 U.S. Supreme Court decision in *Regents of the University of California v. Bakke* held **quotas in public education are illegal**. On July 20, 1995, the University of California Board of Regents voted 14 to 10 to end race-based and gender-based hiring and contracting by January 1, 1996. And, by a vote of 15 to 10 the Regents decided to end race-based and gender-based admissions by January 1, 1997. There is a provision that these actions can be ignored if the federal government would use them to restrict the flow of federal funding now enjoyed by the University of California system. (It is reported that the day following Regent action, the Office of Federal Contract Compliance Programs [OFCCP] was on the phone to the University's Office of the President to discuss the University's intentions under federal regulations. They were told that little change will result from the Regents' action.) There were actually two issues... The first involved student admissions policy and procedures. Well, that had been dealt with under *Bakke*. There can be no set asides or reservations of admission slots based on race. It's that simple. The second issue involved a question of faculty hiring and tenure. That issue must be addressed by the University's affirmative action program under federal requirements. If the University fails to implement its employment affirmative action program, or abandons it altogether, the Department of Labor's OFCCP will find they are not in compliance. Such a condition would jeopardize the University's federal contracts for research and development, including nearly the entire operation of Sandia National Laboratory and Livermore National Laboratory. With hundreds of millions of dollars and thousands of jobs on the line, there is no way the University Regents will allow the government to "pull the plug" on funding of those organizations.

That is why the Regents made the provision for abandoning their resolution if any action on affirmative action would impede the flow of federal funds under its contracts.

Quotas, preferences, set-aside programs are all out, unless mandated by court order.

3. Employment Programs

This is the "original" affirmative action program created in 1965 by President Johnson's Executive Order 11246. Many states, including California, have added their own requirements for these programs for organizations enjoying revenue from contracts with state organizations. Over the years, local, state, and federal programs have created quota requirements based on race or sex. Some courts even supported them. The original intent of affirmative action in employment was not to establish quotas but rather to ensure inclusion of minorities and women in the employment selection process. Today, the Supreme Court of the United States has ruled that affirmative action programs may not be quota systems, nor may they give preferential treatment to anyone based on race or sex. If employment-based affirmative is done according to federal requirements these days, programs will be designed to reinforce non-discrimination under equal employment opportunity law through enhanced outreach and recruiting where underutilization has been identified. Today, these programs require selecting managers to choose the best-qualified applicant to fill each vacancy. Today, these programs require creative effort to identify and solicit sources of qualified minority and female candidates when openings occur in those underutilized job categories.

Both federal and state regulations are unaffected by any of the other actions taken in market place programs or university programs. President Clinton issued guidelines that support the continuation of E.O. 11246 affirmative action programs. Voluntary programs may also continue if they meet his guidelines. Those guidelines are remarkably similar to those written by the Supreme Court in its *Adarand* decision. Affirmative action programs for employment will continue to be valid management tools as long as managers implement them with a non-discriminatory selection process for decisions which impact employees or applicants. Job specific factors must continue to be the focus of all such decision-making.

Summary

In short, there is only one surviving form of "Affirmative Action." That is the employment-related AAP effort. Those programs will continue to be subject to scrutiny from Washington's OFCCP and state enforcement agencies.

Dead, even if some people don't yet recognize it, are M/WBE programs, contract allocation programs and university admissions programs which are based on quotas, preferences or set-asides. Even Small and Disadvantaged Business Enterprise programs (SBE & DBE) that gave preferences to those organizations when bidding for government business have been eliminated. You may still see SBE and DBE programs reaching out to encourage those organizations to participate in government contracting, but the days are past when they receive preferential consideration for selection.

OFFICIAL GOVERNMENT DEFINITION OF AFFIRMATIVE ACTION PROGRAMS

A written, results-oriented program, meeting the requirements of *41 CFR[2] Part 60-2, 60-300.5* and *60-741.5*, in which a federal contractor details the steps it will take to ensure equal employment opportunity.

Some states have their own contractor compliance organizations that oversee vendors and contractors with state-issued contracts.

Regulation Resources

If you have never heard of the *Code of Federal Regulations* (CFR) before, this is an opportunity for you to get acquainted with a new resource. Every action the federal government takes must be authorized by the *Code of Federal Regulations*. That is why, when you receive correspondence from a governmental agency, you will always see in the first paragraph a citation to the CFR section that authorizes them to do what they will tell you about in the balance of their letter. This can be a bit intimidating to anyone who has not experienced it before. It sounds very officious and threatening, especially if you don't know what is in the CFR sections being cited.

As a professional human resources manager, or professional line manager, you can recognize that these are not threats but simply statements of intent to follow the rules in the federal code. On the other hand, if you don't know what those referenced sections of the *Code* contain, it is a good idea to get a copy so you can study the content.

You can get a copy of *41 CFR 60* by calling your nearest office of the OFCCP and requesting a copy. There are two sizes printed. One is 8.5" X 11" and the other is 5.5" X 8.5". Sometimes, if they have both sizes in stock, you can request the size you prefer. If not, you will have to take what they send you. Don't expect to get more than one free copy. If you want extra copies, you will have to purchase them through the government printing office in Washington. Simply tell them you want *41 CFR 60*. You can find the OFCCP office nearest you by looking at the listing in our appendix section at the back of this book.

On the Internet you will find www.regulations.gov a helpful site.
If you are an affirmative action employer, meaning you are required to have a written affirmative action program in your organization, you MUST have a copy of these regulations. They are the

---

[2] CFR is an acronym for "Code of Federal Regulations". It is the "rule book" which lays out how laws passed by Congress will be implemented by designated government departments.

only legal foundation for enforcement. If it is not in the regulations, you cannot legally be expected to do it. If it is in the regulations, you have no choice but to do it. That is...if you wish to be in compliance with the regulations and remain a federal contractor.

If you are a state government contractor, call your state agency responsible for equal employment opportunity laws and ask them whom you should talk with about affirmative action programs. Once you find the right people, ask them to send you a copy of the regulations they use in their compliance review activities. It is also a good opportunity to inquire if they will accept an affirmative action program that meets federal regulatory requirements (*41 CFR 60*). Most will, but then, things change over time. It is always best to check to be sure you are following the proper rules in preparing and implementing your plan.

There are also commercial sources of this federal regulation information. The Bureau of National Affairs, Inc. (BNA) is one such source (www.bna.com). This private organization publishes many resource books, manuals, and binders on subjects having to do with federal government regulation. Their materials are frequently updated, and struggle to reflect the continuing changes brought about by Congressional actions or regulatory alterations. Their materials are not cheap, but if you wish to have a thorough reference at your fingertips, I suggest you take a look at their materials. One such document is called the "Affirmative Action Compliance Manual for Federal Contractors." It is actually a two volume set of three-inch binders that even contains the "Federal Contract Compliance Manual," the document used by OFCCP Compliance Officers to conduct audits of affirmative action plans. This manual expands on the *Code of Federal Regulations* by telling "HOW" to judge successful AAP implementation. Although that's not a guarantee you will be happy with them, at least you can know that your predecessors have been involved in contributing to the development of those regulations through public comments.

For years the agency has been promising itself and the public that it will update the Compliance Manual. So far, budget restrictions have been blamed for the lack of progress on this important task. Nonetheless, you can get what is currently available through one of two commercial sources.

If you are willing to spend the money, and would like to pursue the purchase of a commercially available resource, consider talking with:

The Bureau of National Affairs, Inc.
1231 25th Street, N.W.
Washington, DC 20037   www.bna.com
Voice: 1-800-372-1033   FAX: 1-800-253-0332

CCH Incorporated
4025 West Peterson
Chicago, IL 60646   www.cch.com
Voice: 1-800-835-5224   FAX: 1-800-224-8299

EQUAL OPPORTUNITY - THE FOUNDATION OF AFFIRMATIVE ACTION

FEDERAL LAWS

❑ Civil Rights Act of 1964 (Title VII)

Prohibits failure or refusal to hire an individual on the basis of race, color, religion, sex or national origin. Retaliation, sexual harassment and harassment because of race, religion and national origin are also prohibited. Title VII protects individuals from discrimination in compensation, terms, conditions, and privileges of employment.

The most comprehensive statute on Civil Rights ever enacted in the U.S. Amended in 1978 to prohibit discrimination based on pregnancy.

Case law has interpreted this law to mean than everyone has a race, even Whites. "Title VII, whose terms are not limited to discrimination against members of any particular race, prohibits racial discrimination in private employment against white persons upon the same standards as racial discrimination against nonwhites."[3]

❑ Civil Rights Act of 1991

Allows jury trials for federal employment discrimination cases and sets limits on punitive damage awards allowed in such actions. It also establishes employer requirements for successful defense in discrimination complaints.

---

[3] *McDonald v. Santa Fe Transportation*, 427 U.S. 273 (1976), http://www.supreme.justia.com/us/427/273/

❑ **Age Discrimination in Employment Act of 1967**

As amended, this Act prohibits discrimination in employment against individuals over the age of 40. The act also bans involuntary retirement before age 70 for most employees.

❑ **Equal Pay Act of 1963**

Prohibits employers from paying employees differently on the basis of sex for performance of the same or similar work.

❑ **Rehabilitation Act of 1973**

Prohibits discrimination in employment against people with physical or mental disabilities except where the disabilities would prevent them from performing the major duties of the jobs. Federal contractors are required to take affirmative action to employ and promote qualified disabled individuals and to make reasonable accommodation for their disabilities.

❑ **Americans With Disabilities Act of 1990 (ADA)**

Comprehensive law extending civil rights protections to disabled persons in the area of employment as well as other significant life areas. Requires all employers with 15 or more employees to provide accommodation to disabled workers who are qualified to perform key functions of the job in question.

❑ **Vietnam Era Veterans Readjustment Assistance Act of 1974, Amended 1976 (VEVRAA)**

Employers with federal contracts (or subcontracts) are required to take affirmative action in hiring and promoting Vietnam era veterans as well as disabled veterans of all wars. They must have served some of their duty during the Vietnam era, which began August 5, 1964 and ended May 7, 1975. Veterans of this group must also have received other than dishonorable discharges.

❑ **Jobs for Veterans Act of 2002 (JVA)**

JVA amended VEVRAA by: Raising the dollar amount of the Government contracts that are subject to the requirements of VEVRAA; changing the categories of veterans protected under the law; and changing the manner in which the mandatory job listing requirement is to be implemented. The JVA amendments apply to Government contracts entered into on or after December 1, 2003.

❏ **Genetic Information Nondiscrimination Act of 2008**

GINA, signed into law in May 2008, prohibits discrimination by health insurers and employers based on individuals' genetic information. Genetic information includes the results of genetic tests to determine whether someone is at increased risk of acquiring a condition (such as cancer) in the future, as well as an individual's family medical history. It modified the ADA.

❏ **Employment Opportunities Act (VEOA), 1998, (Public Law 105-339)**

Created new requirements for VETS-100 reporting, including a new category of veterans called "Other Veterans." These are people who served on active duty during a war or in a campaign or expedition for which a campaign badge was authorized.

❏ **Executive Order No. 11246**

Most federal contractors and subcontractors are required to develop and implement written affirmative action programs for women and minority group members. The objective is prompt and full utilization of qualified minority group members and women at each organization location, in all job levels.

How it All Began - Again

In 1964, following the death of President Kennedy, Congress passed and President Johnson signed, the *Civil Rights Act of 1964*, the most sweeping piece of federal civil rights legislation in our country's history.

By no means was it the first federal civil rights law, however. Even today, attorneys are turning to the *Civil Rights Act of 1866* to protect their client's rights in making contracts without regard to race. That was a landmark piece of legislation, too, coming as it did at the end of the American Civil War and recognizing that people of all races have the right to enter into contracts with one another.

There are some wonderful bits of history that can enlighten us about how these laws came to be. For an example, return with me for a moment to 1963. It is an age of open racial conflicts. Viet

Nam was a name known only to a few in the country, because our involvement there had yet to accelerate. Martin Luther King, Jr. was very prominent in national events, leading the August 28, 1963 "March on Washington" in which more than 200,000 people are reported to have participated. It was at the Lincoln Memorial, looking out over the reflection pool toward the Washington Monument that Dr. King delivered his "I have a dream" speech.

Recall, now, that the 24th Amendment to the U.S. Constitution had just been recently passed and was headed for adoption by the necessary number of States later in 1964. This Amendment barred poll taxes in federal elections. Yet in 1963, restaurant owners, hotel owners, and employers could openly discriminate against customers and workers simply because of their race, color, religion or national origin. And, many did.

In the summer of 1963, not only was the Washington weather hot, politics were hot, too. The new civil rights law was finally passed after a 75-day filibuster in the Senate. To this day, it remains one of the longest debates of any single piece of legislation on record. In the end, it subjected employers and public establishments to serve customers and treat employees without regard to **Race, Color, Religion, National Origin or Sex.** Up until the very last, "Sex" was not among the protected categories. Opponents of the legislation added "Sex" as a protected category in an effort to kill the bill. Their thinking was that Congress would never agree to offer women the same protections as it was anticipating offering to minorities. Their strategy backfired, however, when the law was passed with all five categories intact. (Parenthetically, it should be noted that Sexual Harassment is not mentioned anywhere in the *Civil Rights Act of 1964*. It has been defined as a form of Sex discrimination since passage of the law, by federal court action, including U.S. Supreme Court case reviews.) It was in passing the *Civil Rights Act of 1964* that Congress created the Equal Employment Opportunity Commission (EEOC) to enforce the provisions of the new law. Congress knew it couldn't place these requirements on EVERY employer in the land, so it exempted employers who have only one to fourteen workers. When an employer hires its fifteenth worker, and keeps that person on the payroll for 20 weeks, and is involved in interstate commerce, it becomes subject to this federal legislation.

So, the stage has been set by the end of November, 1963 when President Kennedy travels to Dallas and his fateful motorcade. Following the assassination, President Johnson vows to move forward on Kennedy's civil rights agenda. So, as it developed, he called for a review of effectiveness of the new law. In late 1964 to early 1965, the President concluded that employers either weren't taking the law for non-discrimination seriously, or they simply ignored it out of ignorance about the new requirements. In either case, he told his staff that he wanted a means to "force" the implementation of employment-related non-discrimination on that part of the employer community which did business with the federal government. Thus was born the concept of Federal Contractor Compliance. And, it was implemented, not by another Congressional law, but by Executive Order of the President. Since the President is responsible for the Executive branch of government which oversees a goodly amount of purchasing of goods and services for the government, he has the power to direct how the government departments and agencies will conduct that business.

Executive Order 11246 (E.O. 11246 - there were 11,245 executive orders issued by Presidents prior to this one) was signed by President Johnson in 1965 and that was the first time anyone had used the term *affirmative action.*

This Presidential directive ordered certain employers who sold goods or services to the government to take "affirmative action" to assure their workforce looked demographically like the qualified and available workforce in its recruiting territory. That meant contractors had to do two things: **Implement a legitimate non-discrimination program** (equal employment opportunity); and, **create an outreach and recruiting program** to identify sources of qualified candidates which had never been tapped up to current times.

Yet, it wasn't until the Nixon Administration that the U.S. Department of Labor (DOL) issued its first regulations about affirmative action and federal contractor compliance requirements. Only with regulations can the government fully implement and enforce the laws Congress has enacted.

So, to summarize . . . again: Employers can make their own business decision about whether or not they wish to do business with the federal government. Once they decide they want to get some portion of their revenue from government contracts, and that amount exceeds the threshold limit specified in E.O. 11246, **then there is no choice** but to meet affirmative action requirements.

If a federal contractor doesn't abide by regulations on affirmative action, it can lose the contract revenue it has said it wants.

EEO AND AA ARE NOT THE SAME THINGS

Equal Employment Opportunity (EEO) and Affirmative Action (AA) are NOT the same things. Many professionals are even confused by these two subjects.

EEO means *Equal Access*.

Affirmative Action means *Outreach and Recruiting*.

Affirmative Action Programs are NOT set aside programs, nor are they quota programs, nor are they preference programs. Any organization which uses quotas, set asides or preferential treatment based on race or sex is guilty of employment discrimination. Race and sex discrimination are violations of EEO laws, both state and federal. Since Affirmative Action is based on EEO laws and requires they be incorporated into any legitimate AAP, it is not possible for legitimate AAPs to require set asides, preferential treatment or quotas based on race or sex.

A Metaphor

Have you ever been fishing? Let's pretend that you and I are going fishing in the fishing pool shown on the next page. When we get to the fishing pool, and throw our lines in the water, we discover that there is only one kind of fish in the pool.

What will we be able to catch?

Look at Figure 1-1 on the next page.

Fishing Pool

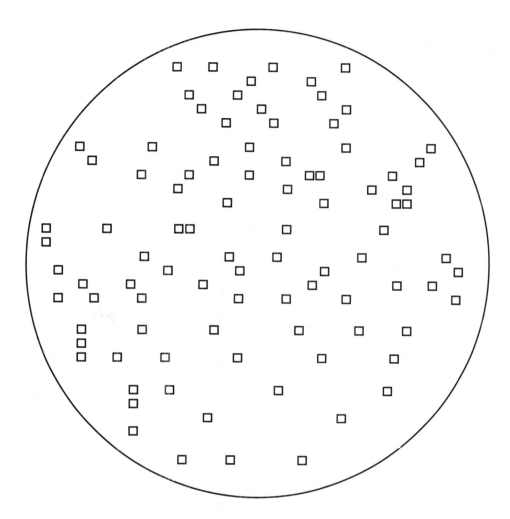

Figure 1-1

QUESTION: If there is only one kind of fish in the pool when we throw our lines in, what kind of fish can we catch?

ANSWER: Whatever that kind of fish happens to be. If there is only one kind of fish in the pool, then that is the only kind that can be caught.

Obviously, if there is only one kind of fish in the pool, that is the only kind of fish we could catch.

Let's say we enjoyed our fishing day so much that we decided to return a few weeks later. When we do, we discover that somehow there are many different kinds of fish now in the pool. What can we catch this time?

The answer is much the same. We can catch whatever happens to be there. Sure, there are lots of variables like what type of bait to use, the time of day, and so forth, but at least in its simplest terms, anything in the fishing pool is fair game for our lines.

Well, if it isn't a fishing pool, but a candidate pool, can you follow the analogy? If there is only one kind of job candidate (person) in the candidate pool, what type of person can we select? Again, it's obvious. We can only select what's there. If that selection must be made from only one type of person, then that is the only choice we have. (See Figure 1-2 on the next page.)

On the other hand, if we have a variety of candidates (people) in the candidate pool, we can have a choice of any of them. (Figure 1-3)

Access to Candidate Pools - Requirement for Equal Opportunity

Historically, white males have had fairly easy access to candidate pools. Minorities and women have not had such easy access.

EQUAL EMPLOYMENT OPPORTUNITY laws tell us that:

- Anyone who is QUALIFIED for the job should have access to the candidate pool. Unqualified people don't get into the pool!
- Employers should use a NON-DISCRIMINATORY SELECTION PROCESS to compare candidates and determine who will be chosen as the successful candidate for placement.

AFFIRMATIVE ACTION REQUIREMENTS expect employers to:

- ASSURE minority and female REPRESENTATION in all candidate pools.
- Follow EEO laws and use a NON-DISCRIMINATORY SELECTION PROCESS.
- AVOID PREFERENCES based on race, sex or any other protected status.
- Develop WRITTEN ACTION PLANS to assess problems of underutilization of minorities and women.

Job Candidate Pool

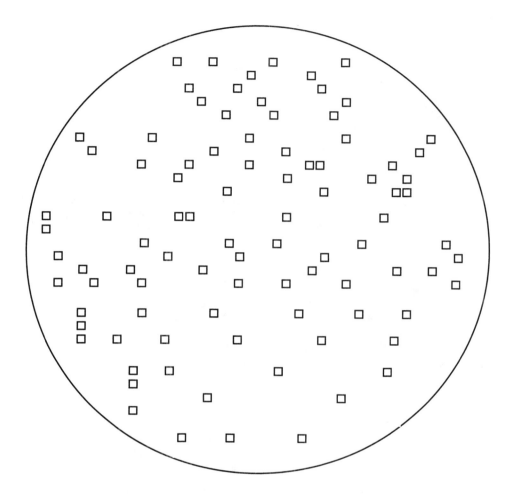

Figure 1-2

QUESTION: If there is only one kind of candidate (person) in the pool when we begin the selection process, what kind of candidate can we select?

ANSWER: Whatever that kind of person happens to be. If there is only one kind of candidate in the pool, then that is the only kind that can be selected.

Job Candidate Pool

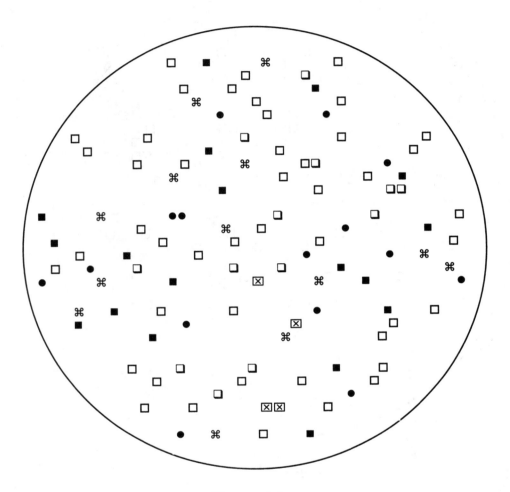

Figure 1-3

QUESTION: If there are many types of candidates in the pool, what can we select?

ANSWER: Whatever type happens to be present can be selected. In terms of job candidates, the best candidate should be the victor.

Job Candidate Pool

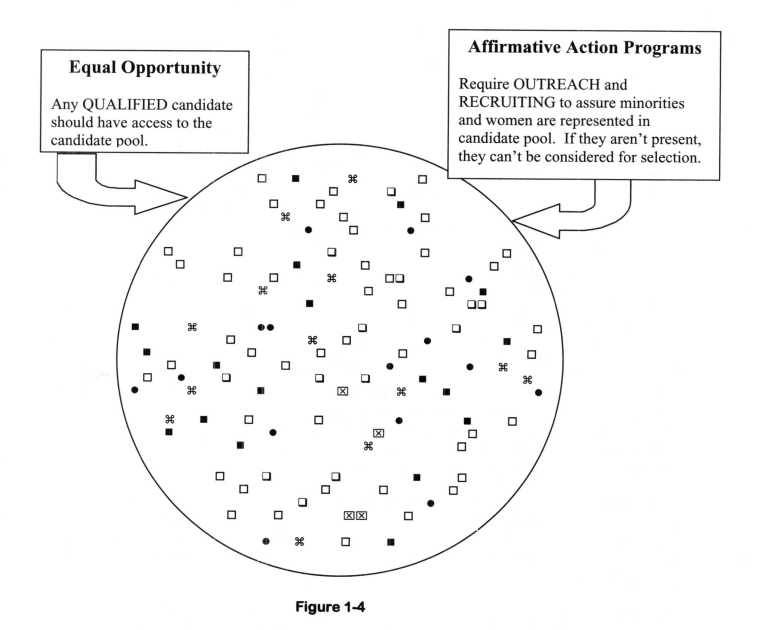

Equal Opportunity

Any QUALIFIED candidate should have access to the candidate pool.

Affirmative Action Programs

Require OUTREACH and RECRUITING to assure minorities and women are represented in candidate pool. If they aren't present, they can't be considered for selection.

Figure 1-4

QUESTION: If there are many types of candidates in the pool, what can we select?

ANSWER: Whatever type happens to be present can be selected.

The EEOC has long offered guidelines on employment selection to assure employers use non-discriminatory procedures in their hiring.

To summarize them briefly:

EEOC Guidelines on Employment Selection

Selection Criteria	Acceptable Selection Criteria
• Religion • National Origin • Color • Pregnancy • Mental Disability • Physical Disability • Age • Veteran Status • Use of Family & Medical Leave • Genetic Information • Retaliation for Filing a Discrimination Complaint • Plus State Protected EEO Categories	• Length of Service • Performance Evaluations • Job Experience • Educational Background • Individual Skills • Demonstration of Skills/Abilities • Attendance/Punctuality • Personal Conduct Record • Training History • Plus Any Other Job-Related Facts

[You will find a Chart of state-enacted EEO Protections in **Appendix A**.]

Selection criteria used by any employer may be different for each job being filled. In the case of executives, job experience may carry more weight than other criteria. In the case of computer hardware engineers, experience with leading edge technology may be balanced by the need for current education or training in the latest technological developments. When filling a laborer job, attendance and punctuality may play the key role.

In the final analysis, any job-related criteria may be used to compare candidates. The comparison process allows the hiring manager to "sort out" the better qualified candidates from the less qualified candidates. The person who should be hired is the one who is "best qualified" for the specific opening without regard to race, age, sex, national origin or any of the other prohibited categories.

Race, age, sex, and the other protected categories should play no role in the individual's success or failure on the job. Personal behavior, job performance, individual skills and the other job-related considerations will play a key role in success or failure. From a business viewpoint, it only makes sense to concentrate on using selection criteria which can assist the hiring manager in making the best possible choice, because that decision will bring the best possible return on investment in the new employee.

If we were to use race as a selection criteria, we would be guilty of employment discrimination. It matters not what race the candidate happens to be. Think about all that has been written in the media in recent years about "reverse discrimination." I would like to suggest that discrimination is discrimination is discrimination. The "reverse" idea got started in the media as a way of

26

describing how white males were being "penalized" by favoritism toward minorities in selection. In fact, there is no such thing as "reverse discrimination." If you decide not to hire me because I am white, that's illegal employment discrimination. We all have a race. And, we are all protected against race discrimination in employment. It is just as illegal for you to use race in your employment decision against me because I am white as it would be to decide against a minority candidate because of his or her race.

Some folks I have come in contact with, even some professional human resource managers, have mistakenly thought that white people were not protected by EEO laws. Hopefully, you are among the enlightened and realize that everyone enjoys protections against race discrimination, regardless of who they are. The EEOC and state EEO enforcement agencies will accept complaints of discrimination from employees who claim they were discriminated against due to their race, even if their race is white.

Diversity in Candidate Pools - Affirmative Action Requirement

With all the media attention to the subject of affirmative action recently, it might be a good idea to begin with a statement of what affirmative action programs are not. That is, presuming they are implemented the way they should be.

Affirmative Action Programs (AAPs) ARE NOT:

- Quota programs
- Set-aside programs
- Preference programs

Quotas, set-asides and preferences are illegal under EEO laws. There are some affirmative action programs which include one or more of these conditions, however, they exist by order of the court. ONLY UNDER COURT ORDER is it legal to have a program which embraces one or more of these conditions. Usually, the court orders special hiring practices in an employer organization because of gross discrimination within that organization in the past. These orders arise as settlements, called consent decrees, to lawsuits over issues of employment-related discrimination.

Employers who are not under such a court order have no defense against charges of discrimination if they implement an affirmative action program which gives preferences to minorities, women, or disabled employees and applicants. The U.S. Supreme Court decisions in *Adarand*[4] reinforced that notion.

So, what ARE affirmative action programs?

Well, they are efforts to identify weaknesses in an employer's recruiting program, needs for greater representation of minorities or women in certain job categories, and then put into place the steps to correct those conditions.

---

[4] Adarand Constructors v. Pena, 515 US 200 (1995) and Adarand Constructors, Inc. v. Mineta, 534 US 103 (2001).

Said simply, AAPs are **outreach and recruiting programs built on a foundation of equal employment opportunity.** If you look at Figure 1-4 again, you can imagine that it might take some effort to identify sources of qualified minority or female candidates for a given type of job. Affirmative Action employers are responsible for the creative thinking necessary to do just that: to find new ways to identify sources of qualified candidates which may not have been used in the past, and which may not even have been known to the employer in the past. Once identified, the employer is responsible for contacting those sources, building a relationship with them and requesting qualified candidates for consideration when job openings occur for which there will be a candidate pool established.

Remember, if minorities and women are not represented in the candidate pool, they can't possibly be selected. Therefore, the employer's job is to assure a representation of minorities and women in the candidate pool in relatively the same proportion as we have computed their availability in the relevant recruiting territory. (This computation process is explained in Chapter 7 on Availability Analysis.)

It often falls to the human resources department to issue job opening announcements, advertise the openings, screen applicant responses, and forward to the selecting manager a slate of candidates who are both qualified and who may deserve to be interviewed. It is the job of the human resources department, in such a scenario, to assure the candidate pool has the proper mix of representation. If the selecting manager is responsible for all of these steps in the process, it falls to the selecting manager to fulfill the organization's obligation to assure a proper mix of candidates.

Once the candidate pool has been established, with proper recruiting for representation of qualified minorities and women, all candidates should be sorted and compared using the organization's non-discriminatory selection process. And, as we know, that will rely on comparison of job-related factors only.

Then, selecting managers should be required to document their selection decision. Why did they pick the person they did?

So, let's review.

- Unqualified people may not be considered candidates.
- Candidate pools should contain a mix of sex and ethnicity.
- Recruiting sources should be identified and relationships with them established.
- All selecting managers should be thoroughly trained in the organization's non-discriminatory selection process.
- All selection decisions should be documented to indicate reasons for choosing the successful candidate.

One final note. In my travels around the country leading seminars on these subjects for both line managers and human resource professionals, someone invariably asked a question about breaking the "tie" when choosing between "equally qualified candidates."

I have to answer them in two ways:

1. It is legal to use an affirmative action goal as the tie breaker. What that means is this. If the job group has a placement rate goal for minorities, and one of the tied candidates is a minority and the other is not, the minority may be given the nod in selection due to the computed affirmative action need. That is legal, but it is not very easily accomplished, in my experience. Remember, if we have been doing our HR job properly we will have been teaching selecting managers their responsibilities for non-discrimination. That means no preference based on ethnicity, right? Then, we turn around and tell them it is OK to use ethnicity as a tie breaker in such a situation? I have never seen it work well. I prefer telling the selecting manager to rethink the criteria and maybe do another round of interviews with the final two candidates. It is always best to find some way to tell the two candidates apart.

2. In my experience of nearly 45 years in management, I have never seen a situation where two candidates were "tied" in their qualifications for the job. I have always found a way to determine which one had the greater qualifications. Here again, creativity and thinking effort are often required, and human nature is to make excuses for not thinking. As HR professionals, we have to work with the selecting managers in our organizations to overcome that tendency.

Thomas A. Edison had a quotation posted in his office which is reported to be his favorite. It said:

> *There is no expedient to which a man will not resort to avoid the real labor of thinking.*
> - Sir Joshua Reynolds

Notes

CHAPTER 2

WHO MUST HAVE A WRITTEN AAP

How Do I Know if I Must Prepare a Written AAP?

There are three types of written affirmative action programs:

- *Minorities & Women*
- *Disabled*
- *Veterans*

What Employers are Required to Have Written AAPs for Minorities and Women?

---

41 CFR 60-1.7
E.O. 11246

Requirements for prime contractors and subcontractors.

There are three conditions that can require an employer to develop and implement a written affirmative action plan. They are:

- Prime contractor or first tier subcontractors with 50 or more employees <u>and</u> $50,000 or more in contract revenue during any 12-month period.
- A depository of Government funds in any amount.
- An issuing and paying agent for U.S. savings bonds and savings notes.

Any one of these conditions will trigger the requirement for a written AAP. Let's look at each one of them briefly.

The 50/50 Condition

This is the condition that captures most federal contractors into a requirement for developing and implementing a written AAP. The requirement is for both 50 employees and $50,000 or more in revenue within 12 months. If you have fewer than 50 employees and more than $50,000 in federal contract revenue, you are not required to have a written AAP. The $50,000 minimum must be in a single contract, not a collection of contracts.

If you are a first tier subcontractor, supplying goods or services to a prime contractor that are directly linked to the prime contract, you must develop your own written AAP if you meet the 50/50 test. As we shall see, the requirement carries with it an obligation to do additional things beyond those required in a written AAP. Output from the subcontract must directly flow to the prime contract goods or services provided to the government.

Both prime contractors and first tier subcontractors are subject to compliance review by the U.S. Department of Labor, Office of Federal Contract Compliance Programs (OFCCP).

The Depository of Government Funds Condition

Virtually any financial institution that is a member of the federal banking system will have government funds deposited from time to time. The OFCCP has determined that all banks fall into this category. Sometimes, savings and loan organizations, and finance institutions will also meet the criteria.

There is no employee headcount criteria. Simply having $1.00 of government deposits at any time captures the organization and requires a written AAP.

The U.S. Savings Bond Condition

Many banks hold transfer authority for U.S. savings bonds. But, for the most part, they are already required to have written AAPs because of the deposit condition. Who else is captured, then, by the U.S. savings bond condition?

How about credit unions? Sometimes credit unions are not depositories for government funds, but they do have transfer agent authority for U.S. savings bonds. If that is the case, the credit union must have a written AAP.

Some private corporations also have transfer agent authority for U.S. savings bonds and offer the sale and redemption of those bonds to employees as a service and courtesy. If such a company is not required to have a written AAP because of the 50/50 rule, it will be required to have a written AAP because of this savings bond transfer authority rule.

It matters not the value of bonds that are transferred, nor over what period of time. If an employer has the transfer agent authority, it must have a written AAP.

Additional Requirements for Construction Contractors

The 50/50 rule applies to subcontracting construction companies, regardless of their position in the subcontracting hierarchy. It doesn't matter how far down the food chain the employer happens to be. If it meets the 50/50 test it must have a written AAP. Construction contractors should see the material in Chapter 19.

What Employers are Exempt from Written AAP Requirements for Minorities and Women?

41 CFR 60-1.5	• Transactions of $10,000 or under.
	• Contracts/subcontracts for indefinite quantities not exceeding $10,000.
	• Work outside the United States.
	• Contracts with State or local governments.
	• Contracts with certain educational institutions.
	• Work on or near Indian reservations.

These exemptions are not only exemptions from written AAP requirements, but also from any contract being subject to the standard government "Equal Opportunity Clause." Every government agency that contracts with non-government organizations for provision of goods or services must include the Equal Opportunity Clause in the contract.

Equal Opportunity Clause - All AAP Employers

A copy of the Equal Opportunity Clause can be found on the next several pages.

"The equal opportunity clause may be incorporated by reference in all Government contracts and subcontracts, including Government bills of lading, transportation requests, contracts for deposit of Government funds, and contracts for issuing and paying U.S. savings bonds and notes, and such other contracts and subcontracts as the Director may designate."
(41 CFR 60-1.4(d))

Actually, there are two clauses. One is for construction contractors and one for everybody else. Be sure you use the proper one in your purchase orders, contracts and bills of lading. Most organizations find that it is easy to print this on the reverse of purchase order pages in a light gray (40% printing screen).

If you wish to avoid printing the entire clause, consider using a statement something like this instead:

"All parties agree that they will abide by the provisions of *41 CFR 60-1.4(a) or 41 CFR 60-1.4(b)*, as appropriate."

Executive Order 13279

On December 12, 2002, President George W. Bush signed Executive Order 13279. Doing so amended Executive Order 11246, Section 204, regarding exemptions and makes the affirmative action clause requirement of Section 202 inapplicable to religious groups that hold government contracts "with respect to the employment of individuals of a particular religion to perform work connected with the carrying on ... of its activities."

This exemption was enacted to permit faith-based organizations to participate in social service programs funded by the federal government. It means, religious employers may use religion as a criteria in employment decisions without concern about running afoul of affirmative action requirements. Title VII of the *Civil Rights Act of 1964* also allows an exemption for religious organizations from complaints of illegal discrimination based on religion. (If you are a religious organization you should heed the counsel of your affirmative action lawyer before plunging forward with selection decisions based on religious preference.)

Equal Opportunity Clause - Government Contracts
41 CFR 60-1.4(a)

"Except as otherwise provided, each contracting agency shall include the following equal opportunity clause contained in section 202 of the order in each of its Government contracts (and modifications thereof if not included in the original contract):

"During the performance of this contract, the contractor agrees as follows:

"(1) The contractor will not discriminate against any employee or applicant for employment because of race, color, religion, sex, or national origin. The contractor will take affirmative action to ensure that applicants are employed, and that employees are treated during employment, without regard to their race, color, religion, sex, or national origin. Such action shall include, but not be limited to the following: Employment, upgrading, demotion, or transfer, recruitment or recruitment advertising; layoff or termination; rates of pay or other forms of compensation; and selection for training, including apprenticeship. The contractor agrees to post in conspicuous places, available to employees and applicants for employment, notices to be provided by the contracting officer setting forth the provisions of this nondiscrimination clause.

"(2) The contractor will, in all solicitations or advertisements for employees placed by or on behalf of the contractor, state that all qualified applicants will receive consideration for employment without regard to race, color, religion, sex, or national origin.

"(3) The contractor will send to each labor union or representative of workers with which he has a collective bargaining agreement or other contract of understanding, a notice to be provided by the agency contracting officer, advising the labor union or workers' representative of the contractor's commitments under section 202 of Executive Order 11246 of September 24, 1965, and shall post copies of the notice in conspicuous places available to employees and applicants for employment.

"(4) The contractor will comply with all provisions of Executive Order 11246 of September 24, 1965, and of the rules, regulations, and relevant orders of the Secretary of Labor.

"(5) The contractor will furnish all information and reports required by Executive Order 11246 of September 24, 1965, and by the rules, regulations, and orders of the Secretary of Labor, or pursuant thereto, and will permit access to his books, records, and accounts by the contracting agency and the Secretary of Labor for purposes of investigation to ascertain compliance with such rules, regulations, and orders.

"(6) In the event of the contractor's noncompliance with the nondiscrimination clauses of this contract or with any of such rules, regulations, or orders, this contract may be canceled, terminated or suspended in whole or in part and the contractor may be declared ineligible for further Government contracts in accordance with procedures authorized in Executive Order 11246 of September 24, 1965, and such other sanctions may be imposed and remedies invoked as provided in Executive Order 11246 of September 24, 1965, or by rule, regulation, or order of the Secretary of Labor, or as otherwise provided by law.

"(7) The contractor will include the provisions of paragraphs (1) through (7) in every subcontract or purchase order unless exempted by rules, regulations, or orders of the Secretary of Labor issued pursuant to section 204 of Executive Order 11246 of September 24, 1965, so that such provisions will be binding upon each subcontractor or vendor. The contractor will take such action with respect to any subcontract or purchase order as may be directed by the Secretary of Labor as a means of enforcing such provisions including sanctions for noncompliance: *Provided however,* that in the event the contractor becomes involved in, or is threatened with, litigation with a subcontractor or vendor as a result of such direction, the contractor may request the United States to enter into such litigation to protect the interests of the United States."

Equal Opportunity Clause - Construction Contracts
41 CFR 60-1.4(b)

"Except as otherwise provided, each administering agency shall require the inclusion of the following language as a condition of any grant, contract, loan insurance, or guarantee involving federally assisted construction which is not exempt from requirements of the equal opportunity clause:

"The applicant hereby agrees that it will incorporate or cause to be incorporated into any contract for construction work, or modification thereof, as defined in the regulations of the Secretary of Labor at 41 CFR Chapter 60, which is paid for in whole or in part with funds obtained from the Federal Government or borrowed on the credit of the Federal Government pursuant to a grant, contract, loan insurance, or guarantee, or undertaken pursuant to any Federal program involving such grant, contract, loan, insurance, or guarantee, the following equal opportunity clause:

"During the performance of this contract, the contractor agrees as follows:

"(1) The contractor will not discriminate against any employee or applicant for employment because of race, color, religion, sex, or national origin. The contractor will take affirmative action to ensure that applicants are employed, and that employees are treated during their employment without regard to their race, color, religion, sex, or national origin, such action shall include, but not be limited to the following: Employment, upgrading, demotion, or transfer; recruitment or recruitment advertising; layoff or termination; rates of pay or other forms of compensation; and selection for training, including apprenticeship. The contractor agrees to post in conspicuous places, available to employees and applicants for employment, notices to be provided setting forth the provisions of this nondiscrimination clause.

"(2) The contractor will, in all solicitations or advertisements for employees placed by or on behalf of the contractor, state that all qualified applicants will receive considerations for employment without regard to race, color, religion, sex, or national origin.

"(3) The contractor will send to each labor union or representative of workers with which he has a collective bargaining agreement or other contract or understanding, a notice to be provided advising the said labor union or workers' representatives of the contractor's commitments under this section, and shall post copies of the notice in conspicuous places available to employees and applicants for employment.

"(4) The contractor will comply with all provisions of Executive Order 11246 of September 24, 1965, and of the rules, regulations, and relevant orders of the Secretary of Labor.

"(5) The contractor will furnish all information and reports required by Executive Order 11246 of September 24, 1965, and by rules, regulations, and orders of the Secretary of Labor, or pursuant thereto, and will permit access to his books, records, and accounts by the administering agency and the Secretary of Labor for purposes of investigation to ascertain compliance with such rules, regulations, and orders.

"(6) In the event of the contractor's noncompliance with the nondiscrimination clauses of this contract or with any of the said rules, regulations, or orders, this contract may be canceled, terminated, or suspended in whole or in part and the contractor may be declared ineligible for further Government contracts or federally assisted construction contracts in accordance with procedures authorized in Executive Order 11246 of September 24, 1965, and such other sanctions may be imposed and remedies invoked as provided in Executive Order 11246 of September 24, 1965, or by rule, regulation, or order of the Secretary of Labor, or as otherwise provided by law.

"(7) The contractor will include the portion of the sentence immediately preceding paragraph (1) and the provisions of paragraphs (1) through (7) in every subcontract or purchase order unless exempted by rules, regulations, or orders of the Secretary of Labor issued pursuant to section 204 of Executive Order 11246 of September 24, 1965, so that such provisions will be binding upon each subcontractor or vendor. The contractor will take such action with respect to any subcontract or purchase order as the administering agency may direct as a means of enforcing such provisions, including sanctions for noncompliance: *Provided however,* That in the event a contractor becomes involved in, or is threatened with, litigation with a subcontractor or vendor as a result of such direction by the administering agency the contractor may request the United States to enter into such litigation to protect the interests of the United States.

"The applicant further agrees that it will be bound by the above equal opportunity clause with respect to its own employment practices when it participates in federally assisted construction work: *Provided,* That if the applicant so participating is a State or local government, the above equal opportunity clause is not applicable to any agency, instrumentality or subdivision of such government which does not participate in work on or under the contract.

"The applicant agrees that it will assist and cooperate actively with the administering agency and the Secretary of Labor in obtaining the compliance of contractors and subcontractors with the equal opportunity clause and the rules, regulations, and relevant orders of the Secretary of Labor, that it will furnish the administering agency and the Secretary of Labor such information as they may require for the supervision of such compliance, and that it will otherwise assist the administering agency in the discharge of the agency's primary responsibility for securing compliance.

"The applicant further agrees that it will refrain from entering into any contract or contract modification subject to Executive Order 11246 of September 24, 1965, with a contractor debarred from, or who has not demonstrated eligibility for, Government contracts and federally assisted construction contracts pursuant to the Executive Order and will carry out such sanctions and penalties for violation of the equal opportunity clause as may be imposed upon contractors and subcontractors by the administering agency or the Secretary of Labor pursuant to Part II, Subpart D of the Executive Order. In addition, the applicant agrees that if it fails or refuses to comply with these undertakings, the administering agency may take any or all of the following actions: Cancel, terminate, or suspend in whole or in part this grant (contract, loan, insurance, guarantee); refrain from extending any further assistance to the applicant under the program with respect to which the failure or refund occurred until satisfactory assurance of future compliance has been received from such applicant; and refer the case to the Department of Justice for appropriate legal proceedings."

Voluntary AAPs

Employers who are not government contractors, yet wish to establish voluntary AAPs may do so, on the condition that they follow all of the regulations set down by the government in 41 CFR Chapter 60. It is not a good idea to approach affirmative action plans thinking that you can pick and choose the portions you wish to use and those you wish to ignore. It's all or nothing for voluntary plans.

Some organizations find that it is advantageous to have a voluntary AAP because it is a requirement of doing business with state or local governments. Without a written AAP, contracting with such customers is not possible in some circumstances. So, the business decision is that a voluntary AAP will be developed and implemented in order to secure the customer's business.

A simple caution should suffice if you find yourself in this situation. Take it upon yourself to digest all of the federal requirements, and any additional requirements placed on you by the governmental entity with which you will be contracting. Be sure that you understand all of the requirements and how your response to them should be tailored.

Other organizations want to create written AAPs as an extension of their culture or management philosophy. Commendable as it is, these organizations must understand they are taking on an obligation to meet all the federal AAP regulations when they make such a decision.

Federal courts and the President have laid out guidelines for us regarding voluntary affirmative action programs. "Strict scrutiny" standards are now applied to federal, state and local affirmative action program requirements. In his July 19, 1995 memorandum to the heads of all federal departments, President Clinton directed the elimination or reform of all programs that use race, ethnicity or gender as a consideration if they:

- Create a quota
- Create preferences for unqualified individuals
- Create reverse discrimination; or
- Continue even after its equal opportunity purposes have been achieved.

To meet court-stated guidelines on affirmative action, employer's programs must follow the federal regulatory guidelines as they are written. Each plan must last for a specified period of time (1 year) and address specific problems of representation in the workforce (utilization analysis and goals).

Public Employer Voluntary AAPs

"…The importance of voluntary affirmative action on the part of employers is underscored by Title VII of the Civil Rights Act of 1964, Executive Order 11246, and related laws and regulations – all of which emphasize voluntary action to achieve equal employment opportunity." (41 CFR 60-3.17(1))

"(b)...Voluntary employer action can play a crucial role in furthering Title VII's purpose of eliminating the effects of discrimination in the workplace, and Title VII should not be read to thwart such efforts." (Johnson v. Transportation Agency, 480 U.S. 616 (1987))

<u>Private Employer Voluntary AAPs</u>

"1. Title VII's prohibition in Section 703(a) and (d) against racial discrimination does not condemn all private, voluntary, race-conscious affirmative action plans." (United Steelworkers of America v. Weber, 443 U.S. 193 (1979))

What is an AAP Establishment?

OFCCP regulations do not define the term "establishment." However, OFCCP has generally accepted definitions from contractors based on either geographic or functional portions of the organization. Then, on March 21, 2002, Charles E. James, Sr., Deputy Assistant Secretary for Federal Contract Compliance, signed OFCCP Directive Number 254.

"Establishments" are important in affirmative action because a separate written plan must be prepared for each establishment. That means the complete narrative and total statistical analysis is required for each of those portions of the enterprise.

The new Directive separates "functional AAP" from the definition of establishment. According to the Directive, "The term 'functional AAP' as used throughout this Administrative Notice refers to the development and preparation of an AAP based on clearly distinct functional or business units within a corporate structure as opposed to an AAP based solely on physical location." Further, it says, "Until the functional AAP agreement is approved, the contractor must continue to develop and maintain AAPs for each establishment."

Generally, an AAP entity is that portion of the organization over which one person has ultimate authority to hire and fire. That person does not have to go to any other manager or executive for approval on a hiring decision, for example. (Even though there may be a need for budget approval at higher levels, the decision about hiring one person versus another is made locally.) Usually, we find the senior establishment executive, if not the Chief Executive Officer (CEO) of the enterprise, is the senior official at the geographic location or for the function represented. That might be a plant's General Manager or the Vice President of Sales and Marketing. (The water gets muddied when people from many departments work at the same campus location, reporting to people at other work sites. To resolve the question, look for the executive who heads the dominant portion of the organization at that location.)

New regulations (12/13/2000) make clear that the OFCCP intends to keep a tight rein on contractors' use of "functional" establishments. [60-2.1(d)(1) says: *"Employees who work at establishments* (meaning locations) *other than that of the manager to whom they report, must be included in the affirmative action program of their manager."*] [60-2.1(d)(2) says: *"Employees who work at an establishment where the contractor employs fewer than 50 employees, may be included under any of the following three options: In an affirmative action program which covers just that establishment; in the affirmative action program which covers the location of the personnel function which supports the establishment; or, in the affirmative action program which covers the location of the official to whom they report."*] [60-2.1(d)(4) says: *"If a contractor wishes to establish an affirmative action program other than by establishment, the contractor may reach agreement with OFCCP on the development and use of affirmative action programs based on functional or business units. The Deputy Assistant Secretary, or his or her designee, must approve such agreements. Agreements allowing the use of functional or business unit affirmative action programs cannot be construed to limit or restrict how the OFCCP structures its compliance evaluations."*]

It is now clear that contractors must seek prior approval of the OFCCP before constructing affirmative action plans based on functions rather than street addresses. You will find a summary of the new Directive in the Appendix of this book on page 331. Requests for approval must be submitted to OFCCP 120 days in advance and, when approved will last for five years. An extension for an additional five years can be requested 120 days prior to expiration of the first agreement.

Geographic Establishments

By far the most common of the two establishment definitions, this is appropriate when there is one address, cluster of addresses or "nearby" employer work locations over which there is one senior executive responsible for the entire workforce at that location or group of locations.

For example, a manufacturing facility may have a large plant located at a single address. It has a "Plant Manager" responsible for all that goes on at that location. It produces products for government contracts, directly or indirectly, which are valued at more than $50,000 per year. And, there are more than 50 employees at the plant. The employer could create one AAP for this plant location as a geographic establishment

Another example could be an industrial "cluster" of addresses in a campus arrangement. In the buildings on the "campus" are housed administrative employees who produce the services associated with a government contract or subcontract. There are more than 50 workers and the contract value exceeds $50,000 per year. The cluster of addresses could be grouped together into one establishment with one AAP if the employer wished to do so. The reasons are: There is one senior official responsible for the employer's operations at all of the buildings in the cluster; and, jobs at this collection of addresses are recruited from the same recruiting territories.

A third example could be several work locations located within a few miles of one another, all of which report to the CEO. They share recruiting territories and the CEO is the senior executive of the AAP establishment. They could all be represented under one AAP document.

Although there are some nuances that are important, these are generally accepted practices when configuring an AAP establishment along geographic lines. If the workforce is extremely large, and individual "divisions," "departments," or other slices of the enterprise can be identified with their own senior executives, it may be more reasonable to create separate AAP documents for those portions of the enterprise.

Ultimately, it is a judgment call the employer must make. There should be some "logic" to the decision, and the reasons for doing it the way you do should be documented. There may well come a time when the OFCCP calls on you to review your AAP in one of your establishments and you will want to be in a position to explain why the establishments are configured the way they are. Still, during a compliance review, you could be directed to reconfigure your AAP boundaries. It becomes a negotiable item at that point, with "you know who" holding the power.

This is the type of establishment you should use if you have folks scattered across the country with only a few here and there. Assume there is a headquarters address where all the core people are located. Sales and marketing people are working out of their homes in 27 different states with only one or two people per address in that group. The rules of the OFCCP require all of the remote people to be "rolled up" into the headquarters establishment, producing one AAP for the entire company and including everyone in the country in that AAP.

Functional Establishments

If your organization is large, and you have more than 50 people in a given function such as sales and marketing, you can seek permission from OFCCP to create a functional establishment containing only those people. Everyone else would be captured in traditional geographic AAP establishments at one or more addresses.

In our example, all of the individuals in that functional area within the enterprise are gathered into the establishment called "Sales and Marketing" or "Customer Service" and it is national in scope.

The problem employers sometimes have with this arrangement is caused by the challenge to be accurate in computing availability for each job group. If professional or sales jobs are truly recruited across a national distance, then the problem is smaller. It is sometimes necessary to increase the number of job groups to accommodate this issue, but we can discuss that further in the Chapter 7 on Availability.

Know for now that you can have a functionally defined establishment if you feel it is in your best interest to do so. Simply define it carefully, document your definition and your rationale for that decision, and prepare to be challenged by the OFCCP during the approval process you must endure.

Standard Affirmative Action Formats (SAAF)

A few years ago, Director Wilcher cancelled all SAAF agreements with major contractors. These were very large employers. There were only a few with approved SAAFs, but they were eliminated. SAAFs allowed a contractor to have a "model" AAP reviewed and approved by OFCCP. Then it replicated that model in each establishment around the country. Contractors with these agreements were exempt from compliance reviews as long as they continued to deliver results data to OFCCP on a scheduled basis.

The new Directive 254 on Functional AAPs goes out of its way to distinguish SAAFs from Functional AAPs. Regulations (*41 CFR 60-1.20(e)*) provide for OFCCP to establish SAAFs with contractors. As of this writing, SAAFs are still not being approved by OFCCP.

Who is Required to Have a Written AAP for Disabled?

---

41 CFR 60-741
Rehabilitation Act of 1973,
Sections 503 & 504

Requirements for contractors and subcontractors.

The following employers must have written AAPs addressing disabled workers.

- Any employer with a contract value or purchase order from the federal government worth $10,000 or more.
- Any employer with bills of lading of $10,000 or more in 12 months.

Employers Exempt from AAP Requirements for Disabled

---

41 CFR 60-741.3

- Contracts or subcontracts not exceeding $10,000 in 12 months.
- Contracts or subcontracts for indefinite quantities not exceeding $10,000.
- Work outside the United States.
- Contracts with State or local governments.

If you are an employer which meets the 50/50 test requiring a written AAP for minorities and women, then you know you must also have a written AAP for disabled. The thresholds are lower for disabled than for minorities and women.

What Individuals Are Covered?

The *Rehabilitation Act of 1973* defines individuals as "disabled" if they:

- Have a physical or mental impairment that substantially limits one or more of a person's major life activities.
- Have a record of such impairment.
- Are regarded as having such impairment.

Individuals are considered "Qualified Disabled" if they are capable of performing a particular job with or without reasonable accommodation to their disability.

PLEASE NOTE: *The term "handicapped" is used in the Rehabilitation Act of 1973, which brought us the need for affirmative action toward that portion of the population. It is a term that has been replaced by the term "disabled." For the purposes of affirmative action, the term "disabled" should now be used.*

Who is Required to Have a Written AAP for Veterans?[5]

---

41 CFR 60-300.4
Vietnam Era Veterans
Readjustment Assistance Act
of 1974 as amended
38 U.S.C. 4212

- Contracts or subcontracts valued at $100,000[6] or more.
- Bills of lading of $100,000 or more in 12 months.
- Indefinite Contracts if the value may reasonably be expected to reach $100,000 in one year, such as open-end contracts, requirement-type contracts, Federal Supply Schedule contracts, call-type contracts, and purchase notice agreements.[7]
- 50 or more employees in addition to contract value.[8]

---

[5] The reference to "veterans" refers to United States of America veterans only. People who served in a foreign government military are not offered any protections or benefits under these laws and regulations. If asked, you must tell them they do not qualify under the provisions for veterans' affirmative action in this country.

[6] 41 CFR 60-300.4 was raised from $25,000 to $100,000 effective September 7, 2007. (Federal Register: August 8, 2007, Volume 72, Number 152, Pages 44393-44416) The new higher limit applies to contracts dated on or after December 1, 2003.

[7] 41 CFR 60-300.4(a)(2)

[8] 41 CFR 60-300.40(a)

Employers Exempt from AAP Requirements for Veterans

---

41 CFR 60-300.4
Vietnam Era Veterans
Readjustment Assistance Act
of 1974 as amended
38 U.S.C. 4212

- Contracts or subcontracts not exceeding $100,000 in 12 months.
- Contracts or subcontracts for indefinite quantities not exceeding $100,000.
- Work outside the United States.
- Contracts with State or local governments.
- Contractors with fewer than 50 employees.

What Individuals Are Covered?

The *Jobs for Veterans Act of 2002* modified the *Vietnam Era Veterans' Readjustment Assistance Act of 1974* (VEVRAA) and it uses five categories of individuals in its definitions.

Disabled Veteran

- A veteran of the U.S. military, ground, naval or air service who is entitled to compensation (or who but for the receipt of military retired pay would be entitled to compensation) under laws administered by the Secretary of Veterans Affairs, or
- A person who was discharged or released from active duty because of a service-connected disability. (41 CFR 60-300.2(n))

Qualified Disabled Veteran

- A disabled veteran who has the ability to perform the essential functions of the employment position with or without reasonable accommodation. (41 CFR 60-300.2(o))

Other Protected Veteran

- A veteran who served on active duty in the U.S. military, ground, naval or air service during a war or in a campaign or expedition for which a campaign badge has been authorized, under the laws administered by the Department of Defense. (41 CFR 60-300.2(p))

Recently Separated Veteran

- Any veteran during the three-year period beginning on the date of such veteran's discharge or release from active duty in the U.S. military, ground, naval or air service. (41 CFR 60-300.2(q))

<u>Armed Forces Service Medal Veteran</u>

- Any veteran who, while serving on active duty in the U.S. military, ground, naval or air service, participated in a United States military operation for which an Armed Forces service medal was awarded pursuant to Executive Order 12985 (61 FR 1209) (41 CFR 60-300.2(r))

<u>Affirmative Action Clause for Veterans</u>

Following is the clause which employers must use in their purchase orders or bills of lading if they are subject to requirements for written AAPs for Disabled and/or Veterans.

Affirmative Action Clause – Special Disabled Veterans and Veterans of the Vietnam Era
41 CFR 60-300.5

[NOTE: Do not put this clause in your AAP document. This statement changed in 2007. Be sure you are using the current wording.]

*"Each contracting agency and each contractor and subcontractor shall **include the following equal opportunity clause in each of its covered government contracts or subcontracts** (and modifications, renewals, or extensions thereof if not included in the original contract):*

Equal Opportunity for Special Disabled Veterans Recently Separated Veterans, Other Protected Veterans, and Armed Forces Service Medal Veterans

1. The contractor will not discriminate against any employee or applicant for employment because he or she is a disabled veteran, recently separated veteran, other protected veteran, or Armed Forces service medal veteran in regard to any position for which the employee or applicant for employment is qualified. The contractor agrees to take affirmative action to employ, advance in employment and otherwise treat qualified individuals without discrimination based on their status as a disabled veteran, recently separated veteran, other protected veteran, or Armed Forces service medal veteran in all employment practices, including the following:
 i. Recruitment, advertising, and job application procedures;
 ii. Hiring, upgrading, promotion, award of tenure, demotion, transfer, layoff, termination, right of return from layoff and rehiring;
 iii. Rates of pay or any other form of compensation and changes in compensation; iv. Job assignments, job classifications, organizational structures, position descriptions, lines of progression, and seniority lists;
 v. Leaves of absence, sick leave, or any other leave;
 vi. Fringe benefits available by virtue of employment, whether or not administered by the contractor;
 vii. Selection and financial support for training, including apprenticeship, and on-the-job training under 38 U.S.C. 3687, professional meetings, conferences, and other related activities, and selection for leaves of absence to pursue training;
 viii. Activities sponsored by the contractor including social or recreational programs; and
 ix. Any other term, condition, or privilege of employment.

2. The contractor agrees to immediately list all employment openings which exist at the time of the execution of this contract and those which occur during the performance of this contract, including those not generated by this contract and including those occurring at an establishment of the contractor other than the one where the contract is being performed, but excluding those of independently operated corporate affiliates, with the appropriate employment service delivery system where the opening occurs. Listing employment openings with the state workforce agency job bank or with the local employment service delivery system where the opening occurs will satisfy the requirement to list jobs with the appropriate

employment service delivery system.

3.   Listing of employment openings with the appropriate employment service delivery system pursuant to this clause shall be made at least concurrently with the use of any other recruitment source or effort and shall involve the normal obligations which attach to the placing of a *bona fide* job order, including the acceptance of referrals of veterans and nonveterans. The listing of employment openings does not require the hiring of any particular job applicants or from any particular group of job applicants, and nothing herein is intended to relieve the contractor from any requirements in Executive orders or regulations regarding nondiscrimination in employment.

4. Whenever a contractor, other than a state or local governmental contractor, becomes contractually bound to the listing provisions in paragraphs 2 and 3 of this clause, it shall advise the state workforce agency in each state where it has establishments of the name and location of each hiring location in the state. As long as the contractor is contractually bound to these provisions and has so advised the state agency, there is no need to advise the state agency of subsequent contracts. The contractor may advise the state agency when it is no longer bound by this contract clause.

5. The provisions of paragraphs 2 and 3 of this clause do not apply to the listing of employment openings which occur and are filled outside of the 50 states, the District of Columbia, the Commonwealth of Puerto Rico, Guam, the Virgin Islands, American Samoa, the Commonwealth of the Northern Mariana Islands, Wake Island, and the Trust Territories of the Pacific Islands.
6. As used in this clause:
   i. *All employment openings* includes all positions except executive and senior management, those positions that will be filled from within the contractor's organization, and positions lasting three days or less. This term includes full-time employment, temporary employment of more than three days' duration, and part-time employment.
   ii. *Executive and senior management* means: (1) Any employee (a) compensated on a salary basis at a rate of not less than $455 per week (or $380 per week, if employed in American Samoa by employers other than the Federal Government), exclusive of board, lodging or other facilities; (b) whose primary duty is management of the enterprise in which the employee is employed or of a customarily recognized department or subdivision thereof; (c) who customarily and regularly directs the work of two or more other employees; and (d) who has the authority to hire or fire other employees or whose suggestions and recommendations as to the hiring, firing, advancement, promotion or any other change of status of other employees are given particular weight; or (2) any employee who owns at least a bona fide 20-percent equity interest in the enterprise in which the employee is employed, regardless of whether the business is a corporate or other type of organization, and who is actively engaged in its management.
   iii. *Positions that will be filled from within the contractor's organization* means employment openings for which no consideration will be given to persons outside the contractor's organization (including any affiliates, subsidiaries, and parent companies) and includes any openings which the contractor proposes to fill from regularly established "recall" lists. The exception does not apply to a particular opening once an employer decides to consider applicants outside of his or her own organization.

7. The contractor agrees to comply with the rules, regulations, and relevant orders of the Secretary of Labor issued pursuant to the Act.

8. In the event of the contractor's noncompliance with the requirements of this clause, actions for noncompliance may be taken in accordance with the rules, regulations, and relevant orders of the Secretary of Labor issued pursuant to the Act.

9. The contractor agrees to post in conspicuous places, available to employees and applicants for employment, notices in a form to be prescribed by the Deputy Assistant Secretary for Federal Contract Compliance, provided by or through the contracting officer. Such notices shall state the rights of applicants and employees as well as the contractor's obligation under the law to take affirmative action to employ and advance in employment qualified employees and applicants who are disabled veterans, recently separated veterans, other protected veterans, or Armed Forces service medal veterans. The contractor must ensure that applicants or employees who are disabled veterans are informed of the contents of the notice (*e.g.*, the contractor may have the notice read to a visually disabled individual, or may lower the posted notice so that it might be read by a person in a wheelchair).

10. The contractor will notify each labor organization or representative of workers with which it has a collective bargaining agreement or other contract understanding, that the contractor is bound by the terms of the Vietnam Era Veterans' Readjustment Assistance Act of 1974, as amended, and is committed to take affirmative action to employ and advance in employment qualified disabled veterans, recently separated veterans, other protected veterans, and Armed Forces service medal veterans.

11. The contractor will include the provisions of this clause in every subcontract or purchase order of $100,000 or more, unless exempted by the rules, regulations, or orders of the Secretary issued pursuant to the Vietnam Era Veterans' Readjustment Assistance Act of 1974, as amended, so that such provisions will be binding upon each subcontractor or vendor. The contractor will take such action with respect to any subcontract or purchase order as the Deputy Assistant Secretary for Federal Contract Compliance may direct to enforce such provisions, including action for noncompliance.

PLEASE NOTE: Listing Job Openings with State Employment Service is Required[9]

As it now stands, __ALL employment openings must be filed__ with the State employment service, EXCEPT:

- *Executive and Senior Management positions*[10]
- *Positions that will be filled from within the organization*[11]
- *Positions lasting three days or less*

America's Job Bank (AJB) ceased its operations on June 30, 2007, due to lack of Congressional funding. That leaves contractors in the position of having to seek out each state's employment service and file job openings with the service where the job is located. Some state employment services will accept job listings only by FAX, some will accept them only by email, and others will accept them only if entered via their on-line web site. This makes a contractor's life complicated if there are job openings in several states. I'm afraid there is little we can do but get in and dig. There are commercial services available to handle the job listing placement with each individual state service, just like AJB used to do for us, but they charge in the five-digit range. We don't recommend any of them because we don't believe they are cost effective. You can hire a full-time clerk for about what it would cost to have one of these services process your job opening announcements.

If you need to find contact information about your state's job placement service, the government maintains a web site that allows you to point to a U.S. map and get what you need. Go to: http://www.jobbankinfo.org/ .

---

[9] The contractor agrees to immediately list all employment openings which exist at the time of the execution of this contract and those which occur during the performance of this contract, including those not generated by this contract and including those occurring at an establishment of the contractor other than the one where the contract is being performed, but excluding those independently operated corporate affiliates, with the appropriate employment service delivery system where the opening occurs. Listing employment openings with the state workforce agency job bank or with the local employment service delivery system where the opening occurs will satisfy the requirement to list jobs with the appropriate employment service delivery system. (41 CFR 60-300.5(a)(2))

All *employment openings* includes all positions except executive and senior management, those positions that will be filled from within the contractor's organization, and positions lasting three days or less. This term includes full-time employment, temporary employment of more than three days' duration, and part-time employment. (41 CFR 60-300.5(a)(6)(i))

[10] *Executive and senior management* means: (1) Any employee (a) compensated on a salary basis at a rate of not less than $455 per week (or $380 per week, if employed in American Samoa by employers other than the Federal Government), exclusive of board, lodging or other facilities; (b) whose primary duty is management of the enterprise in which the employee is employed or of a customarily recognized department or subdivision thereof; (c) who customarily and regularly directs the work of two or more other employees; and (d) who has the authority to hire and fire other employees or whose suggestions and recommendations as to the hiring, firing, advancement, promotion or any other change of status of other employees are given particular weight; or (2) any employee who owns at least a bona fide 20percent equity interest in the enterprise in which the employee is employed, regardless of whether the business is a corporate or other type of organization, and who is actively engaged in its management. (41 CFR 60-300.5(a)(6)(ii))

[11] *Positions that will be filled from within the contractor's organization* means employment openings for which no consideration will be given to persons outside the contractor's organization (including any affiliates, subsidiaries, and parent companies) and includes any openings which the contractor proposes to fill from regularly established "recall" lists. The exception does not apply to a particular opening once an employer decides to consider applicants outside of his or her own organization. (41 CFR 60-300.5(a)(6)(iii))

Why Not Put All Three Plans Into One Document?

When you have had the chance to review the content requirements of all three AAPs (women and minorities, disabled and veteran), you will see that there are some rather significant overlaps. For example, each plan requires a policy statement. Each plan requires a statement of responsibility assignments and how the policy will be disseminated internally and externally. There are other similarities and overlaps as well.

Given those overlaps, why not make the required narrative content work for you by combining all three subjects into one document? My answer to that question is, "It makes a lot of sense." You can save paper, simplify the process, make the document less intimidating to the line managers who will have to use it and generally communicate in a clearer fashion.

There is no guidance to be had from the OFCCP regulations about combining AAPs. We know that each establishment must have its own document. It is the employer's choice as to how that happens.

The employer gets to choose to keep each of the three plans in separate documents, or to combine them into one volume with shared sections. I recommend you consider the combined approach because it can make your life simpler in many ways.

When Do I Have to Complete My AAP?

The regulations tell us that each written AAP must be updated and re-implemented each year. (41 CFR 60-300.40(c)) They don't tell us when the plan year must begin. So, employers get to choose when to begin their plan year.

Assuming the contract value and employee head count qualify, a new contractor has 120 days from the beginning of the first contract to complete development and begin implementation of its AAP. (*41 CFR 60-300.40(b)*) *"Contractors ... shall, within 120 days of the commencement of a contract, prepare and maintain an affirmative action program at each establishment."*

As far as "normal" AAP year is concerned, here are some additional thoughts.

> The employer gets to designate when its AAP year will begin and end. That is not required to be a calendar year. Often, employers want their AAP year to coincide with their financial fiscal year. Other times, subsidiaries are asked by their parent organizations to comport with the parent company's plan year. This might well make summarizing reports on results easier to accomplish. Creating report summaries for different plans on different plan years can be a bit of a headache.

> OFCCP will accept a plan year with any starting and ending dates the employer wishes. The only requirement is that once the plan year is established, it not be changed without a valid business reason for making the change. Much like the IRS requirement for corporate income tax reporting. The company can set its tax year as it chooses, but may only change it for a valid business reason.

If your organization is purchased by another company and the new parent wants you to change your fiscal and AAP years to match the ones it uses, that is a valid business reason for making a change. You should document the reason for the decision and make sure your AAP records and files reflect that documentation. If you are ever audited by the OFCCP you will have to produce the documentation to justify the decision and action.

So, pick whatever year you want. And, then, stick with it. Change it only if you have a valid business reason to do so. Then, be sure you have documented the reasons for any change and that the documentation is in your AAP files.

When making a plan year change, follow the OFCCP's "rule of thumb" which is:

If you are less than six months into your current plan year, you may continue using your existing plan until the new plan year begins. If you are more than six months into your current plan year, update your AAP document at the time you make the plan year change.

Narrative Sections - A Word or Two About Writing Style

Over the years, I have read many AAPs written in many different styles. Some people have told me that the style they used was one they didn't like but they used it because it was "required" by the government.

Nothing in the regulations tells you what style to use in developing your AAP document. You are free to use whatever style is best for you and your organization.

My suggestion to you, however, is that you pick the writing style that will most effectively communicate within your organization. Look at the type of documents you have in your organization which deal with other subjects and analyze the style used in their creation. What style would seem familiar to your management staff? What style would be easiest to use because it is culturally familiar?

Remember, you should be guided by how effectively your AAP can be implemented and understood. Ultimately, you will be judged by the "good faith efforts" you are making to develop and implement an effective affirmative action program. If style will help you demonstrate your "good faith efforts" then focus on that as a reason for your choice of style.

You get to decide.

How Long Will It Take To Prepare My AAP?

It wasn't until April 30, 1999, that the **OFCCP made an official estimate of hours required for preparation of an affirmative action plan**. The agency was required to do so as part of its application for collecting information via the compliance evaluation-scheduling letter. Here is what they said:

a. *Recordkeeping Burden*

A recordkeeping burden is imposed by OFCCP regulations to develop, update, and maintain Affirmative Action Programs. Using contractor estimates of the hours required to annually update an AAP, as well as discussions with District Office staff who regularly assist contractors to comply with the requirements, we have calculated recordkeeping hours for these three functions as follows:

1) *Initial Development of AAP*

It is estimated that only one percent of the contractor universe is first-time contractors required to develop their initial AAPs. However, for the one percent (898), it is estimated that the development time is more than 2½ times greater than the time required for the annual update. Size of the workforce influences the amount of time required. Small employers (50 to 100 employees) generally spend 133 hours. Large employers (1000+ employees) generally spend 366 hours.

Average time required per contractor for initial AAP = 179.5 hours

---

2) *Annual Updating of AAP*

[OFCCP made an] estimate of professional and clerical time required for contractors to accomplish the annual update of their AAPs. Small employers are estimated to spend no less than 32 hours, split equally between professionals and clerical workers. Large employers are estimated to spend about 235 hours, about 2/3 of it by professionals and the remaining 1/3 by clerical workers.

Average time required per contractor for annual updates = 74.9 hours

---

Remember, that's uninterrupted time during which you can concentrate. Let your boss know about these estimates. It is a budget item, particularly if you contract with a consultant or attorney for the development service.

If I Hire Someone to Prepare My AAP, What Will it Cost?

Asking how much it will cost to prepare an affirmative action plan is like asking how long is a piece of string. There are two major variables involved in determining cost:

- What will be included in the deliverables?
- What amount of support will you receive when you begin to implement your plan?

If you ask for bids from several consulting firms for your AAP preparation, you would be well advised to list the deliverables you expect them to provide. Do you want only statistical reports prepared for your minority's and women's AAP? Do you want the narrative sections included in the project? How about the AAPs for disabled and veterans? Are those to be included? What about statistical analysis required for your disparate impact testing of new hires, promotions and terminations? And, how about compensation analysis to determine equal pay discrepancies or illegal discrimination?

You see, what you include will help determine the cost of the project. It is not appropriate to compare bids until you know they have all been developed for the same set of deliverables.

Ask your attorney or consultant how much support they are willing to provide as you begin implementation of your AAP. Is management training included in their bid? Will they accept telephone calls and answer questions that arise during the course of your AAP year? Are any or all of those types of "extra" activities going to cost you more over time?

We know some AAP developers who price their jobs based on what the client is willing to pay. In my view, that is like picking a surgeon based on the amount of money you have in your pocket.

You don't want to waste money, but generally speaking, you get what you pay for.

Can You Give Me a Master Checklist for All I Have to Do to Be In Compliance?

Sure. We all like things to be as simple as possible. Don't let the following table fool you. Many of these items do not represent events or milestones, but rather ongoing activities every federal contractor is responsible for managing throughout their AAP year.

In addition, you will find other checklists in other sections of this book that offer more details.

See the next page.

Master AAP Checklist for Compliance

☒	Action	Citation	Description
	Advertising Tag Line	41 CFR 60-1.41(a)	Add "Equal Opportunity Employer" or something similar to all employment advertising
	EEO Poster & OFCCP Notice	41 CFR 60-1.4 41 CFR 60-1.42(a)	Specific wording is specified within the EO Clause. Must be posted so both applicants and employees may see them.
	EEO-1 Report	41 CFR 60-1.7(a)(1)	Must file report annually if you are an AAP employer.
	Equal Opportunity Clause in Subcontracts	41 CFR 60-1.4(c) 41 CFR 60-741.5 41 CFR 60-300.5	May be incorporated by reference if desired. Must be included in vendor agreements, purchase orders, etc.
	Invitation to Self-Identify	41 CFR 60-741.23(c) 41 CFR 60-741.42 41 CFR 60-300.42	Must invite all new hires to identify as disabled or veterans if they wish.
	Listing Job Openings With State Employment Service	41 CFR 60-300.5(2)	Most job openings must be listed with state employment service or with America's Job Bank.
	Posting Location & Hours When AAP May be Reviewed	41 CFR 60-741.41 41 CFR 60-300.5(2)	Post a notice identifying location & hours when applicants and employees may access the AAP for Disabled and Veterans.
	Prepare/update AAP document for Disabled	*Rehabilitation Act of 1973, Sections 503 & 504* 41 CFR 60-741	Narrative sections speaking to each AAP provision required by the regulations.
	Prepare/update AAP document for Minorities & Women	E.O. 11246 41 CFR 60-1.7	Narrative & statistical analysis of workforce, setting goals & citing goal achievement results from previous year.
	Prepare/update AAP document for Veterans	*Vietnam Era Veterans Readjustment Assistance Act of 1974* 41 CFR 60-300.40	Narrative sections speaking to each AAP provision required by the regulations.
	Provision of non-segregated facilities	41 CFR 60-1.8	Restrooms, dressing rooms, sleeping areas must be separate for each sex.
	Retention of Records (Includes ALL employment-related records including all expressions of interest in employment and all notes of interviews or discussions.)	41 CFR 60-1.12 41 CFR 60-741.80 41 CFR 60-741.23(d) 41 CFR 60-300.80	Personnel & employment records must be kept for one year if employer has fewer than 150 employees or does not have a federal contract of at least $150,000. Requirement is for 2 years if those limits are exceeded.
	Union Notification	41 CFR 60-1.4 41 CFR 60-1.42(b) 41 CFR 60-741.5(a) 41 CFR 60-300.44(g)(vi)	Notify each labor union of employer requirements under EO 11246, Rehabilitation Act & VEVRAA.
	VETS-100 Report and/or VETS-100A Report	41 CFR Part 61	Must file annual VETS-100 and/or VETS-100A Reports with Office of Veterans' Employment & Training, U.S. Department of Labor.

Notes

CHAPTER 3

WHAT NARRATIVE SECTIONS ARE REQUIRED?

Narrative Sections for Minority and Women AAP

On the following pages, you will find an explanation of required content for your Minorities and Women AAP. Each section is identified by a number for the sake of convenience. There is no regulatory requirement that the sections be placed in the sequence we have shown them. On the other hand, this sequence seems to make some sense. You may, however, place the information in any order you wish when writing your AAP. And, you may call the sections by whatever title you like. Numbers are used here because they are easy to use as reference.

At the end of this chapter of the book you will find a sample set of AAP narrative sections. It is very important that you not simply copy these words and adopt them as your own plan. To be in compliance, your plan must fit your organization and your needs. It must contain the specific information appropriate to how your organization operates and plans it has made to correct any identified deficiencies. So, **you will need to modify the sample before you use it.**

Many of the ideas or suggestions for content you will find here can be of help to you in building your own AAP. I have tried to give you a head start in the thinking process by offering ideas you would be able to generate on your own given time, but which might save you some effort in the short run.

Eventually, your AAP development efforts will become much easier as you gain experience with the process.

MINORITY AND WOMEN'S AAP BY SECTION

AAP Narrative Requirements

SECTION 1: **Responsibilities for Implementation of AAP.**

❑ Required Content of This Section

Regulations say, *"The contractor must provide for the implementation of equal employment opportunity and the affirmative action program by assigning responsibility and accountability to an official of the organization. Depending upon the size of the contractor, this may be the official's sole responsibility. He or she must have the authority, resources, support of and access to top management to ensure the effective implementation of the affirmative action program."* *(60-2.17(a))*

The OFCCP's Compliance Manual says, *"to be acceptable, the AAP must identify the person who is responsible for implementation of the policy and must describe how the policy is implemented, in sufficient detail for the (Compliance Officer) to be able to audit compliance...The AAP should identify the EEO Officer by name and/or title, and may describe his or her duties and responsibilities as well as those of line managers with respect to EEO."* *(FCCM, Par. 2G10)*

❑ Employer Suggestions

Since this AAP document is (or can be) a valuable communication tool, I suggest that you consider four categories for your responsibility assignments. Sometimes, we find information about CEO responsibilities and HR Manager responsibilities in other documents. Occasionally, we find managers and employees given responsibilities to follow employer policies in documents such as employee handbooks or policy manuals. Nonetheless, this is an excellent opportunity to reinforce the notion that everyone has a role to play in successful implementation of your affirmative action plan. Don't miss the opportunity.

■ Chief Executive Officer (Required Content)

The Chief Executive Officer (CEO) is the one person who is ultimately accountable for successful implementation of the AAP. In some cases, primarily in very large organizations, an AAP will show the senior executive for the establishment with ultimate responsibility for AAP and policies. That's OK, too. And, that's all you have to say in your AAP document about this person. He or she is responsible for assuring that the plan is properly prepared and properly implemented. Show the name and/or title of the individual in this position.

■ **Affirmative Action Manager (Required Content)**

Actually, the category should probably be titled, "Person responsible for day-to-day implementation activities related to affirmative action." Since that's a bit long, I have defaulted to the Affirmative Action Manager title. Ordinarily, the HR Manager, Director of HR, Personnel Manager or EEO/AA Director will be the person who carries daily implementation responsibilities for AAP. Whoever it is, show that person's name and/or job title in the heading, and then list the responsibilities performed by him/her. Review the required list above, and then consider the following for your list:

- Develop policy statements, AAP, internal and external communication techniques.
- Assist in identification of problem areas.
- Assist line management in solving problems.
- Design and implement audit and reporting systems.
- Liaison between organization and OFCCP.
- Liaison between organization and minority organizations, women's organizations, and community action groups.
- Keep management informed of developments in EEO.
  > Audit training programs, hiring and promotion patterns.
  > Review qualifications of all employees to insure minorities and women are given full opportunity for transfers and promotions.
  > Career counseling for all employees.
  > Posters properly displayed.
  > All supervisors' work performance evaluation based in part on their efforts and results with EEO/AA.
  > Prevent harassment of employees placed through affirmative action efforts.

■ **All Managers and Supervisors (Recommended Content)**

If you look at this as a communication tool, one which managers and supervisors should receive a copy of and use from time-to-time in their management activities, then it is a perfect opportunity to explain again how managers have responsibilities for following organization policies and insuring everyone equal employment opportunity. As a matter of practice, that's about all you have to say.

■ **All Employees (Recommended Content)**

Here, again, is an opportunity to include all employees and to reinforce the expectation that everyone in the enterprise has a responsibility to abide by the equal employment opportunity policy. Don't ever miss the opportunity to communicate, again, and again, and again. Once is never enough.

SECTION 2: **Internal Audit and Reporting Systems**

❏ **Required Content**

Regulations say, *"The contractor must develop and implement an auditing system that periodically measures the effectiveness of its total affirmative action program. The actions listed below are key to a successful affirmative action program:*

> *(1) Monitor records of all personnel activity, including referrals, placements, transfers, promotions, terminations, and compensation, at all levels to ensure the nondiscriminatory policy is carried out;*
>
> *(2) Require internal reporting on a scheduled basis as to the degree to which equal employment opportunity and organizational objectives are attained;*
>
> *(3) Review report results with all levels of management; and*
>
> *(4) Advise top management of program effectiveness and submit recommendations to improve unsatisfactory performance.*

The Federal Contractor Compliance Manual has not yet been revised to reflect the new regulatory content. No doubt, when that happens, more will be said about the issues of monitoring systems.

Currently, the FCCM says, *"The system must permit adequate monitoring of progress made toward goal accomplishment and implementation of other affirmative action commitments... An acceptable audit and reporting system is one which allows the contractor to measure the effectiveness of its total program. Such a system should include specific procedures for monitoring goals progress and analyzing employment activity... Since utilization and availability analysis are conducted by job group, and where problems are identified, goals are established by job group, monitoring of goals progress should be at least by job group... Results of the AAP should be compiled annually... Audit and reporting systems should also monitor personnel activity (e.g., hires, promotions/transfers, terminations, and other activity) at least by job group and, where appropriate, by organizational unit..."* (FCCM, Par. 2G14(a-c)).

❏ **Employer Suggestions**

There is no requirement for computer tracking systems. There is a requirement for tracking systems. As the contractor, you get to decide how best to create the tracking systems you need so your obligations under this section of the regulations are met. This obligation is not new. It contains the same requirements as in the old regulations.

When writing your narrative for this section of the AAP, consider identifying the types of data that you track on personnel activity in your establishment. The minimum should be logs showing applicants by sex and ethnicity within job titles, new hires by sex and ethnicity within job titles, terminations by sex and ethnicity within job titles, and promotions/transfers by sex and ethnicity within job titles.

60

If you have never had a written AAP before, chances are you will have none of these data tracking logs in place when you begin your first AAP year. That's OK. Remember, your obligation is to make a good faith effort to implement your AAP obligations. In the first year, you can be forgiven virtually anything. Simply do this. Identify what reports you intend to implement during the first AAP year so all the data you require will be available for use in modifying your AAP when you begin year two. That's how simple it is. You can't be held accountable for meeting requirements before they applied to you. So, in your first year, you state that you know what the requirements are, and you plan to put yourself in a position to meet them when you begin your next AAP year.

<u>SECTION 3</u>: Identification of Problem Areas

❑ **Required Content**

Regulations say, *"The contractor must perform in-depth analyses of its total employment process to determine whether and where impediments to equal employment opportunity exist. At a minimum the contractor must evaluate:*

(1) The workforce by organizational unit and job group to determine whether there are problems of minority or female utilization (i.e., employment in the unit or group), or of minority or female distribution (i.e., placement in the different jobs within the unit or group);

(2) Personnel activity (applicant flow, hires, terminations, promotions, and other personnel actions) to determine whether there are selection disparities;

(3) Compensation system(s) to determine whether there are gender-, race-, or ethnicity-based disparities;

(4) Selection, recruitment, referral, and other personnel procedures to determine whether they result in disparities in the employment or advancement of minorities or women; and

(5) Any other areas that might impact the success of the affirmative action program. (60-2.17(b))

The Federal Contract Compliance Manual offers, *"To be acceptable, the AAP must provide evidence that the contractor has addressed the following: ...The contractor must examine its basic employment processes (recruitment, hiring, training, promotion, transfer, termination) to identify any impediments to the full utilization of minorities and women. To do so, in its AAP, the contractor may use any analysis that measures how these processes affect minorities and women. For example, the contractor may use Impact Ratio Analysis... The contractor must examine the distribution of minorities and women among its organizational units. To do so, the contractor may use any analysis that identifies any problem areas in such distribution. For example, the contractor may use a Job Area Acceptance Range (JAAR) type analysis to identify areas of minority or female concentration/underrepresentation and/or a utilization analysis applied to job groups within such units."* (FCCM, Par. 2G11(a-b))

❑ Employer Suggestions

This is a tricky section to write in your AAP. If you do disparate impact testing (impact ratio analysis) and discover you may have some discrimination indicated by the result, rather than write that you have discovered disparate impact, write that an investigation has begun into the reasons why certain phases of your employment process appear to be screening out more protected group members than it should. Conceivably, your AAP document could be used as evidence in a lawsuit against the organization based on discrimination charges. You don't want to admit to anything without explaining that you are taking measures to correct the problem indicated.

There are some protections that might be sought from the "critical self analysis" concept in law. Your employment law attorney can help you with that issue if it becomes necessary. As a legal defense, it says basically that you are not to be held liable for results of doing a self-audit in areas such as affirmative action planning and implementation. Critical self-analysis is required by the Federal regulations. You cannot avoid going through the process. Some courts have held that to penalize employer organizations for abiding by the regulations doesn't make any sense. Especially if they subsequently take action to correct the problems uncovered in that analysis.

Still, it makes good sense to carefully craft your words in the AAP document.

To meet the requirements of this section, use the checklist on the following page as a guide in your yearly audit of your AAP implementation efforts. Then, based on the results of your audit, prepare a narrative outlining the problems you discovered.

I always prefer displaying a table of information in this section of the AAP that shows a complete list of job groups in the establishment. Within that matrix is indicated those job groups that are experiencing an underutilization of either minorities or women. It becomes a pictorial summary of the Utilization Analysis you will find discussed in the chapter on Utilization.

So, since we have yet to complete a statistical analysis of our workforce, we are not fully in a position to write this section of our AAP. Only after all the statistical analysis is done can we summarize the results into this narrative section of our plan.

This section offers an excellent opportunity for reviewing last year's AAP goals and our progress toward them. Were our goals reached? If so, which ones? If not, what happened to prevent us from getting to them? If our good faith efforts to reach the goals didn't succeed, why not? We are required to critique our goal achievement for our previous AAP year.

Minority & Women Affirmative Action
Problem Identification
Checklist

Executive Order 11246 Requirements	Completed?
AAP document contains a review of last year's goal accomplishments	
Applicant is defined as required in OFCCP regulations	
Applicant Demographics collected with voluntary request form	✓
Applicant Logs complete for current year	
Apprenticeship Programs nondiscriminatory & include minorities & women	
Disparate Impact Analysis (Impact Ratio Analysis) completed on all applicant and employee activity	
Employee Attitudes monitored regarding EEO/AA	
Employee Data verified for accurate sex & ethnic identification	
Employee Referral Procedures reviewed (producing minority & female candidates)	
Employer Training Programs include minorities & women	
Employment Applications Retained for at least two years after job is filled	
Employment Posters in all work locations	
Employment Screening Tests reviewed (validation data on file if necessary)	
Final Selections documented and filed with candidate papers	
Interview Procedures and interviewer training reviewed	
Job Application Forms reviewed	
Job Description review	
Job Group Analysis by EEO code or job group	
Job Title review	
New Hire Logs complete for current year	
Promotion Logs complete for current year	
Records are retained according to 2005 regulations	
Selection Criteria for Each Job reviewed	
Seniority Practices & Union Contracts nondiscriminatory	
Termination Logs complete for current year	
Training Participation Logs complete for current year	
Transfer & Promotion Practices reviewed	
Transfer Logs complete for current year	
Union Notification Letters on file from current year	
Vendor/Supplier Notification Letters on file from current year	
Workforce Analysis by department or Organizational Profile Chart	

SAMPLE
Minority & Women Affirmative Action
Summary for Analysis of Incumbents vs. Availability

Job Group	B/AA	H	A	P	I	F	# Needed
Officials & Managers - Top							
Officials & Managers - Middle							
Officials & Managers - Lower							
Professionals - Technical							
Professionals - Administrative							
Technicians							
Sales Workers							
Senior Administrative Support Workers							
Junior Administrative Support Workers							
Craft Workers							
Operatives							
Laborers & Helpers							
Service Workers							

Key: B/AA = Black/African American   H = Hispanic   A = Asian   P = Native Hawiian/Pacific Islander I = Native American/Alaska Native   F = Female
Needed = Quantity of additional employees to eliminate the Underutilization at this time.

Using this type of table to summarize the results of your Analysis of Incumbents vs. Availability will give you the option of addressing results from your statistical analysis without having to insert the actual analysis forms into your AAP document if you choose not to do so. There is more advice about the subject in Chapter 4 on Data Analysis.

<u>SECTION 4</u>: Development of Action Oriented Programs

❑ **Required Content**

Regulations say, *"The contractor must develop and execute action-oriented programs designed to correct any problem areas identified pursuant to Section 60-2.17(b) and to attain established goals and objectives. In order for these action-oriented programs to be effective, the contractor must ensure that they consist of more than following the same procedures that have previously produced inadequate results. Furthermore, a contractor must demonstrate that it has made good faith efforts to remove identified barriers, expand employment opportunities, and produce measurable results.* (60-2.17(c)).

The Federal Contract Compliance Manual adds these words, *"The contractor may commit to increasing the number of qualified minorities and women in the appropriate candidate pool, since with more women and minorities in the candidate pool, the logical outcome, absent discrimination, is an increase in the number of minorities and women hired, promoted, etc. [The Compliance Officer must] make a professional judgment as to whether the action-oriented programs are sufficiently specific and result-oriented to accomplish the aims for which they were created, and whether they were properly executed.*

"A specific action oriented program is one that indicates <u>what</u> the action is, <u>who</u> will accomplish it, <u>how</u> it will be accomplished and <u>when</u> it will be accomplished. An action-oriented program without any one of these ingredients cannot be considered specific.

"A results-oriented action program is one tailored in such a way that proper execution will result either in an increase in the minority group/female representation in the job group, if vacancies occur, or clear documentation of contractor action sufficient to constitute good faith effort. An action-oriented program that does not meet this standard cannot be considered results-oriented.

"The AAP's action items must be sufficient, if implemented in good faith, to ensure that each of its specific objectives and the overall intent of equal employment opportunity are achieved." (*FCCM, Par. 2G13(a-d)*)

❑ **Employer Suggestions**

The really surprising thing I have found in about fifteen years of working with employers on affirmative action issues is that the vast majority will look at this task and throw up their hands saying it's too hard. It can't be accomplished. They say they have no idea where to begin the process of identifying sources of minority and female candidates.

If you will forgive me my bias, I think that's simply lazy. Sure, the task may take a bit of energy and creativity, but that's the purpose of the process. The human resources manager, personnel manager, or AAP manager is charged with identifying and then building linkages with these organizations. In the first place, if that is not done, the organization will not be in compliance.

So it is a no-choice task. Second, it doesn't take much real effort to begin the process. The biggest challenge, I find, is getting over the hurdle of believing it's too hard.

Call your local United Way headquarters. They are almost always listed in the white business pages of your local phone book. Ask them which of their member agencies offers job training programs to minorities and women. Ask if any others offer job placement services without training people. Then, look for the telephone number of the local chapters of these organizations: National Organization for Women, Urban League, Hispanic Chamber of Commerce, Chinese for Affirmative Action, and Bureau of Indian Affairs. If you don't find local phone listings, call each organization's national headquarters. Most are in Washington, DC or Virginia. Look at the list of potential sources you will find in Appendix B. Inquire of them if they have a local chapter in your area.

Once you have a list of local organizations, call each one and explain why you are calling. You are attempting to create a list of sources for qualified minority and female candidates for jobs you expect to have available during the coming year. Get acquainted with one of the people at each organization. Establish a personal contact. Ask if it would be all right to send job opening announcements when they are released. Ask if they would be interested in spending a couple hours some day to tour your work facility and see the type of jobs you have on a first hand basis.

Take it one step at a time and you will find the project is not very daunting at all. Just don't give up before you start.

Then, plan your implementation training for your managers and supervisors. Your senior establishment executive should be present at each of the training sessions to emphasize personal commitment to the EEO/AAP program. Remember, that is something you can document as part of your good faith effort. But, for now, identify the planning process in your AAP and, if possible, establish target dates.

List your action plans on a chart like the one below, if you don't already have a personal preference for another format. Remember, the OFCCP will be judging your action plans for thoroughness and completeness as well as measurability and accomplishment.

This is a very simple little action planning matrix. You likely use something similar to it now in your action plan development. I like this approach because it shows at a glance all of the key information about the problem, what steps are to be taken, who will be responsible for each step, and what the objective completion date is. This approach will also meet all of the requirements of the OFCCP.

This is a flexible approach, too. It can be done on a blank piece of paper, on easel paper, or on a white board in the conference room. You don't need to have special forms to do your target setting with this approach. And, it lends itself easily to group discussions. The document can become the output of your group discussion sessions.

Sample Action Planning Form
Affirmative Action Program

Problem Identified	Action Steps	Person Responsible	Target Date
1. Need for local M/W recruiting sources	1. Call United Way 2. Call NOW 3. Call national HQ of other key orgs.	HR Manager	End of 1Q2012
2. AAP training - managers/supervisors	1. Schedule conf rm 2. Develop outline 3. Prepare aides 4. CEO support	HR Manager

CEO | Complete all sessions by end of 1Q2012 |
3. Candidate pools need more M/W representation	1. Target candidate pool demographics at availability %s 2. Personally talk with contacts at M/W recruiting source organizations 3. Don't allow selection in job groups with under-utilization until M/W candidates are in selection pool for consideration	HR Manager	End of January 2012
4. Employees asking about child care	1. Establish study plan to determine if child care program will benefit company and employees	HR Manager Line Managers	End of 2Q2012
5. Transportation problems for some M/W	1. Identify employee concerns with questionnaire 2. Involve line management in survey	HR Staff Line Managers	End of 3Q2012

Remember, this section of your AAP document will become your own set of commitments for actions to be taken during the ensuing 12 months of AAP effort. **You will be judged during a compliance review by whether or not you exhibited good faith efforts to implement your action plans and make the progress you set out to make.** Completing the document and then letting it gather dust on your office bookshelf is a sure way to gain criticism for lack of good faith efforts to implement your AAP. Overall, good faith efforts will carry the day.

❑ Recordkeeping Requirements

Regulations were updated in 2005 with the following requirements effective on February 6, 2006: (41 CFR 60-1.12)

Sec. 60-1.12 Record Retention

*(a) General requirements.   * * * Such records include, but are not necessarily limited to,*
  - *Records pertaining to hiring, assignment, promotion, demotion, transfer, lay off or termination, rates of pay or other terms of compensation, and selection for training or apprenticeship,*
  - *And other records having to do with requests for reasonable accommodation,*
  - *The results of any physical examination*
  - *Job advertisements and postings,*
  - *Applications, resumes, and any and all expressions of interest through the Internet or related electronic data technologies as to which the contractor considered the individual for a particular position, such as on-line resumes or internal resume databases,*
  - *Records identifying job seekers contacted regarding their interest in a particular position (for purposes of recordkeeping with respect to internal resume databases, the contractor must maintain a record of*
    - *Each resume added to the database,*
    - *A record of the date each resume was added to the database,*
    - *The position for which each search of the database was made,*
    - *And corresponding to each search, the substantive search criteria used*
    - *And the date of the search;*
  - *For purposes of recordkeeping with respect to external resume databases, the contractor must maintain*
    - *a record of the position for which each search of the database was made,*
    - *and corresponding to each search, the substantive search criteria used,*
    - *the date of the search,*
    - *and the resumes of job seekers who met the basic qualifications for the particular position who are considered by the contractor,*
    regardless of whether the individual qualifies as an Internet Applicant under 41 CFR 60-1.3
  - *Tests and test results*
  - *And interview notes.*
    [Bullets added for clarity.]

How Long Must We Keep Records?

"Any personnel or employment record made or kept by the contractor shall be preserved by the contractor for a period of not less than two years from the date of the making of the record or the personnel action involved, whichever occurs later. However, if the contractor has fewer than 150 employees or does not have a Government contract of at least $150,000, the minimum record retention period shall be one year from the date of the making of the record or the personnel action involved, whichever occurs later. Such records include, but are not necessarily

limited to, records pertaining to hiring, assignment, promotion, demotion, transfer, lay off or termination, rates of pay or other terms of compensation, and selection for training or apprenticeship, and other records having to do with requests for reasonable accommodation, the results of any physical examination, job advertisements and postings, applications and resumes, tests and test results, and interview notes. In the case of involuntary termination of an employee, the personnel records of the individual terminated shall be kept for a period of not less than two years from the date of the termination, except that contractors that have fewer than 150 employees or that do not have a Government contract of at least $150,000 shall keep such records for a period of not less than one year from the date of termination. Where the contractor has received notice that a complaint of discrimination has been filed, that a compliance evaluation has been initiated, or that an enforcement action has been commenced, the contractor shall preserve all personnel records relevant to the complaint, compliance evaluation or enforcement action. The term "personnel records relevant to the complaint," for example, would include personnel or employment records relating to the complainant and to all other employees holding positions similar to that held or sought by the complainant and application forms or test papers submitted by unsuccessful applicants and by all other candidates for the same position as that for which the complainant unsuccessfully applied. Where a compliance evaluation has been initiated, all personnel and employment records described above are relevant until OFCCP makes a final disposition of the evaluation." (60-1.12(a))

"A contractor establishment required under Section 60-1.40 to develop and maintain a written affirmative action program (AAP) must maintain its current AAP and documentation of good faith effort, and must preserve its AAP and documentation of good faith effort for the immediately preceding AAP year, unless it was not then covered by the AAP requirement." (60-1.12(b))

"(1) For any record the contractor maintains pursuant to this section, the contractor must be able to identify:

> *(i)   The gender, race, and ethnicity of each employee; and*
>
> *(ii)   Where possible, the gender, race, and ethnicity of each applicant or Internet Applicant as defined in 41 CFR 60-1.3, whichever is applicable to the particular position.*

(2) The contractor must supply this information to the Office of Federal Contract Compliance Programs upon request." (60-1.12(c))

*"**Failure to preserve complete and accurate records** as required by paragraphs (a) through (c) [60-1.12] of this section **constitutes noncompliance** with the contractor's obligations under the Executive Order and this part. **Where the contractor has destroyed or failed to preserve records as required by this section, there may be a presumption that the information destroyed or not preserved would have been unfavorable to the contractor**: [Emphasis added.] Provided, That this presumption shall not apply where the contractor shows that the destruction or failure to preserve records results from the circumstances that are outside of the contractor's control."* (60-1.12(d))

"The requirements of this section shall apply only to records made or kept on or after December 22, 1997." (60-1.12(e))

❑ **Employer Suggestions**

Retention requirements have been split into two categories, based on the size of the contract and the size of the contractor's workforce. Here's how it goes: If the contractor has **fewer than 150 employees** or does not have a Government **contract of at least $150,000 the retention period for these records is one year**. **If either of those thresholds is surpassed, then the contractor must retain its records for two years**.

Naturally, there is an exception to the rule. Actually, there are a couple of exceptions. If an employer is notified of a discrimination complaint, it must flag all relevant records for retention until the complaint has been settled. Likewise, if a compliance review has been initiated by the OFCCP, all records must be retained until the successful conclusion of that review and any period of conciliation. In these situations the one or two year periods are not relevant. Record retention is mandated for the life of the compliance review or discrimination complaint investigation and resolution.

Be sure to check with your state and local jurisdictions to be sure they don't have longer retention requirements.

The biggest hazard facing employers/contractors in this regard is that of poor communication. I can't tell you how often I have learned that client managers and supervisors have destroyed records **simply because they were cleaning house and didn't know of the retention requirements.** The solution seems fairly obvious. Communicate the requirements to your managers and supervisors.

All Contractors Must Keep Audit Trail for Records Access

As you read in 60-1.12 above, all contractors are required to maintain databases for resumes, application forms, and other records. More importantly, contractors must maintain an accurate audit trail showing who accessed each database, at what time, and for what purpose.

If you have ever allowed your line managers to have access to your applicant database(s), you might wish to rethink that policy, or at least assure yourself that you have a proper audit trail in place so ANY access will be recorded in some way that you can retrieve at a later time.

This is a budget item. You are required to do this. It is not optional and there are no short cuts. Talk with your CEO and your CFO and determine what budget will be required for your organization to meet its obligation under this regulatory requirement. Then, do what is necessary to bring your organization into compliance with these rules.

(See Footnote #8 at the bottom of page 147.)

Narrative Sections for Disabled

1996 was a busy year for revising Federal regulations governing affirmative action for disabled. The laws didn't change. However, the implementing rules underwent some rather significant alterations. Many of them were good, like those that bring Section 503 of the *Rehabilitation Act* regs into consistency with *The Americans With Disabilities Act* (ADA) regs. Some of the other changes leave us scratching our heads.

For all intents and purposes, the term handicapped has been expunged from the vocabulary of enforcement officials. This, too, is consistent with use of the term "disabled" so common now because of the influence of ADA.

Affirmative Action Programs for Disabled are not required by Executive Order 11246, but rather by an act of Congress in the form of the *Rehabilitation Act of 1973*. Section 503 of that law requires government contractors to take affirmative action to employ and advance in employment qualified disabled individuals. The dollar limit has been adjusted upward to $10,000 from its previous $2,500 level, and is now consistent with the threshold for Veterans AAPs. Any organization with that much or more in yearly Federal contract revenue must comply with this law and OFCCP regulations; which means having a written affirmative action plan for the disabled.

These new rules became effective on August 29, 1996. The OFCCP allowed contractors until December 27, 1996 to comply.

AAP FOR DISABLED BY SECTION

DISABLED AAP SECTION 1: Development or reaffirmation of EEO/AA policy.

❑ **Required Content**

Regulations say, *"The contractor shall include an equal opportunity policy statement in its affirmative action program, and shall post the policy statement on company bulletin boards. The contractor must ensure that applicants and employees with disabilities are informed of the contents of the policy statement...The policy statement should indicate the chief executive officer's attitude on the subject matter, provide for an audit and reporting system and assign overall responsibility for the implementation of affirmative action activities required under this part. Additionally, the policy should state, among other things, that the contractor will: recruit, hire, train and promote persons in all job titles, and ensure that all other personnel actions are administered, without regard to disability; and ensure that all employment decisions are based only on valid job requirements. The policy shall state that employees and applicants shall not be subjected to harassment, intimidation, threats, coercion or discrimination because they have engaged in or may engage in any of the following activities: (1) Filing a complaint; (2) Assisting or participating in an investigation, compliance review, hearing, or any other activity related to the administration of Section 503 of the Rehabilitation Act of 1973...; (3) Opposing any act or practice made unlawful by section 503 or its implementing regulations in this part or any other Federal, State or local law requiring equal opportunity for disabled persons; or (4) Exercising any other right protected by section 503 or its implementing regulations in this part."* (41 CFR 60-741.44(a))

The Federal Contract Compliance Manual says, *"Contractors are required to take affirmative action to employ and advance in employment qualified special disabled veterans, veterans of the Vietnam era, and individuals with handicaps. The contractor must affirm its commitment to this affirmative action requirement by incorporating it in a policy statement included in its AAP (s)."* (FCCM, Par. 2102)

Regulations say, *"Each contractor and subcontractor shall include the ... equal opportunity clause* (see page 41) *in each of its covered government contracts or subcontracts (and modifications, renewals, or extensions thereof if not included in the original contract)."*

❑ **Employer Suggestions**

Since you have already developed a policy statement for your Minority and Women's AAP document, you have two choices now. First, create a new, separate policy statement addressing only disabled applicants and employees. Second, incorporate disabled workers into your existing policy statement by modifying what you already have developed.

My preference is to keep paperwork to a minimum. Posting several policy statements takes up more space. Printing several policy statements takes up more paper. Distributing several policy statements means your managers and supervisors must keep track of more individual policies. I believe it is simpler to implement EEO and AA if we focus everything to make it as easy for the line manager as we possibly can.

Add "physical disability" and "mental disability" to your list of protected categories in your M/W AAP policy statement. Be sure to check your state laws for additional requirements. In California, for example, the Department of Fair Employment and Housing (DFEH), California's EEO/AA enforcement agency, the statement must include: "...physical disability (including HIV and AIDS), mental disability..." You will want to be sure you meet all requirements for any of the states in which you operate.

DISABLED AAP SECTION 2: Dissemination of the Policy - Internal and External

❑ **Required Content**

Regulations say, *"The contractor shall undertake appropriate outreach and positive recruitment activities ... that are reasonably designed to effectively recruit qualified individuals with disabilities. ... The scope of the contractor's efforts shall depend upon all the circumstances, including the contractor's size and resources and the extent to which existing employment practices are adequate.*

"The contractor should enlist the assistance and support of recruiting sources (including State employment security agencies, State vocational rehabilitation agencies or facilities, sheltered workshops, college placement officers, State education agencies, labor organizations and organizations of or for individuals with disabilities) ... Formal briefing sessions should be held, preferably on company premises, with representatives from recruiting sources. Plant tours, clear and concise explanations of current and future job openings, position descriptions, worker specifications, explanations of the company's selection process, and recruiting literature should be an integral part of the briefing. Formal arrangements should be made for referral of applicants, follow up with sources, and feedback on disposition of applicants. The contractor's recruitment efforts at all schools should incorporate special efforts to reach students with disabilities ... The contractor should establish meaningful contacts with appropriate social service agencies, organizations of and for individuals with disabilities, and vocational rehabilitation agencies or facilities, for such purposes as advice, technical assistance and referral of potential employees ... The contractor should include individuals with disabilities when employees are pictured in consumer, promotional or help wanted advertising ... The contractor should send written notification of company policy to all subcontractors, vendors and suppliers, requesting appropriate action on their part ... The contractor should take positive steps to attract qualified individuals with disabilities not currently in the work force who have requisite skills and can be recruited through affirmative action measures ... The contractor, in making hiring decisions, should consider applicants with known disabilities for all available positions for which they may be qualified when the position(s) applied for is unavailable.

"A strong outreach program will be ineffective without adequate internal support from supervisory and managerial personnel and other employees, who may have had limited contact with individuals with disabilities in the past ...

"The contractor should implement and disseminate this policy internally as follows: Include it in the contractor's policy manual; Periodically inform all employees and prospective employees of its commitment to engage in affirmative action to increase employment opportunities for qualified individuals with disabilities; Publicize it in the company newspaper, magazine, annual report and other media; Conduct special meetings with executive, management, and supervisory personnel to explain the intent of the policy and individual responsibility for effective implementation, making clear the chief executive officer's attitude; Discuss the policy thoroughly in both employee orientation and management training programs; Meet with union officials and/or employee representatives to inform them of the contractor's policy, and request their cooperation; Include articles on accomplishments of disabled workers in company publications; When employees are featured in employee handbooks or similar publications for employees, include individuals with disabilities." (41 CFR 60-741.44 (f-g))

The Federal Contract Compliance Manual adds, *"Contractors are required to take affirmative action to employ and advance in employment qualified special disabled veterans, veterans of the Vietnam era, and individuals with handicaps. The contractor must affirm its commitment to this affirmative action requirement by incorporating it in a policy statement included in its AAP (s)."* (FCCM, Par. 2102)

❑ Employer Suggestions

Very simply, I recommend that you take the list of requirements from the regulations and build them into your M/W AAP section on dissemination of policy. Make the one document work for you in all three AAP efforts (Minorities & Women, Disabled and Veterans).

**Dissemination Requirements for Disabled AAP
Checklist**

To Be Included in AAP	Completed?
• Review employment practices for inclusion of disabled people	
• Develop internal communication re: AAP obligation	
• Develop procedures to assure AAP obligation to hire and promote disabled people is being implemented	
• Yearly notice to all employees reminding of AAP efforts	
• Notice to applicants re: AAP obligations for disabled	
• Development of recruiting sources from both public and private sectors	
• Recruiting efforts at educational institutions for disabled	
• Establish relationship with social service agencies	
• Review employment records to determine availability of promotable/transferable employees who are known disabled	
• Include disabled workers in consumer, promotional or help wanted advertising	
• Yearly written notice to subcontractors/vendors	
• Publicity for disabled AAP in employer publications	
• Special meetings with executives & managers with CEO	
• Meet with all employees re: individual responsibilities	
• Include policy in employee orientation and management training	
• Articles on accomplishments of disabled in employer publications	
• Include disabled employees in handbooks, etc.	

DISABLED AAP SECTION 3: Responsibility for
Implementation.

❑ **Required Content**

Regulations say, *"An official of the contractor shall be assigned responsibility for implementation of the contractor's affirmative action activities under this part. His or her identity should appear on all internal and external communications regarding the company's affirmative action program. This official shall be given necessary top management support and staff to manage the implementation of this program."* (41 CFR 60-741.44 (i))

❑ **Employer Suggestions**

I'm sure you have gotten the message by now. Combine. Combine. Combine.

Build into Section 3 of your W/M AAP the disabled AAP assignment of responsibilities you know you must meet. Make the one section work for all your AAP obligations.

DISABLED AAP SECTION 4: Review of personnel processes.

❑ **Required Content**

Regulations say, *"The contractor shall ensure that its personnel processes provide for careful, thorough, and systematic consideration of the job qualifications of applicants and employees with known disabilities for job vacancies filled either by hiring or promotion, and for all training opportunities offered or available. The contractor shall ensure that its personnel processes do not stereotype disabled persons in a manner which limits their access to all jobs for which they are qualified. The contractor shall periodically review such processes and make any necessary modifications to ensure that these obligations are carried out ... The contractor must design procedures that facilitate a review of the implementation of this requirement by the contractor and the Government."* (41 CFR 60-741.44 (b))

"The following is a set of procedures which contractors may use to meet the requirements of 41 CFR 60-741.44 (b):

"1. The application or personnel form of each known applicant should be annotated to identify each vacancy for which the applicant was considered, and the form should be quickly retrievable for review by the Department of Labor and the contractor's personnel officials for use in investigations and internal compliance activities.
2. The personnel or application records of each known individual with a disability should include (i) the identification of each promotion for which the employee with a disability was considered, and (ii) the identification of each training program for which the individual with a disability was considered.
3. In each case where an employee or applicant with a disability is rejected for employment, promotion, or training, a statement of the reason should be appended to the personnel file or application form as well as a description of the accommodations considered. This statement should be available to the applicant or employee concerned upon request.
4. Where applicants or employees are selected for hire, promotion, or training and the contractor undertakes any accommodation which makes it possible for him or her to place an individual with a disability on the job, the application form or personnel record should contain a description of that accommodation." (41 CFR 60-741 Appendix C)

❑ **Employer Suggestions**

If ever there was a strong argument for having current, accurate job descriptions, this is it. Although they are still not "required," they are an integral part of any system an employer can create to meet this requirement for process review. In the absence of job descriptions, for those who still feel they are unnecessary or intrusive, the employer must produce a list of physical and mental requirements for each job. In practical terms, some jobs can be "lumped" together into generic categories. This is acceptable if the description and/or physical and mental requirements are universally applicable to every incumbent position. This requirement is strengthened by the requirements of the next section in our AAP for Disabled. Suffice it to say here that having a system in place which guarantees updates to these job requirements is what we must insure. We must be able to show the OFCCP if necessary that we not only have the job requirements documented, but that they are regularly reviewed and there is a legitimate process in place for changes to be made when job changes require that, even before the next regularly scheduled review.

Watch out here, too. Note that one of the requirements of Appendix C is that we document by statement in the applicant's file or employee's personnel record the reason why the applicant or employee was not selected on each occasion. Then, the requirement is that we show the statement to the applicant or employee on their request. WOW! For years, we have been telling employers to avoid giving specific feedback to individuals when they are rejected during selection processes. Now, at least for disabled candidates, **we are instructed by the federal government regulations that we have to document the reasons for rejection of any person with a disability and then show the statement to the person concerned if they ask to see it**. You can think about this one for a while. You may even wish to discuss it with your AAP legal expert. I can just imagine dozens, scores or hundreds of managers each creating their own documentation with no true consistency from one manager to another. I believe this is a land mine waiting for an employer's footfall.

The best suggestion I can make to you is that you establish some standards for documentation in this circumstance and make sure every manager in your organization knows and understands what those standards are. Train them. Then drill them on their training. Then re-train them to be sure they have it the way you want them to do it. Without consistency in documentation, and employer guidelines on what are acceptable reasons for rejection, and how those should be cited, employers may well be setting themselves up for charges of discrimination for failure to accommodate or worse. We have more to say about documentation in the discussion of the new "definition of job applicant" on page 71.

DISABLED AAP SECTION 5: Physical and mental qualifications.

❑ **Required Content**

Regulations say, *"The contractor shall provide in its affirmative action program, and shall adhere to, a schedule for the periodic review of all physical and mental job qualification standards to ensure that, to the extent qualification standards tend to screen out qualified individuals with disabilities, they are job-related for the position in question and are consistent with business necessity.*

"Whenever the contractor applies physical or mental qualification standards in the selection of applicants or employees for employment or other change in employment status such as promotion, demotion or training, to the extent that qualification standards tend to screen out qualified individuals with disabilities, the standards shall be related to the specific job or jobs for which the individual is being considered and consistent with business necessity. The contractor shall have the burden to demonstrate that it has complied with the requirements ... of this section."

"The contractor may use as a defense to an allegation of a violation of ... this section that an individual poses a direct threat to the health or safety of the individual or others in the workplace." (41 CFR 60-741.44 (c)(1-3))

"Direct threat means a significant risk of substantial harm to the health or safety of the individual or others that cannot be eliminated or reduced by reasonable accommodation. The determination that an individual with a disability poses a 'direct threat' shall be based on an individualized assessment of the individual's present ability to perform safely the essential functions of the job. This assessment shall be based on a reasonable medical judgment that relies on the most current medical knowledge and/or on the best available objective evidence. In determining whether an individual would pose a direct threat, the factors to be considered include: (1) The duration of the risk; (2) The nature and severity of the potential harm; (3) The likelihood that the potential harm will occur; and (4) The eminence of the potential harm." (41 CFR 60-741.2 (y))

The Federal Contract Compliance Manual says, *"To be acceptable, the AAP (s) must affirm that the contractor has reviewed its personnel processes to determine whether its present procedures ensure careful, thorough, and systematic consideration of the job qualifications of known individuals with handicaps, special disabled veterans, and Vietnam era veterans who are applicants for job vacancies filled by employment or promotion, and for all training opportunities offered or available."* (FCCM, Par. 2103)

"The AAP must contain the contractor's schedule for the review of all physical and mental job qualification requirements. (a) To be acceptable, the AAP must either affirm that the review of physical and mental job qualification requirements has been completed, or provide a specific time schedule by which jobs are to be reviewed. Where the AAP indicates that the review has been completed, the contractor is not required to review those physical and mental job qualification requirements again unless there is a change in working conditions. The AAP should state, however, that where there is such a change in working conditions -- for example, through increased automation -- the requirements will be reevaluated. (b) The AAP must affirm that physical or mental job qualification requirements, to the extent that such requirements tend to screen out qualified individuals with handicaps or qualified special disabled veterans, shall be related to the specific jobs for which such individuals are being considered, and shall be consistent with business necessity and the safe performance of the job. (c) To be acceptable, the AAP must affirm that whenever the contractor inquires into an applicant or employee's physical or mental condition or conducts a medical examination prior to employment or change in

employment status, information obtained as a result will be kept confidential, except as otherwise provided for in the regulations." (FCCM, Par. 2104(a-c))

❑ Employer Suggestions

Nowhere in the regulations or in the Federal Contract Compliance Manual is there an absolute requirement for AAP employers to have written job descriptions for each position in the establishment. HOWEVER, it is very difficult to meet the regulatory requirements of reviewing physical and mental job requirements, and knowing if those have changed due to the change in job content, if there are not written job descriptions available.

So, my suggestion to every AAP employer (actually, my suggestion to every employer) is that they develop or update their written job descriptions as the first step in meeting this requirement. Since the advent of the *Americans With Disabilities Act (ADA)* in 1990, there has been more heed paid to this advice. ADA doesn't require job descriptions either. But, it does allow that job descriptions can be used by an employer as a defense against complaints of failure to accommodate disabilities.

Step one, then, is to get current job descriptions.

Step two is to review and DOCUMENT IN EACH JOB DESCRIPTION the list of physical and mental requirements of the job. This text is not focused on the process involved in creating job descriptions or identifying physical and mental requirements. That is sufficiently large as a subject to warrant a separate volume of material. Suffice it to say here, that employers who want to protect themselves and give selecting managers a tool to work within the employment process will gladly step up to this requirement. It makes good business sense.

Step three is to establish or review a procedure for updating job description content when the job responsibilities have changed by a certain amount. That amount is up to you. For many years, I worked with internal clients in a very large organization, consulting on job description writing and job evaluation for compensation purposes. We used to say a 15% change in job content required rewriting the job description. I'm not sure that is a practical target for employers who don't have full time staff working on the function. It may be realistic, however, to require a written job description update if the job changes by 30% or 40%, or any time the physical or mental requirements of the position must be restated. Of course, anytime you take such action, you should put another note into your Affirmative Action File folder to that affect.

Step four is to schedule an annual review of your organizational policies and procedures related to personnel selection, employment interviewing, applicant processing and other similar related activities. Schedule the review for the same time each year, likely toward the end of any given AAP year, so you will be able to say in your new AAP update that the review has been completed as planned. There will not be a change in your policies or procedures each year. All you have to do is say that you have reviewed them and they are acceptable. Then document that effort in your new AAP update and in your affirmative action documentation file.

DISABLED AAP SECTION 6: Reasonable accommodation to physical and mental limitations.

❑ Required Content

Regulations say, *"The contractor shall make reasonable accommodation to the known physical or mental limitations of an otherwise qualified individual with a disability unless it can demonstrate that the accommodation would impose an undue hardship on the operation of its business.* ***If an employee with a known disability is having significant difficulty performing his or her job and it is reasonable to conclude that the performance problem may be related to the known disability, the contractor shall confidentially notify the employee of the performance problem and inquire whether the problem is related to the employee's disability; if the employee responds affirmatively, the contractor shall confidentially inquire whether the employee is in need of a reasonable accommodation."*** *(41 CFR 60-741.44 (d))*

❑ Employer Suggestions

Two things are important here. First, we must place into our AAP document a commitment to making reasonable accommodation to physical and mental limitations when appropriate. Second, recognize that what is printed in bold type in the regulation citation above is new with the 1996 changes. Read it again. If you have to, read it several times until the message sinks in.

We may not take any disciplinary action against anyone who is known to be disabled, until we inquire of that employee if they feel they need an accommodation to help them perform their job. If the employee feels that the performance deficiency is related to the disability, we must attempt to accommodate that disability if at all possible. Whatever you do when you get into one of these situations, document every action you take. Build a record for yourself that demonstrates how you followed the regulatory requirements and took the appropriate actions. It may be that you will need to rely on that record of documentation at some later date, either when defending against a discrimination complaint, or during an OFCCP compliance review.

DISABLED AAP SECTION 7: Harassment.

❑ Required Content

Regulations say, *"The contractor must develop and implement procedures to ensure that its employees with disabilities are not harassed because of disability."* *(41 CFR 60-741.44 (e))*

❑ **Employer Suggestions**

Some employers choose to wrap their EEO/AA non-discrimination and non-harassment policies into one document. Others have taken the approach that separate policies are the best tools for them.

Whichever you decide, be sure you have a non-harassment policy which specifies employee options for complaint procedures and the fact that it is not essential to strictly follow the chain of command in making complaint reports. Remember in disability harassment as well as sexual, racial or religious harassment, it may be the immediate supervisor who is the harasser. Forcing an employee to make a complaint to the immediate supervisor essentially takes away the complaint alternative in that scenario. It is advisable to allow complaints (some even say encourage complaints) to go directly to any management individual, including the Director of Human Resources or the Chief Executive Officer. Spelling out these procedures in the policy statement makes it clear that employees do have "escape avenues" from any harassment they may believe themselves to be suffering.

DISABLED AAP SECTION 8: Training.

❑ **Required Content**

Regulations say, *"All personnel involved in the recruitment, screening, selection, promotion, disciplinary, and related processes shall be trained to ensure that the commitments in the contractor's affirmative action program are implemented."* (*41 CFR 60-741.44 (j)*)

❑ **Employer Suggestions**

A simple paragraph in the AAP to state your commitment to training all key players in the employment process should be sufficient. Then, be sure you keep detailed records of each instance when managers, supervisors, recruiters, and anyone else involved in the selection process is given training in EEO/AA issues and procedures.

TMA, Inc.
123 Main Street
Portland, WI 60000

Job Applicant Self Identification of Race/Ethnicity and Sex

We are an equal opportunity and affirmative action government contractor. In compliance with government regulations we are required to record numbers of job applicants by sex, and ethnic category. We ask that you indicate your race or ethnicity and sex. **DO NOT WRITE YOUR NAME**. This information will NOT be kept with your application and will be used only in accordance with federal and state regulations.

YOU ARE NOT REQUIRED TO PROVIDE THIS INFORMATION. Your application for employment will be considered in the same manner whether or not you fill out this form.

Check One:	**Check One**:[4]
	(Only if Not Hispanic)
__ Female	__ Asian
__ Male	__ Black/African American
	__ Native American/Alaska Native
Check One:	__ Native Hawiian/Pacific Islander
	__ White
__ Hispanic	__ Two or More Races
__ Not Hispanic	

Job Title(s) Applied For:

_____
_____

Date of Job Application:

_____

If you have any questions about the government requirements or this request, please contact our office of Human Resource Management at XXX-555-1234.

This completed form should be returned to:_____

---

[4] Census 2000 allowed people to select multiple ethnic/race categories if they wished.

TMA, Inc.
123 Main Street
Portland, WI 60000

Request for Information from Individuals Receiving Job Offers
Self-Identification for Disabled Individuals and Veterans

1.   [TMA, Inc.] is a U.S. Government contractor subject to 41 CFR 60-741, or 41 CFR 60-300, which require Government contractors to take affirmative action to employ and advance in employment qualified individuals with disabilities. We are also subject to the *Vietnam Era Veterans Readjustment Assistance Act of 1974 (VEVRAA)* and the *Jobs for Veterans Act of 2002 (JVA)*. We are required to take affirmative action to employ and advance in employment qualified disabled veterans, recently separated veterans, other protected veterans, and Armed Forces service medal veterans. If you are a member of one or more of these categories we would like to include you in our affirmative action program. If you would like to be included, please tell us which category you belong to so we can work with you to satisfy all requirements. The term **"recently separated veteran"** refers to any veteran during the three-year period beginning on the date of discharge or release from active duty. The term **"other protected veteran"** refers to a person who served on active duty during a war or in a campaign or expedition for which a campaign badge has been authorized. The term **"Armed Forces service medal veteran"** refers to a person who, while serving on active duty in the Armed Forces, participated in a United States military operation for which an Armed Forces service medal was awarded under Executive Order 12985 (62 FR 1209). The term **"disabled veteran"** refers to a veteran who is entitled to compensation (or who but for the receipt of military retired pay would be entitled to compensation) under laws administered by the Secretary, or was discharged or released from active duty because of a service-connected disability. You may inform us of your desire to benefit under the program at this time and/or at any time in the future.

2.   Telling us about your disability or status as a veteran in one of these categories is voluntary. Refusal to give us information about your disability or veteran status will not subject you to any adverse treatment. Information you give us will be kept confidential. Some people will need to know about any disability accommodation requirements you may have. Those people could include your supervisor, manager, human resources specialist, medical and safety personnel, and government officials engaged in enforcement activities related to affirmative action issues for disabled and veterans.

2.   If you are an individual with a disability or a disabled veteran, it would assist us if you tell us about:
    (i)   Any special methods, skills, and procedures which qualify you for positions that you might not otherwise be able to do because of your disability so that you will be considered for any positions of that kind, and;
    (ii)   The accommodations which we could make which would enable you to perform the job properly and safely, including special equipment, changes in the physical layout of the job, elimination of certain duties relating to the job, provision of personal assistance services or other accommodations.

Employee Name: _____
Job Title: _____ Date: _____
Veteran Status: ❏ Disabled Veteran   ❏ Qualified Disabled Veteran
(U.S. Veterans   ❏ Other Protected Veteran   ❏ Not a qualified veteran
 Only)   ❏ Recently Separated Veteran (within the last three years)
                   ❏ Vietnam Era Veteran (this category is still used on the VETS-100 report)
Disabled Status: ❏ Physical Disability   ❏ Mental Disability   ❏ None
                   ❏ I would like to request the following disability accommodation on my
                     job: _____
                   ❏ At this time, I prefer not to volunteer information about my status as a veteran or any disabilities I may have. I understand I can change my mind at any time in the future.

If you would like a list of campaigns and expeditions that might qualify you as a veteran in the "other veteran" category, go to http://www.opm.gov/veterans/html/vgmedal2.asp.

Handicapped/Disabled AAP
Problem Identification Checklist

Responsibility	Completed?
Policy statement accurate and complete	
Written AAP completed for all sections or requirements	
Managers and supervisors appraised on EEO/AA efforts & results	
Problem areas identified in conjunction with line management	
Audit and reporting systems developed and used	
Known disabled employees participate in employer sponsored training, educational, recreational and social activities	
Each work location is in compliance with posters, policies, AAPs	
Career counseling offered to known disabled employees	
Job applicants requested to provide EEO demographics	
Job applications retained for at least one year	
Unions properly notified	
Outreach/positive recruitment programs in place	
Linkages built with recruiting sources of disabled candidates	
No reduction in compensation for disabled individuals	
Personnel policies and job descriptions properly reviewed & revised	
Requests for accommodation are documented	
Employer investigations/decisions re: accommodation requests are documented	
All job openings listed with State employment service	
Internet application process has been tested for accessibility and contains name and phone number of person to whom accommodation requests should be directed.	

❑ **Self Identification Request Process for Disabled and Veterans**

Changes here have thrown contractor discussion groups into a frenzy. Here is the rule: Contractors are **required** to extend an invitation to self-identify to all applicants **post-offer but prior to employment**. Contractors are permitted to invite self-identification **pre-offer** in only two limited circumstances. (41 CFR 60-741.42) (41 CFR 60-300 Appendix B)

You may no longer ask all applicants for self-identification of either disabled or veteran status before you have made them a job offer. Yet, you still are responsible for gathering the demographic data for your Minority & Women AAP applicants. Therefore, you must now use two separate forms. Look at the form on **page 82** to find a sample request for sex/ethnic identification. This form, or one like it, should be used for all qualified applicants. The form on **page 83** is offered as a model for collecting self identification of disabled employees and veterans. (41 CFR 60-741 Appendix B) (41 CFR 60-300 Appendix B).

Next, work out the specific details of when you will give this self-identification request to your target audience. You <u>may not</u> give it to applicants in general. You <u>may not</u> give it to applicants after they have become employees. **You <u>must</u> give it to applicants who have received a job offer, before they become employees.** For some employers, that is a very narrow window. One possible way to deal with the requirement is to put this invitation on the top of the stack of papers that will be reviewed by new workers when they report on their first day for orientation. It is generally agreed that people are not "employees" (on the payroll) until they have completed all of the necessary employer documents required to award them that status. These include I-9, W-4, Benefit elections, payroll deductions, etc. Until that magic moment, they are still "applicants with a job offer." However you decide to do it, you must be sure you distribute the self-identification request to people between the time they receive their job offer and the time they are officially placed on the payroll as employees.

Be sure your procedures allow people to refuse to identify themselves as either disabled or veterans. Remember, this is a voluntary process, so people must have the option of not disclosing to you (their employer) that they are disabled or a veteran. You should insist on receiving a self-identification form from every employee that will contain their name and the date it was reviewed by the employee. That form should be included in the new employee's official personnel file. It is your proof that you invited each person's self-identification as required by regulations. You will need to produce that proof if you are ever audited by the Department of Labor. One of the options on the form should be, "I would rather not indicate my status at this time."

Be sure your procedures provide for handling forms from new employees who DO identify themselves as being disabled. Anyone who requests an accommodation must receive a follow up from the employer. Your procedures should provide for that follow up. And you will want to maintain a separate file that tracks all requests for accommodation and what was done with them.

❑ Processing Discrimination Complaints

AAP regulations have been brought into line with the ADA, allowing up to 300 days for filing a discrimination complaint based on disability. That period may be extended by the OFCCP when accepting complaints if there is good cause for the extension. Complaints are now processed by the OFCCP in the same way as they are processed by the EEOC.

❑ Accessible Online Applications

On July 10, 2008, then OFCCP Director Charles James issued Directive #281 entitled, *OFCCP Directive on Accessible Online Applications.*

Here is the heart of the new policy from the enforcement agency...

> **POLICY:** *Effective immediately, all compliance evaluations shall include a review of the contractor's online application systems to ensure that the contractor is providing equal opportunity to qualified individuals with disabilities and disabled veterans. The review*

should include whether the contractor is providing reasonable accommodation, when requested, unless such accommodation would cause an undue hardship. In this directive, the term "online system" shall include, but not be limited to, all electronic or web-based systems that the contractor uses in all of its personnel activities.

You can get a PDF copy of the 3-page directive at
http://www.dol.gov/ofccp/regs/compliance/directives/dir281.pdf

What it Means

If you require people to submit their job applications through your web site, to be in compliance with the new directive you must:

o **Prominently display a notice** telling how to get an accommodation if using the online application process is not possible due to a disability. There must be a description of the process you offer for requesting an accommodation in the job application process. There must also be the name and contact information (email link, phone number or such) for the person responsible for receiving and processing requests for accommodation in the application process.

o **Company Kiosks** that offer people equipment needed to input an online job application must also be accessible to the physically disabled. (e.g., Can a wheelchair user reach the keyboard and see the screen?) There must be an alternative method for inputting application information for people who are unable to use the Kiosk facility.

o **Alternative Application Process** - there must be a "fall back" alternative for anyone who is unable to use the company's online application system. You might wish to have a paper-and-pencil application process as an accommodation, or if you run a parallel paper-and-paper application system, you could simply direct people into that process. Whatever you do, it must be timely. People must receive the accommodations needed (as long as they do not present an undue hardship to your business) in time to participate in the selection process for the job opening in question.

Additional Issues for Attention

o **Web sites should use "Interoperable technology"**

(http://en.wikipedia.org/wiki/Interoperability_testing) that permits assistive technology

(http://en.wikipedia.org/wiki/Assistive_technology) to work with the application process. Examples of assistive technology are software programs that read aloud words on a web site, software that magnifies the site content for the vision impaired, programs that allow paraplegics to make site selections and enter text responses. This can involve some budget allocations, so you should conference with your IT professionals to determine how best to accomplish "Interoperability" for your web site. Your site is not required to offer all of these types of assistance, but it should be compatible with software used by visitors to your site. *[See references and tools listed at the end of the message.]*

o **OFCCP Compliance Reviews** will begin including a review of your web site application process, its Interoperability and alternatives you make available to visitors who are unable to input applications on your site.

o **OFCCP will Retain and Investigate Complaints** of illegal discrimination based on disability or disabled veteran status related to online application systems. Normally OFCCP would hand-off to the EEOC individual discrimination complaints. But those originating from disabled veterans or other disabled individuals who are having trouble with your online application system will be investigated by OFCCP from now on.

REFERENCES and TOOLS:

Three agencies have created what is called the Accessible Systems Racing League. It is a metaphor for assessing a web site to determine if it allows easy use by someone dependent upon assistive technology. There are 10 questions and responses can result in a green flag, yellow flag, or red flag, indicating how much work must yet be done to bring the web site into a condition of accessibility.

o Accessible Systems Racing League http://www.earnworks.com/508Racing.asp

o Assistive Technology in the Workplace http://www.earnworks.com/docs/508materials/FS-ER-ATWorkplace.pdf

o Accessibility, Interoperability and Usability in the Workplace http://www.earnworks.com/docs/508materials/FS-ER-Interoperability.pdf

o Assistive Technology and Universal Design Resources Directory http://www.earnworks.com/docs/508materials/FS-ER-ATUDResources.pdf

❑ Definitions Changed

Definitions of certain terms have been changed for consistency with definitions used in the *Americans with Disabilities Act of 1990* (ADA). Two examples are: "Substantially Limits" and "Qualified." They are both now defined in the same way for Disabled Affirmative Action as in the ADA. Definitions of Veteran categories have also changed. Vietnam Era Veteran is no longer one of the categories used for affirmative action plans, although it remains as a category for VETS-100 reporting.

Specific exclusions have also been made to mirror the ADA. **Transvestites, various other psycho-sexual conditions; compulsive gambling; kleptomania; pyromania; homosexuality and bisexuality <u>are not</u> considered disabilities.** (41 CFR 60-741.3 (d) (e))

❑ Medical Examinations

Pre-offer medical exams are prohibited under the regs. Employers may require medical examinations after they make a job offer, before hiring the individual. The job offer may be contingent upon the person passing a medical examination. The same medical examination process must be required of all individuals who are hired into that particular job, not just those with disabilities. (41 CFR 60-741.23)

Although pre-offer medical examinations are prohibited, it is still permitted that contractors may ask applicants if they have the ability to perform job related functions. They may be asked to demonstrate their ability to perform those job functions.

DRUG TESTING is permitted at any time. It is not considered a medical examination. Contractors who have drug testing policies, those who must meet "drug free workplace" standards or Department of Transportation requirements may implement those drug testing programs without fear of complications from their affirmative action requirements. (41 CFR 60-741.24 (b))

Separate files are now required for medical records. In the past, employers were allowed to decide how to store medical information about employees. Some elected to combine personnel files and medical files. That is no longer permitted under the current requirements. All medical records must be stored separately (no co-mingling of medical and other personnel records) and must be kept confidential. "Confidential" should be taken to mean they are only available to individuals who have a specific business need to know the information contained in those records. (41 CFR 60-741.23 (d) (1))

❑ Recordkeeping Requirements

Examples of records which must be maintained by a contractor include: *Requests for reasonable accommodation; the results of any physical examination; job advertisements and postings; applications and resumes; tests and test results; interview notes; and other records having to do with hiring, assignment, promotion, demotion, transfer, lay-off or termination, rates of pay or other terms of compensation, and selection for training or apprenticeship. (41 CFR 60-741.80)*

Retention requirements have been split into two categories, based on the size of the contract and the size of the contractor's workforce. Here's how it goes: If the contractor has **fewer than 150 employees** or does not have a Government **contract of at least $150,000 the retention period for these records is one year. If either of those thresholds is surpassed, then the contractor must retain its records for two years**.

Naturally, there is an exception to the rule. Actually, there are a couple of exceptions. If an employer is notified of a discrimination complaint, it must flag all relevant records for retention until the complaint has been settled. Likewise, if a compliance review has been initiated by the OFCCP, all records must be retained until the successful conclusion of that review and any period of conciliation. In these situations the one or two year periods are not relevant. Record retention is mandated for the life of the compliance review or discrimination complaint investigation and resolution.

Be sure to check with your state and local jurisdictions to be sure they don't have longer retention requirements.

❑ Reasonable Accommodation

Failure to provide reasonable accommodation is expressly termed discrimination and is unlawful unless the employer can show an undue hardship. (41 CFR 60-741.21 (f))

Also under the regulations, undue hardship must consider any tax credits or other offsets which might be available to help the employer reduce its cost of accommodation. (41 CFR 60-741.2 (w) (2))

❑ Discrimination Complaint Remedies

Regulations now provide for the OFCCP to issue Show Cause Notices in the same way as they can for E.O. 11246 (minority and women) affirmative action programs. The enforcement agency has also been given authority to require Conciliation Agreements in settling out-of-compliance conditions with contractors. Although the OFCCP did this as a matter of practice until 1997, the regulations since then have authorized those actions for the first time. (41 CFR 60-741.62 and 41 CFR 60-741.64)

❑ Enforcement Process - Procedures and Sanctions

The process of having an Administrative Law Judge (ALJ) hear cases of enforcement action by the Agency remains the same. Now, however, the final administrative order must be issued by the Agency within a year of the ALJ recommendation or decision. (41 CFR 60-741.65 (b))

Sanctions became more specific under regulations issued in 1997. The agency can still withhold progress payments from contractors, terminate existing contracts and/or debar contractors for an indefinite period of time. **New provisions make it possible for the OFCCP to debar contractors for fixed periods of time ranging from 6 months to 3 years**. The reinstatement and appeal process allow contractors who have experienced fixed-term debarment to request reinstatement after 6 months. (41 CFR 60-741.66 (c) and 41 CFR 60-741.68)

Under provisions, published May 3, 1996, the Administrative Review Board, rather than the Assistant Secretary of Labor, will issue final agency decisions under Section 503.

❑ Employer Suggestions

In a nutshell, requirements for outreach and recruiting of disabled applicants was strengthened in 1997. While the self-identification requirements are flaky, employers will find that it is much easier to have affirmative action requirements parallel those of the ADA.

One recommendation I would offer in addition to all the others is this: Prepare a notice or a hand-out which can be given to job applicants which says, "It is our policy to make reasonable accommodation to all job applicants who request it so they may fully participate in our job application and employment selection process." This is not a request for self-identification, but it is going to help protect the employer against charges that it didn't provide for accommodation of job applicants as required by the ADA.

The best advice I can give for action oriented programs on Disabled AAPs is the same you will find regarding M/W AAPs. Make them detailed and measurable. The OFCCP will be looking for a way to determine that you have made a good faith effort. The best approach for satisfying their interest is to have a written plan which outlines the problem, the action steps to be taken in addressing that problem, an assignment of responsibility to someone for each action step, and a target date for completion. A simple four column chart will serve you well in compiling that information. (A sample of such a chart is located on page 74.)

Be sure to include in your action plans each of the requirements from the regulations:

- Job content review for physical and mental requirements
- Job requirements available to all managers involved in selection decisions
- Assessment of selection process to ensure freedom from stereotyping disabled people
- Training for all managers involved in the selection process
- Site visits, briefing sessions and workplace tours for representatives of recruiting sources to showcase your jobs and job requirements
- Attempt to include disabled workers on HR staff
- Disabled employees involved in career days, school recruiting programs and similar activities
- Attempts to reach disabled students when recruiting at schools
- Sponsorship, participation, or involvement with special training or educational programs related to job training for disabled people
- Establishment of on-the-job training programs

Narrative Sections for Veterans AAP

The third Affirmative Action Plan requirement comes to us for Disabled Veterans, and Other Veterans. All the Federal regulations regarding these efforts can be found in *41 CFR 60-300.*

It is interesting to note that it was the *Vietnam Era Veterans Readjustment Assistance Act of 1974* that originally brought us the requirement to file a listing of all our job openings with the State employment service if those jobs paid under $25,000 per year.

Of course, the *Veterans' Benefits Improvements Act of 1994* changed that requirement to **ALL** job openings (regardless of salary) with only three exceptions:

- Executive and top management positions
- Positions that will be filled from within the organization (or from regularly established recall lists)
- Positions lasting only three days or less

These changes became effective on January 5, 1995 and were reinforced with the publication of 41 CFR 60-300 on August 8, 2007.

All **categories of veterans were redefined in the 2007** regulations. And, rather than publish the list of qualifying medals, ribbons, or campaign badges, we suggest you get the latest information from the government's web site at http://www.opm.gov/veterans/html/vgmedal2.asp

Many of the requirements found in the regulations regarding veterans and affirmative action are similar to those we have reviewed for disabled employee and applicants.

And, employers may consider putting all three affirmative action programs into one written document, if they choose to use that approach to communicate their plans for meeting AAP obligations.

Any employer that has "contracts or subcontracts for the furnishing of supplies or services or for the use of real or personal property (including construction) for $100,000 or more"[5] must have a written AAP for Veterans.

Once meeting eligibility requirements, the employer must have its written AAP for Veterans prepared and implemented within 120 days.[6]

"Each contractor covered by the requirements of *41 CFR 60-300* must report, at least annually, the number of special disabled veterans and the number of veterans of the Vietnam era in its workforce, by job category and hiring location."[7] This is commonly known as the VETS-100 report. A sample may be found in Appendix E. The form was changed in 1999.

You may occasionally see reference to 38 U.S.C. 2012 in the regulations and literature regarding Affirmative Action Programs for Veterans. This United States Code section is the one governing implementation and enforcement of federal contractor compliance with the law and regulations.

---

[5]   *41 CFR 60-300.1*
[6]   *41 CFR 60-300.5*
[7]   *Federal Contract Compliance Manual, Paragraph 3103*

VETERANS AAP BY SECTION

VETERANS AAP SECTION 1: Development or reaffirmation of EEO/AA policy.

❑ **Required Content**

Regulations say, *"...standards for compliance with the Vietnam Era Veterans Readjustment Assistance Act of 1974, as amended, which requires government contractors to take affirmative action to employ and advance in employment qualified covered veterans. Disabled veterans, recently separated veterans, other protected veterans, and Armed Forces service medal veterans are covered veterans under VEVRAA."* [8] (41 CFR 60-300.1)(38 U.S.C. 4212)

"In offering employment or promotions to disabled veterans, recently separated veterans, other protected veterans, or Armed Forces service medal veterans, it is unlawful for the contractor to reduce the amount of compensation offered because of any income based upon a disability-related and/or military-service-related pension or other disability related and/or military-service-related benefit the applicant or employee receives from another source." (41 CFR 60-300.21(i))

"The contractor shall include an equal opportunity policy statement in its affirmative action program, and shall post the policy statement on company bulletin boards. The contractor must ensure that applicants and employees who are disabled veterans are informed of the contents of the policy statement...The policy statement should indicate the chief executive officer's attitude on the subject matter, provide for an audit and reporting system and assign overall responsibility for the implementation of affirmative action activities required under this part...
*Additionally, **the policy should state**, among other things, **that the contractor will recruit, hire, train and promote persons in all job titles, and ensure that all other personnel actions are administered, without regard to disabled veteran, recently separated veteran, other protected veteran, or Armed Forces service medal veteran status**..."* (41 CFR 60-300.44(a))

The Federal Contract Compliance Manual adds, *"Contractors are required to take affirmative action to employ and advance in employment qualified special disabled veterans, veterans of the Vietnam era, and individuals with handicaps. The contractor must affirm its commitment to this affirmative action requirement by incorporating it in a policy statement included in its AAP(s)."* (FCCM, Par. 2I02)

Definition of Veteran Classifications (41 CFR 60-300.2(n), (o), (p), (q), (r))

Disabled veteran means: (1) A veteran of the U.S. military, ground, naval or air service who is entitled to compensation (or who but for the receipt of military retired pay would be entitled to compensation) under laws administered by the Secretary of Veterans Affairs, or (2) A person who was discharged or released from active duty because of a service-connected disability.

---

[8]   United States Code reference to *Vietnam Era Veterans Readjustment Assistance Act of 1974*, as amended.

__Qualified disabled veteran__ means a disabled veteran who has the ability to perform the essential functions of the employment position with or without reasonable accommodation.

__Other protected veteran__ means a veteran who served on active duty in the U.S. military, ground, naval or air service during a war or in a campaign or expedition for which a campaign badge has been authorized, under the laws administered by the Department of Defense.

__Recently separated veteran__ means any veteran during the three-year period beginning on the date of such veteran's discharge or release from active duty in the U.S. military, ground, naval or air service.

__Armed Forces service medal veteran__ means any veteran who, while serving on active duty in the U.S. military, ground, naval or air service, participated in a United States military operation for which an Armed Forces service medal was awarded pursuant to Executive Order 12985. (61 FR 1209)

❑ Employer Suggestions

Because the "old" Veterans Affirmative Action Plan regulations at 41 CFR 60-250 were not eliminated when the "new" Veterans Affirmative Action Plan regulations at 41 CFR 60-300 were implemented, there has been a lot of confusion about which set of rules to follow. Some folks have even suggested that contractors must follow both sets of rules and their convoluted qualifying thresholds, etc.

Consider this…

"Most federal contracts only last a year. Some last a year with the right to extend or renew for another year. In either case, there are few if any contracts that exist dating back to December 2003," said John C. Fox,[12] partner at Fox, Wang & Morgan P.C. in San Jose, California. That means, you can probably not worry about the old Veterans regulations. Focus on the new regs at 60-300 and you will eliminate all that confusion.

Including veterans' affirmative action commitments in one policy along with minorities and women and disabled is an option employers should consider. Since there are three separate written affirmative action plans required, it makes sense to use one document for communication and centralized control over the process of affirmative action. Using three separate plans is permitted, but from a practical point, it complicates the communication process and can easily confuse managers and employees who are less sophisticated about these subjects.

Remember, the same requirements apply to this AAP policy as to the others: Current AAP year date, signature of CEO or senior management executive, and statement of protected categories and the employment actions to which they apply. **Be sure you specify "<u>disabled veteran,</u>**

---

[12] Fox, Wang & Morgan P.C.

recently separated veteran, other protected veteran, or Armed Forces service medal veteran status" as protected categories in your policy statement. They should be spelled out along with race, sex, national origin, religion, etc.

You can find an example of a combined affirmative action policy statement in the sample AAP document at the end of this chapter.

VETERANS AAP SECTION 2: Dissemination of
policy - internal and external.

❑ **Required Content**

Regulations say, *"A strong outreach program will be ineffective without adequate internal support from supervisory and management personnel and other employees. In order to assure greater employee cooperation and participation in the contractor's efforts, the contractor shall develop internal procedures such as ... implement and disseminate this policy internally as follows: (i) Include it in the contractor's policy manual. (ii) Inform all employees and prospective employees of its commitment to engage in affirmative action to increase employment opportunities for qualified disabled veterans, recently separated veterans, other protected veterans, and Armed Forces service medal veterans. The contractor should periodically schedule special meetings with all employees to discuss policy and explain individual employee responsibilities. (iii) Publicize it in the company newspaper, magazine, annual report and other media. (iv) Conduct special meetings with executive, management, and supervisory personnel to explain the intent of the policy and individual responsibility for effective implementation, making clear the chief executive officer's attitude. (v) Discuss the policy thoroughly in both employee orientation and management training programs. (vi) Meet with union officials to inform them of the contractor's policy, and request their cooperation. (vii) Include articles on accomplishments of disabled veterans, recently separated veterans, other protected veterans, and Armed Forces service medal veterans in company publications. (viii) When employees are featured in employee handbooks or similar publications for employees, include disabled veterans. (41 CFR 60-300.44 (g))*

"The contractor shall undertake appropriate outreach and positive recruitment activities, such as [those listed below]...that are reasonably designed to effectively recruit qualified disabled veterans, recently separated veterans, other protected veterans, and Armed Forces service medal veterans. It is not contemplated that contractors will necessarily undertake all the activities listed ... or that their activities will be limited to those listed. The scope of a contractor's efforts shall depend upon all the circumstances, including the contractor's size and resources and the extent to which existing employment practices are adequate.

(1) The contractor should enlist the assistance and support of the following persons and organizations in recruiting, and developing on-the-job training opportunities for, qualified disabled veterans, recently separated veterans, other protected veterans, and Armed Forces service medal veterans, to fulfill its commitment to provide meaningful employment opportunities to such veterans: (i) The Local Veterans' Employment Representative in the local employment service office nearest the contractor's

establishment; (ii) The Department of Veterans Affairs Regional Office nearest the contractor's establishment; (iii) The veterans' counselors and coordinators ("Vet-Reps") on college campuses; (iv) The service officers of the national veterans' groups active in the area of the contractor's establishment; and (v) Local veterans' groups and veterans' service centers near the contractor's establishment.

(2) Formal briefing sessions should be held, preferably on company premises, with representatives from recruiting sources. Plant tours, clear and concise explanations of current and future job openings, position descriptions, worker specifications, explanations of the company's selection process, and recruiting literature should be an integral part of the briefing. Formal arrangements should be made for referral of applicants, follow up with sources, and feedback on disposition of applicants.

(3) The contractor's recruitment efforts at all educational institutions should incorporate special efforts to reach students who are disabled veterans, recently separated veterans, other protected veterans, or Armed Forces service medal veterans. An effort should be made to participate in work-study programs with Department of Veterans Affairs rehabilitation facilities which specialize in training or educating disabled veterans.

(4) The contractor should establish meaningful contacts with appropriate veterans' service organizations which serve disabled veterans, recently separated veterans, other protected veterans, or Armed Forces service medal veterans for such purposes as advice, technical assistance, and referral of potential employees. Technical assistance from the resources described in this paragraph may consist of advice on proper placement, recruitment, training and accommodations contractors may undertake, but no such resource providing technical assistance shall have authority to approve or disapprove the acceptability of affirmative action programs.

(5) Disabled veterans, recently separated veterans, other protected veterans, or Armed Forces service medal veterans should be made available for participation in career days, youth motivation programs, and related activities in their communities.

*(6) The contractor should **send written notification of company policy to all subcontractors, vendors and suppliers, requesting appropriate action on their part.***

(7) The contractor should take positive steps to attract qualified disabled veterans, recently separated veterans, other protected veterans, and Armed Forces service medal veterans not currently in the work force who have requisite skills and can be recruited through affirmative action measures. These persons may be located through the local chapters of organizations of and for disabled veterans, recently separated veterans, other protected veterans, and Armed Forces service medal veterans.

(8) The contractor, in making hiring decisions, should consider applicants who are known disabled veterans, recently separated veterans, other protected veterans, or Armed Forces service medal veterans for all available positions for which they may be qualified when the position(s) applied for is unavailable. (41 CFR 60-300.44(f))

The Federal Contract Compliance Manual adds, *"the contractor must limit its consideration of a covered veteran's military record to only the portion of that record which is relevant to the specific job qualifications for which the veteran is being considered. This should be affirmed in the AAP."* (FCCM, Par. 2I03(b))

❑ Employer Suggestions

As with the requirements for dissemination of policy for Disabled AAPs, I recommend you take the regulatory specifics for Veterans AAP policy dissemination and incorporate them into your M/W AAP section on dissemination. Using the one document for all three AAP efforts will make life simpler in the long run, and will assist in understanding overall AAP obligations when discussing implementation with managers and supervisors.

You should note that **it is the Veterans AAP requirements in VEVRRA that require employers to publish notice to employees and applicants telling when they can review the AAP and who to contact to make that request.** There is no such requirement for the Minority's & Women's AAP nor for the Disabled AAP. (41 CFR 300.41)

VETERANS AAP SECTION 3: Responsibility for implementation.

❑ Required Content

Regulations say, *"An official of the contractor shall be assigned responsibility for implementation of the contractor's affirmative action activities under this part. His or her identity should appear on all internal and external communications regarding the company's affirmative action program.* **This official shall be given necessary senior management support and staff to manage the implementation of this program.** (41 CFR 60-300.44(i))

The Federal Contract Compliance Manual adds, *"An acceptable AAP must affirm that the contractor reviews its employment practices, and must at least state that appropriate outreach and positive recruitment activities are undertaken where indicated by the findings of such reviews. The AAP may also describe in some detail the steps taken by the contractor in its review of employment practices and the resulting outreach and recruitment activities."* (FCCM, Par. 2I07)

Dissemination Requirements for Veterans AAP
Checklist

To Be Included in AAP	Completed?
• Review employment practices for inclusion of veterans	
• Develop internal communication re: AAP obligation	
• Develop procedures to assure AAP obligation to hire and promote disabled veterans (and other veterans) are being implemented	
• Yearly notice to all employees reminding of AAP efforts	
• Notice to applicants re: AAP obligations for veterans	
• Development of recruiting sources from both public and private sectors	
• Recruiting efforts at educational institutions	
• Establish relationship with the veterans employment representative at the State employment service, Veterans Administration Regional Office, National Alliance of Businessmen Jobs for Veterans' Program, veterans counselors at college campuses, service officers of the national veterans groups active in employer recruiting area	
• Review employment records to determine availability of promotable/transferable employees who are known disabled veterans or other veterans	
• Include disabled veterans and other veterans in consumer, promotional or help wanted advertising	
• Yearly written notice to subcontractors/vendors	
• Publicity for veterans AAP in employer publications	
• Special meetings with executives & managers with CEO concerning veterans AAP	
• Meet with all employees re: individual responsibilities	
• Include policy in employee orientation and management training	
• Articles on accomplishments of disabled veterans and other veterans in employer publications	
• Include employees who are disabled veterans and other veterans in employee handbooks, etc.	
• Meet with union officials to inform them of the employer's policy and request their cooperation	
• Include nondiscrimination clauses in all union contracts, and review all contractual provisions to insure they are nondiscriminatory	
• Post the policy on company bulletin boards, including a statement that employees and applicants are protected from coercion, intimidation, interference or discrimination for filing a complaint or assisting in an investigation under the requirements	
• VETS-100A (VETS-100) report completed and filed as required	
• Confirm an alternative application process for disabled individuals	

❏ **Employer Suggestions**

Let me say again. Combine. Combine. Combine.

Build into Section 3 of your W/M AAP the veterans AAP assignment of responsibilities you know you must meet. Make the one section work for all your AAP obligations.

VETERANS AAP SECTION 4: Indication of who is covered.

❏   **Required Content**

Regulations say, *"This part applies to all Government contracts and subcontracts of $100,000 or more, entered into or modified on or after December 1, 2003, for the purchase, sale or use of personal property or non-personal services (including construction)..."* (41 CFR 60-300.1)

Contracts created prior to December 1, 2003 are still governed by the old regulations on Veterans' Affirmative Action and apply to contracts valued at $25,000 or more. *"Any contractor or subcontractor who has contracts for the purchase, sale or use of personal property and non-personal services (including construction) that were entered into before December 1, 2003 (and not modified...) must follow part 41 CFR 60-250.1.* (41 CFR 60-300.1)

"Disabled veteran means (1) A veteran of the U.S. military, ground, naval or air service who is entitled to compensation (or who but for the receipt of military retired pay would be entitled to compensation) under laws administered by the Secretary of Veterans Affairs, or (2) A person who was discharged or released from active duty because of a service-connected disability. (41 CFR 60-300.2(n))
Qualified disabled veteran means a disabled veteran who has the ability to perform the essential functions of the employment position with or without reasonable accommodation. (41 CFR 60-300.2(o))
Other protected veteran means a veteran who served on active duty in the U.S. military, ground, naval or air service during a war or in a campaign or expedition for which a campaign badge has been authorized, under the laws administered by the Department of Defense. (41 CFR 60-300.2(p))
Recently separated veteran means any veteran during the three-year period beginning on the date of such veteran's discharge or release from active duty in the U.S. military, ground, naval or air service. (41 CFR 60-300.2(q))
Armed Forces service medal veteran means any veteran who, while serving on active duty in the U.S. military, ground naval or air service, participated in a United States military operation for which an Armed Forces service medal was awarded pursuant to Executive Order 12985 (61 FR 1209). (41 CFR 60-300.2(r))

❑ Employer Suggestions

If you choose, you may make this a separate section of your "AAP for Veterans" document, or it can be built into your single AAP document at any point you wish. Ordinarily, we find this information either in the policy statement or in a separate section that addresses special AAP issues for veterans that won't fit naturally into other M/W AAP sections.

If you decide to put this definition into your policy statement, you can make it less officious by rewording some of the content. Perhaps, something like this:

> By definition, a "veteran" is almost anyone who served in the U.S. military, ground, naval or air service, or who participated in a United States military operation for which an Armed Forces service medal was awarded by the Defense Department. Disabled veterans are included in this definition.

VETERANS AAP SECTION 5: **Provision for annual review of AAP, personnel policies and practices, physical and mental job requirements.**

❑ Required Content

Regulations say, *"The contractor shall periodically review such [personnel] processes and make any necessary modifications to ensure that these [affirmative action] obligations are being carried out. A description of the review and any necessary modifications to personnel processes or development of new processes shall be included in any affirmative action programs required under this part. The contractor must design procedures that facilitate a review of the implementation of this requirement by the contractor and the Government."* (41 CFR 60-300.44(b))

"The contractor shall provide in its affirmative action program, and shall adhere to, a schedule for the periodic review of all physical and mental job qualification standards to ensure that, to the extent qualification standards tend to screen out qualified disabled veterans, they are job-related for the position in question and are consistent with business necessity...The contractor shall have the burden to demonstrate that it has complied with [these] requirements." (41 CFR 60-300.44(c))

"...as a matter of nondiscrimination the contractor must make reasonable accommodations to the known physical or mental limitations of an otherwise qualified disabled veteran unless it can demonstrate that the accommodation would impose an undue hardship on the operation of its business." (41 CFR 60-300.44(d))

"The contractor shall design and implement an audit and reporting system that will: (i) Measure the effectiveness of the contractor's affirmative action program; (ii) Indicate any need for remedial action; (iii) Determine the degree to which the contractor's objectives have been attained; (iv) Determine whether known disabled veterans, recently separated veterans, other

protected veterans, and Armed Forces service medal veterans have had the opportunity to participate in all company sponsored educational, training, recreational and social activities; and (v) Measure the contractor's compliance with the affirmative action program's specific obligations. (41 CFR 60-300.44(h))

The Federal Contract Compliance Manual adds, *"To be acceptable, the AAP must either affirm that the review of physical and mental job qualification requirements has been completed, or provide a specific time schedule by which jobs are to be reviewed. Where the AAP indicates that the review has been completed, the contractor is not required to review those physical and mental job qualification requirements again unless there is a change in working conditions. The AAP should state, however, that where there is such a change in working conditions -- for example, through increased automation -- the requirements will be reevaluated."* (FCCM, Par. 2104(a))

❑ **Employer Suggestions**

If you have already read about AAP for disabled individuals, you will recall that we discussed the need for written job descriptions. If you wish to review that discussion, turn to page 80.

Establishing a schedule of activities in your review will help you avoid any missed obligations. You can do so easily by planning those steps on a calendar, in your automated activity tracking, or by using some sort of check list, maybe like the one shown below. Use whatever approach your personal style dictates. Just be sure you have done what you are responsible for doing, and that you have made notes about the result of those reviews, so you can place that documentation into your annual AAP implementation file. Each of those notes adds credence to your claim that you are making a good faith effort to implement your plan according to your regulatory obligations.

Annual AAP, Policy and Job Description Reviews
Checklist

Review Activity	Scheduled	Completed
• Annual review of AAP content and obligations		
• Annual review of personnel policies		
• Annual review of personnel practices		
• Annual review of physical & mental job requirements for each job in the establishment		

VETERANS AAP SECTION 6: Inclusion of AA clause in contracts and subcontracts.

❑ **Required Content**

Regulations say, *"Each contracting agency and each contractor and subcontractor shall include the following equal opportunity clause in each of its covered Government contracts or subcontracts (and modifications, renewals, or extensions thereof if not included in the original contract)..."* (41 CFR 60-300.5)

❑ **Employer Suggestions**

The complete affirmative action clause can be found beginning on page 45. Please note that this clause should NOT be placed in your AAP document. It is intended only for use with contracts. You MUST include it as a part of any subcontracts you negotiate with suppliers or vendors that can be directly linked to your contract for federal government goods or services. It may be included by reference to 41 CFR 60-300.5 if you would rather not print the entire clause.

In your AAP document, you simply should reiterate your commitment to include the affirmative action clause in all contracts. And, you will want to keep samples of contracts you have developed which show you have included the affirmative action clause. Remember, Compliance Officers will want you to demonstrate your follow through by showing your documentation of the effort. In other words, keep sample copies of contracts and subcontracts that have the AAP clauses printed on the backs of the contract pages.

VETERANS AAP SECTION 7: Provisions for physical access to employment process and reasonable accommodation of disabled applicants and employees.

❑ **Required Content**

Regulations say, *"... the contractor must make reasonable accommodation to the known physical and mental limitations of an otherwise qualified special disabled veteran unless it can demonstrate that the accommodation would impose an undue hardship on the operations of its business. (41 CFR 60-300.44(d))*

"Factors to be considered. In determining whether an accommodation would impose an undue hardship on the contractor, factors to be considered include: (i) The nature and net cost of the accommodation needed, taking into consideration the availability of tax credits and deductions, and/or outside funding; (ii) The overall financial resources of the facility or facilities involved in the provision of the reasonable accommodation, the number of persons employed at such facility, and the effect on expenses and resources; (iii) The overall financial resources of the contractor, the overall size of the business of the contractor with respect to the number of its employees, and the number, type and location of its facilities; (iv) The type of operation or operations of the contractor, including the composition, structure and functions of the work force of such

contractor, and the geographic separateness and administrative or fiscal relationship of the facility or facilities in question to the contractor; and (v) The impact of the accommodation upon the operation of the facility, including the impact on the ability of other employees to perform their duties and the impact of the facility's ability to conduct business." (41 CFR 60-300.2(u))

❑ Accessible Online Applications

On July 10, 2008, then OFCCP Director Charles James issued Directive #281 entitled, *OFCCP Directive on Accessible Online Applications*.
[See Page 85 for more details.]

❑ Employer Suggestions

Our obligations under affirmative action regulations for veterans are essentially the same as it is under the regulations for disabled. We are obliged to make reasonable accommodation for disabled veterans if we can.

Applicants must be able to access the employment process. As with other disabled candidates, disabled veterans can't very well participate in the employment process equally and fairly if they can't get into our building. We must be sure that all employment offices and other such facilities are accessible to the disabled. ADA had given this requirement an added push with its demand that public buildings be accessible to disabled customers, clients and the general public. There are requirements within ADA that we make modifications to our buildings (or work with our landlord to plan modifications to buildings in which we rent/lease space).

Applicant accommodations are usually not complicated or expensive. For example, many employers use paper and pencil tests to measure clerical aptitude such as English language skills and mathematical abilities. If the applicant is blind and can't read the test, what will you do? Is it possible to accommodate that disability in your employment process? Do you "forgive" or "waive" the test for that applicant? If you do, how will you compare that applicant with the other qualified individuals you have required to take the test?

How about having someone read the test to the blind applicant? If it is necessary to allow more time to complete the test, perhaps you could determine how much extra time would be appropriate as an allowance.

If English language writing and reading are a part of the job requirements, and basic math skills are also required, ask the applicant what accommodation would be required for him or her to be able to perform the job. If the applicant is blind, unable to read text or numbers, it will be necessary to have some means of "reading" information and translating that into auditory input for the individual. There are numerous technologies available today which will do just that, for surprisingly little money.

You get the point, I'm sure. **Good Faith Effort is the key to success** with this affirmative action requirement. We can anticipate that we will be faced with many challenges over time.

They will come from employees and from applicants. How we deal with them is the measure of our good faith effort. Rejecting a need for disability accommodation out of hand is not a demonstration of good faith effort. Studying the problem, involving the disabled individual in determining a reasonable accommodation, and then testing it to see if it will work, are good techniques for making a good faith effort on accommodation.

And, documentation of all your efforts will keep you in a position whereby you can "prove" you have done what you are obligated to do.

VETERANS AAP SECTION 8: Development and execution of affirmative action programs.

❑ Required Content

Regulations say, *"(1) The contractor should enlist the assistance and support of the following persons and organizations in recruiting, and developing on-the-job training opportunities for, qualified special disabled veterans and veterans of the Vietnam era, to fulfill its commitment to provide meaningful employment opportunities to such veterans: (i) The Local Veterans' Employment Representative or his or her designee in the local employment service office nearest the contractor's establishment; (ii) The Department of Veterans Affairs Region Office nearest the contractor's establishment; (iii) The veterans' counselors and coordinators ('Vet-Reps') on college campuses; (iv) The service officers of the national veteran's groups active in the area of the contractor's establishment; and (v) Local veterans' groups and veterans' service centers near the contractor's establishment."* (41 CFR 300.44(f)(1))

"All personnel involved in the recruitment, screening, selection, promotion, disciplinary, and related processes shall be trained to ensure that the commitments in the contractor's affirmative action program are implemented." (41 CFR 60-300.44(j))

The Federal Contract Compliance Manual adds, *"The AAP should include a description of the specific action programs which have been developed and implemented by the contractor."* (FCCM, Par 2I08(c))

❑ Employer Suggestions

As with the other two AAP requirements (M/W and Disabled), Veterans AAP requirements are for detailed and measurable action plans. The OFCCP will want to know that you are indeed making a good faith effort to complete meaningful steps toward furthering employment of disabled veterans and veterans of the Vietnam era. If you have the documentation to support that effort, you are in a good position to face your Compliance Officer during a compliance review.

Be sure to include in your action plans each of the requirements from the regulations:

- Job content review for physical and mental requirements

- Written job descriptions including those physical and mental requirements to support your published job requirements
- Job requirements available to all managers involved in selection decisions
- Assessment of selection process to ensure freedom from stereotyping disabled veterans or veterans of the Vietnam era
- Training for all managers involved in the selection process
- Site visits, briefing sessions and workplace tours for representatives of recruiting sources to showcase your jobs and job requirements
- Attempt to include disabled veterans on HR staff or on advisory committees
- Disabled veteran employees involved in career days, school recruiting programs and similar activities
- Attempts to reach disabled veterans when recruiting at schools
- Sponsorship, participation, or involvement with special training or educational programs related to job training for disabled veterans
- Establishment of on-the-job training programs to support qualification and placement of disabled veterans

---

Disabled Veterans & Vietnam Era Veterans AAP
Problem Identification Checklist

Responsibility	Completed?
Policy statement accurate and complete	
Written AAP completed for all sections or requirements	
Managers and supervisors appraised on EEO/AA efforts & results	
Problem areas identified in conjunction with line management	
Audit and reporting systems developed and used	
Known disabled veterans participate in employer sponsored training, educational, recreational and social activities	
Each work location is in compliance with posters, policies, AAPs	
Career counseling offered to known disabled veterans	
Job applicants requested to provide EEO demographics	
Job applications and interview records retained for at least one year	
Unions properly notified	
Outreach/positive recruitment programs in place	
Linkages built with recruiting sources of disabled veteran candidates	
No reduction in compensation for disabled veterans	
Personnel policies and job descriptions properly reviewed & revised	
Requests for accommodation are documented	
Employer investigations/decisions re: accommodation requests are documented	
All job openings listed with State employment service[13]	

---

[13] Since America's Job Bank (AJB) ceased operations on July 1, 2007, contractors have been placed in the position of having to deal with each individual state employment agency. There is no longer one point of contact provided

❑ Self Identification Request Process

Here, as with similar changes made in regulations governing affirmative action programs for the disabled, self-identification procedures here have thrown contractor discussion groups into a frenzy. The new rule is the same as for disabled: Contractors are **required** to extend an invitation to self-identify to all applicants **post-offer but prior to employment**. Contractors are permitted to invite self-identification **pre-offer** in only two limited circumstances. (41 CFR 60-300.42)

The resulting impact on contractor operations will be immediate.

FIRST: Change your current self-identification request form. You may no longer ask all applicants for self-identification of either disabled or veteran status before you have made them a job offer. Yet, you still are responsible for gathering the demographic data for your Minority & Women AAP applicants. Therefore, you must now use two separate forms, if you didn't before this. Look at the form on **page 83** to find a sample request for sex/ethnic identification. This form, or one like it, should be used for all qualified applicants. The form on **page 84** is modeled on the one found in the regulations at 41 CFR 60-300 Appendix B. There is a requirement for contractors to collect data. Employers are required to complete a VETS-100 report each year. In order to do that, the employer needs to know how many disabled veterans and other veterans are in each of the EEO categories. You will also need to be able to log requests for disability accommodation.

SECOND: Work out the specific details of when you will give this self-identification request to your target audience. You may not give it to applicants in general. You may not give it to applicants after they have become employees. **You must give it to applicants who have received a job offer, before they become employees.** For some employers, that is a very narrow window. One possible way to deal with the requirement is to put this invitation on the top of the stack of papers that will be reviewed by new workers when they report on their first day for orientation. It is generally agreed that there is validity to the argument that people are not "employees" (on the payroll) until they have completed all of the necessary employer documents required to award them that status. These include I-9, W-4, Benefit elections, payroll deductions, etc. Until that magic moment, they are still "applicants with a job offer." However you decide to do it, you must be sure you distribute the self-identification request to people between the time they receive their job offer and the time they are officially placed on the payroll as employees.

Changes in VETS-100 Reporting

As you may know, you must report veterans data by the end of September each year. The original VETS-100 form should be used for contracts valued at $25,000 or more that were created prior to December 1, 2003. VETS-100A is the version you should use if you have contracts valued at $100,000 or more that were created from December 1, 2003 to present. But

---

by the government for listing job openings. It is more work, but without paying a private company to do it for you, you'll have to do it for yourself. As of this writing it is still possible to find a link to each state's employment service through http://www.jobbankinfo.org.

what if you are not sure which form you should use since you have had contracts on both sides of the December 1, 2003 date?

Most government contracts are updated or renewed if they extend beyond a one-year period. That means they have been "updated" or "modified" and you should use the VETS-100A reporting form. You will find that very few, if any, of your contracts have remained unchanged since December 1, 2003.

There are two primary changes in form content when comparing the VETS-100 to the VETS-100A. The first is found in the categories of veterans. The new categories have been in the regulations for several years and you have been inviting new hires to identify themselves using those categories. So, they are the same categories you will use for reporting data on the VETS-100A form.

- o **Disabled veterans**
- o **Other protected veterans** (veterans who served on active duty in the U.S. military during a war or in a campaign or expedition for which a campaign badge is awarded)
- o **Armed Forces service medal veterans** (veterans who, while serving on active duty in the Armed Forces, participated in a United States military operation for which an Armed Forces service medal was awarded pursuant to Executive Order 12985)
- o **Recently separated veterans** (veterans within 36 months from discharge or release from active duty)

The second significant difference in the two forms is that the VETS-100A contains the two job or occupational categories now used on the EEO-1 report for "Officials and Managers." (Executives/Senior Level Officials and Managers; First/Mid-Level Officials and Managers)

So, you will probably conclude that you should be using the VETS-100A form for your reporting. I encourage you to read the Department of Labor's web information about these two reports before making your decision. https://vets100.vets.dol.gov/ . You will also find PDF copies of each form at that location. The regulations require that you submit both forms if you qualify under each set of conditions.

And, remember that the data you report will have been collected from people who volunteer it. They are under no obligation to express to you their status as a veteran or disabled person (disabled veteran or otherwise). So, you will be reporting only the data you have been given. We can assume that it is not complete. So, use what you have. That's the best you can do.

As of 2000, <u>organizations that produce reports for ten or more locations</u> are required to submit their VETS-100 reports in electronic format rather than on hard copy. If you fall into this category, you can retrieve instructions you will need by sending an email to diskfile@vets100.com.

If you have never filed a VETS-100 report before because you are a new federal contractor, you MUST obtain a company number before submitting your report. You can get a company number assigned to your establishment by visiting the web site (http://vets100.cudenver.edu) or by sending an email request for a company number to newcompany@vets100.com. You will also need to have a North American Industry Classification Code (NAICS) for your establishment and a DUNS number before sending in your report. If you don't know your NAICS code you can get information from the web site at http://www.census.gov/epcd/www/naicstab.htm. If you don't know your DUNS (Dun & Bradstreet) number, you can call 1-800-333-0505. Tell them you are a federal contractor or subcontractor.

OFCCP's Good-Faith Initiative for Veterans Employment (G-FIVE)

On July 17, 2008, then OFCCP Director, Charles James issued an Administrative Notice outlining the evaluation factors, processes, and procedures for implementing the G-FIVE Initiative.

This award requires a nomination by one of the OFCCP Region managers. The following factors will be considered when evaluating federal contractor and subcontractor establishments for G-FIVE recognition:

i.   Evidence of covered veterans in the contractor's labor force.
ii.   Evidence of an increase in the number of covered veterans in the contractor's labor force.
iii. The number of partnerships with local veterans' service organizations to employ or advance covered veterans.
iv.   Established liaison with the state workforce agency job bank or the local employment service delivery system representative to facilitate the posting of their job listings. Whether appropriate job openings were sent to the state and/or local employment service delivery system and the number of veterans hired by the contractor during the AAP year.
v.   Recruitment efforts at educational institutions to reach students who are covered veterans.
vi.   The number of job advertisements in the local community targeting veterans; and targeted recruitment of qualified covered veterans during company career days and/or related activities in contractor communities.
vii. For prime contractors, evidence that demonstrates a commitment to encourage their subcontractors to seek qualified covered veterans for employment opportunities.
viii. Affirmative action steps taken to attract qualified special disabled or disabled veterans through the nearest Veterans Administration job placement program.
ix.   The number of on-the-job training opportunities provided to covered veterans.

Nominations can be based on the outcome of a full compliance review including an on-site visit. Regional Directors are asked to make recommendations for the award based on those compliance review outcomes. Contractors and subcontractors may also self-nominate by submitting to the appropriate Regional Director a written statement of their interest in being considered for G-FIVE recognition. **A full compliance review will be conducted if the nominated establishment has not undergone a full compliance review within 24 months of the nomination.**

Sources of Veterans as Job Candidates

One national example of a program that offers training and work for former members of the U.S. military services is **Helmets to Hardhats**. This is a free source for construction trade careers. So, if you are an employer in the construction industry, perhaps receiving contracts under the *American Recovery and Reinvestment Act (ARRA),* here is an organization that can help you with your good faith effort to recruit veterans. The organization offers employment placement services and apprenticeship programs for qualified candidates. It is a program linked to more than a score of industry associations. Get more information from the national office at:

> Helmets to Hardhats
> 815 16th Street NW Suite 600
> Washington, DC 20006
> 866-741-6210
> www.helmetstohardhats.org

Another source for candidates that may be both veterans and disabled is the **Department of Rehabilitation** in your state. In California, for example, the California Department of Rehabilitation has a strong program to help place qualified individuals into jobs that they have the skills to accomplish. For information, Google "Department of Rehabilitation" and scan the results. Chances are you will find a link to the state agency you need.

> California Department of Rehabilitation
> 721 Capitol Mall
> Sacramento, CA 95814
> (916) 324-1313 (VOICE)
> (916) 558-5807 (TTY)
> http://www.rehab.cahwnet.gov/

Chances are good that you will find a Department of Rehabilitation office in your county. Aside from the quality of candidates you can find through this resource, you will be pleased to hear that it costs the employer nothing. In fact, if a placement is made with your organization and the individual requires an accommodation in order to perform the job, the Department of Rehabilitation will often pick up the expense for that accommodation if there is any. There may be other state-provided benefits for the employer as well. Talk with your state's representative to learn more.

And, a resource you should never overlook is the state employment service. Almost always, you will find a Coordinator of Veterans Services within that state agency. That is because the U.S. Department of Labor provides funds to state employment agencies that support activities involved with placing military veterans in jobs for which they qualify.

Called by various names, depending on the state, you will find them listed as the Employment Development Department in California, the Department of Job and Family Services in Ohio, the Department of Employment Security in Illinois, and the Office of Employment and Training in Kentucky. Google "Employment Services Department" to find the agency in your state. All services are free to employers.

**Sample AAP
Narrative Sections**

Modify and Use

_____

If you have worked your way through all the material preceding this page, you have a pretty good idea of what information should be placed into your AAP documents.

If you recall:

- One AAP document is required for each establishment.
- Three AAP target populations must be addressed, either in separate AAPs or together in one AAP -- (1) minorities and women, (2) disabled, and (3) veterans.
- Statistical analysis is required for minorities and women AAP.
- EEO-1, EEO-4, or EEO-2 must be filed annually, but should not be placed into the AAP document. (EEO-5 and EEO-6 have been combined with Department of Education forms and are not filed separately any longer.)
- VETS-100 form must be completed and filed annually, but should not be placed into the AAP document.
- EEO Clauses must be printed, or included by reference, in all contracts, purchase orders, and similar business documents.

You will also recall that you will not be considered in compliance with federal regulations on Affirmative Action unless you have customized your plan to meet your establishment's needs, problems and analysis.

That means, quite simply, you cannot expect to take the following sample plan, copy it directly and be in compliance. It doesn't work that way. We have included the sample here, as a model for you to use in creating your own affirmative action document. Nothing more. We do not guarantee that its content is sufficient to place you in a compliance condition with the OFCCP.

You will have to take each section of the plan and rewrite it to fit your needs in your establishment. That's not because we have done a poor job on our sample, but because no sample can by itself place you in a position of compliance with the regulations.

Affirmative action requires you to analyze the condition of your workforce, management staff and upcoming conditions for job openings during the next twelve months. Without that analysis process, and resultant narrative explanation of the results, you will have a plan that may sound nice, but which has no relevance to the real-world needs in your establishment.

A word about "boilerplate." I can say without hesitating that most of the HR managers I talk with about affirmative action view it as a document containing standardized wording or boilerplate text. Boilerplate, as you know, is the thick metal casing used to contain the extraordinary pressures inside a water heater. I must tell you that affirmative action plans that are written with "boilerplate" text and not changed from year to year will have to be extraordinarily magic to contain the pressures generated by a compliance officer during an audit. With the exception of the section dealing with compliance with government guidelines on religious, national origin and sex discrimination, all other narrative sections of an AAP document must be updated each year. If those government guidelines should ever change, that section of the AAP will also have to be updated. Don't get trapped by the "boilerplate" argument. It can get you into hot water. (I couldn't resist completing the metaphor. Sorry.)

So, get to work. Analyze your data. Re-write your policy. Identify additional recruiting sources you can use. Make your AAP a living document, and you will find your management staff will be more willing to use it as it is intended.

Remember, you should always have your AAP reviewed by an employment attorney or HR consultant who specializes in this subject area. Please believe me when I tell you, an expert in discrimination law may know nothing about AAP regulations. Don't use an attorney who is a discrimination expert when you want a review of your AAP unless he/she is also an expert in the requirements of affirmative action plans. That would be as bad as using a real estate attorney to review your plan. Certain duties fall to you as the HR expert in your organization. One of them is the proper selection of legal and consulting advisors.

Sample Affirmative Action Plan
for TMA, Inc.
Plan Year: 1/1/2015 through 12/31/2015

CONTENTS

Section 1. Policy Statement[14]

It is the policy of TMA, Inc. to encourage and support equal employment opportunity for all employees and applicants for employment without regard to sex, race, color, ancestry, religious creed, national origin, physical disability (including HIV and AIDS), mental disability, medical condition (Cancer, genetic disposition), age (over 40), marital status, political affiliation, sexual orientation, disabled veteran, recently separated veteran, other protected veteran, or Armed Forces service medal veteran status. Employment decisions will be evaluated on the basis of an individual's skills, knowledge, abilities, job performance and, other legitimate qualifications, and where appropriate in promotion or transfer, seniority. Equal Employment Opportunity is among the very highest priorities for TMA, Inc.

Affirmative action requirements of the federal government are designed to enhance employment opportunities for females and ethnic minorities (Black, Hispanic, Asian, Hawiian Native and Native American), people with disabilities and disabled veterans, recently separated veterans, other protected veterans, or Armed Forces service medal veteran status. Affirmative action programs provide for fuller utilization and development of all human resources. Affirmative action and equal employment opportunity affects all employment practices at TMA, Inc. including recruiting, hiring, transfer, promotion, training, compensation, benefits, discipline and termination of employment.

The **Board of Directors holds me responsible for EEO and Affirmative Action performance** in this company. As the President, **I have appointed Katherine E. Nelson** of the Human Resources Department the responsibility to develop and monitor affirmative action and other equal employment opportunity programs. **She is our Affirmative Action Officer.** However, management personnel at every level must share in the responsibility for promoting affirmative action and equal employment opportunity to ensure that compliance is achieved.

Harassment of any kind, including sexual harassment, is strictly prohibited. Complaints of harassment will be investigated rapidly and thoroughly and employees who are found to have behaved in such a way will be disciplined, including the possibility of dismissal from the payroll. Harassment is considered a serious behavior problem and will not be tolerated at TMA, Inc. If you have a complaint of harassment, you may see your immediate supervisor, the HR Director, any management person, or the President. You can be assured that we will do all we can to maintain confidentiality, but an investigation will be conducted. Retaliation for filing a complaint of discrimination (of any kind) is not permitted and will not be tolerated.

Equal opportunity must be part of the fabric of all personnel decisions at the TMA, Inc. Successful performance on our affirmative action goals will provide benefits to the company to the full utilization and development of previously underutilized human resources.

Date: 1/1/2015

T A Smith

T. A. Smith, President

---

[14] Including your policy statement within your AAP document is a requirement of the Disabled and Veterans AAP regulations. It is not a requirement of the Minorities and Women AAP regulations.

Section 2. Responsibility For Implementation (41 C.F.R. 60-2.17(a))

A. Chief Executive Officer

As CEO, T.A. Smith has overall responsibility and accountability for proper implementation of TMA, Inc. policies on equal employment opportunity and affirmative action. For management efficiency, he has delegated responsibility for day-to-day management of the functions to the Director of Human Resources.

B. EEO/AA Administrator

Katherine E. Nelson, Director of Human Resources, has been appointed EEO/AA Administrator. In this capacity, she is responsible for the following:

1.   Developing policy statements, affirmative action programs and both internal and external communication programs.

2.   Ensuring the consistency and completeness of TMA, Inc.'s Affirmative Action Plan with federal, state and local agencies' rules and regulations.

3.   Assisting line management in collecting and analyzing employment data, identifying problem areas, setting goals and time tables, and developing programs to achieve goals.

4.   Providing feedback to line managers on their affirmative action progress.

5.   Designing, implementing and monitoring internal audit and reporting systems to measure program effectiveness and to determine where progress has been made and where further action is needed.

6.   Ensuring that action is initiated to remedy areas of underutilization.

7.   Reporting once each quarter to senior management on the progress of each reporting unit in relation to company goals.

8.   Serving as a liaison between the company, government regulatory agencies, minority and women's organizations and other community groups serving women and minorities.

9.   Ensuring that current legal information affecting affirmative action is disseminated to appropriate personnel.

C. Managers and Supervisors

Managers and supervisors have the ultimate responsibility for decisions affecting progress toward achieving affirmative action goals. Their responsibilities include:

1.   Assisting in identifying problem areas.

2.   Being actively involved with local minority and community service programs designed to promote equal employment opportunity.

3.   Reviewing qualifications of all employees to ensure minorities and women are given full opportunity for transfers and promotions.

4.   Taking action to prevent or correct any harassment of employees.

5.   Conducting and supporting career counseling for all staff members.

6.   Ensuring that posters and notices are properly displayed.

7.   Ensuring that minority and female employees are afforded full employment opportunities and are encouraged to participate in all company sponsored educational, training, and social activities.

8.   Ensuring that their department fully complies with the spirit and policies of the Affirmative Action Program.

9. Accountability to senior management for personal support of the company's EEO policies and for personal contributions toward achieving its Affirmative Action goals. Management performance evaluations will, in part, be based on individual manager EEO/AA performance.

D. All Employees
All employees of TMA, Inc. are expected to support and abide by the policies of our company, including our EEO/AA policy. No one may use their lack of knowledge about these policies as an excuse for inappropriate behavior or decisions. All employees will be held accountable for their behavior under this policy.

Section 3. Internal Audit and Reporting System (41 C.F.R. 60-2.17(d))

To assure that the company's Affirmative Action Program is fully implemented and is progressing towards accomplishing its goal, the following internal audit system has been established:
1. All employment activities are monitored using the following tracking systems:
   - Applicant Flow Log
   - Hiring Log
   - Transfers/Promotions Log
   - Salary Actions Log
   - Disciplinary Actions Log
   - Terminations Log
2. Detailed data on these logs areas are compiled by department managers quarterly and are submitted to the EEO Administrator for review.
3. Formal reports from department managers regarding progress made towards goals are submitted to the EEO Administrator on a quarterly basis.
4. Quarterly staff meetings are held by the EEO Administrator to update all management and supervisory personnel on affirmative action issues and to identify and resolve problem areas.
5. A summary of key activities and accomplishments in implementing the affirmative action plan is submitted to the Chief Executive Officer quarterly.
6. Each year the company will file its EEO-1 (Standard Form 100) report with the EEOC's Joint Committee on Reporting, as required by federal regulations.

Section 4. Identification Of Problem Areas (41 C.F.R. 2.17(b))

[Insert here your summary of statistical analysis, utilization analysis, department reviews, etc.]

Secrets of Affirmative Action Compliance

Section 5.   Action Oriented Programs (41 C.F.R. 60-2.17(c))

The following programs have been designed to meet the company's affirmative action goals:

Problem Area	Action Steps	Whose Responsibility	Target Completion Date

Section 6.   Affirmative Action For The Disabled (41 C.F.R. 60-741)

A.   General

TMA, Inc. supports community programs designed to provide employment opportunities for the disabled. Recognizing that disabled individuals are a valuable human resource, the company has formalized its support of these programs by implementing an affirmative action plan for the employment and advancement of qualified physically and mentally disabled individuals.

B.   Definition of Disabled Applicants and Employees

The law defines "Disabled Individual" as any person who (1) has a physical or mental impairment which substantially limits one or more of such person's major life activities, (2) has a record of such impairment, or (3) is regarded as having such an impairment. For purposes of this part, a disabled individual is "substantially limited" if he or she is likely to experience difficulty in securing, retaining or advancing in employment because of a disability. The terms "handicapped" and "disabled" are intended to have the same meaning within this Plan.

C. Consideration of Qualifications

1.   All applicants applying for employment with the company are invited to voluntarily identify themselves as disabled and indicate any reasonable accommodation that can be made to enable them to perform a job that they would not otherwise be able to do.

2.   Whenever disabled applicants are considered for employment, the employment applications are annotated to identify positions for which they are considered.

116

3.   If a disabled applicant or employee is not selected for employment, promotion or training, the reason for the nonelection is documented and maintained in the personnel file, or with the application.

4.   Whenever an accommodation is made for the hire, promotion or training of a disabled individual, a description of the accommodation is documented and kept with the personnel file, or with the application.

D.   Physical and Mental Requirements

1.   Selection processes involved in hiring, promotions and training opportunities are reviewed annually to ensure that no qualified disabled individual is screened out.

2.   Job requirements are reviewed and updated periodically to ensure that they are realistic and do not contain unnecessary qualifications which serve to screen out disabled individuals.

E.   Accommodations to Physical and Mental Limitations of Employees

TMA, Inc. will try to reasonably accommodate the physical and mental limitations of qualified, disabled applicants or employees so as to ensure that each one is afforded equal opportunity for employment and advancement. In determining the degree of accommodations that may be reasonably undertaken, business necessity and expenses will be considered with such other related factors as: efficiency, health and safety, the essential functions of each specific job, etc. Each decision regarding request for accommodations will be determined on an individual basis.

The company will consider the following types of accommodations:
1.   Architectural Modifications:
   a. Curb accessibility
   b. Entrance door accessibility
   c. Ramps
   d. Distance from parking lot to building entrance
   e. Restroom facilities that accommodate wheelchairs
2.   Work Environment Modifications:
a. Lowered or raised work surfaces
b. Special lighting
c. Rearranged shelves
3.   Work Schedule Modifications:
   a.   Flex-time
   b.   Off shifting
   c.   Part-time schedules
4.   Job Task Modifications:
   a.   Sequencing changes
                         b.   Functional
      rearrangements
5.   Equipment Modifications
   a.   Telephone equipped with amplifiers
   b.   Altered controls to accommodate left or right hand or
foot

operation

F. Compensation

When offering employment or promotion to a qualified disabled person, the company will not consider disability income, pension income, or other benefits received by the applicant or employee as relevant to determination of his/her salary. No deductions from company pay will be made for any other income of that nature.

G. Outreach and Positive Recruitment

1.   The company works with local recruiting sources and special service agencies to ensure that disabled individuals are aware of openings and are submitting applications. These agencies include:
> a. The State Employment Development Department
> b. Social Services Department
> c. State Department of Rehabilitation

2.   All company recruiters, interviewers and supervisors responsible for employment decisions have been given training for interviewing the disabled.

3.   The EEO Administrator serves on the board of the Regional Occupation Program.

4.   Our employment records are reviewed periodically to determine the availability of promotable and transferable disabled employees. Additionally, the same review is made to determine whether disabled employees' present and potential skills are being utilized and/or developed.

H. Development and Execution of Affirmative Action Programs

1.   At least annually, all aspects of selection, training and promotion are reviewed to ensure freedom from stereotyping disabled persons that limits their access to jobs for which they are qualified.

2.   Schools from which we recruit are informed of our commitment to employ disabled individuals.

3.   Disabled employees are encouraged to participate in community sponsored programs designed to provide career related information.

Section 7.   Affirmative Action Plan For Disabled Veterans, Veterans Of The Vietnam Era, Recently Separated Veterans, and Other Veterans (41 C.F.R. 60-300)

A.   General

TMA, Inc. supports community programs designed to provide employment opportunities for disabled veterans and veterans of the Vietnam Era. Recognizing that veterans are a valuable human resource, the company has formalized its support of these programs by implementing an affirmative action plan for the employment and advancement of qualified disabled veterans, recently separated veterans, other protected veterans, or Armed Forces service medal veterans.

B.   Definition of Veterans

Disabled Veteran means: (1) A veteran of the U.S. military, ground, naval or air service who is entitled to compensation (or who but for the receipt of military retired pay would be entitled to compensation) under laws administered by the Secretary of Veterans Affairs, or (2) A person who was discharged or released from active duty because of a service-connected disability.

Recently separated veteran means any veteran during the three-year period beginning on the date of such veteran's discharge or release from active duty in the U.S. military, ground, naval or air service.

Other protected veteran means a veteran who served on active duty in the U.S. military, ground, naval or air service during a war or in a campaign or expedition for which a campaign badge has been authorized, under the laws administered by the Department of Defense.

Armed Forces service medal veteran means any veteran who, while serving on active duty in the U.S. military, ground, naval or air service, participated in a United States military operation for which an Armed Forces service medal was awarded pursuant to Executive Order 12985 (61 FR 1209).

C.   Identification of Veterans in the Workforce

1.   The company maintains a listing of all employees who are known to be covered under veterans' regulations. The company invites those and any other individuals believing themselves to qualify in any of the defined veteran categories to voluntarily identify themselves.

2.   Each job applicant who is given a job offer by the company is also invited to voluntarily identify his or her status as a disabled veteran, veteran of the Vietnam era or other veteran, and to indicate any reasonable accommodation that can be made to enable the successful performance of job duties.

3.   Whenever a job applicant is known to be a disabled veteran, a veteran of the Vietnam era, recently separated veteran, or other veteran, the employment application is annotated to identify positions for which the candidate was considered.

4.   If a disabled veteran, veteran of the Vietnam era, or other veteran is not selected for employment, promotion or training, the reason for the non-selection is documented and maintained in the personnel file, or with the job application.

5.   Whenever an accommodation is requested and made for the hiring, promotion or training of the disabled veteran, a description of the accommodation is documented and kept with the personnel file, or with the application.

D. Physical and Mental Requirements

1. Selection processes involved in hiring, promotions and training opportunities are reviewed annually to ensure that no qualified disabled veteran is screened out.

2. Job requirements are reviewed and updated periodically to ensure that they are realistic and do not contain unnecessary qualifications which would serve to screen out qualified disabled veterans.

E. Job Listings

1. In compliance with statute and U.S. Department of Labor regulations, all of the company's job openings will be listed with the state employment service. **Exceptions include:** executive and top management positions, positions that will be filled from within the organization, and positions lasting three days or less.

F. Compensation

1. When offering employment or promotion to a known veteran, the company will not consider disability income, pension income, or other benefits received by the applicant or employee as relevant to determination of his/her salary. No deduction from company pay will be made for any other income of that nature.

G. Outreach and Positive Recruitment

1. The company works with local recruiting sources and social service agencies to ensure that disabled veterans and other veterans are aware of openings and are submitting applications. These agencies include:
    a. The State Employment Department
    b. Veterans' Assistance Center
2. All company recruiters, interviewers and supervisors responsible for employment decisions have been given training for interviewing disabled veterans.
3. Our employment records are reviewed annually to determine the availability of promotable and transferable disabled veterans and other veterans. Additionally, the same review is made to determine whether veteran employees' present and potential skills are being fully utilized and/or developed.

H. Development and Execution of Affirmative Action Programs

1. At least annually, all aspects of selection, training and promotion are reviewed to ensure freedom from stereotyping disabled veterans and other veterans in a manner which limits their access to jobs for which they are qualified.
2. Schools from which we recruit are informed of our commitment to employ disabled veterans and other veterans.
3. Disabled veterans and other veterans are encouraged to participate in community sponsored programs designed to provide career related information.

4.   The company meets its annual obligation to file a VETS-100 reporting form showing the number of veterans in our workforce.

I. Records Retention

1. We maintain our records of job applicants and employees as required by federal regulations (41 C.F.R. 60-300.80). Records are retained for a period of two years past the date of the personnel action and include all requests for accommodation of disability and the company's responses to those requests.

J. Complaint Review Procedure

1. If an applicant or employee files a complaint based on disqualification because of a demonstrated disability, or status as a veteran, it will be referred to the Human Resources office for review of all pertinent factors and disposition within a reasonable time after referral.

Notes

CHAPTER 4

INTRODUCTION TO ANALYSIS OF DATA
FOR MINORITY/WOMEN's AAP

AAP ACTIVITY
FLOW CHART

On the next page you will find a flow chart outlining the activities that must take place during the course of development of an Affirmative Action Plan for Minorities and Women.

Minority & Women's AAP
Affirmative Action Planning
Activity Flow

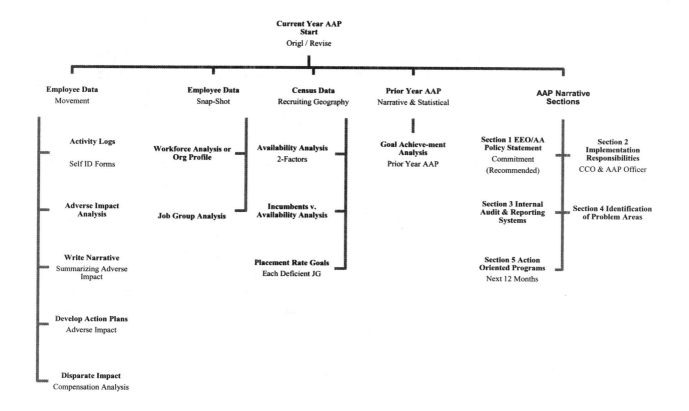

Current Year AAP
Start
Origl / Revise

Employee Data	**Employee Data**	**Census Data**	**Prior Year AAP**	**AAP Narrative Sections**
Movement	Snap-Shot	Recruiting Geography	Narrative & Statistical	

Activity Logs
Self ID Forms

Workforce Analysis or Org Profile

Availability Analysis
2-Factors

Goal Achieve-ment Analysis
Prior Year AAP

Section 1 EEO/AA Policy Statement
Commitment
(Recommended)

Section 2 Implementation Responsibilities
CCO & AAP Officer

Adverse Impact Analysis

Job Group Analysis

Incumbents v. Availability Analysis

Section 3 Internal Audit & Reporting Systems

Section 4 Identification of Problem Areas

Write Narrative
Summarizing Adverse Impact

Placement Rate Goals
Each Deficient JG

Section 5 Action Oriented Programs
Next 12 Months

Develop Action Plans
Adverse Impact

Disparate Impact
Compensation Analysis

AAP ANALYSIS REPORTS CHART

On the following page is a flow chart showing reports that must be considered a part of your AAP document. Although it is not necessary for them to be in the same binder with the narrative sections of your plan, it is necessary for you to send copies of these reports to the OFCCP when you get notice of a compliance review.

Some employers prefer to publish only the narrative sections of their AAP for distribution to managers and employees. As you get more acquainted with the data contained in each of these statistical reports, you will be able to understand the concern of these employers.

A Workforce Analysis contains sex/ethnicity headcount information for each job title in each department of the establishment. If this information were public, competitors might be able to find it of interesting use. For example, if my Research and Development Department had a large expansion of engineers and my Regulations Management Department had a big increase in the number of government permit processors, one might deduce that I was onto something in the way of a new product. At the very least, it could foretell increase in future marketplace activity that my competitors would be delighted to know about.

Recall that Section 4 of our M/W AAP is a narrative summary of the identified problem areas within our establishment. Since we have summarized all of the data analysis in narrative form, we are permitted to hold back the distribution of the basic analysis reports if we choose.

When the time comes for a compliance review, we must consider the statistical reports as an integral part of our AAP, and copies must be sent to the Compliance Officer for review as part of our Plan.

**Minority & Women's AAP
Affirmative Action Planning
AAP Analysis Reports**

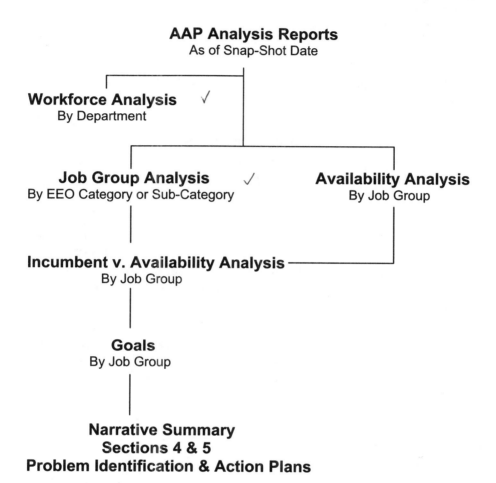

WHAT THE FEDERAL REGULATIONS HAVE TO SAY

There are requirements for the following reports as part of the AAP document:
- Workforce Analysis or Organizational Profile
- Job Group Analysis
- Availability Analysis
- Incumbent v. Availability Analysis
- Goals

In addition, affirmative action employers must also complete and submit to the federal government two reports required of many employers who are not federal contractors:
- Standard Form 100 (EEO-1, EEO-4, etc.)
- VETS-100

We will briefly review the regulatory requirements so you will know why these things are necessary, and then we'll be off to inspect each of the reports in detail and discuss how to assemble them.

❑ **Required Data**

In order to complete development (or updating) of your AAP you will need to have the following information:

- Employee data file showing the following information for each employee (at a minimum)
  - Employee ID
  - Last Name
  - First Name
  - Job Title
  - EEO-1 Category (EEO-4 Category)
  - Department Name
  - Wage Type (annual, monthly, semi-monthly, bi-weekly, weekly, daily, or hourly)
  - Grade (Wage grade if grades are used)
  - Race (W, B, H, A, I)
  - Sex (M, F)
  - Job Group (Assigned by Job Title)

- Census Data (EEO-File for each geographical jurisdiction considered a recruiting territory for each job group)
- Employee Movement Data (12-month Logs of New Hires, Promotions, Terminations)

❑ Employer Suggestions

<u>What about employee movement data?</u>

Data gathering requirements can be satisfied by keeping logs of employment activity. There is no regulatory requirement that employers maintain an expensive electronic or computerized data tracking system if they don't wish to or can't afford it. Data may be tracked manually using these logs, if that is the preference of the employer.

Minimum requirements then are for the following activity tracking logs:

- Applicant Log
- New Hire Log
- Transfer/Promotions Log
- Terminations Log
- Training Participation Log

The fact that these are "activity" logs indicates they will contain data accumulated over a period of time. Usually that period of time is a full AAP year. However, it is a good idea to set up your logs in a way that you can isolate calendar quarters or fiscal quarters of data if you need to, perhaps for compliance review purposes.

At the end of this chapter are examples of these log forms. You may copy them and use them for your data tracking efforts if you wish.

You may also convert these logs to computer reports if you have a computerized human resource information system (HRIS) that allows you to electronically sort and report on data in your employee database. The problem you must guard against encountering, though, is that job applicants are not yet employees and usually will not be found in an employee database. There are many applicant tracking computer programs on the market that allow for management of data regarding job applicants. This data can also be handled manually on the applicant log, if you choose.

Be sure you arrange to keep all required records for the minimum two years (or one year if you qualify for the exemption).

Summary of Data Log Content Requirements

Employment Applicant Log

Each applicant for employment should be logged, regardless of the job being applied for, or the job requisition used for recruiting. Data may be collected manually on the log form or, in an electronic database.

CAUTION: Applicants should NOT be questioned about race or national origin. Data should be gathered by an anonymous, tear-off sheet from the application form or separate Request for Self Identification.

Information needed includes:

- Date applied for job

This is the date the applicant "walked in" to the employment/personnel office, or the date a resume was received and logged. Unsolicited resumes may or may not constitute an "application" depending upon the employer's stated policy. Policy will impact the amount of data to be collected.

- Name of applicant
- Race

    Standard five EEO categories (White, Black, Hispanic, Asian/Pacific Islander, American Indian/Alaska Native)

- Sex
- Job applied for

    Job applicant says (s)he wants or job applicant cites as the opening applied for, or job interviewer cites as possible match for candidate.

- EEO-1 category
- Source
    - Walk-in
    - Referral (note from whom)
    - Newspaper ad (name of newspaper)
    - Agency (employment agency)
    - Other
    - Handicapped (special candidate sources)
      Note made to indicate self identification
      or observation by applicant receptionist
    - Veteran (special candidate sources)
      Note made to indicate self identification

- Disposition
    - Application taken
    - Turned down
    - Hired
    - Pending

- Offer refused
- Not qualified
- <u>Hire Date (if hired)</u>
- <u>Title/Department (job assignment if hired)</u>

Hire Log

This is the place to put detailed information about the people who are actually made job offers whether or not the offer is accepted. You may take credit for a job hire, even though the candidate selected may have found employment elsewhere. The fact you selected that person to fill the position is enough to give you credit. Data may be collected manually on the log form or, in an electronic database.

<u>CAUTION</u>: Applicants should NOT be questioned about race or national origin. Data should be gathered by observation, or by an anonymous, tear-off sheet from the application form.

Information needed includes:

- <u>Date hired (the payroll effective date)</u>
- <u>Name</u>
- <u>Race</u>
    - Standard five EEO categories
- <u>Sex</u>
- <u>Job title assigned</u>
- <u>EEO-1 category</u>
- <u>Job group</u>
    - Within EEO-1 categories, which job group is this job title a part of?
- <u>Department in which job is located</u>

Transfer Log

Movement of employees within the organization can be tracked using this transfer log. On it will be information about the old job and the new job assignment. This data is important to the analysis of feeder groups. Data may be collected manually on the log form or, in an electronic database.

Information needed includes:

- <u>Effective date</u>
    - Date payroll change is in effect

- Name
- Race
    - Standard five EEO categories
- Sex
- Present job (old job)
    - Job title
    - EEO-1 category
    - Job group
- New job
    - Job title
    - EEO-1 category
    - Job group

Promotion Log

Similar to the transfer log, the promotion log tracks information about the "from" and "to" jobs involved in employee movement. Anything considered by policy to be a promotion should be recorded on this form. Data may be collected manually on the log form or, in an electronic database.

Information needed includes:

- Effective date
    - Date payroll change is in effect
- Name
- Race
    - Standard five EEO categories
- Sex
- Present job (old job)
    - Job title
    - EEO-1 category
    - Job group
- New job (position promoted into)
    - Job title
    - EEO-1 category
    - Job group

Training Log

Training information is important to affirmative action as an indicator of equal treatment in the preparation of personnel for higher responsibilities. The data will be analyzed using the "80% Rule" to be sure there is no disparate impact on any protected class of employees. Data may be collected manually on the log form or, in an electronic database.

Information needed includes:

- Selection date
  - May be defined as the date of approval to attend training, the course start date, graduation date, or any other date as long as the application is consistent for all entries.
- Name
- Race
  - Standard five EEO categories
- Sex
- Present job (old job)
  - Job title
  - EEO-1 category
  - Job group
- Department in which employee is located
- Course title
- Completed - Yes/No

Termination Log

This information concerns employee separations from the payroll. Every individual who leaves the payroll should be logged on this form, regardless of the reason for leaving. This data is used in affirmative action to test for disparate impact of protected groups. Data may be collected manually on the log form or, in an electronic database.

Information needed includes:

- Effective date
  - Date payroll change is in effect
- Name
- Race
  - Standard five EEO categories
- Sex
- Last job (prior to separation)
  - Job title
  - EEO-1 category
  - Job group
- Department in which employee was last assigned
- Reason for termination
  - Voluntary reasons
    - > Dislike for work
    - > Salary reasons
    - > Another position
    - > Health
    - > Resume schooling

133

> Family
> Temporary job
> Retirement
> Leaving the area
> Unsuited for the position
> Other
- Involuntary reasons
> Performance
> Attendance/punctuality
> Code of conduct
> Poor job match
> Death
> Other

Who (What) is an Applicant?

A key question for years has been, "Who is an applicant?"

Until 2004, the only official input we have on that issue is found in the <u>Questions and Answers to Clarify and Provide a Common Interpretation of the Uniform Guidelines on Employee Selection Procedures</u>. These "Q & A's", as they're called, were issued by the Equal Employment Opportunity Commission (EEOC), with agreement from the Department of Labor (OFCCP), the Department of Justice, the Office of Personnel Management, and the Treasury Department's Office of Revenue Sharing. They were first printed in the March 2, 1979 Federal Register. Question #15 asks, "What is meant by the terms 'applicant' and 'candidate' as they are used in the Uniform Guidelines?" The answer follows:

*"The precise definition of the term **'applicant'** depends upon the user's recruitment and selection procedures. The concept of an applicant is that of **a person who has indicated an interest in being considered for hiring, promotion, or other employment opportunities**. This interest might be expressed by completing an application form, or might be expressed orally, depending upon the employer's practice.*

*"The term **'candidate'** has been included to cover those situations where the **initial step by the user involves consideration of current employees for promotion, or training, or other employment opportunities, without inviting applications**. The procedure by which persons are identified as candidates is itself a selection procedure under the Guidelines.*

*"**A person who voluntarily withdraws formally or informally at any stage of the selection process is no longer an applicant or candidate for purposes of computing adverse impact**. Employment standards imposed by the user which discourage disproportionately applicants of a race, sex, or ethnic group may, however, require justification. Records should be kept for persons who were applicants or candidates at any stage of the process."*

[Editor's Note: Bold emphasis added.]

The United States Supreme Court has given us some small amount of guidance in its ruling on *McDonnel Douglas Corporation v. Green*, which involved a Title VII race discrimination suit. In that ruling, the court held that a plaintiff, in order to establish a Title VII claim, must prove that "**he applied and was qualified for a job for which the employer was seeking applicants** ..."

There are some basic differences between applicant definitions acceptable to the U.S. Department of Labor's (DOL) Office of Federal Contract Compliance Programs (OFCCP) and the Equal Employment Opportunity Commission (EEOC).
The EEOC has issued guidelines. The OFCCP has issued final rules. Rules have the weight of law. Guidelines do not. If you are a federal contractor, you would be best served if you adopted the OFCCP approach to defining "job applicant."

EEOC GUIDELINES

On February 24, 2004, the Equal Employment Opportunity Commission and several other agencies published in the Federal Register a set of questions and answers that will be added to the 1979 Q & A's associated with the Uniform Guidelines on Employee Selection (41 CFR 60.3). The Office of Federal Contract Compliance Programs (OFCCP) through the Department of Labor, Employment Standards Division, and the Civil Rights Division of the Department of Justice also signed the proposal and request for comments from the public. Here are the additional questions and answers as proposed in this filing:

["UGESP" = Uniform Guidelines on Employee Selection Procedures]

On March 25, 2008, the EEOC asked the Office of Management and Budget (OMB) for permission to extend its Uniform Guidelines without the new Q & A's. There are no changes to the way EEOC defines job applicant. Virtually anyone who expresses interest can be considered a job applicant under EEOC interpretations.

OFCCP RULE

The OFCCP (Office of Federal Contract Compliance Programs in the U.S. Department of Labor) is responsible for enforcement of affirmative action and equal employment opportunity laws and regulations related to federal contractors. OFCCP has finalized its rules about the definition of Internet applicant. On October 7, 2005, OFCCP posted its final rule in the Federal Register. It is not identical to the EEOC and Department of Justice guidelines.

Here is what the OFCCP has to say:

An Internet applicant is someone who...

- has submitted an expression of interest in employment through the Internet or related technology
- the employer has considered as a job seeker for a particular open position

- expresses interest that indicates he or she possesses the advertised, basic qualifications for the position
- and, did not subsequently indicate no longer having an interest in employment in that position.

Federal contractors will have to provide race, ethnicity and gender information for those individuals who the contractor considers for a particular position and who possess basic qualifications. The rule also requires contractors to retain all expressions of interest by individuals considered and specifies records to be maintained about searches of internal and external databases. OFCCP retains the ability to assess whether selection criteria used by federal contractors are discriminatory.

Clearly, it is important to the OFCCP that the issue of qualifications be addressed in the definition of job applicant.

On a practical level, OFCCP says applicant vs. new hire data can be analyzed statistically at any stage in the employment process PRIOR to the interview stage. It is universally agreed in the enforcement community that an "applicant" is created some time before a decision is made about which people to interview.

If you are an affirmative action employer supplying contracted goods and/or services to the federal government, you may need to have a written affirmative action plan. We can help. Call us to discuss your needs, toll-free at 1-888-671-0404.

If you are any employer with 15 or more people on the payroll and you are involved in interstate commerce (ship goods across state lines), you are obligated to abide by 41 CFR 60-3, the Uniform Guidelines on Employee Selection Procedures. That involves validating any written employment test and performing statistical testing on data associated with each step of your employment selection process. The purpose is to determine if there is any unintended disparate impact against any protected group. If you need help with this testing process, call us. We can help with that also.

Clearly, the government has drawn a fine distinction between Internet applicant and other applicants. It has been very specific about the definition for Internet applicant and less specific about the definition of other applicants.

And, we should also remember, we are required to retain all resumes, applications, letters, interview records, correspondence logs, demographic self-identification logs, and other employment-related records for one year after the position is filled to satisfy EEOC requirements. We must keep those same records for a minimum of two years to satisfy OFCCP requirements. The same records must be kept indefinitely once a discrimination complaint or compliance evaluation begins. Only after resolution of a complaint or compliance evaluation may records exceeding the retention limits be destroyed. We'll have more information about retention requirements later.

Recommendations for Defining "Job Applicant"

There are two different record requirements built into the 2005 applicant/record retention regulations. One is the codification of the contractor obligation to extend an invitation to self-identify race/ethnicity and sex once someone becomes a job applicant. And, the second is to retain records on a much broader universe of people. Let's start with the definition of job applicant and then we can later address the question of what records we should retain.

1. Use the same definition for traditional applicants as for Internet applicants

    Follow the OFCCP's definition for job applicant in all processing, whether Internet derived or traditionally sourced.

    An applicant is someone who:
    - Submits an application, resume, or other expression of interest in employment
    - Has been considered for a specific job opening
    - Possesses all the basic job qualifications for the open job
    - Did not self-eliminate from consideration by taking another job elsewhere, stating she/he was no longer interested, or failing to respond to employer communications.

2. Establish a formal application process.

    Many organizations, particularly those with an entrepreneurial bent, eschew the thought of having formal job application forms. That's too much paper work. It represents too much structure of the process. It flies in the face of creating a culture that is warm, friendly, relaxed, responsive, unburdened, and quick-to-respond. All that is true. Yet, the government has given us little option but to design a system which allows us to protect ourselves from criticism due to the lack of such structure.

    OFCCP will try to identify if an individual communicated a clear interest in being considered for a position. Their position, almost always, will be that an unsolicited resume, an e-mail message, an Internet posting and letters of inquiry are clear indications of interest in being considered. Therefore, according to the OFCCP's logic, each of those individuals must be considered a job applicant. Unless the employer establishes documented procedures that prohibit that type of interpretation, there will be an expanded obligation to collect demographic data.

    If you establish a policy that says no one will be considered a job applicant unless they submit a completed copy of your organization's "Job Application Form," then you have reason to reject an argument which would count unsolicited resumes, e-mail messages and the like.

    You can further strengthen your policy if you take the position that you will only accept job applications for open positions. That is, you don't accept job applications unless there is an open position available which you are trying to fill.

    Such a definition won't work for some organizations. They hungrily collect every resume they can get their hands on, just because the types of people they use in their company are so hard to recruit. In reality, you must meet the business need first. In this example, establish a policy of accepting unsolicited resumes. Just recognize that everyone of them you deem to be qualified should be sent a request for demographics and you should retain their records.

3.   <u>Always have specific job qualifications identified to determine who is basically qualified</u>.

Since, by OFCCP definition, no one is an applicant until they are determined to be basically qualified, be sure you know what qualifications each job requires for successful performance. [Please Note: There is likely a difference between "basic" qualification and "minimal" qualification…at least to the lawyers.] Consider basic qualifications to be those skills and abilities, education and experience that are must-haves for success. If any one is missing, the individual could not possibly succeed in the position, and therefore must NOT be considered for the position.

Here's a suggestion for reducing the group of records you must keep under the new regulations. You must retain records for anyone who expresses interest in employment with your company. But, what if you can reduce the level of data in the contact to eliminate even a person's name? Confused? Well, consider this…

If you use pre-qualifying questions to determine who has the "basic" qualifications for a job, you don't even have to allow the individual to submit an application form if they are missing something the job requires. For example:

Job Opening: Accounting / Payroll Clerk
Basic Job Requirements: Intermediate skill with arithmetic, basic English language skills, 2 years of accounting experience, preferably in payroll.

A pre-qualifying question might be, "Do you have at least 2 years of accounting experience?" If the answer is no, the person can't go any farther in the process. Unless the answer is "Yes" there can be no job applicant and the only record you would have to maintain would be the contact and response to the pre-qualifying question. There is certainly no race/sex data transmitted for which a candidate might charge the employer with illegal discrimination. The more you can reduce the record retention obligation through procedures for processing job applicants the better off you will be.

When To Invite Job Applicants to Self Identify Race & Sex

The new regulations are extensive. Attorneys will be having fun with interpretation of these records retention requirements for many years. Part of that requirement involves when to ask a job applicant to identify race and sex. We have provided the invitation form on page 85 if you wish to use such a format. But, when do you send it and to whom do you send it? The answer isn't easily arrived at if you try to interpret the 2005 regulations.

Our friends and colleagues at Maly Consulting LLC have come up with a unique pictorial explanation of the new requirements. Here is what they offer:

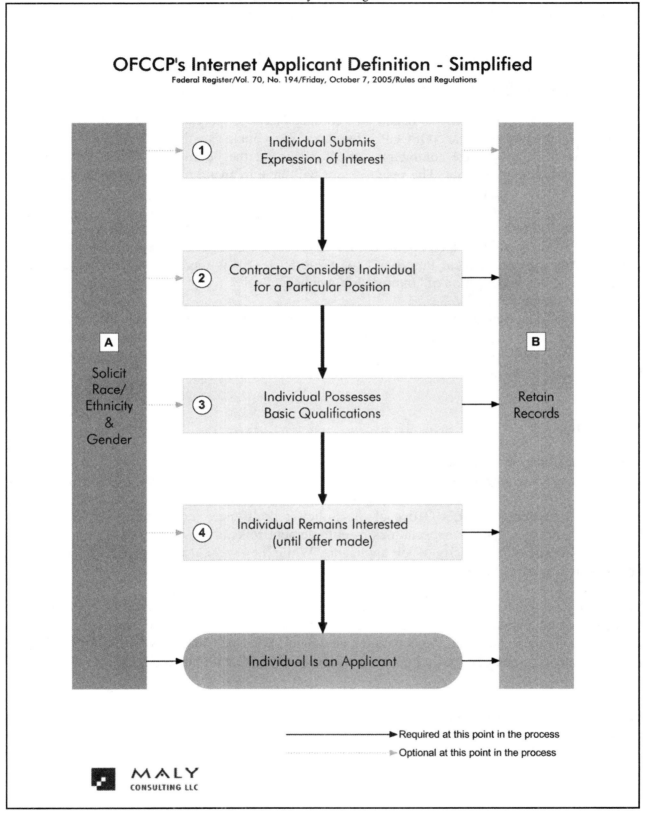

Secrets of Affirmative Action Compliance

In the diagram on the previous page, the center items (1-4) represent the four OFCCP criteria for defining an Internet job applicant. It is only when all of these criteria have been met that a job applicant is created. And, every job applicant must be invited to self identify their race and sex.[15]

New OFCCP Regulations Contain Explosion of Record Maintenance Requirements

New record keeping requirements began on February 6, 2006. They are much more complex than anyone has dreamed possible. (OFCCP offered an olive branch to the contractor community by saying it would not penalize contractors for 90 days after the February 6th effective date of the regulatory data requirements.) The result is you will have to spend much more money to comply than you may have originally believed. Here's why.

On October 7, 2005, the U.S. Department of Labor's Office of Federal Contract Compliance Programs (OFCCP) published its Final Rule for contractors' "Obligation to Solicit Race and Gender Data for Agency Enforcement Purposes." (41 CFR 60-1.3) It is the same set of regulations that contain the agency's definition of "Internet Job Applicant."

To understand the changes these new regulations are making and the impact they will have on federal contractors and subcontractors (employers), it's necessary to step back and look at the context in which all this is happening. It's also a good idea to understand something about the way things are done in the agency.

Background

Begin by realizing that in 2005, and for the past few years prior to that, the Department of Labor (DOL) is a civilian agency operating in an environment of a war mentality in Washington, DC. Within the government, attention is being paid to the war effort and not much is left for civilian agencies. Nonetheless, DOL's Office of the Solicitor drafts new regulations to define "Internet Applicant" and spell out the expectations of enforcement folks about collecting and retaining data about the sex and race/ethnicity of job applicants. While they were at it, they threw in some words about what they expect contractors to retain in the form of other records.

During the George W. Bush Administration (2001-2008) the agency was led by Charles James, Sr. Mr. James had extensive experience in the community of federal contractors and understood affirmative action issues from the contractor viewpoint. Because Congress continued to reduce the agency's budget, some new procedural systems were needed that would allow the agency to operate smarter.

Mr. James decided that changes to the way OFCCP approached its enforcement responsibilities could yield greater results and waste less efforts if they turned more toward enforcement of Title VII and focused less on the mechanics of affirmative action plans.

---

[15] Our thanks to Edward T. Correro and Anna Mae Maly at Maly Consulting LLC for allowing us to reproduce their work here. They can be reached at www.malyconsulting.com or by email at etc@malyconsulting.com. Also by telephone at (415) 883-7058.

Expensive Monster Waiting Down the Road

Actions to refocus its efforts will bring OFCCP more visible results, allowing it to create a positive report to Congress. What is so positive? Money, of course. Money collected in settlements from employers. Here's how it will work.

Currently, a contractor who fails to have an Affirmative Action Plan in place when it is required is subject to one of two remedies by OFCCP. Either the agency can proceed through the process of seeking debarment for the contractor or the contractor can acquiesce and sign a Conciliation Agreement. That agreement will simply require the contractor to put a plan in place, report periodically to OFCCP on its progress and be off the hook after a couple of years. There isn't usually any financial penalty, except in the case of debarment.

The agency has been doing thousands of compliance reviews and constructing many Conciliation Agreements with contractors that don't involve any monetary settlement in the remedy.

So, Mr. James has decided that it will be more productive for his group to begin looking more closely at contractor organizations for signs of illegal discrimination. After all, OFCCP has as part of its mission the enforcement of Civil Rights laws such as the Civil Rights Act of 1964, Title VII, the Vietnam Era Veterans Readjustment Assistance Act and the Rehabilitation Act.

The Civil Rights Act provides for financial remedies to illegal discrimination. These can include back pay, front pay, expense reimbursement, punitive damages, reinstatement, retroactive promotion, and more. Back pay can be calculated for two years in most cases. So, let's see … If OFCCP discovers some pay discrepancies between minorities and non-minorities, it can push for two years' back pay representing the gap amount which would have been earned if the employer had paid everyone correctly. Depending on the number of folks affected, these dollars can grow rapidly. They are cash flow dollars, being paid out at the time of settlement. Often amounts total in the 6 and 7 digit ranges. Now, I've been a manager for 45 years. In all that time, I've never seen a company budget money for a line item such as "Potential Discrimination Settlements." These things just aren't a part of financial planning efforts. One reason is such a budget item would be tantamount to admission that the employer is illegally discriminating. So, when such settlements hit an employer, the impact can be felt on the bottom line profit levels and in earnings per share. Mr. James may be on to something. He's found a way to get the attention of federal contractors by going after employer errors that can be expensive. And, there is another weapon in his arsenal we have yet to discuss. That is the public press release.

Every time OFCCP reaches a Conciliation Agreement with a contractor, it sends a press release to all the local news media where that contractor is headquartered, to the financial press and to key national press contacts. Each of these press releases explains that the contractor has agreed to pay to settle allegations of illegal discrimination, whether or not the contractor denies that discrimination took place. And, it cites the amount of the agreement. If there are other key provisions of the agreement, they will also be included in the press release.

This type of negative publicity is usually unwelcome to employers.

So, Mr. James has concluded that seeking out systemic discrimination within contractor organizations will produce settlements involving large amounts of money that will prove to

Congress his agency is performing its function well. That, in a nut shell, is why Mr. James and the OFCCP are trying to employ more statistical analysis of contractor compensation data. They are looking for cases of illegal discrimination they can then remedy with Conciliation Agreements. The name of the game is now "discrimination" and not so much "affirmative action."

You should create your own estimate of the financial burden these record retention rules will place on your organization. Once you have quantified everything, be sure you discuss the result with your CEO and CFO. They both need to know why you are requesting additional budget dollars.

A New Sherriff in Town

About nine months into his administration, President Obama appointed Patricia A. Shiu as the Director of OFCCP. Shortly thereafter, Labor Secretary Hilda L. Solis announced the elimination of the Employment Standards Administration (ESA). OFCCP has resided within the ESA. Now, the OFCCP Director, Patricia A. Shiu, reports directly to Secretary Solis.

In the first couple of months of Ms. Shiu's tenure, there was widely held belief that she would want to make her mark on the agency by chancing something significant. It was thought that "something" would be the elimination of Charles James'-created Compliance Scheduling Announcement Letter (CSAL). It turned out that she actually modified the letter and proceeded to send it out, although it was a bit late for Fall 2009. CSAL alerts large employers that they may be subject to 2 to 25 establishment audits in the coming year. It is not required by regulations and can be easily removed from the OFCCP procedure with the stroke of the Director's pen. It seems the Director will choose something else on which to make her mark.

An Expanded Record-Keeping Requirement

OFCCP regulations finalized in October 2005, provide significant modifications to the record retention requirements for federal contractors. We're talkin' a lot more records! Here are some key items from 60-1.12 as it is now written.

Contractors must keep and maintain:

- Any record created by the employer pertaining to hiring, assignment, promotion, demotion, transfer lay off or termination, rates of pay or other terms of compensation and selection for training or apprenticeship
- Other records having to do with request for reasonable accommodation, and results of any physical examination
- Job advertisements or postings
- Applications
- Resumes
- Any and all expressions of interest through the Internet or related electronic data technologies … such as on-line resumes or internal resume databases
- Records identifying job seekers contacted regarding their interest in a particular position

- The Contractor must maintain a record of each resume added to its internal resume databases, a record of the date each resume was added to the database
- A record of each position for which a search of the database was made and corresponding to each search, the substantive search criteria used and the date of the search
- When using external databases, contractors must maintain a record of the position for which each search of the database was made, and corresponding to each search, the substantive search criteria used, the date of the search, and the resumes of job seekers who met the basic qualifications for the particular position who are considered by the contractor.

All of this is required, "regardless of whether the individual qualifies as an Internet Applicant under 41 CFR 60-1.3."

But wait …there's more …

Records retained must now also include:

- Tests and test results
- Interview notes

Those are some rather sweeping requirements encompassing many more records than have been included in the past.

But…

The new regulations require us to maintain records on ALL of the people who express interest in employment, not just job applicants. It says we must invite self identification from job applicants. It also requires that we retain ALL resumes, job application forms, letters and other indications of interest in employment. That could be a lot of records, especially for a large employer. (Presumably, government attorneys could make a claim that even voice mail and email messages expressing interest in employment are subject to these retention requirements.)

Some Examples of Record Retention Requirements

Let's just look at three of these new requirements as examples.

1. Records identifying job seekers contacted regarding their interest in a particular position.

   The employer must now maintain a record of EVERY contact made with ANYONE who has expressed a job seeker's desire for employment. Contents of the "record" are not specified in the regulations. However, a record might contain a date the contact was made, the name of the individual job seeker, the job involved, and why the contact was made. Contractors should NOT collect race and sex data on these people unless they fall into the category of "job applicant" or "Internet applicant."

2. A record of each position for which a search of the database was made and corresponding to each search, the substantive search criteria used and the date of the search.

If you search your own database for candidates, you must maintain a log of each search. Here the regulations are specific about content. Required components are the date, the position involved, and the search criteria used. There is no provision for limiting the log of searches to those done only by Human Resources. If you allow operations managers to search your databases those searches, too, must now be logged.

3. When using external databases, contractors must maintain a record of the position for which each search of the database was made, and corresponding to each search, the substantive search criteria used, the date of the search, and the resumes of job seekers who met the basic qualifications for the particular position who are considered by the contractor.

Here is another log maintenance requirement. But, it doesn't say it is limited to searches done by you as the employer. What about searches done by your agent, the executive search specialist or placement firm? All those records are subject to record retention requirements as well.

Consequences of a Cavalier Approach

In the past year, we have heard several federal contractors say, "We aren't going to update our affirmative action plan this year. We don't want to spend the money. Let them catch us." That's quite a shift from a policy of full compliance that was most common only a few years ago. There is no question about the cost of being a federal contractor just having increased. If you want to be in compliance, your data management systems must be able to keep resumes, job applications, interview notes, lists of selection criteria at a minimum.

Up to this point it has been common for contractors to ignore the requirement to collect job applicant data and perform disparate impact testing on new hires, promotions and terminations.
As you can imagine, there have been many excuses created for why those logs didn't exist at the end of the year. Now, the OFCCP may be getting more aggressive in its enforcement efforts by employing a provision that has existed in the regulations for many years.

If you look at 41 CFR 60-3.4 (D) you will find the following at the end of that section:

Where the user has not maintained data on adverse impact as required by the documentation section of applicable guidelines, the Federal enforcement agencies may draw an inference of adverse impact of the selection process from the failure of the user to maintain such data...(emphasis added).

Disparate or adverse impact is illegal discrimination. If OFCCP may infer by default that absence of data means the data would have shown illegal discrimination, they have all they need to force any contractor to the negotiation table and insist on a Conciliation Agreement containing dollar remedies.

We will be encouraging our clients to establish the proper record management systems so they can avoid the most unpleasant consequences of being found to have discriminated illegally because of the "inference" provision.

Recommendations for Employers[16]

1. Make a list of records you are currently keeping. Then make a list of records you are required to keep under this new regulation. Identify any new records you must maintain and make plans for how that will be done.
2. Review the requirements with your Chief Financial Officer and Chief Executive Officer. Identify additional budget requirements resulting from the new record keeping requirements.
3. Train your management staff in the requirements and enroll them in the process so, when appropriate, they are creating and protecting required records.
4. Be sure you have a retention process that allows for destruction of records once they are no longer required. It will be bad enough having to store three years worth of paper and electronic data (the current year plus two previous years), saving it for longer than that would be unnecessary expense.

What About Third Party Recruiters?

The new regulations from OFCCP place an additional burden on contractors. They are likely going to be held accountable by OFCCP for having data about individuals considered by recruiters for any of the job openings for which recruiters were engaged to supply candidates.

John C. Fox, attorney at Fox, Wang & Morgan P.C.[17] presents numerous seminars around the country each year. His subject is affirmative action compliance and he consistently works with the National Employment Law Institute (NELI)[18] to provide updates at an advanced level. If you are a policy maker in your organization, you should consider attending these sessions. If you are looking for a seminar to teach you how to write an affirmative action plan, NELI can help with that, too.

According to Mr. Fox, "Employers which outsource their recruitment and hiring procedures should exercise caution since they may be jointly and severally liable for any unlawful recruitment and

---

[16] We must counsel every contractor to comply with the regulatory requirements. Most of our affirmative action clients fall into the 100 to 500 employee range and they are far from membership in the Fortune 100, hopes notwithstanding. They are angry about the new records retention requirements because they are so outrageously expensive to implement and offer so little value in return. Contractors will not use these records. And, the only time OFCCP will want the records is if they schedule a compliance evaluation on the contractor's establishment. Even then, there are questions about how much value these records will offer to OFCCP. Analysis will be exceedingly time consuming, and therefore expensive. It is not likely that OFCCP will want to spend the time required to really analyze all the retained records. While we will have to wait for years to learn through experience with OFCCP's application of the new regulations what the contractor risk really is, we may assume that with a 2% to 5% chance of audit, smaller contractors may wish to wait for a while to see what OFCCP actually does about the new requirements before implementing programs to collect and maintain all these records. Taking such action will place your organization "out of compliance" and subject to settlement through cash payment if discrimination is presumed by the government. Be sure you discuss such a position with your labor attorney before taking such action.

[17] John C. Fox, Esq. was previously Executive Assistant to the Director of OFCCP, where he was in charge of all policy and enforcement matters. He has defended hundreds of class-wide compensation discrimination investigations, both in and out of the courts, most involving the definition of "Who is an Applicant?" He can be reached at Fox, Wang & Morgan P.C., 160 West Santa Clara St., Suite 700, San Jose, CA 95113.

[18] National Employment Law Institute (NELI), 1601 Emerson Street, Denver, Colorado 80218, 303-861-5600, neli@neli.org

selection procedures their delegate may occasion. The federal government has remained active in monitoring such practices, and even an unintended, discriminatory impact on minorities or women in the selection process can lead to substantial potential economic liability for back pay damages."

"Furthermore," he continues, "the so-called and little known *nondelegable duty doctrine* generally prevents an employer from avoiding liability for discrimination by attempting to delegate the recruitment, hiring and/or promotion procedures to a third party. Rather, various courts have settled the question by holding that liability for discriminatory hiring practices must rest with the employer, itself." Recruiters are typically not agents of the employer under traditional legal thinking because most employers do not control their recruiters or consent to their unlawful acts. Rather, many recruiters will find that they are bound by the *nondelegable duty doctrine* to collect data and avoid illegal employment discrimination as if they were on the employer's payroll rather than a contractor of services.

Mr. Fox offers as support for that position, the following court decisions that have held employers liable for the actions of their recruiters or others:

- *Powers v. Alabama Dep't of Education*, 854 F.2d 1285 (11th Cir. 1988), the State of Alabama Department of Education's Disability Determination Service ("DDS") delegated its <u>promotion</u> selection process to the Personnel Board of the State of Alabama ("SPD"). The SPD gathered and ranked applicants on the basis of three criteria: (1) 45% based on applicant's training and education; (2) 45% on experience, the length of time an applicant had worked in disability determination, and the positions in which he or she had served [this 90% formed the 'training and experience' or 'T&E' score]; and (3) 10% based on supervisor evaluations while at DDS. The SPD then further culled applicants, placing the most desirable candidates on a list of "Certificate of Eligibles." The DDS then only considered such "eligible" applicants for promotion. Plaintiffs alleged that the T&E evaluation criteria (worth 90% of the total promotion criteria) had a disparate impact on Black applicants.

  The Eleventh Circuit Court of Appeals rejected the DDS' attempt to avoid liability by alleging that it had delegated its promotion mechanism to the SPD. The Court held that "an employer cannot delegate several aspects of its promotion procedure to another agency such as SPD and then escape liability if that agency develops discriminatory practices."

- *Moskowitz v. City of Chicago*, 1993 U.S. Dist LEXIS 16402, *10-11 (N.D. Ill. 1993)("[U]nder either Title VII or the ADEA, an employer cannot simply delegate portions of its hiring or promotion procedure to a third party and escape liability if the third party develops discrimination problems.")

- *Scott v. City of Topeka Police and Fire Civil Service Comm'n*, 739 F. Supp. 1434, 1438 (D. Kan. 1990) ("To hold that the City of Topeka could avoid liability for employment discrimination by delegating certification decisions to a commission would be contrary to the broad scope of the definition of "employer" under Title VII and would eviscerate Title VII's protection for municipal employees. Therefore, the court finds that the City of Topeka can be held liable under Title VII for the gender discriminatory practice of its Police and Fire Civil Service Commission in this issue.")

- *Terbovitz v. Fiscal Court of Adair County,* 825 F.2d 111, 116 (6th Cir. 1987) (disapproved on other grounds) (holding, in a case involving hiring for emergency medical technician positions, that "[a]n employer … may not avoid Title VII liability by delegating its discriminatory programs to third parties.")

- *Town of South Whitley v. Cincinnati Ins. Co.,* 724 F. Supp. 599, 603-04 (N.D. Ind. 1989) (holding that town and its governing board acted as a single entity in not hiring employee. Because governing board exercised so much authority in the name of the town [including setting town employee salaries, hiring and firing town employees])

- *Eldredge v. Carpenters 46 Northern Cal. Counties Joint Apprenticeship and Training Ctte.,* 833 F.2d 1334, 1337 (9th Cir. 1987) ("[The joint labor-management committee] cannot avoid liability for the effects of its own admission procedures by pointing to the discriminatory practices of those to whom it has delegated the power to select apprentices.")

- *Lam v. Univ. of Hawaii,* 40 F.3d 1551, 1561 (9th Cir. 1994) ("…where a university has delegated employment decisions to a committee and members of that committee have engaged in discriminatory treatment, the university is liable.)

So, be advised that OFCCP is very likely to take the position both that the federal contractor or subcontractor is jointly liable with the third party recruiter for any discriminatory acts and that the federal contractor or subcontractor must also retain and make available all records for those job seekers your recruiters considered on the contractor's behalf. That goes well beyond the common practice of retaining only those records of job seekers the recruiter forwards to the employer for final consideration.

Recommendations for Contractors (& Subcontractors)

Obviously, most contractors will have to change the way they have been working with recruiters. Some recruiters have standard contracts that absolve them of any liability for acts or omissions related to the work they do for an employer. Further, most recruiters strongly resist any requests for documentation on people they may have considered in their searches. They consider that proprietary information.

Well, proprietary or not, federal contractors are now faced with the need for those data. And, the most likely method of obtaining it is by contract with the recruiter. According to Mr. Fox, you should consider including at least the following in your recruiter contracts:

- Cooperation Clause – recruiter agrees to cooperate in any investigation of complaints, grievances, claims or other issues.
- Adverse Impact Data Collection – recruiter agrees to collect and report to the employer appropriate complete adverse impact information and underlying raw data related to any search done on behalf of the employer.
- Discrimination Prohibition – agreement from the recruiter to abide by all state, federal and local laws and regulations governing equal employment opportunity.
- Indemnity – provision for the recruiter to hold harmless the employer from any liabilities created by the recruiter in not collecting or reporting as required.

What is an Employee?

What employees should I count and include in my AAP analysis?

No sooner have we settled all the upset about applicant definitions than we have to ask for a definition of "employee." In the old days, an employee was someone who worked for you. The relationship defined the term. There weren't a lot of alternatives. If I worked for you, you paid me. If you paid me, I was considered your employee. But, life was simpler in those days.

Today, we have temporary agency employees, co-employment relationships through Professional Employer Organizations (formerly called employee leasing companies), people who are hired for part-time work and people who are hired for only a specified period of time or "term." When their project is completed, "term" employees are removed from the payroll. And, of course, there is the big controversy about "contractors." When can someone work for you, but not be your employee? When they are a contractor, naturally.

Well, there has been a bit of confusion added to the issue over the past several years. We now are faced with the problem of determining which noses to count when we determine our "snapshot" date for affirmative action workforce analysis. If I take a picture of my workforce on a given date so I can analyze its characteristics, what do I take a picture of? Said differently, whom do I count as an employee in my workforce on that day?

In early 1997 the U.S. Supreme Court issued a ruling in *Walters v. Metropolitan Educational Enterprises* (1997 WL 9783). In this case, a worker filed a discrimination complaint against the employer. The employer said it didn't meet the Title VII requirement of "15 or more employees for each working day in each of 20 or more calendar weeks in the current or preceding calendar year." The employer explained by saying it only counted workers on days they were being compensated. Therefore, people who worked part-time were only counted on the days they worked. People who were on vacation weren't counted if the vacation time was unpaid. Any other unpaid or uncompensated status would cause Metropolitan Educational Enterprises to overlook someone in their count. The Supreme Court said we should count people based on whether or not they have an employment relationship on the day in question. That is to say, **are they on our payroll?** The Court said the payroll method of counting employees represents a fair interpretation of Title VII. Therefore, if someone goes on unpaid leave of absence (for any reason), yet remains on your payroll, you should probably count that person in your workforce. You will find you begin counting folks who are on disability leave, sabbatical, scheduled days off, suspension, or on jury duty. If somebody goes into the federal witness protection program and can't come to work any longer, but you keep them on your payroll, you will likely have to count them in your workforce as an employee for affirmative action purposes as well as for Title VII purposes.

There are no regulatory guidelines for us in the question of employee definition. However, in its 2000 regulations, the OFCCP printed in its preamble the following, *"The term 'employees' is broad enough to include part-time, temporary and full time employees. Therefore the final rule adopts paragraph (b) of the proposal without change."*[19]

---

[19] Federal Register, Vol. 165, No 219, Monday, November 13, 2000, page 68024, third column. (41 CFR 60-2.1(b))

Temporary workers, if they are on your payroll on the day you take the "snapshot" of your workforce, should be included. Our experience indicates that your data analysis will be more accurate, and often more favorable, if you include everyone who is on the payroll. Independent contractors and agency employees who are not part of your payroll should not be included in the AAP analysis. And, anyone on your payroll who is stationed at a location outside the United States should NOT be counted.

Any non-employee should be excluded from your AAP. That includes folks such as consultants, agency temps, off-shore contractors, and others who are not on your payroll.

We recommend you include everyone in the United States in one or more of your AAP establishments. If you have someone working on the payroll but stationed outside the country, they do not have to be counted. Employees are defined as those who are full-time, part-time, temporary, project, or other classification, embracing someone for whom you produce a paycheck.

To answer the question about who must be included in your AAP establishment, we can say any job in the U.S. for which you have a placement opportunity should the incumbent leave.

OK. So, we have to count noses based on payroll. But what about independent contractors. What about people who are long-term temps, technically on some agency's payroll? The answer, I think, is this. If they are on your payroll, count them. If they are on someone else's payroll, you may argue they don't have to be, or should not be, counted in your workforce. You are stuck for the co-employment condition in which you share employer status with a co-employer under a Professional Employer Organization (PEO) contract. Those people are still officially considered your employees. It so happens that they are also employees of the PEO at the same time. "Temps" don't have to be considered part of your workforce, however, as long as they are not on your payroll.

What a bucket of worms. As I said, life used to be simpler in years past. Now, it is very important for human resource managers to think these things through carefully. Because, liabilities are now often attached to the definitions we use.

Employee Data Required

On the date you have chosen as your "snap shot" date, determine for each employee the following information:

- Employee Name
- Current Job Title
- Current Supervisor
- Current Department
- Sex
- Ethnic Code
- Disability status
- Disabled veteran/Vietnam era veteran status

While employers may not require job applicants to respond to requests for sex and ethnic data, employers are held accountable for having sex and ethnic identification of all of their employees.

If an employee says to you, "I don't want to give you that information," or something equally eloquent, you will have to make the identification yourself, by observation. Be sure you use the current government-specified categories[20]:

<table>
<tr><td colspan="2"><u>Sex</u></td><td colspan="2"><u>Race/Ethnicity</u></td></tr>
<tr><td>(M)</td><td>Male</td><td>(H)</td><td>Hispanic</td><td><u>Non-Hispanic</u></td></tr>
<tr><td>(F)</td><td>Female</td><td></td><td></td><td>(B) Black</td></tr>
<tr><td></td><td></td><td></td><td></td><td>(A) Asian</td></tr>
<tr><td></td><td></td><td></td><td></td><td>(P) Hawiian/Pacific Islander</td></tr>
<tr><td></td><td></td><td></td><td></td><td>(I) American Indian/Alaska Native</td></tr>
<tr><td></td><td></td><td></td><td></td><td>(W) White</td></tr>
<tr><td></td><td></td><td></td><td></td><td>(2) 2 or More Races (Multiple)</td></tr>
</table>

If, for some reason, you believe you must track data about your employees in some other group of categories, be sure you are able to reassemble your data into these categories. They are the ones you MUST use for your AAP data analysis.

And, remember, for employees, "Other" or "Unknown" is not an option.

Now, go forth and count!

What is a Promotion or Transfer?

Who should be counted and logged as having had a promotion or transfer during the year? Well, you get to decide. You define promotion. You define transfer. But once you do, be consistent in how you apply those definitions for data gathering purposes.

Some employers say a promotion occurs only when an employee receives a change in job assignment that qualifies for a bonus payment under the compensation plan. Other employers say a promotion is movement from one salary grade to a higher salary grade. Other employers use other definitions. You get to use the definition that is best for your organization and its business needs. It is a good idea to write it down, and make sure whoever is involved in data tracking, knows what it says and how to apply it.

Do the same thing for your definition of transfer. Write it down and make sure those who must refer to it understand how to apply it.

---

[20] New EEO-1 categories as published in the Federal Register, Vol. 70, No. 227, Monday, November 28, 2005, Notices, Page 71302.

WHAT REMAINS
TO BE COVERED

In the following chapters, you will find detailed information about each of the analysis reports that must be completed and considered a part of your AAP document (whether or not you decide to distribute copies with the narrative sections).

While personnel activity logs track how people move over time, these other data analysis reports will look at information representing a specific date's profile of your organization.

I call it the "snap shot" date. It is the date on which we take a picture of our organizational demographics and then analyze what we see. We must look at a specific date because if we look at a span of time, there would be no way to make sense of what we see. People are being hired and fired all the time. People are being promoted and transferred all the time. We can't analyze something that keeps changing its makeup. So, we have to make the organization "hold still" to determine what it looks like.

Your "snap shot" date should be the last work day of the previous AAP year, or the first work day of the current AAP year...or as near as you can come to either of those two dates.

Consistency in your "snap shot" date will allow you to compare data profiles from one year to the next, knowing that each year the data is the RESULT of all the activity which has transpired during the previous twelve months.

Using Your Applicant Log to Meet Recordkeeping Requirements

The importance of your Applicant Flow Log has grown since the increase in responsibility for records retention. You are now responsible for demonstrating the disposition of each individual who shows interest in employment with your organization. To do that easily means some modification to your Applicant Log.

Everyone who shows interest in employment is not necessarily qualified for the job you wish to fill. And, everyone who is qualified may not still be on the list of available applicants when you get to the final steps of selection. So, knowing who to invite to self-identify their race and sex is vital. Only those who meet the definition of "Job Applicant" rise to the level when you must extend that invitation.

And, along the path to a final selection, some of your job applicants may drop out of the race. They may get jobs elsewhere, or simply not show up for one or more of the interviews or testing appointments in your selection process. That is a disqualifier and they would thus become a non-applicant as a result. You are only required to use "applicants" in your statistical analysis of new hires. Disparate impact can only be determined by comparing those who are hired with those who are in the pool of justly qualified job applicants for those open positions.

So, disposition codes are critical to your recordkeeping success. I urge you to do whatever it takes to modify your job applicant log to allow proper tracking of disposition on everyone who expresses interest in employment with your organization. That is the only way you can "prove" to the OFCCP that you have done the proper analysis.

Some Possible Disposition Codes
For Your Applicant Log

Code	Disposition
1	Hired
2	Meets Basic Qualifications
3	Rejected Job Offer
4	Failed Background Check
5	Failed Written Test(s)
6	Not Most Qualified – Telephone Interview
7	Not Most Qualified – Personal Interview
8	Does Not Meet Basic Qualifications
9	Does Not Have Authorization to Work in the U.S.
10	No Openings – Position Filled with Rehire
11	No Openings – Position Cancelled
12	Unsolicited And Not Considered
13	Withdrew - No Show for Telephone Interview
14	Withdrew - No Show for Personal Interview
15	Withdrew – Accepted Another Job
16	Withdrew – At Interview
17	Withdrew – Failure to Respond
18	Withdrew – Compensation Related
19	Insufficient Information for Processing
20	Insufficient Age
21	Received from Agency But Not Approved for Agency Expense
22	Not Local Candidate – No Relocation Authorized
23	Other: (Explain)
24	Other: (Explain)
25	Other: (Explain)

You are invited to modify this list as you wish. Make it fit your organization and your employment process. Whatever you use should allow you the opportunity to isolate people who rise to the level of "Job Applicant" from those who never were or no longer are applicants. Remember, a job applicant is defined by the OFCCP this way:

An applicant is someone who:
- Submits an application, resume, or other expression of interest in employment
- Has been considered for a specific job opening
- Possesses all the basic job qualifications for the open job
- Did not self-eliminate from consideration by taking another job elsewhere, stating she/he was no longer interested, or failing to respond to employer communications.

CAUTION:

I see two recurring problems with applicant data. Please be alert to them and avoid them.

1) <u>Inconsistency of Recordkeeping</u> – If you have multiple internal and/or external people processing job applicants, having everyone treat recordkeeping with the proper attention is a critical orchestration process. If one of your recruiters is not filling in the form with disposition codes, it jeopardizes your ability to prove your data are accurate. Fail that and you will be subject to back pay awards if you are unfortunate enough to be audited at that time. Constantly check to be sure your recruiters are all using the same system and that they all understand the disposition codes to mean the same thing.

2) <u>Failure to Show New Hires on BOTH the Applicant Flow Log and the New Hire Log</u> – Much too frequently, people think that people cease being considered applicants when they are given a job offer and placed on the New Hire Log. In actuality, for your analysis to come out correctly, you must have those hired also appear as applicants. They were in the pool from which they were picked and without them represented your pool demographics will be skewed.

APPLICANT FLOW LOG

Location: _____   Period Covered: _____

Date	Name	Referral Source	Solicited Y/N	Position Applied For	Inter-viewed Y/N	RACE (1)	Dis/* Vet	SEX	Disposition Code (4)	AAP Job Group (2)	EEO-1 Cat. (3)

(The last two columns, "AAP Job Group (2)" and "EEO-1 Cat. (3)", are grouped under the heading **Personnel Use Only**.)

*Complete only if the information is volunteered or determined by visual or other legal means. Dis/Vet = Disabled or Veteran (D or V)

(1) 0 = White; 1 = Black; 2 = Hispanic; 3 = Asian; 4 = American Indian; 5 = Hawiian/Pacific Islander; 6 = 2 or more races
(2) See Affirmative Action Plan for Job Group defined as job having similar content, skills, wage rates and promotional opportunities.
(3) 1.1 = Executive/Senior Level Officials and Managers; 1.2 = First/Mid Level Officials and Managers; 2 = Professionals; 3 = Technicians; 4 = Sales Workers; 5 = Administrative Support Workers; 6 = Craft Workers; 7 = Operatives; 8 = Laborers and Helpers; 9 = Service Workers.
(4) Disposition Code – Use Company Provided List of Disposition Codes

Applflow.doc

155

Secrets of Affirmative Action Compliance

NEW HIRE LOG

Location: _____   Period Covered: _____

Date	Name	Position Hired Into	EEO (1)	Dis/* Vet	SEX	Personnel Use Only	
						AAP Job Group (2)	EEO-1 Cat. (3)

*Complete only if the information is volunteered or determined by visual or other legal means. Dis/Vet = Disabled or Veteran (D or V)

(1) 0 = White; 1 = Black; 2 = Hispanic; 3 = Asian; 4 = American Indian; 5 = Hawiian/Pacific Islander; 6 = 2 or more races
(2) See Affirmative Action Plan for Job Group defined as job having similar content, skills, wage rates and promotional opportunities.
(3) 1.1 = Executive/Senior Level Officials and Managers; 1.2 = First/Mid Level Officials and Managers; 2 = Professionals; 3 = Technicians; 4 = Sales Workers; 5 = Administrative Support Workers; 6 = Craft Workers; 7 = Operatives; 8 = Laborers and Helpers; 9 = Service Workers.

NEWHIRE.DOC

156

TRANSFER & PROMOTION LOG

Location: _____   Period Covered: _____

Eff. Date	TRANSFERRED OR PROMOTED FROM						TRANSFERRED OR PROMOTED TO								
	Name	Department	Title	Pay Grade	AAP Job Group (1)	EEO-1 Cat. (2)	Department	Title	Pay Grade	AAP Job Group (1)	EEO-1 Cat. (2)	Race (3)	Sex	Dis/ *Vet

* Dis/Vet = Disabled or Veteran (D or V)

(1) See Affirmative Action Plan for Job Group defined as job having similar content, skills, wage rates and promotional opportunities.

(2) 1.1 = Executive/Senior Level Officials and Managers; 1.2 = First/Mid Level Officials and Managers; 2 = Professionals; 3 = Technicians; 4 = Sales Workers; 5 = Administrative Support Workers; 6 = Craft Workers; 7 = Operatives; 8 = Laborers and Helpers; 9 = Service Workers.

(3) 0 = White; 1 = Black; 2 = Hispanic; 3 = Asian; 4 = American Indian; 5 = Hawiian/Pacific Islander; 6 = 2 or more races

TrsPrmLg.doc

Secrets of Affirmative Action Compliance

TRAINING LOG

Location: _____   Period Covered: _____

Date	Name & Job Title	Course/Seminar Title & Length	RACE (1)	Dis/* Vet	SEX	Personnel Use Only	
						AAP Job Group (2)	EEO-1 Cat. (3)

*Complete only if the information is volunteered or determined by visual or other legal means. Dis/Vet = Disabled or Veteran (D or V)

(1) 0 = White; 1 = Black; 2 = Hispanic; 3 = Asian; 4 = American Indian; 5 = Hawiian/Pacific Islander; 6 = 2 or more races
(2) See Affirmative Action Plan for Job Group defined as job having similar content, skills, wage rates and promotional opportunities.
(3) 1.1 = Executive/Senior Level Officials and Managers; 1.2 = First/Mid Level Officials and Managers; 2 = Professionals; 3 = Technicians; 4 = Sales Workers; 5 = Administrative Support Workers; 6 = Craft Workers; 7 = Operatives; 8 = Laborers and Helpers; 9 = Service Workers.

158

TERMINATION LOG

Location: _____   Period Covered: _____

Date	Name	Job Title	EEO (1)	SEX	Volunt/ Invol	AAP Job Group (2)	EEO-1 Cat. (3)

The last two columns (AAP Job Group and EEO-1 Cat.) are grouped under the heading "Personnel Use Only".

(1) 0 = White; 1 = Black; 2 = Hispanic; 3 = Asian; 4 = American Indian; 5 = Hawiian/Pacific Islander; 6 = 2 or more races

(2) See Affirmative Action Plan for Job Group defined as job having similar content, skills, wage rates and promotional opportunities.

(3) 1.1 = Executive/Senior Level Officials and Managers; 1.2 = First/Mid Level Officials and Managers; 2 = Professionals; 3 = Technicians; 4 = Sales Workers; 5 = Administrative Support Workers; 6 = Craft Workers; 7 = Operatives; 8 = Laborers and Helpers; 9 = Service Workers.

Notes

CHAPTER 5

WORKFORCE ANALYSIS

WORKFORCE ANALYSIS

Workforce Analysis is the first of the statistical analysis documents that must be in your AAP for minorities and women. It contains information about the sex and ethnic distribution of headcount for all job titles in the establishment, broken down by departments.

Workforce Analysis is a VERTICAL SLICE of your organization. Remember, we are talking about a physical address where 50 or more people are working. It might even be a "campus" or cluster of buildings within a complex that can be considered an "Establishment." If your establishment is "Functional" (and you have had it approved by OFCCP), your geography will probably be national, or at least regional.

Outline of Content Requirements

As you read in the last chapter, OFCCP regulations are very concise about how a Workforce Analysis must be prepared. The new revisions, however, allow you a choice about how you will display your Workforce Analysis. December 13, 2000, regulations say affirmative action programs must contain the following information:

(a) *An organizational profile is a depiction of the staffing pattern within an establishment. It is one method contractors use to determine whether barriers to equal employment opportunity exist in their organizations. The profile provides an overview of the workforce at the establishment that may assist in identifying organizational units where women or minorities are underrepresented or concentrated. The contractor must use either the organizational display or the workforce analysis as its organizational profile:*

(b) *(1) An organizational display is a detailed graphical or tabular chart, text, spreadsheet or similar presentation of the contractor's organizational structure. The organizational display must identify each organizational unit in the establishment, and show the relationship of each organizational unit to the other organizational units in the establishment. (2) An organizational unit is any component that is part of the contractor's corporate structure. In a more traditional organization, an organizational unit might be a department, division, section, branch, group or similar component. In a less traditional organization, an organizational unit might be a project team, job family, or similar component.*

The term includes an umbrella unit (such as department) that contains a number of subordinate units, and it separately includes each of the subordinate units (such as sections or branches). (3) For each organizational unit, the organizational display must indicate the following: (i) The name of the unit; (ii) The job title, gender, race, and ethnicity of the unit supervisor (if the unit has a supervisor); (iii) The total number of male and female incumbents; and (iv) the total number of male and female incumbents in each of the following groups: Blacks, Hispanics, Asians/Pacific Islanders, and American Indians/Alaskan Natives.

(c) *(1) A workforce analysis is a listing of each job title as appears in applicable collective bargaining agreements or payroll records ranked from the lowest paid to the highest paid within each department or other similar organizational unit including departmental or unit supervision. (2) If there are separate work units or lines of progression within a department, a separate list must be provided for each such work unit, or line, including unit supervisors. For lines of progression there must be indicated the order of jobs in the line through which an employee could move to the top of the line. (3) Where there are no formal progression lines or usual promotional sequences, job titles should be listed by department, job families, or disciplines, in order of wage rates or salary ranges. (4) For each job title, the total number of incumbents, the total number of male and female incumbents, and the total number of male and female incumbents in each of the following groups must be given: Blacks, Hispanics, Asians/Pacific Islanders, and American Indians/Alaskan Natives. The wage rate or salary range for each job title must be given. All job titles, including all managerial job titles, must be listed. (60-2.11)*

Traditional Workforce Analysis

A separate Workforce Analysis Form must be prepared for each Department in the organization.

That requirement brings us to the question, "What is a Department?" You get to answer, as the employer. Your business organization is designed to allow your business to function in the best possible way, so your organization can accomplish the things it has been created to do. Therefore, your organization will likely be different from other organizations, even though it may share some similarities.

For example, some contractors have a Finance and Administration Department. It houses all of the administrative support functions of the organization: accounting, human resources, mail handling, reception, utilities management, and the like. Other contractors have these functions divided into separate departmental entities. A lot depends on the size of the company and the quantity of people in each part of the group.

Begin with the definition of Department you ordinarily use. If you have a Sales and Marketing organization you call a Department, then use that designation.

Be sure you are able to identify all information required in your Workforce Analysis:

- Department Entity
- Separate page for each separate line of progression within Department
- Job Titles in order of compensation from highest to lowest
- Compensation for each job title
- EEO category of each job title
- Total number of incumbents in the title
- Women incumbents identified by ethnic group
- Men incumbents identified by ethnic group
- Totals for each category, for each page, for each line of progression, and for the Department as a whole

Take a blank Workforce Analysis Form and begin listing job titles within that Department. You will need compensation data for each incumbent in the Department because you must show job titles on the Workforce Analysis Form in compensation order. That means from lowest compensation to highest, or from highest to lowest. Regulations say to rank job titles from lowest paid to highest paid within the Department, but they don't say where to begin the ranking. That is, they aren't clear whether the highest paid job should be at the top of the list or at the bottom of the list. Therefore, you get to choose which way you list your job titles. Just be sure they are in compensation order.

Next, you must show the compensation for each job title. You may either show actual dollars paid to each job title, or as some employers prefer doing, code the salary ranges. (See "Salary Range Charts" on page 157.)

Next, you must show the EEO category of each job title. EEO categories are specified and defined by the government as part of the "Standard Form 100" series of documents. All employers in the country with 100 or more workers on payroll must file an EEO report by October 31st each year. All employers who are federal contractors, required to have a written affirmative action plan, must also file an EEO report by October 31st each year. So, if you only have 50 workers on payroll, but you are an affirmative action employer, you must file the report.

Appendix C contains a copy of the EEO-1 report and its instructions.

Appendix D contains a copy of the EEO-4 report and its instructions.

Different EEO categories have been created for different segments of the economy. Private sector companies should use EEO-1 categories, of which there are nine. Public sector organizations should use EEO-4 categories, of which there are eight. There are differences, based on the type of work done in each sector of the economy. For example, private sector firms have "Sales Workers" which are shown in EEO-1, category 4. In the public sector, however, we don't find sales workers. We do find "Protective Service

Workers" such as firefighters, police officers, and so forth. Category 4 for the public sector EEO-4 report is relabeled "Protective Service Workers."

TITLE VII REPORTS

STANDARD FORM 100

Report Form	Who Must File
EEO-1 Active	1) All employers covered by Title VII that have 100 or more employees; 2) government contractors covered by Executive Order 11246 that have 50 or more employees and government contracts of $50,000 or more. Annual.
EEO-2 (Discontinued)	1) Joint labor-management committees that have five or more trainees in their programs and at least one employer having 25 or more employees; 2) union sponsor having 25 or more members covered by Title VII. Annual.
EEO-2E (Discontinued)	Every establishment with 25 or more employees by each employer who (1) has a total company-wide employment of 100 or more employees, (2) conducts and controls an employer-operated apprenticeship program, and (3) has five or more apprentices in the establishment. Annual.
EEO-3 Active	Local unions that have had 100 or more members at any time since the previous December 31. An international union is not required to file a report unless it operated a local union under a trusteeship or other arrangement or performs any functions of a local. BiAnnual in even numbered years. Due December 31 of the survey year.
EEO-4 Active	State and local governmental jurisdictions with 100 or more employees. (States, cities, counties, and special districts such as water, sewer, fire districts.) Bi-annual in odd numbered years.
EEO-5 Active	Formally known as the **Elementary-Secondary Staff Information Report**, is a joint requirement of the EEOC, and the Office for Civil Rights (OCR) and the National Center for Education Statistics (NCES) of the Department of Education. It is conducted biennially, in the even numbered years, and covers all public elementary and secondary school districts with 100 or more employees in the United States.
EEO-6 (Discontinued)	Colleges and universities with 15 or more employees. Was required every two years. Now incorporated into Department of Education report. Bi-annual.

For current information about Title VII reports go to:
http://www.eeoc.gov/employers/surveys.html

EEO-6 reports have been discontinued as stand-alone documents. They are now contained within another report required by the U.S. Department of Education.

Whichever Standard Form 100 you use in your organization, become familiar with the definitions of each job category it offers. You will find examples of job functions within each job category within the instructions for your proper Standard Form 100. This is important. EEO categorization will impact your statistical analysis.

And, it is a good idea to request a new copy of the government's instructions for your Standard Form 100 every year, just to make sure those categories have not changed. They do shift from time to time. And definitions of ethnic categories also shift from time to time. For example, in the '60s when the affirmative action requirement first came into existence, Asian did not include people from India in its definition. Today, people from India, and all others from the Asia continent are considered Asians. And, people from Portugal are excluded from the definition of Hispanic today. (I'm not here to defend the reasoning. Frankly, I'm not sure I could. It is my role, however, to help you understand the need to keep pace with whatever changes the government might offer as time goes by.)

2005 Changes to EEO-1 Report

On November 28, 2005, the Equal Employment Opportunity Commission (EEOC) published a Notice of Submission for OMB Review containing its final version of the updated EEO-1 Report. If you don't have 100 or more employees in the private sector or are not an affirmative action employer with 50 or more workers, you don't need to go any farther. You are not required to submit an EEO-1 Report.

Qualifying employers must file demographic data each year by September 30th that tells the government the makeup of their workforce by sex and race/ethnicity. This is further divided into occupational categories called EEO-1 Groups.

Specific Changes in EEO-1

Several changes are being made in the race/ethnic categories for which reporting will be required. See the "before and after" look at the tracking categories below.

Former EEO-1 Race/Ethnic Categories	New EEO-1 Race/Ethnic Categories
• Hispanic	• Hispanic or Latino (includes all employees who answer "Yes" to the question, are you Hispanic or Latino?)
• White (not of Hispanic origin)	• White (not Hispanic or Latino)
• Black (not of Hispanic origin)	• Black or African American (not Hispanic or Latino)

Former EEO-1 Race/Ethnic Categories	New EEO-1 Race/Ethnic Categories
• Asian or Pacific Islander	• Native Hawiian or Other Pacific Islander (not Hispanic or Latino)
• American Indian or Alaskan Native	• Asian (not Hispanic or Latino)
	• American Indian or Alaska Native (not Hispanic or Latino)
	• Two or More Races (not Hispanic or Latino)

One major change has been made in the occupational categories. And, as you can see from the content of the table below, some cosmetic differences have also occurred. Of primary importance is the splitting of EEO Category 1. It will become two groups, one for executives and senior level managers and the other for mid level managers and supervisors.

Former EEO-1 Job Categories	New EEO-1 Job Categories
1. Officials and Managers	1.1 Executive/Senior Level Officials and Managers
	1.2 First/Mid Level Officials and Managers
2. Professionals	2. Professionals
3. Technicians	3. Technicians
4. Sales Workers	4. Sales Workers
5. Office and Clerical	5. Administrative Support Workers
6. Craft Workers (Skilled)	6. Craft Workers
7. Operatives (Semi-Skilled)	7. Operatives
8. Laborers (Unskilled)	8. Laborers and Helpers
9. Service Workers	9. Service Workers

Gathering Data

The new instructions offer some specific guidance about how employers are to collect this data from their employees.

Self-identification is the preferred method of identifying the race and ethnic information necessary for the EEO-1 report. Employers are strongly encouraged to use self-identification to complete the EEO-1 report. If an employee declines to self-identify, employment records or observer identification may be used.[21]

---

[21] Federal Register, Vol. 70, No. 227, Monday, November 28, 2005, Notices, Page 71302.

However a determination of Race/Ethnicity and Sex identification is made, employers are held accountable for having and maintaining that information about all employees. However, it is not necessary to resurvey your workforce for the purposes of converting to the new EEO-1 race categories. The EEOC has specifically said it does not require employers to resurvey existing.

Next Step

You should be using the new EEO-1 categories for all new self-identification invitations you give applicants and new employees.

OFCCP has said that it will not penalize contractors who choose to use the new seven race category array in their affirmative action plans. While, at this writing, there is no official regulatory proposal for changing the five-race-category AAP analysis requirement, they have published their guidelines on their official web site at http://www.dol.gov/regs/compliance/ofccp/EEO1_Interim_Guidance.htm.

We recommend you transition to the new 7-category configuration for your AAP. Trying to maintain two data sets, one with 5 categories and one with 7 categories is beyond reason.

For more information about the changes being proposed you may visit the EEOC web site at www.eeoc.gov/eeo-1/qanda.html.

Our sample company uses EEO-1 categories. They are:

- Executive and Senior Officials and Managers
- First and Mid Level Officials and Managers
- Professionals
- Technicians
- Sales Workers
- Administrative Support Workers
- Craft Workers
- Operatives
- Laborers
- Service Workers

Finally, spread the incumbent headcount across sex and ethnic categories as shown in the sample forms at the end of this chapter.

Be sure to total each page. Total each separate line of progression, and total the department overall when it is complete. Check your arithmetic. It is very easy to make errors on a Workforce Analysis Form. Verify columns and then verify rows to be sure everything adds up as it should.

Lines of Progression

The regulations tell us that each line of progression must be placed on a separate Workforce Analysis Form. Great. Be happy to do that. What's a line of progression?

"Line of Progression" is defined as the natural family of job titles through which one may progress in a career over time. We find such job families in functional areas of engineering, programming, accounting, and other similar affinity groups.

For example, there is a natural hierarchy of skills and responsibilities in the family of jobs associated with computer programming. At the lowest, or entry level, are the basic "coder" functions. Higher skill requirements are found in "programmer" jobs, which are often segmented into sub-titles such as "Programmer I," "Programmer II," "Programmer III," and so forth. Higher still, are jobs that begin to get involved in system design, and sometimes even hardware integration. These are often referred to as "System Analyst" positions. They may also be broken into sub-titles if there are enough of them and the job content is actually varied enough. So, you see, there can be a vertical ladder of job titles available to employees for career advancement. At the top of the ladder is the manager responsible for the programming function or department. That job represents the "king of the programming mountain."

People can spend their entire careers in jobs within a "Line of Progression" hierarchy. It represents a functional specialty.

Sample Line of Progression

- Manager - Software Programming
- Systems Analyst
- Programmer III
- Programmer II
- Programmer I
- Software Coder

Except in very large organizations, it is unusual to find more than one line of progression in any one Department. Some Departments will not have any lines of progression. They are normally found where incumbent count is among the highest for the organization.

Salary/Wage Range Charts

Usually this is expressed as a compensation (wage or salary) "range." Some employers object to having dollars on the Workforce Analysis Forms. However, it is required that compensation be indicated somehow. One alternative to using actual dollars, is to use a compensation range code of your own design. If you already use salary/wage grades in your organization, those will work nicely. If you don't use salary/wage grades, you might consider building a chart of compensation code ranges like that shown below. However you do it, be sure you include compensation information for each job title on your list.

If you choose to use a Salary/Wage Range Chart, remember that it must be considered part of your AAP document if you ever are audited and asked to provide the OFCCP copies of your AAP. A copy of your Salary/Wage Range Chart must travel with your AAP. You may omit it from other copies you distribute to managers and employees if you wish.

The advantage of using such range codes in your published AAP document is quite simple. It helps preserve the confidential nature of your compensation structure. Even in publicly owned companies that must disclose compensation of elected officers, disclosure of other management compensation is a sensitive subject.

Sample Salary/Wage Range Chart

Compensation Code Ranges

Code	Hourly Rate	Yearly Rate
A	$84.13 - $96.15	$175,000 - $200,000
B	60.10 - 84.12	125,000 - 175,000
C	48.08 - 60.09	100,000 - 125,000
D	36.06 - 48.07	75,000 - 100,000
E	24.04 - 36.05	50,000 - 75,000
F	12.00 - 24.03	25,000 - 50,000
G	9.62 - 11.99	20,000 - 25,000
H	7.21 - 9.61	15,000 - 20,000
I	4.81 - 7.20	10,000 - 15,000
J	4.25 - 4.80	8,840 - 10,000

*** Caution ***

Confidential Information

**Not for use or disclosure outside _____
Under Any Circumstances Without Written Authorization**

Organizational Profile Option

In its original regulatory proposal, OFCCP suggested that the Organizational Profile should replace the traditional Workforce Analysis. There was such an outcry of objection from contractors and others that the agency relented in the final rule and now permits contractors to choose one or the other. I prefer the traditional Workforce Analysis, but you get to make your own selection.

If you choose to display your workforce using an Organizational Profile, you may do so using a graphical chart format or a "tabular chart, text, spreadsheet, or similar presentation of ..." your organizational structure. On the following page is a sample of a graphical format. On the page following is a tabular format for the same information. You are able to display this information in any format you wish as long as all the information required by the regulations is included.

Workforce Analysis Required Content

- The name of the organizational unit being represented.
- The job title, gender, race, and ethnicity of the unit supervisor.
- The total number of male and female incumbents.
- The total number of male and female incumbents in each of the minority groups: Black, Hispanic, Asian/Pacific Islander, and American Indian/Alaskan Native.

Examples from Sample Company

Following examples of the Organizational Profile you will find examples of traditional Workforce Analysis Forms for TMA, Inc. (a fictitious federal contractor). They show how you might use the form to meet the requirement. Note that there is a Line of Progression indicated for the Manufacturing Department.

There is also a basic organization chart at the beginning of the forms to help you understand how TMA, Inc. is structured.

Blank Workforce Analysis Form for Your Use

The very last page in this chapter is a blank copy of the Workforce Analysis Form for you to copy and use, if you wish.

Secrets of Affirmative Action Compliance

TMA, Inc.
2010 Establishment Organization

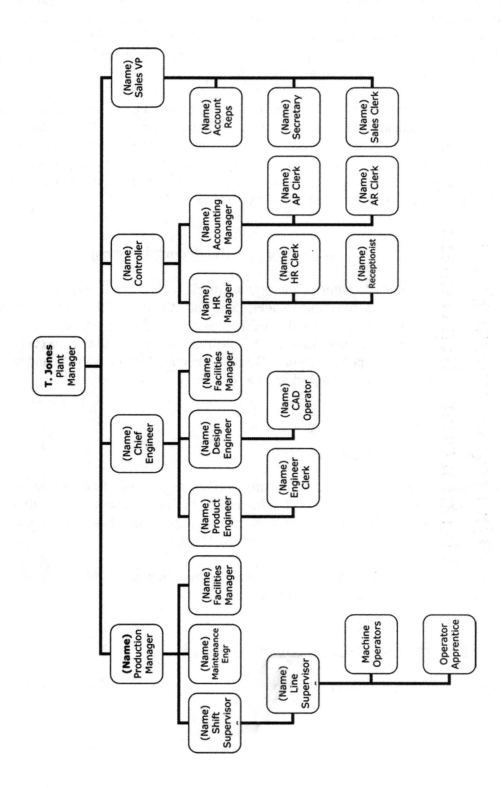

172

TMA, Inc.
2010 Organizational Profile
Manufacturing Department

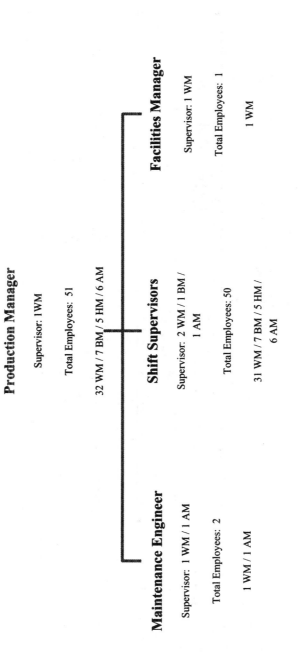

Production Manager

Supervisor: 1 WM

Total Employees: 51

32 WM / 7 BM / 5 HM / 6 AM

Maintenance Engineer

Supervisor: 1 WM / 1 AM

Total Employees: 2

1 WM / 1 AM

Shift Supervisors

Supervisor: 2 WM / 1 BM / 1 AM

Total Employees: 50

31 WM / 7 BM / 5 HM / 6 AM

Facilities Manager

Supervisor: 1 WM

Total Employees: 1

1 WM

TMA Inc.
2010 Organizational Profile
Manufacturing Department
(Tabular Format)

Job Title	Supervisor	Total Employees	Sex/Ethnic Breakdown	Notes
Production Manager	1WM	51	32WM/7BM/5HM/6AM	
Maintenance Engineer	1WM/1AM	2	1WM/1AM	
Shift Supervisors	2WM/1BM/1AM	50	31WM/7BM/5HM/6AM	
Facilities Manager	1WM	1	1WM	

WORKFORCE ANALYSIS
As of 12-31-10

Department: ___Finance & Administration___

Employee Headcount: _____

Line of Progression: _____

Job Titles	Comp	EEO	Total		Men							Women						
				White	Black	Hisp	Asian	Hawaii	AI/AN	2+	White	Black	Hisp	Asian	Hawaii	AI/AN	2+
Controller	B	1A	1														
HR Mgr	F	1B	1								1						
Acctg Mgr	F	1B	1	1													
Accts Payable Clk	G	5	1														
Accts Receivable Clk	G	5	2														
HR Clk	H	5	1														
Receptionist	J	5	1														
Totals			8	1	-	-	-	-	-	-	1	-	-	-	-	-	-
Percents			100.0	12.5	-	-	-	-	-	-	12.5	-	-	-	-	-	-

A word about new race/ethnic categories for EEO-1 reporting…. The OFCCP so far has not created new regulations requiring contractors to record and analyze incumbents using the new **Hawaiian/Pacific Islander** or **Two or More Races** categories that now appear on the EEO-1. However, they have promised that those regulatory changes will be forthcoming and have issued notice that they will not penalize contractors for using the new 7 race/ethnic categories in their AAPs. We recommend that you convert to the new categories for your analysis rather than maintain two databases with different race-category information.

WORKFORCE ANALYSIS

As of 12-31-10

Employee Headcount

Department: _____ Sales & Marketing _____

Line of Progression: _____

Job Titles	Comp	EEO	Total	Total White	Total Black	Total Hisp	Total Asian	Total Hawaii	Total AI/AN	Total 2+	Men White	Men Black	Men Hisp	Men Asian	Men Hawaii	Men AI/AN	Men 2+	Women White	Women Black	Women Hisp	Women Asian	Women Hawaii	Women AI/AN	Women 2+
Sales VP	A	1A	1	1							1													
Acct Reps	C	4	5	4	1						4													
Secretary	G	5	1															1						
Sales Clerk	H	5	4															3		1				
Totals			11	5	1	-	-	-	-	-	4	-	-	-	-	-	-	4	-	1	-	-	-	-
Percents			100.0	45.5	9.1	-	-	-	-	-	36.4	-	-	-	-	-	-	36.4	-	9.1	-	-	-	-

176

WORKFORCE ANALYSIS

As of 12-31-10

Employee Headcount

Department: _____ Engineering

Line of Progression: _____

Job Titles	Comp	EEO	Total	Men							Women						
				White	Black	Hisp	Asian	Hawaii	AI/AN	2+	White	Black	Hisp	Asian	Hawaii	AI/AN	2+
Chief Engineer	B	1A	1	1													
Product Engineer	D	2	3	2	1												
Design Engineer	D	2	7	3			1				1			2			
Test Engineer	D	2	5				3				1			1			
Engineering Aide	G	3	8	4	1							1	2				
CAD Operator	G	3	8	4							4						
Engineering Clerk	H	5	4								4						
Totals			36	14	2	-	4	-	-	-	10	1	2	3	-	-	-
Percents			100.0	38.9	5.6	-	11.1	-	-	-	27.8	2.8	5.6	8.3	-	-	-

Secrets of Affirmative Action Compliance

WORKFORCE ANALYSIS
As of 12-31-10

Employee Headcount

Department: _____ Manufacturing _____   Line of Progression: _____ Machine Management _____

Job Titles	Comp	EEO	Total	Men							Women						
				White	Black	Hisp	Asian	Hawaii	AI/AN	2+	White	Black	Hisp	Asian	Hawaii	AI/AN	2+
Shift Supervisor	F	1B	4	2	1		1										
Line Supervisor	F	1B	6	2	2		2										
Maintenance Engr	F	3	2	1			1										
Machine Operator	F	6	32	25	3	1	3										
Operator Apprentice	H	6	8	3	1	4											
Totals - LOP			52	33	7	5	7	-	-	-	-	-	-	-	-	-	-
Percents			100.0	63.5	13.5	9.6	13.5	-	-	-	-	-	-	-	-	-	-

178

WORKFORCE ANALYSIS

As of 12-31-10

Employee Headcount

Department: ____Manufacturing____

Line of Progression: _____

Job Titles	Comp	EEO	Total	Men							Women						
				White	Black	Hisp	Asian	Hawaii	AI/AN	2+	White	Black	Hisp	Asian	Hawaii	AI/AN	2+
Plant Manager	A	1A	1	1													
Production Manager	D	1A	1	1													
Facilities Manager	E	1B	1	1													
Machine Mgmt LOP			52	33	7	5	7	-	-	-	-	-	-	-	-	-	-
Totals			55	36	7	5	7	-	-	-	-	-	-	-	-	-	-
Percents			100.0	65.5	12.7	9.1	12.7	-	-	-	-	-	-	-	-	-	-

Secrets of Affirmative Action Compliance

WORKFORCE ANALYSIS

As of _____

Employee Headcount

Department: _____

Line of Progression: _____

Job Titles	Comp	EEO	Total	Men							Women						
				White	Black	Hisp	Asian	Hawaii	AI/AN	2+	White	Black	Hisp	Asian	Hawaii	AI/AN	2+
Totals																	
Percents																	

180

CHAPTER 6

JOB GROUP ANALYSIS

JOB GROUP ANALYSIS

Job Group Analysis is the second of the statistical analysis documents that must be in your AAP for minorities and women. It contains information about the sex and ethnic distribution of headcount for all job titles in the establishment, broken down by job function.

Job Group Analysis is a HORIZONTAL SLICE of your organization. It cuts across Departmental lines, accumulating information about job titles regardless of their location in the establishment.

Outline of Content Requirements

If you look at the Job Group Analysis form at the back of this chapter, you will likely think it looks just like the Workforce Analysis Form we just finished discussing. And you'd be correct.

The difference between Workforce Analysis and Job Group Analysis lies with the content of jobs reported in each. Workforce Analysis is a study of jobs within each Department. It shows a VERTICAL SLICE of the organizational structure. Job Group Analysis is a study of jobs by functional alignment, regardless of their departmental affiliation. It shows a HORIZONTAL SLICE of the organizational structure.

Each Job Group must be represented by a Job Group Analysis Form, and they must all be part of the AAP document. Here is what the new regulations have to say about requirements for a Job Group Analysis:

(a) *A job group analysis is a method of combining job titles within the contractor's establishment. This is the first step in the contractor's comparison of the representation of minorities and women in its workforce with the estimated availability of minorities and women qualified to be employed.*

(b) *In the job group analysis, jobs at the establishment with similar content, wage rates, and opportunities, must be combined to form job groups. Similarity of content refers to the duties and responsibilities of the job titles that make up the job group. Similarity of opportunities refers to training, transfers, promotions, pay, mobility, and other career enhancement opportunities offered by the jobs within the job group.*

(c) *The job group analysis must include a list of the job titles that comprise each job group. If, pursuant to Section 60-2.1(d) and (e) the job group analysis contains jobs that are located at another establishment, the job group analysis must be annotated to identify the actual location of those jobs. If the establishment at which the jobs actually are located maintains an affirmative action program, the job group analysis of that program must be annotated to identify the program in which the jobs are included.*

(d) *Except as provided in Section 60-2.1(d), all jobs located at an establishment must be reported in the job group analysis of that establishment.*

(e) *Smaller employers: If a contractor has a total workforce of fewer than 150 employees, the contractor may prepare a job group analysis that utilizes EEO-1 categories as job groups. EEO-1 categories refers to the nine occupational groups used in the Standard Form 100, the Employer Information EEO-1 Survey: Officials and managers, professionals, technicians, sales, office and clerical, craft workers (skilled), operatives (semiskilled), laborers (unskilled), and service workers. (60-2.12)*

Configuring Job Groups is a critical step in the analysis process. The reason is simple. Everything done from now on in our analysis effort will be done based on Job Groups. Therefore, if we don't get the Job Groups configured correctly, everything else we do, and all the work we put in on the subsequent steps will be for naught.

There are three criteria specified in the regulations for development of Job Groups. All of them must be met for Job Group configuration to be acceptable to the OFCCP.

Job Group Criteria

- **Jobs have similar levels of responsibility.**
- **Jobs have similar levels of compensation.**
- **Jobs have similar developmental opportunities**

The OFCCP has created a new acronym for these Job Group Criteria. It is "COW." [22]

- C = Content
- O = Opportunity
- W = Wage

If you wish, you can use that to help you remember how to construct your job groups. Or, not.

These criteria are helpful, for example, to help in our understanding that management jobs at the senior executive level may not belong in the same job group with first line supervisor jobs. They have different levels of responsibility, different levels of compensation, and their developmental (promotional) opportunities are also different. Certainly in larger organizations, we see management jobs sub-divided into three job groups: Senior (Executive) Managers, Middle Managers, and Lower Level Managers (and Supervisors).

If you are in a smaller organization, you may decide that breaking your few management jobs into separate job groups would be inappropriate. There are some considerations to be given to headcount in each job group due to the need for statistical analysis later on. If you configure your Job Groups and the result is fewer than 5 individuals in those jobs, you might want to take another

---

look at the configuration. When you hit the level of only three incumbents in a Job Group, you lose statistical significance in your mathematical testing later on.

So, if you have a choice, put at least five people into each Job Group.

Unfortunately, you won't always have a choice. When you only have five managers (or less) in the entire establishment, there will be nothing you can do. You must not mix management jobs with other jobs in your Job Group configurations. More about that later.

Interestingly, problems can also develop when the number of incumbents in a Job Group becomes too large. It may be an indication that we have combined more job titles than we should. That is, it may be possible for us to sub-divide the larger group based on the three Job Group Criteria so that we have two or more Job Groups emerge from the original one.

An example of this comes from one client's experience. A large software development company has many AAP establishments due to its division-oriented structure. In one of the divisions, there were a total of 500 employees. Of those, 300 were programmers. In the initial design of Job Groups, the company put all the programmers into one Job Group. When we looked at that arrangement, and discussed the implications, we decided to take another look at the jobs in that group. Ultimately, we broke those jobs into three separate Job Groups: Senior Programmers & Analysts; Advanced Programmers; and Basic Programmers. Three Job Groups reflected a closer representation of the three criteria at work than did the one Job Group.

If You Have Fewer than 150 Employees

The regulations give you an official blessing if you have fewer than 150 employees in your establishment and wish to use EEO-1 categories as your job groups. Establishments with more than 150 workers may not use this consolidated approach. You will have to establish specific job groups.

Rules for Counting Employees by Job Group

Begin your Job Group configuration with your basic EEO categories. List your EEO-1 categories. Or, list your EEO-4 categories. Whichever, use what is appropriate for your situation.

These are the basic building blocks of your Job Groups. You may not use categories that are larger than one EEO category. That means, you may not combine jobs from Professionals with jobs from Officials and Managers. You should not combine jobs from more than one EEO category.

You do not have to use each of the EEO categories if you don't have jobs representative of each of those categories. Use only the categories you need to accommodate the types of job functions you have in your organization. Assign each of your job titles to one of the EEO categories. Once you have done that, step back and take another look at what you have accomplished. If you have only one person in a janitor job, and no other jobs in the Service Worker EEO category, you must move forward with a Job Group of only one job and one incumbent. You will not be able to do any statistically significant testing on that Job Group, but you have no choice. Service Workers may not be combined with any other EEO category, even if we have too few of them.

In your review, look for both large groups and small groups. By group, I mean population size. If you have many employees in the Professional category, ask yourself if it is possible to reconfigure those job titles into sub-groups by reassessing them using the three Job Group Criteria.

_____

EEO-1 Categories
Examples of Jobs in Each Category

EEO-1 Category	Job Examples (Functions)
Officials & Managers **1-Executive/Senior Level** Officials & Managers and	Officials, executives, senior management. Individuals who plan, direct and formulate policies, set strategy and provide the overall direction of enterprises/organizations for the development and delivery of products or services, within the parameters approved by boards of directors or other governing bodies.
Officials & Managers **2-First/Mid Level** Officials & Managers	Mid-level managers and supervisors. Individuals who serve as managers, other than those who serve at the Executive level. Includes those who oversee and direct the delivery of products, services or functions at group, regional or divisional levels of organizations. These managers receive direction from senior management and typically lead major business units.
Professionals	Accountants, auditors, airplane pilots, navigators, architects, artists, chemists, designers, dietitians, editors, engineers, lawyers, librarians, mathematicians, natural scientists, registered professional nurses, personnel and labor relations specialists, physical scientists, physicians, social scientists, teachers, surveyors, etc.
Technicians	Computer programmers, drafters, engineering aides, junior engineers, mathematical aides, licensed, practical or vocational nurses, photographers, radio operators, scientific assistants, technical illustrators, technicians (medical, dental, electronic, physical science), etc.
Sales Workers	Advertising agents, sales workers, insurance agents and brokers, real estate agents and brokers, stock and bond sales workers, demonstrators, sales workers and sales clerks, grocery clerks, cashiers/checkers, etc.
Administrative Support Workers	These jobs involve non-managerial tasks providing administrative and support assistance, primarily in office settings. Examples of these types of positions include: bookkeeping; accounting and auditing clerks cargo and freight agents dispatchers couriers; shipping, receiving and traffic clerks' word processors and typists; proofreaders; desktop publishers; and general office clerks.
Craft Workers	Most jobs in this category include higher skilled occupations in construction (building trades craft workers and their formal apprentices) and natural resource extraction workers. This category also includes occupations related to the installation, maintenance and part replacement of equipment, machines and tools, and production occupations requiring a high degree of skill and precision.
Operatives	Most jobs in this category include intermediate skilled occupations and include workers who operate machines or factory-related processing equipment. Most of these occupations do not usually require more than several months of training. This category also includes occupations of generally intermediate skill levels that are concerned with operating and controlling equipment to facilitate the movement of people or materials such as bridge and lock tenders; truck, bus or taxi drivers, etc.
Laborers	Jobs in this category include workers with more limited skills who require only brief training to perform tasks that require little or no independent judgment.
Service Workers	Jobs in this category include food service, cleaning service, personal service, and protective service activities. Skill may be acquired through formal training, job-related training or direct experience.

EEO-4 Categories
Examples of Jobs in Each Category

EEO-4 Category	Job Examples (Functions)
Officials & Administrators	Department heads, bureau chiefs, division chiefs, directors, deputy directors, controllers, wardens, superintendents, sheriffs, police and fire chiefs and inspectors, examiners (bank, hearing, motor vehicle, warehouse), inspectors (construction, building, safety, rent-and-housing, fire, A.B.C. Board, license, dairy, livestock, transportation), assessors, tax appraisers and investigators, coroners, farm managers, etc.
Professionals	Personnel and labor relations workers, social workers, doctors, psychologists, registered nurses, economists, dietitians, lawyers, systems analysts, accountants, engineers, employment and vocational rehabilitation counselors, teachers or instructors, police and fire captains and lieutenants, librarians, management analysts, airplane pilots and navigators, surveyors and mapping scientists, etc.
Technicians	Computer programmers, drafters, survey and mapping technicians, licensed practical nurses, photographers, radio operators, technical illustrators, highway technicians, technicians (medical, dental, electronic, physical sciences), police and fire sergeants, inspectors (production or processing inspectors, testers and weathers), etc.
Protective Service Workers	Police patrol officers, fire fighters, guards, deputy sheriffs, bailiffs, correctional officers, detectives, marshals, harbor patrol officers, game and fish wardens, park rangers (except maintenance), etc.
Paraprofessionals	Research assistants, medical aids, child support workers, policy auxiliary welfare service aids, recreation assistants, homemakers aides, home health aides, library assistants and clerks, ambulance drivers and attendants, etc.
Administrative Support (including Clerical and Sales)	Bookkeepers, messengers, clerk-typists, stenographers, court transcribers, hearing reporters, statistical clerks, dispatchers, license distributors, payroll clerks, office machine and computer operators, telephone operators, legal assistants, sales workers, cashiers, toll collectors, etc.
Skilled Craft Workers	Mechanics and repairers, electricians, heavy equipment operators, stationary engineers, skilled machining occupations, carpenters, compositors and typesetters, power plant operators, water and sewage treatment plant operators, etc.
Service-Maintenance Workers	Chauffeurs, laundry and dry cleaning operatives, truck drivers, bus drivers, garage laborers, custodial employees, gardeners and ground keepers, refuse collectors, construction laborers, park rangers (maintenance), farm workers (except managers), craft apprentices/ trainees/helpers, etc.

There has been no indication from the EEOC that it plans to modify these job categories.

It is not uncommon to find larger organizations dividing their Job Groups along the following lines:

Management	Senior, Middle, Lower Levels
Professionals	By skill level or specialty
Technicians	By skill level or specialty
Sales Workers	By skill level or territory
Protective Service Workers	By skill level or specialty

Finally, take a look at your Job Groups with an eye on recruiting geographies. The territory from which we recruit new employees will sometimes be different from one job group to another. And, it will usually be different from lower level EEO categories to higher level EEO categories.

Think about your Office and Clerical jobs, for example. It is not very likely that you have to go much outside your headquarters' city or county to find people to fill those jobs. Even if you did recruit from a wider territory, it is not likely you could get people to commute unreasonable distances to clerical work at clerical wages. And, you are not likely to pay relocation expenses for clerical workers, right?

On the other hand, you probably recruit from a wider geography for your Officials and Managers (Officials and Administrators). You may not be able to locate exactly the management talent you want by restricting your search to your headquarters' city or county. You likely will be doing state-wide, regional, or national searches for employees at this level. And, you will likely be more willing to pay for relocation expenses when you find someone in a remote location who is the perfect match for your job opening.

Recruiting geography expands as we move upward on the list of EEO categories.

So, geography plays an important part in our recruiting of new employees. Because it does, it also plays an important part in our AAP development and analysis efforts.

In your final review of the Job Groups you have developed, identify any work location differences. You may find that you have several offices located great distances from one another -- too far for someone to commute. And, you will also find in all likelihood that you actually recruit from "local" candidates at each work location. Recruiting territories are isolated from one another. This is common with clerical jobs. Even if all your work locations are in the same part of a state, like the San Francisco Bay Area, for example, that geography is sufficiently large that commuting from one end to another is not reasonable or practical.

You will probably find in such instances that you actually target your recruiting efforts to the general locale surrounding your work locations.

When this is the case, you can create a different job group for each of the work locations. In our clerical example, we might have a job group called Clerks - Location A, another called Clerks - Location B, etc. While each of these Job Groups has the same titles in it, each pulls its recruited candidates from a different geography, which we will see is an important distinction when we begin our discussion of Availability Analysis. That distinction can mean it is to our advantage to maintain separate Job Groups in such a case.

You may find that splitting up your clerical workforce by work location results in each sub-group having a very small incumbent population. If that happens, you must make a judgment call. You have to decide if giving up some statistically significant analysis is outweighed by the ability to focus more realistically on an ability to design target recruiting strategies in different geographies.

As with most of AAP development, you have to assess the pros and cons of each question to find the approach that is best for you in your circumstance. When you do look at alternatives, you can sometimes discover "a better way of approaching the problem" than might have been available if you hadn't explored alternatives.

Examples from Sample Company

On the following pages are the Job Group Analysis Forms for TMA, Inc. (our fictitious federal contractor). They show how you might use the form to meet federal requirements.

Blank Job Group Analysis Form for Your Use

The very last page in this chapter is a blank copy of the Job Group Analysis Form for you to copy and use, if you wish.

Everything we do from now on, in analyzing our data, will be based on our Job Group configurations.

Secrets of Affirmative Action Compliance

JOB GROUP ANALYSIS

As of 12-31-10

Employee Headcount
EXECUTIVES AND SENIOR MANAGERS

Job Titles	EEO	Total	Men							Women						
			White	Black	Hisp	Asian	Hawaii	AI/AN	2+	White	Black	Hisp	Asian	Hawaii	AI/AN	2+
Plant Manager	1A	1	1													
Sales VP	1A	1	1													
Chief Engineer	1A	1	1													
Controller	1A	1								1						
Totals		4	3	-	-	-	-	-	-	1	-	-	-	-	-	-
Percents		100	75.0	-	-	-	-	-	-	25.0	-	-	-	-	-	-

A word about new race/ethnic categories for EEO-1 reporting... The OFCCP so far has not created new regulations requiring contractors to record and analyze incumbents using the new **Hawaiian/Pacific Islander** or **Two or More Races** categories that now appear on the EEO-1. However, they have promised that those regulatory changes will be forthcoming and have issued notice that they will not penalize contractors for using the new 7 race/ethnic categories in their AAPs. We recommend that you convert to the new categories for your analysis rather than maintain two databases with different race-category information.

JOB GROUP ANALYSIS
As of 12-31-10

Employee Headcount
MID-MANAGERS AND SUPERVISORS

Job Titles	EEO	Total	Men							Women						
			White	Black	Hisp	Asian	Hawaii	AI/AN	2+	White	Black	Hisp	Asian	Hawaii	AI/AN	2+
Production Manager	1B	1	1													
HR Manager	1B	1								1						
Accounting Manager	1B	1	1													
Facilities Manager	1B	1	1													
Shift Supervisor	1B	4	2	1		1										
Line Supervisor	1B	6	2	2		2										
Totals		14	7	3	-	3	-	-	-	1	-	-	-	-	-	-
Percents		100	50	21.4	-	21.4	-	-	-	7.1	-	-	-	-	-	-

191

Secrets of Affirmative Action Compliance

JOB GROUP ANALYSIS
As of 12-31-10

Employee Headcount

PROFESSIONALS

Job Titles	Total		Men							Women						
	EEO		White	Black	Hisp	Asian	Hawaii	AI/AN	2+	White	Black	Hisp	Asian	Hawaii	AI/AN	2+
Production Engineer	2	3	2	1												
Design Engineer	2	7	3			1				1			2			
Test Engineer	2	5				3				1			1			
Totals		15	5	1	-	4	-	-	-	2	-	-	3	-	-	-
Percents		100	33.3	6.7	-	26.7	-	-	-	13.3	-	-	20.0	-	-	-

192

JOB GROUP ANALYSIS
As of 12-31-10

Employee Headcount

TECHNICIANS

Job Titles	EEO	Total	Men							Women						
			White	Black	Hisp	Asian	Hawaii	AI/AN	2+	White	Black	Hisp	Asian	Hawaii	AI/AN	2+
Maintenance Engineer	3	2	1			1										
Engineering Aide	3	8	4	1							1	2				
CAD Operator	3	8	4							4						
Totals		18	9	1	-	1	-	-	-	4	1	2	-	-	-	-
Percents		100	50.0	5.6	-	5.6	-	-	-	22.2	5.6	11.1	-	-	-	-

193

JOB GROUP ANALYSIS
As of 12-31-10

Employee Headcount

SALES WORKERS

Job Titles	Total		Men							Women						
	EEO	Total	White	Black	Hisp	Asian	Hawaii	AI/AN	2+	White	Black	Hisp	Asian	Hawaii	AI/AN	2+
Account Representatives	4	5	4	1												
Totals		5	4	1	-	-	-	-	-	-	-	-	-	-	-	-
Percents		100	80.0	20.0	-	-	-	-	-	-	-	-	-	-	-	-

194

JOB GROUP ANALYSIS
As of 12-31-10

Employee Headcount

ADMINISTRATIVE SUPPORT

Job Titles	EEO	Total	Men							Women						
			White	Black	Hisp	Asian	Hawaii	AI/AN	2+	White	Black	Hisp	Asian	Hawaii	AI/AN	2+
Engineering Clerk	5	4								4						
Secretary	5	1								1						
HR Clerk	5	1								1						
Accounts Payable Clerk	5	1									1					
Accounts Receivable Clerk	5	2								2						
Sales Clerk	5	4								3		1				
Receptionist	5	1											1			
Totals		14	-	-	-	-	-	-	-	11	1	1	1	-	-	-
Percents		100	-	-	-	-	-	-	-	78.6	7.1	7.1	7.1	-	-	-

Secrets of Affirmative Action Compliance

JOB GROUP ANALYSIS
As of 12-31-10

Employee Headcount

CRAFT WORKERS

Job Titles	EEO	Total	Men							Women						
			White	Black	Hisp	Asian	Hawaii	AI/AN	2+	White	Black	Hisp	Asian	Hawaii	AI/AN	2+
Machine Operator	6	32	25	3	1	3										
Operator Apprentice	6	8	3	1	4											
Totals		40	28	4	5	3	-	-	-	-	-	-	-	-	-	-
Percents		100	70.0	10.0	12.5	7.5	-	-	-	-	-	-	-	-	-	-

JOB GROUP ANALYSIS

As of _____

Employee Headcount
(Job Group Title)

Job Titles	EEO	Total	Men								Women							
			White	Black	Hisp	Asian	Hawaii	AI/AN	2+		White	Black	Hisp	Asian	Hawaii	AI/AN	2+	
Totals																		
Percents																		

Notes

CHAPTER 7

AVAILABILITY ANALYSIS
(The Dreaded 2-Factor Analysis)

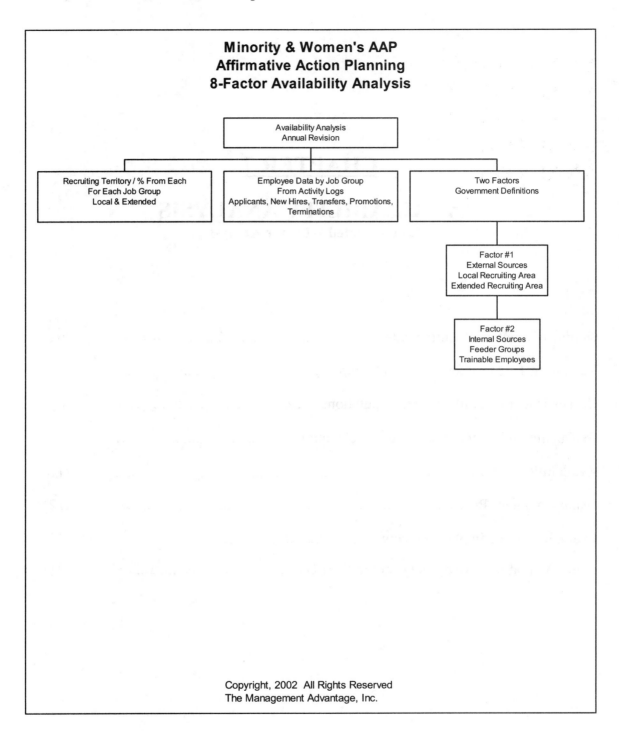

**Minority & Women's AAP
Affirmative Action Planning
8-Factor Availability Analysis**

Availability Analysis
Annual Revision

Recruiting Territory / % From Each
For Each Job Group
Local & Extended

Employee Data by Job Group
From Activity Logs
Applicants, New Hires, Transfers, Promotions,
Terminations

Two Factors
Government Definitions

Factor #1
External Sources
Local Recruiting Area
Extended Recruiting Area

Factor #2
Internal Sources
Feeder Groups
Trainable Employees

AVAILABILITY ANALYSIS

2-FACTOR ANALYSIS

For over 20 years, this part of the process was referred to as the 8-factor Analysis. It was incorrectly named because most contractors only used two or three of the factors in their final computation of availabilities. With the regulation changes made effective 12/13/2000, the government has yielded to the practical nature of the exercise and now only requires contractors to consider those sources actually used in recruiting job candidates.

Calculating availability is the way to establish a benchmark of "qualified, available candidates" for each job group. Against this benchmark we can measure our own job group make up.

Job Group Analysis gives us the demographic picture of actual minority and female representation in our workforce, expressed as a HORIZONTAL SLICE of the organization. We isolate job groups by function.

Once we know what our actual workforce looks like in each job group, and we have computed the availability of qualified candidates, we can measure how close we are to that availability. Measuring that distance is expressed in affirmative action terms as "Comparison of Incumbents to Computed Availability."

So, we need to create our benchmarks for each job group. The "stake in the ground" from which we can measure our own accomplishments at influencing the sex and ethnic composition of our job groups.

Outline of Content Requirements

The regulations tell us: *"(a) Availability is an estimate of the number of qualified minorities or women available for employment in a given job group, expressed as a percentage of all qualified persons available for employment in the job group. The purpose of the availability determination is to establish a benchmark against which the demographic composition of the contractor's incumbent workforce can be compared in order to determine whether barriers to equal employment opportunity may exist within particular job groups.*

(b)   The contractor must separately determine the availability of minorities and women for each job group.

(c)   In determining availability, the contractor must consider at least the following factors:

   1)   The percentage of minorities or women with requisite skills in the reasonable recruitment area. The reasonable recruitment area is defined as the geographical area from which the contractor usually seeks or reasonably could seek workers to fill the positions in question.

   2)   The percentage of minorities or women among those promotable, transferable, and trainable within the contractor's organization. Trainable refers to those employees within the contractor's organization who could, with appropriate training which the contractor is reasonably able to provide, become promotable or transferable during the AAP year.

(d)   The contractor must use the most current and discrete statistical information available to derive availability figures. Examples of such information include census data, data from local job service offices, and data from colleges or other training institutions.

(e)   The contractor may not draw its reasonable recruitment area in such a way as to have the effect of excluding minorities or women. For each job group, the reasonable recruitment area must be identified, with a brief explanation of the rationale for selection of that recruitment area.

(f)   The contractor may not define the pool of promotable, transferable, and trainable employees in such a way as to have the effect of excluding minorities or women. For each job group, the pool of promotable, transferable, and trainable employees must be identified with a brief explanation of the rationale for the selection of that pool.

(g)   Where a job group is composed of job titles with different availability rates, a composite availability figure for the job group must be calculated. The contractor must separately determine the availability for each job title within the job group and must determine the proportion of job group incumbents employed in each job title. The contractor must weigh the availability for each job title by the proportion of job group incumbents employed in that job group. The sum of the weighted availability estimates for all job titles in the job group must be the composite availability for the job group. (60-2.14)

Availability computations draw from U.S. Census Bureau data and from data that represent internal candidate sources. The preamble to the new regulations has some further comments about external source data.

"...decennial census data or some variant thereof often will satisfy the requirement to use the most current information 'available.'"

"Data on college and university graduates are readily available in private publications, from the U.S. Department of Education, and from the schools themselves."

"The regulation retains the requirement that contractors determine the availability of total minorities. The language in the proposal [initially proposed changes to the regulations], which does not require calculating availability separately by individual minority subgroup, was not modified and has been adopted in this final rule."

Let's look at each of the two factors to start.

Availability Factors

Factor	Definition	Data Source
1 Percentage of minorities and women among those having requisite skills in a reasonable recruitment area.	Those actually employed in occupations matching our job group functions in a larger recruiting area.	U.S. Census Data - 2000
2 Percentage of minorities and women among those promotable, transferable and trainable within the facility.	Internal "feeder groups" which supply qualified candidates to this job group.	Internal Job Group Analysis Forms for feeder groups.

Recruiting Territory for Each Job Group

It is clear from the chart that we will need to gather certain data before we are able to complete our Availability Analysis. Before we can be sure of what data we need, there is one more question we must answer: Where do we recruit for candidates in each Job Group?

"Where" is important for two reasons. Regulations talk about "reasonable recruiting area." And, it is likely that we have a wider recruiting territory for Officials and Managers, for example, than for Office and Clerical or Service Workers. So, each Job Group will rely on data from its own recruiting territory.

How do we determine what the recruiting area is for any one Job Group? Well, we can guess, or we can look at history. Look at your actual experience over the past year. Where did the people come from whom you hired for each job group? You have a source for that data, remember?

Sure. Your "New Hire Log" will tell you who has been hired into each job title. If you know job title, you know Job Group, right?

Another way you can find out where both applicants and new hires are coming from is to do a ZIP CODE analysis on their home addresses. Zip Codes are geographic indicators and, using them, you can scribe a circle on a map to indicate all of the people you hired into any given Job Group. Once you have drawn your circle so it captures everyone who was hired, look at all the applicants and new hires to find out where the greatest density came from. If you actually plot each new hire and applicant on a map, representing each one with a dot, you will discover that most often the cluster of dots around your work location is greatest and that density diminishes the further out you go from the work location. That map can help you draw a circle indicating ALL the applicants and new hires in your "reasonable recruiting area."

If you recruit mostly from colleges and universities into certain job groups (usually Professional and Technical), you might want to substitute data about the university's demographics for the Census data. Or, you could use both, weighting them to determine an overall contribution from external sources.

When you have completed that analysis for each of your Job Groups, you can display the information on a simple chart like the one below:

External Sources of Candidates by Job Group

Job Group	Other External Recruiting Source		Reasonable Recruiting Census Area	
Executives & Senior Level Managers	(Source)	%	(Area)	%
Mid Level Managers & Supervisors				
Professionals	(Source)	%	(Area)	%
Technicians	(Source)	%	(Area)	%
Sales Workers	(Source)	%	(Area)	%
Admin Support Workers	(Source)	%	(Area)	%
Craft Workers	(Source)	%	(Area)	%
Operatives	(Source)	%	(Area)	%
Laborers	(Source)	%	(Area)	%
Service Workers	(Source)	%	(Area)	%

Census 2000 Special EEO Tabulation
Occupational Crosswalk to EEO Occupational Groups & EEO-1 Job Categories
go to
http://www.census.gov/hhes/www/eeoindex/jobgroups.pdf

Census Data for Availability Computations

A few words about the Census information you will need.

You want the 2000 Census **EEO Special File** reports or its comparable file from the 2010 Census when it becomes available. (That is not expected to happen until at least 2013 or later.) When you negotiate for Census reports with the provider you select, be sure you confirm that you will be getting copies of the EEO File. This is the only Census file that contains the specific information we need for availability computation. (In years past, State Employment Services used to offer updates on the EEO File in years between Census reports. Budget restraints being what they are, many State Employment Services have discontinued this service.)

In practical terms, Census data is not available immediately after it is collected. It takes time for the Bureau to compile the data and output it in reports that we can use.[23]

When requesting data, ask for the EEO Special File. Then, ask for each geographical jurisdiction you need. You have determined which geographical jurisdictions you recruit from, so those are the reports you should ask for. The Census Bureau publishes thousands of jurisdictional reports from across the country. The U.S. as a whole is one jurisdiction. Each state is another. That's 51. Every county in the country is another Census jurisdiction. And, some combined metropolitan areas are each reported as separate jurisdictions.

Be sure you get the report content you need. Some State Data Centers publish their EEO File reports differently from the format used by the Census Bureau. You want to receive data for each of your requested jurisdictions containing:

- Detailed occupational category reports by sex and ethnicity
- Summary of occupational groups (EEO report category summary) by sex and ethnicity

There are 472 occupational categories in the 2000 census reports. Each is represented by a 3-digit code and a title. Every EEO File report will contain the same 472 categories using the same 3-digit codes to describe the same occupations. They will not vary from one data source to another. All State Data Centers will report the same information, although they often alter how that information is displayed on the output report. Formatting is not consistent from one report source to another. **For your state data center go to: http://www.census.gov/sdc/www/**

---

[23] It is possible to extract data for all seven race categories from the Census 2000 EEO Special File. Some AAP software vendors are offering data files based on the 7-Category mix. If you wish to use the 5-Category mix, you may continue to do so until such time as the OFCCP publishes final regulations to the contrary. We suggest you consider migrating to the 7-Category mix because you are required to use that blend of data in your EEO-1 report and keeping separate databases is impractical at best.

Occupational Categories in the 2010 Census

Number of occupation categories in the 2000 and 2010 Standard Occupational Classification				
SOC Edition	Major Groups	Minor Groups	Broad Occupations	Detailed Occupations
2000	23	96	449	821
2010	23	97	461	840
Change	0	1	12	19

http://www7.nationalacademies.org/cfe/Sommers%20SOC%20homepage.pdf

The 1980 Census EEO Special File contained a list of fewer than 400 occupational categories. The 1990 Census EEO file held 512 occupational categories for civilians. You can find the new list on the web at http://www.eeoc.gov/stats/census/variables.html. "Standard Occupational Classifications (SOC) as they are known, must be approved by the Office of Management and Budget (OMB).[24]

Here are the major categories that will be seen in the 2000 Census:

The current Census 2000 compendium of 472 job categories sounds like a lot. Actually, the specific list leaves a lot to be desired. There are some "catch all" occupations that lump together everything left over after the specifics have been removed. For example, with manager jobs, there are 27 specific occupations cited, then category #043 is for "Managers, All Other."

Once you receive your Census reports for the jurisdictions you need, spend some time scanning through the list of occupational categories to acquaint yourself with the list. Part of our job in computing Availability for our AAP involves matching our Job Group functions to these occupational categories in the Census. The more accurate the match, the more accurate will be our Availability computation. And, accuracy is the name of the game. You will be frustrated (and may be legally liable) for inaccurate targets set with inaccurate Availability computations. This process is called "mapping" by some people.

As you can imagine, getting a hard copy of each of the thousands of census jurisdictions would result in a lot of paper being dropped at your doorstep. You might even have to move out of your office (or the building) to make room for the volume. For access to specific data sets, go to http://www.census.gov/hhes/www/eeoindex/eeoindex.html.

If you take a look at the "Recruiting Territory by Job Group" matrix for our sample company at the back of this chapter, you will notice that we will be using Census data from three geographical jurisdictions: State of California, San Francisco MSA and

---

[24] You should note that the Race/Ethnic categories in the Census 2000 EEO Special File are now available in all 7 race categories used by the EEO-1 report. If you wish to configure your AAP analysis so it is consistent with your EEO-1 report, then be sure you are using a form of the Census report that contains all 7 race codes.

Contra Costa County. So, we must obtain from one of the data centers a copy of each of those three Census Reports from the EEO File.

Explanation of Factors Specified in Regulations

Factor 1: Percentage of minorities and women among those having requisite skills in reasonable recruiting labor area.

Here, we are going to identify the quantity of people in our recruiting territory who have the skills and qualifications for the type of work done in this Job Group. This is based on another presumption, but an important one. The presumption is this: If you were counted as performing a given job when the Census was taken, you are presumed *qualified* for that job. Theoretically, if you are not qualified for the job you hold, you should not be in that job.

To find the data I need, I will scan the list of 472 occupational categories looking for one which approximates the content of the Job Group I am working on at the moment. If my Job Group is a composite of titles that can best be described as an entire EEO category, then I should look for Census data which has been summarized by EEO category.

If my job group has job titles in it that are representative of quite varied duties and responsibilities, the regulations require that I use data for each job group and compute a weighted sum for those sources.

In addition to Census data, your external sources might include:

- College or University demographics for graduating specialists you recruit
- Union demographics for qualified people you must hire through union sources
- State employment agency data for those qualified in the job group work
- Trade school demographics for graduates in the specialties you seek (e.g., culinary specialists, carpenters, welders, truck drivers, artists, etc.)

Since the regulations say we must enter data for each job title if possible, we must understand how to weight that data and derive a composite demographic for qualified workforce in each Job Group. Here's an example:

Example of Census Data Weighting

Feeder Group	Total	Female	Min'ty	Black	Hisp	Asian	AI/NA	Hawaii	2+
Step 1: Identify Individual Job Title Demographics									
Accounting Managers * (012 Financial Managers)	11068	5419	3483	275	730	2270	29	15	164
%	100	48.96	31.47	2.48	6.60	20.51	0.26	0.14	1.48
Human Resource Managers * (013 Human Resource Managers)	4227	2418	1257	270	370	525	24	0	68
%	100	57.20	29.74	6.39	8.75	12.42	0.57	0	1.61
Step 2: Compute Individual Job Group Contribution to Total Feeder Group									
Total population of **combined supply is 15,295 people**. Compute percentage of each category based on this total of 15295.									
Accounting Managers	11068 / 15295	5419 / 15295	3483 / 15295	275 / 15295	730 / 15295	2270 / 15295	29 / 15295	15 / 15295	164 / 15295
% Contribution	72.36	35.42	22.72	1.79	4.77	14.84	0.19	0.01	1.07
Human Resource Managers	4227 / 15295	2418 / 15295	1257 / 15295	270 / 15295	370 / 15295	525 / 15295	24 / 15295	0	68 / 15295
% Contribution	27.64	15.81	8.22	1.77	2.42	3.43	.16	0	.44
Step 3: Add Individual Job Group Contributions to Determine Total Group Demographics									
Accounting Managers	72.36	35.42	22.72	1.79	4.77	14.84	0.19	0.01	1.07
Human Resource Managers	27.64	15.81	8.22	1.77	2.42	3.43	0.16	0	.44
Total Job Group %	**100**	**51.23**	**30.94**	**3.56**	**7.19**	**18.27**	**0.35**	**0.01**	**1.51**

* Data comes from Census data for these job titles. We are using San Francisco, CA PMSA as the recruiting territory in our example.

The **"Total Job Group %"** is what we would enter into our Availability Factor Analysis Form" on the line for Factor 1 in the "Raw Data" columns.

Factor 2: Percentage of minorities and women among those promotable, transferable or trainable within the facility.

Census data won't help us here. This is an internal supply – promotable, transferable or trainable from within the facility. Well, how do we know who is transferable, promotable or trainable...as a group?

The most reliable way to determine these internal "feeder groups" is to look at our most recent year's experience in movement of people into this Job Group. That is on our Promotions and Transfers Log, right? Look at the P/T Log and determine how many people moved into this Job Group during the most recent twelve months.

Then identify what Job Groups they came from. You may find, for example, if you have Junior Clerical and Senior Clerical Job Groups, that Junior Clerical is a feeder group for Senior Clerical. Those are logical kinds of feeder group flows one might expect to find. What is not always obvious, however, are the feeder arrangements between Professionals and Officials and Managers or Technicians and Officials and Managers. Other inter-EEO category feeder relationships may exist which are not immediately obvious until you examine the P/T Log data.

We should also consider apprenticeship programs, classes of trainees and any other formal training program demographic.

What happens if you have more than one feeder group supplying candidates to the current Job Group? Well, you identify each feeder Job Group and then weight its contribution to the total of the internal candidate supply. Here is an example:

Weighting Multiple Internal Feeder Groups into Factor 2

Feeder Job Group	Total	Female	Tot Min	Black	Hisp	Asian	AI/AN	Hawaii	2+
Step 1: Identify Individual Job Group Demographics									
Source Job Group "A" *	40	30	11	3	5	2	1	-	-
%	100	75.0	27.5	7.5	12.5	5.0	2.5	-	-
Apprenticeship Program *	50	30	16	4	8	2	2	-	-
%	100	60.0	32.0	8.0	16.0	4.0	4.0	-	-
Step 2: Compute Individual Job Group Contribution to Total Feeder Group									
Total population of combined supply is 90 people. Compute percentage of each category based on this total of 90.									
Source Job Group "A"	40/90	30/90	11/90	3/90	5/90	2/90	1/90	-	-
% Contribution	44.4	33.3	12.2	3.3	5.6	2.2	1.1	-	-
Apprenticeship Program	50/90	30/90	16/90	4/90	8/90	2/90	2/90	-	-
% Contribution	55.6	33.3	17.8	4.4	8.9	2.2	2.2	-	-
Step 3: Add Individual Job Group Contributions to Determine Total Group Demographics									
Group "A" Contribution	44.4	33.3	12.2	3.3	5.6	2.2	1.1	-	-
Apprenticeship Program	55.6	33.3	17.8	4.4	8.9	2.2	2.2	-	-
Total Source Group %	100	66.7	30.0	7.7	14.5	4.4	3.3	-	-

* Data comes from Job Group Analysis profiles already completed for this establishment and from the demographic data that represents makeup of our apprenticeship program.

The **"Total Source Group %"** is what we would enter into our Availability Factor Analysis Form" on the line for Factor 2 in the "Raw Data" columns.

Availability Analysis Form

Assembling All the Pieces You Need

If you have ever baked a cake from scratch, you know the easiest approach is to first get all the ingredients you need spread out on the counter within easy reach. When you start to mix things up, you won't have to waste time and risk spoiling the batter by stopping every few minutes to fetch another ingredient. Having everything handy to your work area is the smart way to bake.

Completing Availability Factor Forms is much the same as baking a cake. It is important to have each of the multiple ingredients within easy reach as you get ready to start filling in the form. It makes no more sense to start Availability computations without a vital piece of data than it would to start mixing cake batter without having the flour you need.

Assemble all the raw data you need before you begin.

Data Needed for Availability Computations

- Census Data - EEO File for Each Recruiting Geography
- Job Group Analysis forms for this establishment
- Promotion and Transfer Logs from previous year
- Hew Hire Logs from previous year
- Sex/Ethnic Demographics of Training Institutions used as supplier of candidates for any Job Group
- Sex/Ethnic Demographics of Internship or Apprenticeship groups which supply candidates to any Job Group

Materials Needed for Availability Computations

- Supply of blank Availability Factor Forms
- Supply of pencils
- Pencil sharpener
- Large eraser
- Calculator with fresh batteries
- Scratch paper

Once you have assembled all you need at your desk, arrange for some uninterrupted time. As you will see, there is nothing mysterious about Availability calculations. They are detailed, however. And, you will be involved in multiple arithmetic calculations for several hours if you are doing Availability for more than one or two Job Groups. You need some quiet time so you can concentrate. If you can't get it, be very careful about how you complete your Availability forms. Errors are VERY EASY to make.

If you are not used to working on spreadsheets or long strings of calculations, give yourself permission to get up from the desk and stretch periodically so you can clear your head. It won't take long to feel like you are tired of "number crunching." When that feeling hits you, take a break. Walk around the office for a while or go out for some fresh air. Do anything you can to allow your head to clear. Then go back and hit it again. You will make fewer mistakes if you give yourself these short periods of recovery.

I have heard some people say that Availability Analysis is so complex that they are the only ones in their entire organization who can understand how to do it. That sounds a lot like job security positioning to me.

There is no secret to Availability Analysis. It is very simple and straight forward. And, it is tedious as the dickens (&%*&^).

Using Computer Programs

If you have the luxury of having a computer program that will do all of these arithmetic computations for you, you are a lucky HR Manager. Only in recent years have these computer tools been fairly user friendly. There are roughly a dozen on the market nationally. Usually, they come in modules that will do individual parts of the AAP statistical requirement. For example, it is possible to purchase software to do only Workforce Analysis and Job Group Analysis reports. Separate modules can be obtained for producing Availability Analysis, Analysis of Incumbents to Computed Availability and Goals, as well as Goals Progress Reports. You will find they range in price from a few hundred dollars to hundreds of thousands of dollars. Cost is determined by how many computers and people will be accessing and using the data at any given moment. For a very reasonable price at or below the $3000 range,[25] you can obtain a PC Windows-based program suite that will do all of your AAP reports and your disparate impact testing reports. With such a suite, at one computer, you can produce AAP reports for as many AAP establishments as you might require. We have looked at nearly all the programs available (and actually used several to produce AAPs) and have concluded that two of the easiest to use and the most cost effective are published by Biddle Consulting Group of Sacramento, California and Peopleclick Software of Raleigh, North Carolina. If you are interested in more information about those products, please call our office. We are authorized resellers for each of them.

For your benefit, we have compiled contact information about the most popular software packages on the market. All are PC-based and designed to automate the number

---

[25] The leaders in PC-based AAP software publishing are now charging federal contractors one price and consultants and attorneys another price for the same software package. Their feeling is that attorneys and contractors are competitors since they have consulting portions of their business trying to secure AAP preparation business from clients. Your guess is as good as mine as to what the future holds. If you are an attorney or a consultant wanting to purchase AAP software, be prepared to pay more than your client would pay. How much often depends on the number of plans you will be preparing each year. More plans, equals higher purchase price.

crunching involved in statistical report preparation. Of course, with any of the software packages, you will have to be familiar with the AAP development process. (That's why you got this book, after all.)

- With the changes made to regulations governing preparation of AAPs, you can expect that all the software publishers will be making updates of their programs available to users.

Let's use our Sample Company to actually complete an Availability Factor Form.

Now, the first thing we have to do is load "Raw Data" into our Availability form.

Executives & Senior Managers
Availability Factor Form

		RAW DATA							
		Total Female	Total Min	Black	Hisp	Asian	AmInd	* NHPI	2 +
1	Percentage of minorities and women with requisite skills in the reasonable recruitment area. (Census data)								
1	Other external sources of minorities and women with requisite skills. (Colleges/Universities, Unions, Trade Schools, etc.)								
2	Percentage of minorities and women among those promotable or transferable within the establishment.								
2	Percentage of minorities and women among those who are trainable within the establishment.								
2	Other internal sources of minorities and women with requisite skills.								

*NHPI = Native Hawaiian or Pacific Islander

Let's use Executives and Senior Managers as our current Job Group. One note about using percentages from Census data. Census reports show percentages carried to one decimal place. That is a sufficient level of accuracy for AAP. computations. I recommend you **round off all numbers before transferring them**. If you use only one decimal place in your numbers, always rounding, you will find you are able to maintain your accuracy at an acceptable level for AAP work and save yourself a lot of time in doing the calculations.

PC-Based Software
for AAP Statistical Report Preparation

Product Name	Publisher	Address	Telephone/ E-Mail
• *AutoAAP* *RECOMMENDED*	Biddle Consulting Group	193 Blue Ravine Rd. Suite 270 Folsom, CA 95630	916-294-4250 888-671-0404 sales@hrwebstore.com Separate pricing for consultants and attorneys.
• *Easy AAP Software* *RECOMMENDED* Free unlimited phone support	C. Alexander & Associates, Inc.	460 Vista Roma Newport Beach, CA 92660-3513	800-433-3761 calexander9@cs.com
• *AAPlanner 7.0* • *Adverse Impact Monitor* • *PayStat* *RECOMMENDED*	Peopleclick (Formerly PRI Associates, Inc.)	Two Hannover Square 7th Floor Raleigh, NC 27601	972-401-0600 888-671-0404 info@hrwebstore.com Separate pricing for consultants and attorneys.
• *JOBase* • *AAPbase*	Gerst Software, Inc.	20370 Town Center Suite 155 Cupertino, CA 95104	800-700-0937 jobase@gerstco.com **Not Sold to Consultants**
• *The Complete AAP* *RECOMMENDED*	Yocom & McKee, Inc.	15401 W. 9th Ave. Golden, CO 80401	800-765-1176 aap@yocom-mckee.com
• *Great AAP*	Berkshire Associates, Inc.	8930 Route 108 #D Columbia, MD 21045	800-882-8904 sales@berkshire-aap.com **Not Recommended due to Pricing Policy**

Our *RECOMMENDED* rating is for software that is not restricted in its sales. Some of the recommended software has different pricing for consultants and attorneys who will be producing numerous AAPs for many clients. We assign a "Recommended" rating to software only if it is available to everyone in the marketplace. Those publishers whose products are restricted and not sold to consultants will not receive a "Recommended" rating. *Great AAP* is not recommended because its license only grants the right to produce ONE AAP.

You should also be aware that you can purchase the entire Census 2000 EEO Special File directly from the Bureau of the Census. You can order it on line at https://censuscatalog.mso.census.gov. It will cost you $200 and you will need a computer programmer familiar with databases in order to use it.

Examples from Sample Company

Now, for **Factor 1**. If you don't have access to commercially available AAP software and its accompanying Census data, you will have a rather large task ahead whenever you find it necessary to combine occupational codes for a representation of availability for your organization's job titles. We will leave it to you to decide how you wish to access the Census data, manually or by computer. Using commercial software will offer you more data access features, but it will cost money. Therein lies the dilemma. Spend money for convenience or save money and live with the increased time requirement.

Whatever you decide, transfer the statistics about management people in this territory to our **Factor 1** on the Availability form.

Executives & Senior Managers
Availability Factor Form

		RAW DATA							
		Total Female	Total Min	Black	Hisp	Asian	AmInd	* NHPI	2 +
1	Percentage of minorities and women with requisite skills in the reasonable recruitment area. (Census data)	34.2	25.2	1.8	5.3	16.3	0.6	0.1	1.0
1	Other external sources of minorities and women with requisite skills. (Colleges/Universities, Unions, Trade Schools, etc.)								
2	Percentage of minorities and women among those promotable or transferable within the establishment.								
2	Percentage of minorities and women among those who are trainable within the establishment.								
2	Other internal sources of minorities and women with requisite skills.								

*NHPI = Native Hawaiian or Pacific Islander

Factor 1 should also take into consideration other sources of qualified minorities and women external to the business. Do we hire into our Management Job Group directly from colleges or universities? Do we go to some special source of management candidates such as "40 Plus" or the military? If so, we should obtain the demographic data on those sources and include it on line two of the Availability Factor Form. Since we have no alternative source for our management candidates, we will leave that line blank in our example.

Factor 2 represents our internal supply of candidates. If we were to look at our Promotions and Transfers Log for the past year we would discover that we did in fact have people promoted from one job title in this job group to another. So, we will use the demographics of the Executives and Senior Managers Job Group as a picture of the internal supply. (There is nothing wrong with using a Job Group to "feed" itself in this way.) If we discovered that we drew candidates from more than one job group, we should combine the demographics for those source groups by the same weighting method we showed you earlier.

Transferring the percentages of representation from our Job Group Analysis form for this Job Group, we can enter those numbers onto the first **Factor 1** line of our Availability Factor Form.

Executives & Senior Managers
Availability Factor Form

		RAW DATA							
		Total Female	Total Min	Black	Hisp	Asian	AmInd	*NHPI	2 +
1	Percentage of minorities and women with requisite skills in the reasonable recruitment area. (Census data)	34.2	25.2	1.8	5.3	16.3	0.6	0.1	1.0
1	Other external sources of minorities and women with requisite skills. (Colleges/Universities, Unions, Trade Schools, etc.)								
2	Percentage of minorities and women among those promotable or transferable within the establishment.	7.1	42.9	21.4	-	21.4	-	-	-
2	Percentage of minorities and women among those who are trainable within the establishment.								
2	Other internal sources of minorities and women with requisite skills.								

*NHPI = Native Hawaiian or Pacific Islander

We have no formalized and structured apprenticeship or internship program for these jobs. Therefore, we have no supply that we can consider for **Factor 2** other than Promotions and Transfers. We must leave the other two Factor 2 lines empty, but I like to place a "dash" into each box on the form just so I know I didn't forget the data. Never put zeros into this section of your Availability Factor Form unless you actually have data that indicates there are no representatives of that category. Zero is data. If you have no data, leave the box blank or put a dash into it. Don't use zeros to indicate the absence of information.

Executives & Senior Managers
Availability Factor Form

		RAW DATA							
		Total Female	Total Min	Black	Hisp	Asian	AmInd	*NHPI	2 +
1	Percentage of minorities and women with requisite skills in the reasonable recruitment area. (Census data)	34.2	25.2	1.8	5.3	16.3	0.6	0.1	1.0
1	Other external sources of minorities and women with requisite skills. (Colleges/Universities, Unions, Trade Schools, etc.)	-	-	-	-	-	-	-	-
2	Percentage of minorities and women among those promotable or transferable within the establishment.	7.1	42.9	21.4	-	21.4	-	-	-
2	Percentage of minorities and women among those who are trainable within the establishment.	-	-	-	-	-	-	-	-
2	Other internal sources of minorities and women with requisite skills.	-	-	-	-	-	-	-	-

*NHPI = Native Hawaiian or Pacific Islander

That completes the "raw data" portion of our Availability Factor Form for the Executives and Senior Managers Job Group. We need to do the same thing for each of our other Job Groups.

Then, we will consider the column on our Availability form that is labeled, "Factor Weight."

Factor Weights are indicators of how many of our placements into this Job Group came from each source, represented by both factors. To determine Factor Weights we must look at information on both our New Hire Log and our Promotion and Transfer Log.

First ask, how many people did we place into this Job Group in total during the past twelve months. Then ask how many of those placements came from inside the organization and how many of them came from outside the organization.

Of those who came from outside the organization, as new hires, how many came from an identifiable supplier such as a university and how many came from non-specific sources represented by general census data? The **"Factor Weight"** column allows us to indicate how much contribution was made by each factor. Because it does, it must always account for all of our placements, and total 100%. We will be showing placement sourcing in this column in terms of percent.

Availability Factor Form - Weighting of Data

		Factor Weight
1	Percentage of minorities and women with requisite skills in the reasonable recruitment area. (Census data)	
1	Other external sources of minorities and women with requisite skills. (Colleges/Universities, Unions, Trade Schools, etc.)	
2	Percentage of minorities and women among those promotable or transferable within the establishment.	
2	Percentage of minorities and women among those who are trainable within the establishment.	
2	Other internal sources of minorities and women with requisite skills.	

I've said all this to make a point. In all of the seminars I have taught on this subject, somebody will invariably raise a hand and say, "The OFCCP told me I had to put some weight into each of the factors." While it may be true that someone at the OFCCP said that, it is not true that it is required of us. Regulations tell us we should use each of the factors in relation to its contribution to staffing the Job Group.

For Executives and Senior Managers, we are using only Census data for Factor 1 and only Promotions and Transfers data for Factor 2. Therefore I have entered dashes in those boxes under the "Factor Weight" heading on lines where I have no raw data. I have determined that 10% of my placements into this Job Group come from inside the organization (promotions and transfers), and 90% of the placements come from outside the organization (new hires). I have no institutional sources, nor do I have intern or apprentice sources for Executives and Senior Managers. Consequently, my **"Factor Weight"** data will look like this:

Officials and Managers - Factor Weighting
Based on Actual Placements During Prior Year

		Factor Weight
1	Percentage of minorities and women with requisite skills in the reasonable recruitment area. (Census data)	90%
1	Other external sources of minorities and women with requisite skills. (Colleges/Universities, Unions, Trade Schools, etc.)	-
2	Percentage of minorities and women among those promotable or transferable within the establishment.	10%
2	Percentage of minorities and women among those who are trainable within the establishment.	-
2	Other internal sources of minorities and women with requisite skills.	-

Don't forget that the total of each **"Factor Weight" column MUST always equal 100%.**

What if this is my first year preparing my AAP and I don't have last year's employment activity logs? **How do I come up with factor weights if there is no history to turn to?** The answer is: Make your best-educated judgment as the HR professional for your organization. And, then document your judgment in addition to assigning weights to the factors you intend to use on each Availability Factor Form. You can't avoid doing Availability computations. They are a required part of the AAP document. And, you can't complete an Availability Factor Form without having factor weights. So, in the absence of historical data, guess. Of course, the absence of data logs will be cited in your narrative on problem identification as one of the problems to be corrected during the current plan year. By the end of the current plan year, we should have our employment activity properly tracked so we can improve the accuracy of our Availability computations for next year's AAP.

The next step we must take is to determine how much of each factor will be included in the "Weighted Data" portion of the Availability Factor Form. To do that, we multiply each number in each column of "Raw Data" by the "Factor Weight" for that factor. The result will be placed into the corresponding column in the "Weighted Data" side of the form.

Look at the form on the next page for an example. We are only using the basic Factors 1 & 2. For each of those factors we will carry out these calculations. Start with Factor 1.

It is weighted at 90%. Multiply .90 X each of the percentages in the columns containing raw data. Enter the results in their respective columns to the right side of the form.

Move to Factor 2. Multiply the Factor 2 weight of 10% X each of the raw data columns, just as you did with the external information. Answers go into the respective columns on the right side of the form.

Do you see how you can kind of get into a rhythm as you perform these calculations?

As the final step in our Availability computation process, we must add each column of numbers in the "Weighted Data" area of the form and enter the totals at the bottom of the page in the boxes which are part of the "Final Availability (%)" row.

Therefore our final availability for Executives and Senior Managers looks like this:

	Total Female	Total Min	Black	Hisp	Asian	AmInd	*NHPI	2 +
Total Availability %	31.5	27.0	3.7	10.1	16.8	0.5	0.1	0.9

*NHPI = Native Hawaiian or Pacific Islander

You can see the completed Availability Factor Form on the next page.

That's all there is to it. You have now done an Availability Analysis. There is nothing mysterious or mystical about it. There is nothing secret about it. As we have already said, it is tedious. And, it requires care as you move numbers around.

In the end, it requires patience and a lot of data. It may also require some expert judgment on your part if you don't have all of the data you need.

If this is your first Affirmative Action Plan you will have missed compiling an Availability Analysis under the old regulations. That involved 8 factors rather than the two we now have. Actually, the two we now have were part of the original eight. The government finally realized that contractors were really only weighting two of the factors into their availability anyway, so decided to eliminate the others. It was a good decision.

Some folks have been very successful setting this form up on a computer spread sheet template. Building in the formulas for multiplication and addition will allow you to avoid having to do all of the computations by hand for every separate Availability form.

One last comment, before we move on. Be sure you complete the notations that are necessary to indicate where each of the raw data entries originated on every Availability form. For our Sample Company we have made one list of notes covering the entire set of Availability Factor Forms. You can make your notes however you wish. It really is a matter of style. Just be sure you make them.

Think about the process of computing availability. We are weighting data based on the sources of staffing we use for this Job Group. If a large portion of total placements come from inside the organization we can influence the Census data significantly. Picture a situation in which we pull from Junior Clerical Job Group and promote people into the Senior Clerical Job Group. When we look at the demographics for our Junior Clerical Job Group we discover we have hardly any minorities. So, when we use the low-minority representation and give it a heavy weighting in our factor analysis, we can mathematically over power any minority representation that may exist in the Census data. According to the new regulations, we may not define our feeder pools of promotable, transferable and trainable people in such a way that we effectively exclude minorities and women. Neither may we define our external recruiting area in a way that excludes minorities and women.

You will want to put yourself in a position that you can defend. And, you will want to document the decisions you make along the way. Do what you think is right.

Another Glitch in Managers' Thinking

Frequently, after having completed the Availability Factor Forms for each of our Job Groups and polishing off all the other AAP developmental requirements, I sit with line managers in the client's organization and discuss what it all means. In those sessions, it is not uncommon for a line manager to look at a particular Job Group's availability and say, "No way! There aren't that many qualified minorities available for these jobs. I know. We've looked!" You can substitute the word "women" for the word "minorities" in the previous sentence. It doesn't matter. I hear both.

It's a difficult argument to counter without explaining in some detail how Availability is calculated. The most important message to help line managers receive is that the Census data represents people who were counted in the jobs, doing the work. They are real people. They were really in those jobs when the Census was compiled. They are in our recruiting area. Therefore, they are considered available. The fact that we don't have them on our payroll, doesn't mean they aren't available. They may work for one of our competitors, but they are considered available.

Secrets of Affirmative Action Compliance

AVAILABILITY FACTOR FORM

Job Group: ___Executives & Senior Managers___

Analysis Date: ___12/31/2010___

		RAW DATA							Factor Weight	WEIGHTED DATA								Source
	Total Female	Total Min	Black	Hisp	Asian	AmInd	NHPI*	2 +		Total Female	Total Min	Black	Hisp	Asian	AmInd	NHPI*	2 +	
1 Percentage of minorities and women with requisite skills in the reasonable recruitment area. (Census data)	34.2	25.2	1.8	5.3	16.3	0.6	0.1	1.0	90	30.8	22.7	1.6	4.8	14.7	0.5	0.1	0.9	Note 1
1 Other external sources of minorities and women with requisite skills. (Colleges/Universities, Unions, Trade Schools, etc.)	-	-							-	-	-							-
2 Percentage of minorities and women among those promotable or transferable within the establishment.	7.1	42.9	21.4	-	21.4	-	-	-	10	0.7	4.3	2.1	-	2.1	-	-	-	Note 2
2 Percentage of minorities and women among those who are trainable within the establishment.	-	-	-	-	-	-	-	-	-	-	-	-	-	-	-	-	-	-
2 Other internal sources of minorities and women with requisite skills.	-	-	-	-	-	-	-	-	-	-	-	-	-	-	-	-	-	-
FINAL AVAILABILITY (%)									100%	31.5	27.0	3.7	10.1	16.8	0.5	0.1	0.9	

Note 1: 2000 Census Data, EEO File, San Francisco PMSA.

Note 2: Job Group 1B: Mid-Managers & Supervisors in this establishment.

* Native Hawaiian or Pacific Islander

222

Don't allow yourself to get all wrapped up in the confusions associated with questions like, "What about all the changes that have happened since the Census data was collected? A lot has changed in the years since then." People who don't want to use the process are people who either have no interest in complying with the federal regulations or are lazy about making an effort to identify recruiting sources, or actually have some bias in their thinking about women and minorities.

We can't change the frequency of the Census collection system. We can't change the fact that Census data ages and becomes less accurate the farther we get from the date it was collected. We can, however, exercise our judgment to place greater emphasis whenever possible on data which relates to people who have "requisite skills" for our Job Groups.

And, we can help line managers in the hunt for recruiting sources. Leaving them to their own devices in this arena is not a good idea.

Availability Analysis tells us what we can reasonably expect to find among qualified, available candidates in our recruiting territory.

Examples from Sample Company

On the following pages are the Availability Factor Forms for each Job Group in our Sample Company.

Blank Availability Analysis Form for Your Use

The very last page in this chapter is a blank copy of the Availability Factor Form for you to copy and use, if you wish.

Secrets of Affirmative Action Compliance

AVAILABILITY FACTOR FORM

Analysis Date: _____ 12/31/2010

Job Group: _____ Executives & Senior Managers

	RAW DATA								Factor Weight	WEIGHTED DATA								Source
	Total Female	Total Min	Black	Hisp	Asian	AmInd	NHPI*	2 +		Total Female	Total Min	Black	Hisp	Asian	AmInd	NHPI*	2 +	
1 Percentage of minorities and women with requisite skills in the reasonable recruitment area. (Census data)	34.2	25.2	1.8	5.3	16.3	0.6	0.1	1.0	55	34.2	25.2	1.8	5.3	16.3	0.6	0.1	1.0	Note 1
1 Other external sources of minorities and women with requisite skills. (Colleges/Universities, Unions, Trade Schools, etc.)	43.7	24.8	4.9	9.0	0.5	10.3	-	2.5	35	15.3	8.7	1.7	3.2	0.2	3.6	-	0.9	Note 2
2 Percentage of minorities and women among those promotable or transferable within the establishment.	7.1	42.9	21.4	-	21.4	-	-	-	10	0.7	4.3	2.1	-	2.1	-	-	-	Note 3
2 Percentage of minorities and women among those who are trainable within the establishment.	-	-	-	-	-	-	-	-	-	-	-	-	-	-	-	-	-	-
2 Other internal sources of minorities and women with requisite skills.	-	-	-	-	-	-	-	-	-	-	-	-	-	-	-	-	-	-
FINAL AVAILABILITY (%)									100%	50.2	38.2	5.6	8.5	18.6	4.2	0.1	1.9	

Note 1: 2000 Census Data, EEO File, San Francisco PMSA.

Note 2: MBA program at California State University at SF

Note 3: Job Group 1B: Mid-Managers & Supervisors in this establishment.

* Native Hawaiian or Pacific Islander

224

AVAILABILITY FACTOR FORM

Job Group: Mid-Managers & Supervisors

Analysis Date: 12/31/2010

	RAW DATA								Factor Weight	WEIGHTED DATA								Source
	Total Female	Total Min	Black	Hisp	Asian	AmInd	NHPI*	2+		Total Female	Total Min	Black	Hisp	Asian	AmInd	NHPI*	2+	
1 Percentage of minorities and women with requisite skills in the reasonable recruitment area. (Census data)	41.9	39.1	2.8	11.4	21.9	0.4	0.5	2.0	80	33.5	31.3	2.2	9.1	17.5	0.3	0.4	1.6	Note 1
1 Other external sources of minorities and women with requisite skills. (Colleges/Universities, Unions, Trade Schools, etc.)	-	-	-	-	-	-	-	-	-	-	-	-	-	-	-	-	-	-
2 Percentage of minorities and women among those promotable or transferable within the establishment.	33.3	53.3	6.7	-	46.7	-	-	-	20	6.7	10.7	1.3	-	9.3	-	-	-	Note 2
2 Percentage of minorities and women among those who are trainable within the establishment.	-	-	-	-	-	-	-	-	-	-	-	-	-	-	-	-	-	-
2 Other internal sources of minorities and women with requisite skills.	-	-	-	-	-	-	-	-	-	-	-	-	-	-	-	-	-	-
FINAL AVAILABILITY (%)									100%	40.2	42.0	3.5	9.1	26.8	0.3	0.4	1.6	

Note 1: 2000 Census Data, EEO File, San Francisco PMSA.

Note 2: Job Group 2: Professionals

* Native Hawaiian or Pacific Islander

Secrets of Affirmative Action Compliance

AVAILABILITY FACTOR FORM

Job Group: Professionals   **Analysis Date:** 12/31/2010

		RAW DATA									WEIGHTED DATA								
		Total Female	Total Min	Black	Hisp	Asian	AmInd	NHPI*	2+	Factor Weight	Total Female	Total Min	Black	Hisp	Asian	AmInd	NHPI*	2+	Source
1	Percentage of minorities and women with requisite skills in the reasonable recruitment area. (Census data)	17.5	31.8	1.4	8.1	21.5	0.1	0.6	0.2	50	8.8	15.9	0.7	4.1	10.8	0.1	0.3	0.1	Note 1
1	Other external sources of minorities and women with requisite skills. (Colleges/Universities, Unions, Trade Schools, etc.)	49.0	24.7	5.3	8.9	10.0	-	.5	1.0	50	24.5	12.4	2.7	4.5	5.0	-	0.3	0.5	Note 2
2	Percentage of minorities and women among those promotable or transferable within the establishment.	38.9	27.8	11.1	11.1	5.6	-	-	-	0	-	-	-	-	-	-	-	-	Note 3
2	Percentage of minorities and women among those who are trainable within the establishment.	-	-	-	-	-	-	-	-	-	-	-	-	-	-	-	-	-	-
2	Other internal sources of minorities and women with requisite skills.	-	-	-	-	-	-	-	-	-	-	-	-	-	-	-	-	-	-
	FINAL AVAILABILITY (%)									100%	33.3	28.3	3.4	8.6	15.8	0.1	0.6	0.6	

Note 1: 2000 Census Data, EEO File, San Francisco PMSA.

Note 2: California State University at SF Engineering Department Graduates 2010

Note 3: Job Group 3: Technicians

* Native Hawaiian or Pacific Islander

226

AVAILABILITY FACTOR FORM

Job Group: Technicians

Analysis Date: 12/31/2010

	RAW DATA									WEIGHTED DATA								
	Total Female	Total Min	Black	Hisp	Asian	AmInd	* NHPI	2 +	Factor Weight	Total Female	Total Min	Black	Hisp	Asian	AmInd	* NHPI	2 +	Source
1 Percentage of minorities and women with requisite skills in the reasonable recruitment area. (Census data)	24.6	49.1	5.0	9.3	33.2	0.7	0.2	0.7	100.0	24.6	49.1	5.0	9.3	33.2	0.7	0.2	0.7	Note 1
1 Other external sources of minorities and women with requisite skills. (Colleges/Universities, Unions, Trade Schools, etc.)	-	-	-	-	-	-	-	-	-	-	-	-	-	-	-	-	-	-
2 Percentage of minorities and women among those promotable or transferable within the establishment.	38.9	27.8	11.1	11.1	5.6	-	-	-	0	-	-	-	-	-	-	-	-	Note 2
2 Percentage of minorities and women among those who are trainable within the establishment.	-	-	-	-	-	-	-	-	-	-	-	-	-	-	-	-	-	-
2 Other internal sources of minorities and women with requisite skills.	-	-	-	-	-	-	-	-	-	-	-	-	-	-	-	-	-	-
FINAL AVAILABILITY (%)									100%	24.6	49.1	5.0	9.3	33.2	0.7	0.2	0.7	

Note 1: 2000 Census Data, EEO File, San Francisco PMSA.

Note 2: Job Group 3: Technicians

* Native Hawaiian or Pacific Islander

Secrets of Affirmative Action Compliance

AVAILABILITY FACTOR FORM

Job Group: _____ Sales Workers

Analysis Date: _____ 12/31/2010

	RAW DATA							Factor Weight	WEIGHTED DATA						
	Total Female	Total Min	Black	Hisp	Asian	AmInd	NHPI*	2 +		Total Female	Total Min	Black	Hisp	Asian	AmInd	NHPI*	2 +	Source
1 Percentage of minorities and women with requisite skills in the reasonable recruitment area. (Census data)	36.1	23.0	2.4	6.9	11.6	0.4	-	1.7	100.0	36.1	23.0	2.4	6.9	11.6	0.4	-	1.7	Note 1
1 Other external sources of minorities and women with requisite skills. (Colleges/Universities, Unions, Trade Schools, etc.)	-	-	-	-	-	-	-	-	-	-	-	-	-	-	-	-	-	-	-
2 Percentage of minorities and women among those promotable or transferable within the establishment.	-	-	-	-	-	-	-	-	-	-	-	-	-	-	-	-	-	-	-
2 Percentage of minorities and women among those who are trainable within the establishment.	-	-	-	-	-	-	-	-	-	-	-	-	-	-	-	-	-	-	-
2 Other internal sources of minorities and women with requisite skills.	-	-	-	-	-	-	-	-	-	-	-	-	-	-	-	-	-	-	-	-
FINAL AVAILABILITY (%)									100%	36.1	23.0	2.4	6.9	11.6	0.4	-	1.7	

Note 1: 2000 Census Data, EEO File, San Francisco PMSA.

* Native Hawaiian or Pacific Islander

228

AVAILABILITY FACTOR FORM

Job Group: Administrative Support

Analysis Date: 12/31/2010

	RAW DATA								Factor Weight	WEIGHTED DATA								Source
	Total Female	Total Min	Black	Hisp	Asian	AmInd	NHPI*	2 +		Total Female	Total Min	Black	Hisp	Asian	AmInd	NHPI*	2 +	
1 Percentage of minorities and women with requisite skills in the reasonable recruitment area. (Census data)	72.5	46.8	5.6	13.4	24.9	0.6	0.9	1.5	75	54.4	35.1	4.2	10.1	18.7	0.5	0.7	1.1	Note 1
1 Other external sources of minorities and women with requisite skills. (Colleges/Universities, Unions, Trade Schools, etc.)	73.9	38.6	9.6	12.8	15.5	0.5	-	1.8	25	18.5	9.7	2.4	3.2	3.9	0.1	-	0.5	Note 2
2 Percentage of minorities and women among those promotable or transferable within the establishment.	-	-	-	-	-	-	-	-	-	-	-	-	-	-	-	-	-	-
2 Percentage of minorities and women among those who are trainable within the establishment.	-	-	-	-	-	-	-	-	-	-	-	-	-	-	-	-	-	-
2 Other internal sources of minorities and women with requisite skills.	-	-	-	-	-	-	-	-	-	-	-	-	-	-	-	-	-	-
FINAL AVAILABILITY (%)									100%	72.9	44.8	6.6	13.3	22.6	0.6	0.7	1.6	

Note 1: 2000 Census Data, EEO File, San Francisco PMSA.

Note 2: Heald Business College graduate population 2010

* Native Hawaiian or Pacific Islander

229

Secrets of Affirmative Action Compliance

AVAILABILITY FACTOR FORM

Job Group: ___Craft Workers___   **Analysis Date:** ___12/31/2010___

	RAW DATA									Factor Weight	WEIGHTED DATA									Source
	Total Female	Total Min	Black	Hisp	Asian	AmInd	NHPI *	2 +			Total Female	Total Min	Black	Hisp	Asian	AmInd	NHPI *	2 +		
1 Percentage of minorities and women with requisite skills in the reasonable recruitment area. (Census data)	6.8	49.0	3.5	24.1	17.6	0.7	0.7	2.4	100.0		6.8	49.0	3.5	24.1	17.6	0.7	0.7	2.4	Note 1
1 Other external sources of minorities and women with requisite skills. (Colleges/Universities, Unions, Trade Schools, etc.)	-	-	-	-	-	-	-	-	-		-	-	-	-	-	-	-	-	-
2 Percentage of minorities and women among those promotable or transferable within the establishment.	-	-	-	-	-	-	-	-	-		-	-	-	-	-	-	-	-	-
2 Percentage of minorities and women among those who are trainable within the establishment.	-	-	-	-	-	-	-	-	-		-	-	-	-	-	-	-	-	-
2 Other internal sources of minorities and women with requisite skills.	-	-	-	-	-	-	-	-	-		-	-	-	-	-	-	-	-	-
FINAL AVAILABILITY (%)									100%		6.8	49.0	3.5	24.1	17.6	0.7	0.7	2.4	

Note 1: 2000 Census Data, EEO File, San Francisco PMSA.

* Native Hawaiian or Pacific Islander

230

AVAILABILITY FACTOR FORM

Job Group: _____

Analysis Date: _____

			RAW DATA						Factor Weight		WEIGHTED DATA							Source
	Total Female	Total Min	Black	Hisp	Asian	AmInd	* NHPI	2 +		Total Female	Total Min	Black	Hisp	Asian	AmInd	* NHPI	2 +	
1	Percentage of minorities and women with requisite skills in the reasonable recruitment area. (Census data)																		Note 1
1	Other external sources of minorities and women with requisite skills. (Colleges/Universities, Unions, Trade Schools, etc.)																		-
2	Percentage of minorities and women among those promotable or transferable within the establishment.																		Note 2
2	Percentage of minorities and women among those who are trainable within the establishment.																		-
2	Other internal sources of minorities and women with requisite skills.																		-
	FINAL AVAILABILITY (%)								100%										

Note 1:

Note 2:

* Native Hawaiian or Pacific Islander

231

Notes

CHAPTER 8

COMPARISON OF INCUMBENCY TO AVAILABILITY ANALYSIS

Notes

COMPARISON OF INCUMBENCY TO COMPUTED AVAILABILITY ANALYSIS

Comparison of Incumbency to Availability Analysis is the third statistical analysis document that must be in our AAP for minorities and women. It contains information comparing what we have in our workforce (Job Group Analysis demographics) with what we have computed is available as qualified workforce within our recruiting area (Availability Factor Analysis demographics).

Comparison of Incumbency to Availability Analysis gives us the opportunity to determine if we are currently fully utilized (at or above computed Availability levels) or underutilized for minorities or women in any of our Job Groups.

Outline of Content Requirements

The term "Underutilization" has been used for years to describe the condition in which there are fewer women or minorities in the job group than one would reasonably expect based on their computed availability. With the changes in December 2000, the terms "Underutilization" and "Utilization" were **<u>deleted</u>** from the regulations. We now refer to that analytical requirement as "Comparison of Incumbency with Availability Analysis." It is much more cumbersome, but I suspect the government embraced the deletion because "underutilized" had become synonymous with "quota." It was time to dump that psychological baggage.

The regulations say, *"When the percentage of minorities or women employed in a particular job group is less than would reasonably be expected given their availability percentage in that particular job group, the contractor must establish a placement goal in accordance with Section 60-2.16."* (41 CFR 60-2.15(b))

That tells us a couple of things: (1) Comparison of Incumbency to Availability Analysis compares actual workforce in a Job Group with computed Availability for that Job Group, and (2) Comparison is only required for Total Minorities and Females in each Job Group. That means we don't have to compute utilization of individual ethnic categories, right? Well, that's what the regulations say.

Don't get too excited, just yet. Further along in the regulations is a clinker. 41 CFR 60-2.16(d) tells us:

> *"The placement goal-setting process described above contemplates that contractors will, where required, establish a single goal for all minorities. In the event of a substantial disparity in the utilization of a particular minority group or in the utilization of men or women of a particular minority group, a contractor may be required to establish separate goals for those groups."* (What a "substantial disparity" might be is left unexplained.)

So, I guess we might as well do our Comparison of Incumbency to Availability Analysis for ethnic groups and Total Minorities as well as Females. At least we will have a chance to see a level of detail that might give us some insight into the types of problems that exist in our Job Groups, if we have any.

Before we go about the business of actually doing the Comparison of Incumbency to Availability Analysis, there is one more important point I would like to make. It, too, has to do with the regulations.

> *"...Where the user has not maintained data on adverse impact as required by the documentation selection of applicable guidelines, the **Federal enforcement agencies may draw an inference of adverse impact of the selection process from the failure of the user to maintain such data**, if the user has an underutilization of a group in the job category, as compared to the group's representation in the relevant labor market or, in the case of jobs filled from within, the applicable work force."* (*41 CFR 60-3.4(D)*) (Bold emphasis added.)

Those few words represent a great big "GOTCHA!" to federal contractors. We will discuss Disparate Impact Analysis (Impact Ratio Analysis, 80% Testing, 4/5's Rule) in another chapter. Illegal discrimination comes from violating one of the Civil Rights Laws. Suffice it to say here that violation of EEO laws such as *Title VII* of the *Civil Rights Act of 1964* can be very costly. It can cause payment of actual damages, compensatory damages (pain and suffering and emotional distress) and punitive damages (as punishment for such terrible behavior). Although there is now a limit to the amount of punitive damages allowed under Federal EEO law, Congress is working on legislation that would eliminate the ceiling. (Some states currently allow unlimited recovery of punitive damages through their state court systems.)

OK, that's important...Illegal discrimination is BAD!

Next...

There are only two types of illegal employment discrimination. Disparate Treatment and Disparate Impact. Disparate Treatment usually happens to one person at a time. "I was treated differently than (cohort), even though circumstances were essentially the same, and I believe it was because of my (protected category membership)." Disparate Impact, on the other hand, usually happens to groups of people. It is most often unintentional discrimination that occurs because of what appear to be fair, honest and even-handed policies and procedures, when in fact they are discriminatory. The attorneys call these "facially neutral" policies that have gone wrong. Usually, Disparate Impact is shown through statistical analysis. (Are the bells starting to go off for you?)

Regulations require us to perform Disparate Impact testing on our employment activities each year. That means we have to use our logs of activity to develop statistics that we can then analyze to determine if we have any Disparate Impact against any protected group. Maybe a particular employment test is screening out females at a rate that is greater than it screens out males. If that is true, we could be facing a problem of discrimination against women.

All right. Stay with me for another minute or so. Let's recap. Discrimination is BAD! Disparate Impact is discrimination. We are required to test (statistically) for Disparate Impact.

Now the kicker. **In the absence of favorable Disparate Impact Analysis data, any deficiency may be used to conclude discrimination on the part of the employer.**

So, in a scenario where we have no logs of activity, aren't tracking employment applicants, or some other such folly, we charge into updating our AAP and our Incumbent vs. Availability Analysis indicates we have some differences between actual representation and our computed Availability. So what's the big deal? All we have to do is set goals to rectify the imbalance.

Unfortunately, that's not all we have to do. Because we have no activity logs and have failed to do our statistical testing for Disparate Impact, we have set ourselves up to be <u>PRESUMED GUILTY OF DISCRIMINATION</u> if we have any computed disparity between incumbency and availability.

Take if from me. That's not a good thing. Consequently, we can conclude that having fewer incumbents than availability calls for is probably not a good thing either. And, generally speaking, that's true.

As AAP employers we should attempt to eliminate that condition for two reasons:

1. That is the objective of affirmative action.
2. So it can't be used against us as "proof" of discrimination.

Let's look at how we determine if we have any computed need for minorities or women in any of our Job Groups.

Regulations are mute on the method we should use to determine if we are in balance or out of balance in our Job Groups. The preamble to the new regulations do make some comments, however. Here is what they say:

The current regulation refers to the difference between availability and incumbency as 'underutilization,' defined as 'having fewer minorities or women in a particular job group than would reasonably be expected by their availability.' When this condition exists, the contractor must establish a goal. ...OFCCP traditionally has permitted contractors to identify underutilization using a variety of methods, including: The 'any difference' rule, i.e., whether any difference exists between the availability of minorities or women for employment in a job group and the number of such persons actually employed in the job group; the 'one person' rule, i.e., whether the difference between availability and the actual employment of minorities or women equals one person or more; the '80 percent rule,' i.e., whether actual employment of minorities or women is less than 80 percent of their availability; and a 'two standard deviations' analysis, i.e., whether the difference between availability and the actual employment of minorities or women exceeds the two standard deviations test of statistical significance."

"...OFCCP believes that retaining the current practice of permitting various methods for determining availability is the appropriate approach to take. OFCCP further believes that the proposed wording of Section 60-2.15 is sufficient to suggest to the contractor community when there exists the need to establish a goal. Therefore, the provision, Section 60-2.15(b), is adopted without change (from the proposal).*"*

A HINT FROM LEGAL EXPERTS

Legal experts tell us that Disparate Impact Analyses are being requested more and more frequently during discovery in lawsuits involving claims of illegal discrimination. **Ask your attorney to direct an external consultant or legal expert to perform the disparate impact analysis as Attorney Work Product.** *Your attorney can give you the details, but hopefully you can protect the Disparate Impact Analysis from disclosure*

We will begin with a visual inspection of our data to determine if there is "any difference" between availability and incumbency. We will go a few steps further though because we are legally allowed to test further, and avoid declaring underutilization in some circumstances.

Back to Comparison of Incumbents to Availability.

In our **Mid-Managers & Supervisors Job Group**, we see the following relationships:

Mid-Managers & Supervisors Job Group

	Total Employees	Total Female	Total Min	Black	Hisp	Asian	AI/AN	NHPI	2 +
Employees (#) JG Analysis	14	1	6	3	0	3	0	0	0
Employees (%) JG Analysis	100.0	7.1	42.9	21.4	0	21.4	0	0	0
Availability (%) 2-Factor	-	40.2	42.0	3.5	9.1	26.8	0.3	0.4	1.6
Visual Deficiency? (Any Difference)		YES	NO	NO	YES	YES	YES	YES	YES

These numbers tell us we have need for Hispanics, Asians, American Indians, Hawaiians, 2 or more races, and Females in the Mid-Managers & Supervisors Job Group. If you compare the numbers on the second and third lines of the chart, you will see how that is determined. Where our actual workforce representation is at or greater than Availability level, we have no underutilization. Said differently, we are fully utilized in that protected group. Our incumbent group has demographics like we would expect based on our computed Availability for that group. Where our actual workforce representation falls below computed Availability, we are underutilized by definition. That is a simple visual inspection. Assessment of "any difference" in rates of representation.

If we think about those categories where we have written "YES" on the "Visual Deficiency?" line, we can go further in our analysis. Look at the American Indian, Hawaiian, and 2 or more race columns, for example. We have no incumbents and small numbers of availability.

The "One Person" Rule

If we ask, "How much will it take to fix the problem if we go out to recruit American Indians?" The answer is 0.3%. When we think of recruiting however, we generally think in terms of "whole people." And, even the OFCCP acknowledges that we can't recruit less than one whole person. So, if the difference between what we have and what we should have is less than one whole person, we do not have to declare a goal. The question then becomes, how much is one whole person in percentage terms.

The answer will vary for each Job Group based on how many people are in the Job Group. In a Job Group of 14 people, one whole person equals 7.1%. In a Job Group of 50 people, one whole person would equal 2%. We can determine what one whole person is worth in percentage terms by simply dividing the number of people in the Job Group into 1. Therefore, 1/50 = 2%. 1/14 = 7.1%. 1/100 = 1%. You get the picture.

In our Mid-Managers & Supervisors Job Group, we have 14 people. Therefore, one person in that group is worth 7.1% (1/14). Because any incumbent gap of less than 7.1% is less than one person's value of 7.1%, we can say we are within one whole person of fully utilizing people in the category, and we therefore do not have a need to declare a goal for increasing the headcount.

<u>Mid-Managers & Supervisors Job Group</u>

	Total Employees	Total Female	Total Min	Black	Hisp	Asian	AI/AN	NHPI	2 +
Employees (#) JG Analysis	14	1	6	3	0	3	0	0	0
Employees (%) JG Analysis	100.0	7.1	42.9	21.4	0	21.4	0	0	0
Availability (%) 2-Factor	-	40.2	42.0	3.5	9.1	26.8	0.3	0.4	1.6
Visual Deficiency? (Any Difference)		YES	NO	NO	YES	YES	YES	YES	YES
% Under		33.1			9.1	5.4	0.3	0.4	1.6
1 Person Equals		7.1			7.1	7.1	7.1	7.1	7.1
More than 1 Person Under?		YES			YES	NO	NO	NO	NO
Statistical Significance (Z=)		2.52			.12				
Need More?		YES			NO				
Practical Significance		>2							
Need More?		YES							

We can extend our analysis chart a few more lines to accommodate the additional tests. You see we have entered 7.1% as the amount of value one whole person has for this Job Group. Because that determined we were not still in need of more Asians, Native Hawaiians, American Indians, or Two or More Races, we stop our analysis at that point in those protected categories. For Hispanics and Females, though, we must go a step or two farther, applying additional tests.

Case Law Allows Statistical Significance Testing

Aside from the preamble you read above, there is no reference to statistical significance testing in the Federal regulations for affirmative action. Nor, is there any mention of the subject in the Federal Contract Compliance Manual. The permission for us to take these extra steps in our Comparison of Incumbents to Availability Analysis comes from case law. That is to say, court cases in which appellate courts or the Supreme Court have ruled and created a precedential decision. Precedent means everyone else within the Court's jurisdiction should abide by the same ruling.

Statistical significance has been addressed in at least two U.S. Supreme Court cases: *Castaneda v. Partida*, *97 USSC 1,272, March 23, 1977* and *Hazelwood School District v. U.S.*, *14 EPD 7,633, June 27, 1977.*

Without going into all the details of each case, let's just say that the U.S. Supreme Court agreed that employers should only be held accountable for numbers that are **statistically significant, meaning "beyond chance."**

To determine statistical significance, we first have to determine the standard deviation of our sample. Standard deviation...you know...the **bell-shaped curve**. Standard deviation is a measure of distance from the midpoint on the bell curve. Going out two standard deviations on either side of center will take us to the "tails" of the curve. Anything occurring in the "tail" sections of the curve could happen by pure chance. Anything falling within ± 2 standard deviations doesn't happen by chance. It is predictable. **In terms of probability, roughly 95% of all occurrences will fall within ± 2 standard deviations**. The other 5% represents chance occurrences in the two tails of our bell curve (2.5% on each side of the curve at the far end, or tail). They are described by positive and negative numbers.

So, how do we determine the standard deviation for our utilization analysis? I'm glad you asked.

Standard Deviation Formula

$$S.D. = \sqrt{(p)(n)(1-p)}$$

(p) = availability %   (n) = # in job group

This says, the standard deviation is equal to the square root of availability times the number of people in the Job Group times the reciprocal of availability. (It helps to have a calculator that figures square roots. Try to do it by hand and your teeth will start to itch.)

That's not the end of it. To determine if our numbers are statistically significant, we must work through one more formula.

Statistical Significance Formula

$$Z = \frac{\text{expected \# - observed \#}}{S.D.} = \frac{(pn) - (o)}{S.D.}$$

(p) = availability %   (n) = # in job group   (o) = # in Minority or Female group

Want to take an example? Oh, good.

In Mid-Managers & Supervisors Job Group again, let's look at the Female representation.

(p) = .402   (n) = 14   (o) = 1

$$S.D. = \sqrt{(.402)(14)(1-.402)}$$

Crunch those numbers and you will find

$$S.D. = \sqrt{3.3655} = \mathbf{1.83}$$

The next step is to use our standard deviation value to **determine whether or not we have statistically significant numbers**. Here's how the numbers fit into that formula:

$$Z = \frac{\text{expected \# - observed \#}}{S.D.} = \frac{(pn) - (o)}{S.D.}$$

$$Z = \frac{(.402)(14) - (1)}{1.83} = \mathbf{2.52}$$

Any statement of statistical significance which exceeds 2.0 indicates the numbers are valid. In this instance, it says we have underutilization of Females in our Mid-Managers & Supervisors Job Group.

Let's do another job group…this time, Executives and Senior Managers.

Executives & Senior Managers Job Group

	Total Employees	Total Female	Total Min	Black	Hisp	Asian	AI/AN	NHPI	2 +
Employees (#) JG Analysis	4	1	-	-	-	-	-	-	-
Employees (%) JG Analysis	100.0	25.0	-	-	-	-	-	-	-
Availability (%) 2-Factor	-	50.2	38.2	5.6	8.5	18.6	4.2	0.1	1.9
Visual Deficiency? (Any Difference)		YES	YES	YES	YES	YES	YES	YES	YES
% Under		25.2	38.2	5.6	8.5	18.6	4.2	0.1	1.9
1 Person Equals		25.0	25.0	25.0	25.0	25.0	25.0	25.0	25.0
More than 1 Person Under?		YES	YES	NO	NO	NO	NO	NO	NO
Statistical Significance (Z=)		.67	.58						
Need More?		NO	NO						
Practical Significance									
Need More?									

A brief note about the size of populations you are testing. Here is the "rule of thumb."

If a group is less than 30, statistical significance will not be very accurate. Fisher's Exact Probability test should be used. If a group is only 5 or less, nothing will accurately measure the significance of your data.

It is the problem of small group size that bedevils the OFCCP. They hate it when a contractor creates groups that are too small to analyze. From their viewpoint, this is only done because the contractor wants to "get away with something." OFCCP has yet to acknowledge that it is not realistic to "roll up" different groups to create a population of 30 or more simply so it can be analyzed statistically. That is at the heart of the ongoing battle over Similarly Situated Employee Groups (SSEGs) in compensation analysis which you will find discussed later. You should be clear about how you construct your data sets for analysis, even if you know a small group will escape statistical analysis because of what you do.

But, lest you drift off to sleep, we aren't done with our analysis of this category yet. There is one more step to go. It is called the **Test for Practical Significance**. Although it is not a test mentioned in OFCCP's regulatory preamble, it is still a valid application.

This comes to us via a case known as *U.S. v. Commonwealth of Virginia, 454FSupp 1077 (1978)*. In basic terms that case said, **if it only takes one or two additional people in the category to change statistically significant numbers into statistically insignificant numbers, there is no Practical Significance**. And, the employer need not declare a goal.

In our example (Page 244), one person is equal to 7.1% and our difference between Availability and actual representation of women is 33.1%. Dividing 7.1% into 33.1% will tell us how many equivalent people we are away from Availability. And the answer is...

$$33.1/7.1 = 4 + \text{people away from parity}$$

It seems fairly clear that another one or two people will not change our condition in this instance. Therefore we have to say we are greater than 2 people from resolving the underutilization and we must carry our declaration to the final line of our chart.

Examples from Sample Company

On the following pages are the Utilization Analysis Forms for TMA, Inc. (our fictitious federal contractor). They show how you might use the form to meet the requirements.

Also included is a chart showing our statistical significance testing for each Job Group.

Blank Incumbency Analysis Form for Your Use

The very last page in this chapter is a blank copy of the Incumbency Analysis Form for you to copy and use, if you wish.

Comparison of Incumbency to Availability
ANALYSIS FORM

Executives & Senior Managers Job Group

	Total Employees	Total Female	Total Min	Black	Hisp	Asian	AI/AN	NHPI	2 +
Employees (#) JG Analysis	4	1	-	-	-	-	-	-	-
Employees (%) JG Analysis	100.0	25.0	-	-	-	-	-	-	-
Availability (%) 2-Factor	-	50.2	38.2	5.6	8.5	18.6	4.2	0.1	1.9
Visual Deficiency? (Any Difference)		YES	YES	YES	YES	YES	YES	YES	YES
% Under		25.2	38.2	5.6	8.5	18.6	4.2	0.1	1.9
1 Person Equals		25.0	25.0	25.0	25.0	25.0	25.0	25.0	25.0
More than 1 Person Under?		YES	YES	NO	NO	NO	NO	NO	NO
Statistical Significance (Z=)		.67	.58						
Need More?		NO	NO						
Practical Significance									
Need More?									

Mid-Managers & Supervisors Job Group

	Total Employees	Total Female	Total Min	Black	Hisp	Asian	AI/AN	NHPI	2 +
Employees (#) JG Analysis	14	1	6	3	0	3	0	0	0
Employees (%) JG Analysis	100.0	7.1	42.9	21.4	0	21.4	0	0	0
Availability (%) 2-Factor	-	40.2	42.0	3.5	9.1	26.8	0.3	0.4	1.6
Visual Deficiency? (Any Difference)		YES	NO	NO	YES	YES	YES	YES	YES
% Under		33.1			9.1	5.4	0.3	0.4	1.6
1 Person Equals		7.1			7.1	7.1	7.1	7.1	7.1
More than 1 Person Under?		YES			YES	NO	NO	NO	NO
Statistical Significance (Z=)		2.52			.12				
Need More?		YES			NO				
Practical Significance		>2							
Need More?		YES							

Comparison of Incumbency to Availability
ANALYSIS FORM

Professionals Job Group

	Total Employees	Total Female	Total Min	Black	Hisp	Asian	AI/AN	NHPI	2 +
Employees (#) JG Analysis	15	5	8	1	-	7	-	-	-
Employees (%) JG Analysis	100	33.3	53.3	6.7	-	46.7	-	-	-
Availability (%) 2-Factor	-	33.3	28.3	3.4	8.6	15.8	0.1	0.6	0.6
Visual Deficiency? (Any Difference)		NO	NO	NO	YES	NO	YES	YES	YES
% Under					8.6		0.1	0.6	0.6
1 Person Equals					6.7		6.7	6.7	6.7
More than 1 Person Under?					YES		NO	NO	NO
Statistical Significance (Z=)					.613				
Need More?					NO				
Practical Significance									
Need More?									

Technicians Job Group

	Total Employees	Total Female	Total Min	Black	Hisp	Asian	AI/AN	NHPI	2 +
Employees (#) JG Analysis	18	7	5	2	2	1	-	-	-
Employees (%) JG Analysis	100	38.9	27.8	11.1	11.1	5.6	-	-	-
Availability (%) 2-Factor	-	24.6	49.1	5.0	9.3	33.2	0.7	0.2	0.7
Visual Deficiency? (Any Difference)		NO	YES	NO	NO	YES	YES	YES	YES
% Under			21.3			27.6	0.7	0.2	0.7
1 Person Equals			5.6			5.6	5.6	5.6	5.6
More than 1 Person Under?			YES			YES	NO	NO	NO
Statistical Significance (Z=)			1.33			2.16			
Need More?			NO			YES			
Practical Significance						>2			
Need More?						YES			

Comparison of Incumbency to Availability
ANALYSIS FORM

Sales Workers Job Group

	Total Employees	Total Female	Total Min	Black	Hisp	Asian	AI/AN	NHPI	2 +
Employees (#) JG Analysis	5	-	1	1	-	-	-	-	-
Employees (%) JG Analysis	100	-	20.0	20.0	-	-	-	-	-
Availability (%) 2-Factor	-	36.1	23.0	2.4	6.9	11.6	0.4	-	1.7
Visual Deficiency? (Any Difference)		YES	YES	NO	YES	YES	YES	NO	YES
% Under		36.1	3.0		6.9	11.6	0.4		1.7
1 Person Equals		20.0	20.0		20.0	20.0	20.0		20.0
More than 1 Person Under?		YES	NO		NO	NO	NO		NO
Statistical Significance (Z=)		1.55							
Need More?		NO							
Practical Significance									
Need More?									

Administrative Support Job Group

	Total Employees	Total Female	Total Min	Black	Hisp	Asian	AI/AN	NHPI	2 +
Employees (#) JG Analysis	14	14	3	1	1	1	-	-	-
Employees (%) JG Analysis	100	100	21.4	7.1	7.1	7.1	-	-	-
Availability (%) 2-Factor	-	72.9	44.8	6.6	13.3	22.6	0.6	0.7	1.6
Visual Deficiency? (Any Difference)		NO	YES	NO	YES	YES	YES	YES	YES
% Under			23.4		6.2	15.5	0.6	0.7	1.6
1 Person Equals			7.1		7.1	7.1	7.1	7.1	7.1
More than 1 Person Under?			YES		NO	YES	NO	NO	NO
Statistical Significance (Z=)			1.37			1.40			
Need More?			NO			NO			
Practical Significance									
Need More?									

Comparison of Incumbency to Availability
ANALYSIS FORM

Craft Workers Job Group

	Total Employees	Total Female	Total Min	Black	Hisp	Asian	AI/AN	NHPI	2+
Employees (#) JG Analysis	40	-	12	4	5	3	-	-	-
Employees (%) JG Analysis	100	-	30.0	10.0	12.5	7.5	-	-	-
Availability (%) 2-Factor	-	6.8	49.0	3.5	24.1	17.6	0.7	0.7	2.4
Visual Deficiency? (Any Difference)		YES	YES	NO	YES	YES	YES	YES	YES
% Under		6.8	19.0		11.6	10.1	0.7	0.7	2.4
1 Person Equals		2.5	2.5		2.5	2.5	2.5	2.5	2.5
More than 1 Person Under?		YES	YES		YES	YES	NO	NO	NO
Statistical Significance (Z=)		2.03	1.74		1.56	1.62			
Need More?		YES	NO		NO	NO			
Practical Significance		>2							
Need More?		YES							

Comparison of Incumbency to Availability
ANALYSIS FORM

Job Group: _____   **Analysis Date:** _____

	Total Employees	Total Female	Total Min	Black	Hisp	Asian	AI/AN	NHPI	2 +
Employees (#) JG Analysis									
Employees (%) JG Analysis									
Availability (%) 2-Factor									
Visual Deficiency? (Any Difference)									
% Under									
1 Person Equals									
More than 1 Person Under?									
Statistical Significance (Z=)									
Need More?									
Practical Significance									
Need More?									

Job Group: _____   **Analysis Date:** _____

	Total Employees	Total Female	Total Min	Black	Hisp	Asian	AI/AN	NHPI	2 +
Employees (#) JG Analysis									
Employees (%) JG Analysis									
Availability (%) 2-Factor									
Visual Deficiency? (Any Difference)									
% Under									
1 Person Equals									
More than 1 Person Under?									
Statistical Significance (Z=)									
Need More?									
Practical Significance									
Need More?									

CHAPTER 9
GOALS

Secrets of Affirmative Action Compliance

CHAPTER 9
GOALS

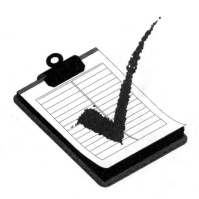

Notes

GOALS

Goals are the final piece of the statistical section for your Minority/Women's AAP. It is here that we identify what placement opportunities we expect during the coming year, and what portion of them we expect to be able to use for reduction of any staffing need.

Outline of Content Requirements

The regulations say: *(a) Purpose: Placement goals serve as objectives or targets reasonably attainable by means of applying every good faith effort to make all aspects of the entire affirmative action program work. Placement goals also are used to measure progress toward achieving equal employment opportunity.*

    (b) A contractor's determination under Section 60-2.15 that a placement goal is required constitutes neither a finding nor an admission of discrimination.

    (c) Where, pursuant to Section 60-2.15, a contractor is required to establish a placement goal for a particular job group, the contractor must establish a percentage annual placement goal at least equal to the availability figure derived for women or minorities, as appropriate, for that job group.

    (d) The placement goal-setting process described above contemplates that contractors will, where required, establish a single goal for all minorities. In the event of a substantial disparity in the utilization of a particular minority group or in the utilization of men or women of a particular minority group, a contractor may be required to establish separate goals for those groups. [Bold emphasis added]

    (e) In establishing placement goals, the following principles also apply:

      1) Placement goals may not be rigid and inflexible quotas, which must be met, nor are they to be considered as either a ceiling or a floor for the employment of particular groups. Quotas are expressly forbidden.

      2) In all employment decisions, the contractor must make selections in a nondiscriminatory manner. Placement goals do not provide the contractor with a justification to extend a preference to any individual, select an individual, or adversely affect an individual's employment status, on the basis of that person's race, color, religion, sex, or national origin.

      3) Placement goals do not create set-asides for specific groups, nor are they intended to achieve proportional representation or equal results.

      4) Placement goals may not be used to supersede merit selection principles. Affirmative action programs prescribed by the regulations in this part do not require a contractor to hire a person who lacks qualifications to perform the job successfully, or hire a less qualified person in preference to a more qualified one.

> *(f)   A contractor extending a publicly announced preference for American Indians as is authorized in 41 CFR 60-1.5(a)(6) may reflect in its placement goals the permissive employment preference for American Indians living on or near an Indian reservation.* (41 CFR 60-2.16)

It bears repeating that ***"Goals may not be rigid and inflexible quotas which must be met."***

<u>Quotas are illegal</u>, unless your organization happens to be operating under a court order (consent decree). <u>Set asides are illegal</u>. <u>Preferences are illegal</u>. All of those fly in the face of EEO laws and principles. <u>An employer who practices affirmative action using quotas, set asides or preferences is placing itself in jeopardy of legal challenges through discrimination suits</u>. And, hopefully, such an employer will be challenged in court. Those practices are just plain wrong. They should not be foisted upon any employee group anywhere.

Why people persist in thinking that Affirmative Action Programs require quotas and preferential treatment is beyond me. It must be the misinformation conveyed by the mass media. Or, maybe it's just a hyperactive rumor mill that flashes misinformation back and forth across the country. Whatever, I wish we could stop it. It's like shoveling sand against the tide. I fear there's no way we're going to overcome these misconceptions.

Of course, the government has done a lot of damage to affirmative action programs by its own actions. Politicians proclaimed very loudly that the Civil Rights Act of 1990 was a "quota bill" and brought enough pressure on President Bush that he vetoed the bill, agreeing that it required quotas. A funny thing then happened. The following year, the same piece of legislation was passed by Congress and President Bush signed it into law saying that it was no longer a "quota bill." It was the same bill. What happened in the intervening months?

A couple of things took place, of course. These things seem to happen because of the emotional reactions from the American public. There is little logic and much less real thought behind any campaign for or against proposed social legislation. In August of 1991, we had the Grand Duke of the Ku Klux Klan making headlines in a political race of his own which received national attention from the media. And, then, there were the Clarence Thomas hearings on confirmation for his appointment to the Supreme Court. If you recall, Anita Hill received a lot of attention when she charged that Mr. Thomas had sexually harassed her. Put those two things together, and the mood of the country shifted nearly overnight. The President signed the new civil rights legislation, the *Civil Rights Act of 1991,* and it became law.

I have concluded that civil service (Federal, state and local government employers) are among the worst offenders of affirmative action prohibition against preferences and employment quotas. Many managers don't really know any better, so when they are confronted by militant minorities or women, they say they will be happy to "keep their affirmative action commitments and offer preferential hiring to minorities or females." You know that's nonsense. And, you know that's illegal. And, you know, that it happens. Just like you know we still have some managers taking out their personal biases against minorities and women in the workplace. Unfortunately, after more than 40 years, employment discrimination is alive and well in this country. People are just much more subtle about it today than they were 40 years ago. (Did you know that the Equal

Employment Opportunity Commission – EEOC – created by the *Civil Rights Act of 1964* – was originally intended to exist for only one year? It was believed by politicians at the time that all discrimination complaints would be handled within one year and the Commission could then be disbanded.)

So, how does all that impact our setting of goals for our AAP? Well, believe it or not, there is a lot of impact when we get to the point of implementing the plan because we have to take it to our line management staff and convince them that they should support it.

You might consider starting with a quotation from the regulations. 41 CFR 60-2.35 says, ***"No contractor's compliance status shall be judged alone by whether or not it reaches its goals. … Each contractor's compliance with its affirmative action obligations will be determined by reviewing the nature and extent of the contractor's good faith affirmative action activities as required under Section 60-2.17***, and the appropriateness of those activities to identified equal employment opportunity problems. Each contractor's compliance with its nondiscrimination obligations will be determined by analysis of statistical data and other non-statistical information which would indicate whether employees and applicants are being treated without regard to their race, color, religion, sex, or national origin."* (41 CFR 60-2.35) (Bold face type added for emphasis.)

Good faith efforts. That is the measure by which we should be judged in our AAP efforts. If any OFCCP official or anyone else tells you differently, read them the quote from section 60-2.35.

---

b. ***Prohibition against Quotas and Preferential Treatment.***

The numerical goals component of affirmative action programs is not designed to be, nor may it properly or lawfully be interpreted as, permitting unlawful preferential treatment and quotas with respect to persons of any race, color, religion, sex or national origin. The regulations at 41 CFR 60-2.12(e), 60-2.15 and 60-2.30, specifically prohibit discrimination and the use of goals as quotas.

(Notice Number 207, December 13, 1995, signed Shirley J. Wilcher, Deputy Assistant Secretary for Federal Contract Compliance.)

As far as AAP goals are concerned, they are a recognition that more must be done to remedy one or more underutilized conditions in the establishment. So, we need one goal for every underutilization we identify in our Utilization Analysis. The "more" which must be done is NOT to implement quotas, set asides or preferential treatment. Rather, it is to implement a soundly constructed recruiting program that will increase the number of qualified candidates who are minority and/or female.

Forecasting Placement Opportunities – Time Tables

What happened to Time Tables? The revised regulations do not mention time tables. In ***Adarand Constructors Inc. v. Pena*** (115 S.Ct. 2097 U.S. 1995), the Supreme Court said affirmative action programs are acceptable if they are "narrowly tailored." Most experts have agreed that plans developed for one year are narrowly tailored. Plans exceeding a one-year period of time go beyond the narrowly tailored requirement. Therefore, I believe, the **OFCCP eliminated the requirement to develop five-year-long time tables for goal achievement. Time tables are no longer part of the regulations and you don't have to prepare them as part of your AAP.**

Part of our analysis involves determining if we have a chance to reach our goals this year. If we look at our forecast of placement opportunities in each job group we can see quickly whether or not there will be hope of reaching our goals. If we have no placement opportunities, there is no way we can reach our goals.

Placement Opportunities

A goal is fine, but by itself, it tells us little about the reality of our reaching it. To know if we even have a chance of influencing an underutilized condition, we need to know whether or not there will exist any placement opportunities during the current AAP year.

Placement opportunities can be forecast, and usually are, whether we label them that or not. Think about the idea of "placement opportunities" for a moment. Where do they come from?

Placement Opportunities = Turnover + Growth

Most of us prepare budgets each year. Those budgets usually include a forecast of our headcount in various segments of the organization over which we have management control. We forecast growth for budget purposes, and we forecast turnover for budget purposes, too, because we have to allow for the cost of training replacements.

On the outside chance that the HR department doesn't have budget forecasts or headcount forecasts, where can the HR Manager get such information? Line managers (your internal clients) have that information for their portion of the enterprise, because they are preparing a budget for the coming year also. Asking line managers to tell HR the number of placement opportunities in each Job Group (or Job Title which can be converted to Job Group data) during the coming year ought to be a fairly simple request for them to fill.

When we know <u>what</u> our AAP goals are for each Job Group and we know <u>how many placement opportunities</u> we anticipate, we can draw a conclusion about <u>the chances for influencing</u> the placement needs during the coming twelve months. NEVER...NEVER...NEVER...write that you will "fix" a placement deficiency when you know darned well that there isn't a snowball's chance in Hades that it will happen.

Goals Should Be Set for <u>Total Minorities</u> and <u>Women</u>

Why set our goal as a placement rate and not as a headcount target?

For the answer, let's look to an example. If I forecast 10 openings and my placement rate goal is 25%, I can hit my goal by placing either 2 or 3 of the type person I need. So, let's say I set my goal as a target of 3 people. Then, for some unanticipated reasons, business just goes wild and we are growing at twice the anticipated rate. Now, instead of 10 openings, I have 20 openings. If my goal is 3 people, I should be able to make that easily given the extra opportunities. But will I really have made a worthwhile advance on my problem of incumbent vs. availability deficiency? Actually, I will have been slipping further behind.

If my goal is a placement rate percentage, instead of a headcount, my target will shift automatically regardless of the adjustments reality brings to my forecast of openings. I can hit my goal by placing 25% of 10 or by placing 25% of 20. In numbers of people, the adjustment happens automatically. My focus must be on the placement rate for that to happen.

I have a consultant friend who used to work for the OFCCP. He says he always suggests to his clients that they not set placement-rate goals, but goals for candidate pool composition. If we meet availability in our candidate pool composition, we will have a better chance of a minority or woman being selected based on qualifications. While I agree with his argument, the federal regulations still require "Placement-Rate Goals."

That brings up another obvious question. What about downsizing? What do I do when I have no placement opportunities during the coming year, and in fact may be shrinking the organization? How do I set AAP goals in that situation?

It is an all too common problem. I have heard HR Managers literally cry when describing how hard they have worked to improve the representation of minorities and women in their organizations, only to have most of their work march out the door during a downsizing which depended on seniority...last in...first out.

I can't take away the pain of downsizing. Nor, can I take away the sense of despair these HR Managers are feeling about having lost all the ground they had gained over the prior years. All I can do is explain that the Affirmative Action process can accommodate that condition. It is dynamic. It is designed to adjust every year to new conditions. Every year we reassess our Job Group status. Every year we re-compute our Availability and put another "stake in the ground" from which to measure our current incumbency equilibrium with availability. And based on the difference between the two, we establish new goals for the following year.

The process accommodates all of these vagaries of economics and business cycles. It doesn't make it any easier to swallow as the HR Manager, however. I know that. I have helped take 24,000 people off the payroll. I understand the pain involved in that process.

Goals Achievement Report

Each year, when updating your AAP, you are required to identify the progress you made during the previous AAP year in your goal attainment efforts. That means identifying all of the placements you made into categories for which you had established goals in the previous year.

If you have not reached your goal in any given category, you should be sure you specify the good faith efforts you made in the attempt. Remember, it is not your success in reaching your numerical goals that is the measure of affirmative action accomplishment, but your good faith efforts to implement your planned activities during the year. Once you have identified a problem, and you have set action plans to address it, taking those steps is critical. On the chance that business needs interfered with your plans, you should document that interference.

From one year to the next, you may discover that you have placement needs in the same categories. If that is the case, and you have been adamant about implementing your action plan, you might want to review the number of placement opportunities you had in that category during the past year. It is possible that you could not have reached your goal because you lacked sufficient placement opportunities. It could be that the action steps you took got you part way to your goal, but there are other actions you can take in the coming year that will help further.

Examples from Sample Company

On the following pages you will find the Goals for TMA, Inc. (our fictitious federal contractor). They show how you might use the form to meet the requirements.

Putting together these numerical Goals is not very difficult. You know that Availability is the minimum placement rate goal you can set, and that is usually the default goal.

The more difficult of our tasks, now is to take the numerical goals and assess them in terms of how we plan to accomplish them.

We have to return to our narrative Section 4 and write some specific action plans that will allow us to measure how well we did in our good faith efforts to achieve these goals.

Blank Goals Form for Your Use

The very last pages in this chapter are blank copies of the Goals Form and the Goals Achievement Report Form for you to copy and use, if you wish.

GOALS FORM
(TMA, Inc.)

Job Group	Placement Needs	Additional # Needed	# Openings Forecast	Placement Rate Goal
Technicians	Asian	5	2	33.2%*
Craft Wkrs	Female	3	15	6.8%

* Goals are only required for TOTAL MINORITYES and TOTAL WOMEN. Setting goals for placements within individual race categories is something you may wish to do, but it is usually not required. (41 CFR 60-2.16(d))

GOALS FORM

Job Group	Placement Needs	Additional # Needed	# Openings Forecast	Placement Rate Goal

REPORT ON GOAL ACHIEVEMENT

Report based on AAP year:

Job Group	Total Placed	Prior Year Placements						Comments
		Minorities			Females			
		#	%	Goal	#	%	Goal	

Notes

CHAPTER 10

IMPACT RATIO ANALYSIS

Disparate Impact Testing
80% Testing
4/5ths Rule

IMPACT RATIO ANALYSIS

Impact Ratio Analysis (IRA) is also known as the "**4/5ths Rule**," "**Disparate Impact Testing**," and the "**80% Test**." Any of these terms can be used to describe the legally acceptable process of analyzing potential discrimination against protected groups of people. With the exception of Age Discrimination, this test is used nearly universally for all other types of discrimination in testing for Disparate Impact.

Disparate Impact is the form of discrimination that occurs inadvertently, against protected groups rather than individuals. And, almost always, it is suggested by statistical analysis. You can have what the attorneys call "facially neutral policies" and still have disparate impact. The court records are full of such cases. That's why we do disparate impact testing.

CAUTION:

Conducting an Impact Ratio Analysis (IRA), otherwise known as a Disparate Impact Test, is not an exact process, regardless of the appearance of mathematical certainty. Courts are still in disagreement about what constitutes disparate impact from a mathematical perspective. The general rule of thumb is anything greater than a standard deviation of 2.0 should be thought of as a red flag requiring more investigation. Statisticians even disagree about the accuracy of specific formulas used to compute disparate impact.

Suffice it to say, it you are ever unfortunate enough to be involved in a legal battle over the question of disparate impact, your attorney will be working with a Ph.D.-level statistician so generate the most accurate analysis possible. For our purposes in affirmative action planning, we can use less precise methodology, because it is good enough for our management of the program.

Outline of Content Requirements

Regulations say, *"A selection rate for any race, sex, or ethnic group which is less than four-fifths (or eighty percent) of the rate for the group with the highest rate will generally be regarded by the Federal enforcement agencies as evidence of adverse impact, while a greater than four-fifths rate will generally not be regarded by Federal enforcement agencies as evidence of adverse impact. Smaller differences in selection rate may nevertheless constitute adverse impact, where they are significant in both statistical and practical terms or where a user's actions have discouraged applicants disproportionately on grounds of race, sex, or ethnic group. Greater differences in selection rate may not constitute adverse impact where the differences are based on small numbers and are not statistically significant, or where special recruiting or other programs cause the pool of minority or female candidates to be atypical of the normal pool of applicants from that group. Where the user's evidence concerning the impact of a selection procedure indicates adverse impact but is based upon numbers which are too small to be reliable, evidence concerning the impact of the procedure over a longer period of time and/or evidence concerning the impact which the selection procedure had when used in the same manner in similar circumstances elsewhere may be considered in determining adverse impact. Where the user has not maintained data on adverse impact as required by the documentation section of applicable guidelines, the Federal enforcement agencies may draw an inference of adverse impact of the selection process from the failure of the user to maintain such data, if the user has an underutilization of a group in the job category, as compared to the group's representation in the relevant labor market or, in the case of jobs filled from within, the applicable work force."* (*41 CFR 60-3.4(D)*)

The Federal Contractor Compliance Manual adds several paragraphs of instruction to Compliance Officers which are important to AAP employers:

"The Impact Ratio Analysis (IRA) is a method for identifying personnel activity which should be investigated further onsite. The IRA is a ratio between two selection rates, one for minorities or women, and one for others. Generally, a selection rate for minorities or women which is less than 80% of the selection rate for nonminorities or men, as appropriate, for a particular personnel activity (e.g., hiring, promotion, termination) should be investigated further during the onsite. Although related, adverse IRAs should not be confused with the term "adverse impact." (FCCM, Par. 2000)

"Selection Rates: The first step in calculating the IRA is to find the selection rate for minorities or women and the selection rate for others.

"Focus on Unfavorable Selection Rate of Minorities/Women: The next step is to compare the selection rate for minorities/women to the rate for others. As a matter of administrative discretion in compliance reviews, OFCCP will focus on situations in which the selection rate for minorities or women is less favorable than the rate for others.* For positive actions, such as hires or promotions, this will be where the minority or female rate is lower; for negative actions, such as terminations, it will be where the minority or female rate is higher

"*Finding the Impact Ratio*: Consistent with [the paragraph on Focus], the IRA is calculated when the selection rate for minorities or women is less favorable. Therefore, for positive personnel actions the IRA is found by dividing the lower minority or female rate by the rate for others. The IRA for negative personnel actions is found by dividing the rate for others by the higher minority or female rate.*

"*Number of Persons Potentially Affected*: For adverse IRAs, the SCRR Worksheet...provides an additional calculation to determine how many minorities or women are potentially affected. This information may be useful in setting investigative priorities.*

"* The [Compliance Officer] should be aware, however, that sometimes a *more* favorable rate for minorities or women may indicate 'channeling' into different -- and perhaps, less favorable -- jobs than others.*" (FCCM, Par. 2001)

"*It is important to remember that an adverse IRA is only a *preliminary* indicator of a potential discrimination problem. It is not proof, in and of itself, of discrimination, or of the existence of an affected class. For example, an adverse IRA in a job group may have been computed using an insufficiently refined candidate pool. Only further investigation onsite can determine whether discrimination has occurred.*" (FCCM, Par. 2003)

"Where adverse IRAs are identified, and further investigation is needed, the [Compliance Officer] should describe the problem on the [Summary of Potential Discrimination Problems Form] and indicate that will be needed on site to determine whether the adverse IRA represents apparent discrimination."

"*Maintenance of Records*: ...contractors with 100 or more employees [are required to] maintain records by job title sufficient to disclose the impact which its selection procedures (including hiring, promotion and termination) have on the employment opportunities of women and on each minority group for whom EEO-1 reporting is required.*

"*Analysis of Impact*: [Guidelines] require that contractors with 100 or more employees annually analyze these data to determine whether the total selection process for each job is having adverse impact. These determinations are required by sex and for each race/national origin group (e.g., Black, Hispanic, Asian/Pacific Islander, American Indian/Alaskan Native) which constitutes 2% or more of the labor force in the relevant labor area or 2% or more of the applicable workforce (i.e., for jobs filled internally.)*" (FCCM, Par. 2004)

There are additional details about certain circumstances a Compliance Officer may encounter. The "bottom line" on IRAs is this: Adverse IRAs will <u>always</u> be followed up by on-site investigation to determine if there is discrimination in the employer's selection processes, and any complaint of discrimination from an employee will be investigated on-site, regardless of the favorable or unfavorable outcome of IRA calculations.

Employer Recommendations:

When we discussed computing incumbents vs. availability, I mentioned that the volume of discovery requests for disparate impact analysis reports has increased dramatically in recent times.

There is no way you can avoid performing the analysis required by the Uniform Guidelines on Employee Selection Procedures, but you can do it in a way that might offer you protection from releasing all that data, good or bad, to plaintiff's counsel.

Talk with your company attorney. If you already have an outside consultant or outside attorney performing the analysis for you, ask your attorney to write the outside experts a letter directing them to perform the required analysis. You should be specific about including job applicants vs. new hires, promotions, transfers and terminations in the list of analysis reports required. Your attorney should also be clear that all reports, backup materials, input worksheets and any other related materials should be delivered to your attorney, not to you. If your attorney receives the analysis reports, he or she can decide how to present them to you and what legal advice to give you in addition to the analytical results. In that way, you may be able to protect the materials from discovery because they are **Attorney Work Product**. Don't think you can protect the AAP(s) from disclosure. It is not likely to happen. The fact that you summarize the Disparate Impact Analysis in your AAP narrative is something you will have to live with. Choose your words carefully. If in doubt, have a talk with your attorney and ask for wording suggestions.

Example of IRA Calculation from Sample Company

Calculating **Impact Ratio Analysis** is a two step process. In the first step, we must determine the selection rates for each group which has been processed through the employment activity (hiring, promotion, etc.)

IRA - Step #1

Determine the selection rate for each group processed.

Hiring Example

Job Group:__Administrative Support__   Employment Action:_____Hires_____

Group	# Applicants (Applicant Log)	# New Hires (New Hire Log)	Selection Rate Hires/Applicants
White	85	35	41.2%
Black	22	8	36.4%
Hispanic	41	14	34.1%
Asian	60	16	26.7%
American Indian	0	0	-
Hawaiian / Pacific Islander	0	0	-
Male	61	48	78.7%
Female	147	25	17.0%
TOTAL	208	73	35.1%

Applicant count and New Hire Logs provide a count of participants in the applicant and new hire activities. Selection Rates in the last column of the table contains calculated information. For each line (category) divide the number of New Hires by the Number of Applicants in the same category. That tells us the selection rate for each group. While this may be interesting information, in and of itself it doesn't tell us very much. It is the **relationship between the selection rates** that is important to us.

PLEASE NOTE: There is no group called "2 or More Races" on the list in our table. That's because you should NEVER attempt to do a disparate impact analysis on that category. "2 or More Races" is not a category offered protection by any of the Civil Rights laws.

IRA - Step #2

Compare the selection rates for protected groups with the selection rate for the most favorably treated group.

IRA - Selection Rate Comparisons

Job Group:__Office & Clerical_____   Employment Action: ____Hires_____

Most Favorably Treated Group	Protected Group	Selection Rate Ratio
White (41.2%)	Black (36.4%)	36.4 / 41.2 = 88.3%
White (41.2%)	Hispanic (34.1%)	34.1 / 41.2 = 82.8%
White (41.2%)	Asian (26.7%)	26.7 / 41.2 = 64.8%
Male (78.7%)	Female (17.0%)	17.0 / 78.7 = 21.6%

Now, we have some comparisons that tell us something. Let's see what that is.

We have already determined that in this example, White was the most favorably treated group. So, if we divide the selection rate for White into the selection rate for each of the protected ethnic groups, we can see a comparison of the two selection rates in each case.

The result: The Black selection rate was 88.3% of the White selection rate. Federal guidelines tell us that in a positive employment action, like New Hires, we can presume that there is no disparate impact if the result is at or above the 80% mark. So, we have no disparate impact against Blacks in this example. The Hispanic selection rate was 82.8% as great as the White selection rate. No disparate impact against Hispanics in this example. Asians, however are another matter. Asians were only selected at a rate 64.8% as often as Whites. Therefore, because that falls below our 80% target, we will want to investigate our hiring process to determine why Asians are being screened out at a higher-than-acceptable rate.

Looking at Male vs. Female we see there are some potentially serious problems. Not only is the Female selection rate only 21.6% of the Male selection rate, but the gap between our 80% target and the 21.6% is substantial. We have some serious investigating to do.

Example of IRA Calculation for Terminations

Testing data for terminations is a bit different from the way tests are done for new hires and promotions. New hires and promotions are positive employment actions. Terminations, on the other hand are negative employment actions. In testing, the numbers have to be reversed. Let's see if we can make sense of it through use of an example.

Termination IRA – Step #1

Determine the selection rate for each group processed.

Termination Example

Job Group:____Office & Clerical_____   Employment Action: _____Terminations_____

Group	# Terminations (Termination Log)	# in JG at start of year + hires (Eligible Pool)	Selection Rate Terminations / Eligible Pool
White	10	46	21.7%
Black	2	9	22.2%
Hispanic	1	15	6.7%
Asian	4	17	23.5%
American Indian	0	0	-
Hawaiian / Pacific Islander	0	0	-
Male	11	48	22.9%
Female	6	39	15.4%
TOTAL	17	87	19.5%

Now that we have our selection rates determined, we can move to the next step which is to compare those selection rates. In the case of terminations, however, the most favorably treated group is the one with the **lowest** selection rate rather than the highest. So our comparisons would look like this:

Termination IRA – Step #2

IRA - Selection Rate Comparisons

Job Group:___Office & Clerical_____   Employment Action:_____Terminations_____

Most Favorably Treated Group	Protected Group	Selection Rate Ratio
Hispanic (6.7%)	White (21.7%)	6.7 / 21.7 = 30.9%
Hispanic (6.7%)	Black (22.2%)	6.7 / 22.2 = 30.2%
Hispanic (6.7%)	Asian (23.5%)	6.7 / 23.5 = 28.5%
Female (15.4%)	Male (22.9%)	15.4 / 22.9 = 67.2%

It appears that we have a potential for disparate impact against White, Black, and Asian groups and against men as well. None of the selection rate comparison ratios reached 80% or more. That being the case we have to begin an investigation to determine why Hispanics and females are terminated at rates so much lower than Whites, Blacks, Asians and males.

What Questions Do You Ask Yourself During An IRA Investigation?

Whenever we are dealing with the subject of Applicants vs. New Hires, I believe we should begin our investigation with the issue of data reliability. Here are some possible questions for us to ask:

- Have we properly isolated Applicants for this job group?
- Have we invited every Applicant to self-identify race/ethnicity and sex?
- Did we accurately summarize all the appropriate log pages? Are there pages missing?
- Who filled in the Applicant Log and New Hire Log? Were there two or more people entering data? Did they interpret the definition of "Applicant" the same way?
- Did all Applicants and New Hires actually get entered?
- How did we determine "race" category for Applicants?
- If the receptionist handles our Applicant Log, what happens when that person goes on a break or off to lunch? Who takes over? Does the relief person do data entry and categorization the same way as the receptionist?
- How many steps are there in our employment process for Office & Clerical jobs?

- Is one of those employment steps screening out Females and Asians more than others?
- Etc.

Be creative with your questioning. After all, you will likely be asking the questions of yourself, anyway. Pull your employment screening process apart. Diagram it if you must so you are sure of each separate step along the way. Some typical employment process steps include:

- Employment Office reception
- Complete employment application form
- Preliminary interview
- Schedule paper-and-pencil test
- Conduct paper-and-pencil test
- In-depth interview by Employment Office
- Interview by selecting department manager
- Background and reference check
- Job offer

Add to the list (or subtract from it) so it represents your own employment process. Then look at the numbers of each group that "pass" each stage of the screening process. You will find there are one or more points along the way where Asians and Females are not doing well. A bunch "wash out" at that "choke point." Finding the "choke point" is what your investigation is supposed to do. If you can identify where it is, you can study what happens there and why the specific protected groups aren't doing so well.

Then, make whatever changes you must to "fix" your Impact Ratio results. If that means cleaning up your data gathering so it is consistent throughout the year, do that. If it means better training for relief people who take over for those normally logging applicant data, arrange for the training.

Then, document your actions. After all, you have just made some substantial good faith efforts to identify a problem and repair it. Take credit for the work you did in your AAP documentation file for the current year.

Although this example and discussion have centered on the application and hiring process, this same approach can also be used to explore unsatisfactory IRA results in any other employment activity. You will want to calculate IRA results for promotions and transfers, training participation, and terminations.

Tracking and Analyzing Data on Self-Eliminations

You might also be interested in tracking those people who self-eliminate from further consideration in your process. If it is always a particular minority group that drops out, you might investigate and discover some selecting manager has a reputation for giving that minority group a hard time in the selection process. Discovering such a bias will help you in your management efforts. It gives you an opportunity to take corrective action before a court orders that same action.

IRA Forms You Can Use

IRA Calculation - Step #1

Job Group:_____ Employment Action: _____

Group	Selection Pool (Source)	# Selected (Source)	Selection Rate Pool / # Selected
White			
Black			
Hispanic			
Asian			
American Indian			
Hawaiian / Pacific Islander			
Male			
Female			
TOTAL			

IRA - Selection Rate Comparisons

Job Group:_____ Employment Action: _____

Most Favorably Treated Group	Protected Group	Selection Rate Ratio

CHAPTER 11

MANAGING
COMPLIANCE EVALUATIONS

Notes

COMPLIANCE EVALUATIONS

Compliance evaluations are the government's way of testing to see if all regulatory requirements concerning affirmative action are being met. They should be straightforward and manageable in most cases. However, because we are all humans, with the foibles humans possess, there is the occasional problem to be addressed. You already know that AAP compliance is not a "cook book" issue. There is a great deal of our AAP effort that is simply checked for completion: "Yes, the contractor did it" or "No, the contractor did not do it." There is also a large measure of judgment that goes into our meeting AAP requirements. What we judge to be excellent examples of good faith efforts, the Compliance Officer may not agree with. It is at these moments that interpersonal management skills become critical.

Remember this about your compliance evaluation experience: The OFCCP is a law enforcement agency. In that regard it is like your local police or highway patrol. It is charged with enforcing federal laws on EEO and affirmative action. And, as with local officials and laws, if we violate these federal laws, there are penalties to be paid. Compliance evaluations are a serious business. Treat them that way.

Reasons for Compliance Evaluations

Contractors who are new to government contracting, and thus to affirmative action requirements, sometimes think that they have to "file a copy" of their AAP with the government. It's a logical assumption, because we ARE required to file other documents, with the government each year, such as our EEO-1 and the new EEO Survey.

There is, however, no need for contractors to send a copy of their AAP anywhere outside their organization until they are notified that they have been scheduled for a compliance evaluation. AAP documents are intended to be working management plans used throughout the year. Although, we are obligated to tell outside people and organizations about our EEO/AA policy, we are not obligated to give them a copy of the AAP document.

All managers in the organization, especially those involved in making selection decisions in hiring or promotion situations, should have their own copy of the complete AAP document. They should have attended training on its content, and ought to be able to explain that content to their subordinates.

Many managers and executives I have talked with over the years feel that affirmative action is an imposition on their freedom to manage their organizations the way they want to manage. And, I have to agree with them up to a point. There are restrictions placed on managers by AAP regulations. Managers may not make "people decisions" by shooting from the hip or arbitrarily picking their favorites. They must spend time to document their decisions about people selection to justify the equity of those decisions. They must discuss the subjects of equal opportunity and affirmative action with their subordinates. They must occasionally take a bit more time than they would like to be sure candidate pools have the proper "mix" of candidates from which they can choose. They may find they are required to plan more and that they are held accountable for their accomplishments or shortcomings.

Some managers believe that affirmative action "requires" them to hire unqualified minorities and women so they can meet their "quotas." You and I know that isn't so, and it is our job to explain to our management clients how affirmative action really works.

I have proven to myself during my 40+ year management career, that using principles of equal opportunity, affirmative action, and sound management skills like communication, leadership and performance management, lead to successful employee performance. Americans have one basic expectation in common. It matters not who you are or what you do for a living. Every one of us expects to be treated fairly. When that doesn't happen for some reason, we say "It wasn't fair." Well, I find it interesting that I have never been able to find a way to measure fairness on the job. I can measure equal opportunity though. And, I can measure how well I am achieving a proper mix of candidates in my selection pools. The things offered us by equal employment and affirmative action are management tools that will help us do our management jobs better.

People cry loudly when they are excluded from something they believe they should have had access to. It might be a new job, or a promotion, or to not be terminated. "It isn't fair." These cries can be heard every time a manager violates equal opportunity laws. Not because employees are all lawyers and they are skulking around trying to catch management in a violation. But, rather because they know how they feel about the way they are treated. Sometimes, we have to help them understand WHY certain actions were taken. Employees don't always have all the facts at first. But, if they watch minorities and women hired and promoted into jobs they have no qualifications for, they will say that's not fair. And, you know, they are right. It is even unfair to those selected, because unqualified people have very little chance of success.

Managers who make decisions to give preferential treatment to minorities and women are just as guilty of illegal discrimination as are managers who are biased against minorities and women. Neither is right. Neither is legal. And, neither action makes good business sense. Somehow, we must convince our managers of that.

Compliance evaluations are designed to allow the government to determine if we are abiding by the laws of equal employment opportunity and the regulations associated with affirmative action. They exist for one purpose...to see if we should be allowed to continue to enjoy the benefits of selling goods and/or services to the federal government, and to punish us if we should not.

In 1997, the OFCCP formalized its right to remove records from the contractor's worksite and take them to its federal offices.

(iii) Where necessary, an off-site analysis of information supplied by the contractor or otherwise gathered during or pursuant to the on-site review.
*(2) **Off-site review of records.** An analysis and evaluation of the AAP (or any part thereof) and supporting documentation, and other documents related to the contractor's personnel policies and employment actions that may be relevant to a determination of whether the contractor has complied with the requirements of the Executive Order and regulations;*
*(3) **Compliance check.** A visit to the establishment to ascertain whether data and other information previously submitted by the contractor are complete and accurate; whether the contractor has maintained records consistent with Section 60-1.12; and/or whether the contractor has developed an AAP consistent with Section 60-1.40; or*
*(4) **Focused review.** An on-site review restricted to one or more components of the contractor's organization or one or more aspects of the contractor's employment practices.*

* * * * * * *

*(d) **Preaward compliance evaluations.** Each agency shall include in the invitation for bids for each formally advertised nonconstruction contract or state at the outset of negotiations for each negotiated contract, that if the award, when let, should total $10 million or more, the prospective contractor and its known first-tier subcontractors with subcontracts of $10 million or more shall be subject to a compliance evaluation before the award of the contract unless OFCCP has conducted an evaluation and found them to be in compliance with the Order within the preceding 24 months. The awarding agency will notify OFCCP and request appropriate action and findings in accordance with this subsection. Within 15 days of the notice OFCCP will inform the awarding agency of its intention to conduct a preaward compliance evaluation. If OFCCP does not inform the awarding agency within that period of its intention to conduct a preaward compliance evaluation, clearance shall be presumed and the awarding agency is authorized to*

proceed with the award. If OFCCP informs the awarding agency of its intention to conduct a preaward compliance evaluation, OFCCP shall be allowed an additional 20 days after the date that it so informs the awarding agency to provide its conclusions. If OFCCP does not provide the awarding agency with its conclusions within that period, clearance shall be presumed and the awarding agency is authorized to proceed with the award.

*…The contractor must provide full access to all relevant data on-site as required by Section 60-1.43. **Where necessary, the compliance officer may take information made available during the on-site evaluation off-site for further analysis.*** (Bold emphasis added.) *An off-site analysis should be conducted where issues have arisen concerning deficiencies or an apparent violation which, in the judgment of the compliance officer, should be more thoroughly analyzed off-site before a determination of compliance is made. The contractor must provide all data determined by the compliance officer to be necessary for off-site analysis. Such data may only be coded if the contractor makes the key to the code available to the compliance officer. **If the contractor believes that particular information which is to be taken off-site is not relevant to compliance with the Executive Order, the contractor may request a ruling by the OFCCP District/Area Director.*** (Bold emphasis added.) *The OFCCP District/Area Director shall issue a ruling within 10 days. The contractor may appeal that ruling to the OFCCP Regional Director within 10 days. The Regional Director shall issue a final ruling within 10 days. Pending a final ruling, the information in question must be made available to the compliance officer off-site, but shall be considered a part of the investigatory file and subject to the provisions of paragraph (g) of this section. The agency shall take all necessary precautions to safeguard the confidentiality of such information until a final determination is made. Such information may not be copied by OFCCP and access to the information shall be limited to the compliance officer and personnel involved in the determination of relevancy. Data determined to be not relevant to the investigation will be returned to the contractor immediately.*
*(g) **Public access to information.** The disclosure of information obtained from a contractor will be evaluated pursuant to the public inspection and copying provisions of the Freedom of Information Act, 5 U.S.C. 552, and the Department of Labor's implementing regulations at 29 CFR Part 70."* (41 CFR 60-1.20)

Selecting Contractors for Review

Your organization can be selected for a compliance evaluation in one of several ways:

As of mid-2009, there are two different types of compliance evaluation being performed by the OFCCP:

1) The "Old Standard" Compliance Evaluation for Supply and Service Contractors

You will learn more on the following pages about the standard Federal Contractor Selection System. It is still being used for non-ARRA contracts.

2) Compliance Evaluations under the *American Recovery and Reinvestment Act of 2009 (ARRA)*[26]

To increase transparency and accountability of ARRA spending, OFCCP is obligated to track its ARRA-related and non-ARRA-related enforcement activities separately. Accordingly, OFCCP has established separate scheduling procedures to provide for compliance evaluations of ARRA funded contractors.

An ARRA-funded contractor is a contractor that has entered into a Federal contract, in which the terms of the contract satisfy OFCCP's jurisdiction (i.e., total dollar amount meets the coverage threshold and the funding is Federal or, in the case of construction contracts, federally assisted).

Supply and Service

ARRA funded contractor establishments that have recently undergone a compliance evaluation scheduled using standard Federal Contractor Selection System (FCSS) procedures will be excepted from being scheduled and reviewed under ARRA procedures for six (6) months from the date of the compliance evaluation closure.

ARRA funded contractor establishments that have undergone a compliance evaluation scheduled using ARRA procedures will not be eligible for another evaluation using ARRA scheduling procedures. ARRA funded contractor establishments that have undergone an evaluation using ARRA scheduling procedures will also be excepted from scheduling for a compliance evaluation using standard FCSS procedures for 24 months from the date of closure of the evaluation using the ARRA procedures.

Construction

An ARRA funded or assisted construction contractor that has undergone an OFCCP review using non-ARRA scheduling procedures will be excepted from an OFCCP evaluation using ARRA procedures, in the same geographical area, for a period of 6 months.

ARRA funded construction contractors that have undergone a compliance evaluation scheduled in a geographical area using ARRA procedures will not be eligible for another evaluation in the same geographical area using ARRA scheduling procedures.

---

[26] http://www.dol.gov/ofccp/arra_data/ARRA_FAQs.pdf

Similar to OFCCP's Federal Contractor Selection System (FCSS), OFCCP uses an administratively neutral selection system[27] that uses multiple information sources to identify ARRA funded Federal contractor establishments for evaluation. The ARRA-FCSS process may include the analysis of external Federal contract databases to better establish jurisdictional coverage.

Once identified by the ARRA-FCSS, establishments selected for evaluation appear on a computer-generated list developed by the OFCCP National Office. To ensure consistent and fair application of OFCCP's administratively neutral selection process, contractors are selected for review from the list in sequential order. If an office rejects an establishment for evaluation, it must identify the reason for the rejection. Information regarding the selection or rejection of contractor establishments is maintained by OFCCP in a centralized electronic database.

Key Difference Between ARRA Contract Selection and Non-ARRA Contract Selection

There is virtually no difference between a normal supply and service contractor audit and an audit of an ARRA supply and service contractor. If it had the resources, OFCCP may conduct more ARRA audits than traditional non-ARRA audits. Although its budget has been increased for FY-2010 future budget levels are not guaranteed. In FY-2010 it is hiring about 200 more Compliance Officers and that will help the agency deal with its increased responsibilities under ARRA.

How Do We Get Picked For A Normal Audit? (Non-ARRA)

- Random number selection from OFCCP data base of contractors

  Unreasonable search and seizure is prohibited by the 4th Amendment to the U.S. Constitution. Over the years, that has been interpreted to mean the government may not target companies for audit without specific reasons. Otherwise, a random number selection must be used so everyone's chances are the same. Since the 1970's only two systems have been used by OFCCP to determine which federal contractors will receive audit visits from Compliance Officers (CO). Beginning in July 2004, the agency abandoned the Equal Employment Data System (EEDS) and began using its new system, identified as the **Federal Contractor Selection System (FCSS)**. It was devised to help OFCCP better identify contractors who were likely to be illegally discriminating against women or minorities in their employment decision making.

---

[27] OFCCP has declined to reveal what its selection system includes for consideration and "random" selection.

Like EEDS, FCSS begins with input from EEO-1 filings that contractors send to the Joint Committee on Reporting every September. Dropped from the database were establishments that had undergone a compliance evaluation within the past two years or had an open review ongoing. Other input includes data like identification of establishments with Conciliation Agreements during the last 10 years that have resulted in settlements of $100,000 or more.

Beginning in 2008, OFCCP will begin implementation of its **"Contracts First Initiative."** According to Director Charles James, this initiative was intended to create a comprehensive database of federal contractors. The Federal Procurement Data System (FPDS) will capture the status of federal contracts and will be used as a cross-reference to the EEO-1 form where companies are asked to check a box if they are a federal contractor. Apparently, the number of companies with federal contracts that don't check the box has not diminished. Mr. James and his agency believe they must "validate" the process by making sure all federal contractors are included in the audit selection process. That is why he has created the "Contracts First" initiative, asking other agencies to help him create a database of federal contracts (and thus contractors) that will allow accurate identification of audit prospects.

- Your organization experiences a sudden surge of discrimination complaints

    EEO-1 (Standard Form 100) reports are shared between the OFCCP and the EEOC. They are received by the "Joint Committee on Reporting" in Virginia and entered into a huge database. Also in this database can be found information about discrimination complaints filed against employers with either federal or state enforcement agencies. Yup, the states input that information to this data base. That's how the OFCCP knows you have a sudden increase in discrimination complaints. We're not talking about one or two more than normal. We're talking about getting three dozen complaints when your normal yearly total is one or two. The computer will flag that activity and output a report to the OFCCP that allows them to decide if they wish to conduct a compliance evaluation on your establishment.

- Community constituency groups cause focus on your organization

    Even though it is a law enforcement organization, the OFCCP is also a government agency that takes direction from the political leaders of the Executive Branch of our federal government. That reporting relationship guarantees there will be sensitivity to political pressures when those pressures get strong enough. So, you can expect a compliance evaluation if you are seeing your organization on the evening news every day as the focal point for complaints about your hiring or termination practices. If community groups representing minorities or women are leading the attacks against you, it increases your exposure to compliance evaluation. And, you can bet that OFCCP will respond when the White House says it wants to focus on a certain segment of the economy, such as High Technology. (This is known as political heat.)

- ## You are in the construction industry

  Since the inception of affirmative action, contractors in the construction industry have had difficulty with the affirmative action process, and some with equal opportunity itself. Attitudes and management styles have been slow to change in that industry. Consequently, construction industry contractors have always had a high risk of compliance evaluation. That is still true today. Construction is an industry targeted by the OFCCP for compliance activity.

  If you are an ARRA construction contractor you can expect to be audited. Of course, you will not have the same type of affirmative action plan as would a supply and service contractor. You can learn more about that in the chapter on construction affirmative action plans. All construction contractor audits involve on-site visits. The Compliance Officer will be knocking on your door wanting to come in. Invite them. Show them the records they request and help them understand how you are serving the federal government. And, go over the 16-points in your AAP so they are clear that you are complying with the regulatory requirements.

  If you are in the construction industry but are a supply and service contractor, like an engineering firm or concrete provider, you will be selected from the FCCS system. The selection rate for construction-related firms has been higher than for contractors not involved in the construction industry.

- ## You are a "first time" federal contractor and must undergo a "pre-award" review if your contract is worth $10,000,000 or more

  Although regulations allow contractors to have up to 120 days after awarding of their federal contract to get their affirmative action plan developed and implemented, they also allow for "pre-award" reviews. In this situation, contractors must demonstrate they are in compliance even before they are awarded the contract. If you wish to learn whether or not you are subject to a "pre-award" audit, you can now check the OFCCP's web site and look at the list of contractors who have received Letters of Compliance within the past two years. If you are on the list, you need not be concerned about a "pre-award" review. Go to: http://dol.gov/dol/public/ofcp_org.htm

- <u>You are selected for review by the local District or Region Director</u>

In "olden days," most compliance reviews were made by selection of local District and Region Directors. Those days are long gone. They vanished in the Clinton Administration when then OFCCP Director, Shirley Wilcher, pulled all audit selection activities into the headquarters office. Her successor, Charles James, continued the centralized selection practice. Now, if a District or Region Director wishes to conduct an audit at a contractor establishment that is not on the list produced by headquarters, they must get approval from Washington, DC before sending the scheduling letter.

Are Functional AAPs Exempt from Review?

In the first few years OFCCP dealt with formalized functional AAPs they didn't have a methodology for conducting compliance evaluations on them. Then, they realized that things are not very much different from normal physical establishments. They are just more spread out and involve more locations.

As OFCCP has set up the approval process for functional AAPs, the national office will be in control of all functional plans. That means the national office will be in control of selecting functional establishments for evaluation as well.

So, the answer now is, "No. Functional AAPs are not exempt from audits."

From the OFCCP's web site under the Q & A involving Functional Affirmative Action Plans (FAAP) come the following words...

A functional compliance evaluation differs chiefly in the logistics necessary to carry it out. Since a functional unit's managers, employees and personnel records can be spread widely across a region or even the entire country, OFCCP may need to travel to more than one contractor facility to conduct an onsite review. For example, the pertinent supervisors and employees who must be interviewed to address a potential issue may work in different cities. Consequently, onsite reviews may be conducted in phases at different locations, and national office and local compliance officers may work together onsite. Alternatively, OFCCP's efficient use of resources may sometimes dictate that staff from a nearby regional, district, or area office perform certain aspects of a compliance evaluation on behalf of the national office. In still other cases, e-mailing, faxing, or shipping records, along with conducting interviews by telephone or teleconference, will address logistical challenges. Depending on where relevant employees or personnel files reside, it may make sense for OFCCP to conduct an onsite review at a facility other than the functional headquarters or where the function managing official works.

Reviews in Companies with Multiple Establishments

Some contractors literally have hundreds of AAP establishments around the country. Think of the large national banks, for example. There are many other industries that have large contractors. And, in those companies, it was not uncommon in past years to have scores of compliance evaluations going on at the same time, or at least within the same year. The agency recognized that it was creating an excessive burden on some companies, and therefore agreed to limit its total number of reviews within a single company in any given year.

Here is what the OFCCP web site Frequently Asked Questions says about the issue:[28]

Is there a limit on the number of evaluations that can be scheduled per contractor?

FCSS limits the number of identified establishments per contractor to no more than 25 new evaluations per Fiscal Year. Compliance evaluations scheduled as a result of contract award notices, directed reviews, conciliation agreement monitoring, or credible reports of an alleged violation of a law or regulation, including complaints, are not counted towards this limit.

Please Note: This limit does not apply to contractors who have contracts under the *American Recovery and Reinvestment Act of 2009.*

Under the Charles James administration, OFCCP placed an upper limit of 25 audits per year on any one contractor. Very large companies can have hundreds of AAP establishments. Having an audit in a lot of those establishments can be an overwhelming burden. So, by policy, OFCCP placed a limit on the number any one company would have to undergo in any single year.

As we are preparing this edition of *Secrets of Affirmative Action Compliance*, there is some indication that OFCCP will not abide by that policy in the future. It is quite possible that there will again be an unlimited number of audits and corporate exposure just went back up.

---

[28] http://www.dol.gov/esa/regs/compliance/ofccp/faqs/fcssfaqs.htm#Q3

How Many Reviews Are Conducted Each Year?

In Fiscal Year (FY) 2008 (from October 1, 2007 through September 30, 2008), OFCCP conducted over 4,000 compliance evaluations. They collected a record $67,510,982 in financial remedies that year, an increase of 14% over the prior year. These back pay settlements were collected on behalf of 24,508 individuals. Clearly, the agency is focused on quality rather than quantity when it comes to audits. There is no doubt they are out to get discrimination remedies in the form of a check from contractors who behave badly.

How Long Do Reviews Take?	
Construction contractor reviews	60 hours of OFCCP time
Non-construction contractor reviews	140 hours of OFCCP time (70% on the desk audit phase)
University reviews	2,000 hours of OFCCP time

A Word About OFCCP Focus in Audits

There is no secret about OFCCP's push to uncover "Systemic Discrimination" so it can be remedied. Charles James and his agency cohorts are rewarded based on the politics of recovery. The more money they are able to obtain for employees and the more cases they can process, the better chance they have of being given those rewards.

These days, OFCCP is doing a cursory review of AAP documents. They still have to fill out the SCRR form and check off the content as required by regulations. But that is routine. They will really spend the bulk of their audit hours looking at Disparate Impact Analysis for employee movement and for employee compensation. Compensation discrimination is a gold mine for them. Be sure you use the OFCCP's new compensation analysis protocol BEFORE you send in your audit response package. You should know ahead of time whether or not the agency will be asking for a large settlement because of a specific issue. If identified early, you can usually save dollars by implementing an appropriate remedy on your own.

At the very least, you should be prepared to explain to the agency's Compliance Officer why the results indicate as they do.

So, if your technical AAP content is not correct, you will get a Conciliation Agreement. It won't cost you any money, though. What will cost you money is a Conciliation Agreement designed to remedy discrimination discovered in your employee movement (usually hiring) and compensation.

Active Case Management (ACM)

A short time before leaving his job as the Director of OFCCP, Charles James signed an OFCCP Directive called "Active Case Management." It is number 285, dated September 17, 2008. Since then, the agency has been managing its compliance evaluations according to its instructions. It applies to non-construction compliance audits only.

> *The chief purpose of Active Case Management (ACM) is to concentrate Agency resources on identifying and remedying cases of systemic discrimination, thereby enabling the Agency to use its resources in a more effective and efficient manner. ACM also aims to quickly and efficiently close out reviews where there are no indicators of systemic discrimination present. As most compliance reviews will require only an abbreviated desk audit, as opposed to the full desk audit and on-site, the ACM approach necessitates specific desk audit procedures and closure letters ... The focus on systemic discrimination under ACM has led OFCCP to have record enforcement results (in terms of back pay and annualized salary and benefits and of number of workers recompensed who had been subjected to unlawful employment discrimination) for three consecutive years, FY 2005-2007.*

ACM directs the Compliance Officer to determine if the proper data has been received as was requested in the Scheduling Letter. If it has and the Compliance Officer does not find "indicators" of systemic discrimination, the ACM directs that the audit be closed.

Take a look at the Active Case Management Directive in the Appendix section of this volume.

Red Flags During An Audit

In one of the most recent fiscal year posting of recovery, OFCCP extracted over $58 million from contractors, most of it related to failure to maintain proper applicant records. This is a BIG issue that you should be concerned about.

- Applicant-to-Hire Ratio of Less than 3-to-1

  Anything that falls into this category will be questioned according to Mickey Silberman, an attorney with Jackson Lewis LLP.[29] You will be asked to show your recruiting records and list of job announcement recipients. Gone are the days when the CEO's next door neighbor can get a job without opening a job requisition to other candidates. You need to help senior management understand they are risking their government contract revenues when they ask you to do such a thing.

- More than 30% of Applicants are "Unknown" Race/Sex

---

[29] Mickey Silberman, Managing Partner, Jackson Lewis, 950 17th Street, Suite 2600, Denver, CO 80202, (303) 225-2400.

The OFCCP will likely assume that a contractor with a high percentage of race/gender unknowns probably did not invite applicants to provide such information. It will be necessary to "prove" you have extended the invitations and not gotten a response. You do that by maintaining lists of individuals you have invited with one copy of the invitation you sent.

- Large Differences From Representation in Applicant Pool

  A "sizable discrepancy" between the representation of females and minorities in the applicant pool in comparison to their overall labor pool availability may also prompt follow-up questions from OFCCP.

- Internet Applicant Accommodation Offers Not Made

  All contractors are required to make their on-line application process accessible to persons with disabilities. If there is not a name and phone number posted at the top of a contractor's web site showing the person to contact for applicant accommodation request, the OFCCP will judge the process to be out of compliance.

  If you use an on-line job application process, be sure the contact information is both shown and current. Out-of-date information is also non-compliant. The OFCCP has cited several areas of concern in that regard. Sometimes, people are not able to read the graphics on a web site. Others find that the employer's web site does not function well with their adaptive technology (zooming in on graphics and text to make them more readable, or converting graphics and text to voice for the sight impaired), or not being able to get a wheel chair or scooter up to a Kiosk application facility so the keyboard can be properly used. The key action OFCCP will be looking for from contractors is the clear posting of name and contact information for the person who will handle requests for reasonable accommodation in the application process. The notice should also indicate an alternate method of application if the web site is the only normal avenue and it is unusable for some reason by an individual applicant.[30]

OFCCP Will Visit On-Site in Every 50th Audit

As a matter of policy, and quality control, OFCCP will make an on-site visit to every 50th compliance evaluation contractor. It doesn't matter if they have found any "indicators" during the desk audit phase of the evaluation. They will come on-site anyway because they wish to inspect I-9 Forms, check posters, review records, and interview employees to be sure they are drawing the proper conclusions from their desk audits. They may also

---

[30] OFCCP webinar, September 10, 2008

request documentation that supports every compensation decision made by the contractor in the past two years.

Immigration Service Audits

While they have nothing to do with affirmative action enforcement, federal contractors should be aware that the U.S. Citizenship and Immigration Services (USCIS) has begun accelerating its program of audits to capture employers that are using immigrant benefit programs to bring illegal aliens into the United States. These audits have been conducted for some time, but the number of them will be increasing over the coming years.

Some of the fraud being detected involves:

- Religious organizations hiring foreign ministers, volunteers and other workers when the organization does not have physical facilities.
- Companies hiring foreign engineering, medical or other specialty occupation workers under the H-1B visa program when there is no actual job opening they will fill.

You can expect, if you use H-1B or other work-related visas, that immigration auditors will be making on-site visits to inspect records supporting your applications. Some visa status, like the H-1B, require a public file be available for review by anyone. The auditors will also be checking on compensation rates for visa holders.

So, what should you do if an auditor shows up at your reception desk? Be cordial and direct that person to the single individual who has been designated by your organization as the contact point for all government officials. Whatever you do, don't let the receptionist make decisions about admitting an auditor or sending him/her away. Decide in advance who you want to handle this type of government request. And, understand that you are entitled to advance notice of a records review. So, if it is not "convenient" for you to have the auditor admitted to review your records when they request to do so, make an appointment for them to return at a later time to conduct their review. You probably can't block their access to your records, but you can request them to do their work at a time that meets with your business needs.

Contractor Requirements Under E-Verify and the No-Match Rule

All new federal contracts awarded after September 8, 2009, are required to include the Federal Acquisition Regulation (FAR) E-Verify clause (73 FR 67704).

There has been a long-running battle over the Department of Homeland Security (DHS) use of the "No-Match" rule on Social Security Numbers (SSN) for new workers. When an employer reports a new employee, the Social Security Administration (SSA) compares the reported SSN with its records and determines that it matches or does not match with the individual on the employer's records. The SSA sends out "no-match" letters to employers when the SSN and other employee data do not appear to belong together. The controversy has involved what employers are supposed to do as a result of the "No-Match" letters.

There are some key facts you may wish to note:

o Prime Contracts valued at $100,000 are covered IF the performance period is 120 days or longer.

o Contracts for off-the-shelf products are usually exempt.

o Subcontracts valued at $3,000 or more are covered if the prime contract contains the new E-Verify requirement provision.

o Contractors and subcontractors have 30 days to enroll following the effective date of their first contract that qualifies.

o Within 90 days after enrollment, the contractor must begin verification inquiries for existing staff who are working on contract-related duties. Within the same period, the contractor/subcontractor must begin submitting all new employees to the verification system. New employees must be submitted within 3 days of their start date.

o Contractors/subcontractors who wish to submit existing employees who DO NOT work on federal contracts must submit a request to the Department of Homeland Security (DHS) through the company profile page on the E-Verify web site.

o No one working on federal contracts outside the U.S. (50 States, the District of Columbia, Guam, Puerto Rico and the U.S. Virgin Islands) should be submitted to E-Verify.

o Anyone hired who has a U.S. government security clearance or HSPD-12 compliant credential is exempt from the E-Verify requirement.

o There are two new Mandatory-to-Post poster requirements associated with E-Verify. One poster is a notice provided by DHS indicating the employer participates in the E-Verify program. The other is an anti-discrimination notice issued by the Office of Special Counsel for Immigration-Related Unfair Employment Practices at the Department of Justice. Both are available for free at the "On-line Resources" section of the E-Verify web site. You may access that section after you have registered for the program.

Once you are required to use E-Verify, you must input all new employees as required. The rules concerning what employers must do when there is no valid match between the new worker's SSN and SSA records are still evolving. Be sure you keep track of the latest requirements and that you are working with your management attorney to be sure you meet the requirements as they change.

Sequence of Events In an OFCCP Compliance Evaluation

So, how do you find out you've been selected for a compliance evaluation? And, what happens after that? You can experience any of the following audit types. Here's a brief outline:

> **Compliance Review** - Starts with a desk audit of your written affirmative action plan (AAP) and other documentation you will be asked to send to the Compliance Officer. Then comes an on-site review to investigate problems the CO believes your documents point out. There may be an off-site review to further analyze your AAP achievements, measure your results, etc. This is the most comprehensive evaluation you can receive under the new program.

> **Indicators of Systemic Discrimination Present**

> If the Compliance Officer discovers through analysis that there is some indication of disparate impact in either employee movement (new hires, promotions or terminations) or compensation programs, then the CO will send out a request that the contractor deliver a data file containing 12 items of information for every employee in the establishment.

> (Contractors who are good negotiators are sometimes able to narrow the focus of this data file to the specific job groups or job titles the CO is having some difficulty with.)

> There is more information about the Mini-Regression analysis in the chapter on Compensation Analysis.

Let's presume you have received notice that you are being scheduled for the entire audit process in what is now called a "Compliance Review." Here is what you can expect:

- **Corporate Scheduling Announcement Letter (CSAL)**

  OFCCP has engaged in the practice, since 2004, of sending letters out to contractors in October notifying them that they may have two to or more audits in their establishments in the coming year. It's not fool proof, however. It is still possible for you to receive a Scheduling Letter even if you don't get the CSAL. You will find a copy in Appendix G. In recent years, the agency has sent the CSAL out twice a year.

- **Scheduling letter**

  You will receive what is called a "scheduling letter." You can see a sample of one in Appendix H. On December 3, 1999, the Office of Management and Budget (OMB) approved OFCCP's request to add the requirement that contractors submit consolidated compensation data with their other AAP documents. The contractor community is generally unhappy with that development, but for now, it is a requirement. The scheduling letter will outline for you that you have been selected, when the review will begin, the establishment which will be reviewed, what documents you are to send to the Compliance Officer, and the deadline for your response. That deadline will be 30 days from the day you receive your letter. It will request copies of your AAP document (all narrative sections and all statistical sections), union contracts, report on AAP goal achievement for the previous AAP year, and data on your employment activity for the previous AAP year (applications, new hires, promotions and terminations.) If you are more than six months into your current AAP year, it will require that you re-compute all of your statistical sections and re-determine underutilizations and submit a report on your goal achievement to the present in your current AAP year.

  In June, 2005, OFCCP updated all of its regulations concerning compliance evaluations. They published their final rule in the Federal Register (Vol. 70, No. 119, June 22, 2005, Pages 36262-36266) As of this publication, OFCCP is no longer obligated to make a physical visit to a contractor's premises to conduct a compliance evaluation. Everything may now be done off-site.

- **Delivery of your documents to Compliance Officer**

  Don't miss the deadline for delivery of your documents to the Compliance Officer. The Federal Contractor Compliance Manual tells the Compliance Officer: *"If there is no reason to believe that the AAP is en route, or if an AAP reported en route has not been received at the end of 5 calendar days following the 30th day, a Show Cause Notice should generally be issued."* (*FCCM, Par. 2C01*) If you absolutely cannot deliver your package of documents by the deadline, contact your Compliance Officer or the District Director and request an extension of time. If you have a really good story they may go for it.

A Show Cause Notice is a nice legal way of saying you have an additional 30 days to show the OFCCP a reason why you should not be immediately taken to enforcement proceedings. That is a very fast route to such penalties as suspension of payments for current contracts, and prevention of participating in future contracts. If you get a Show Cause Notice, you are 30 days from disaster! There are two phone calls you should make immediately. The first is to your CEO to let him/her know that all of your federal contracts and revenues are in danger of being suspended. The second is to your employment attorney. You need your AAP legal specialist to help you out of this one.

If you don't have your AAP document in place (in current condition for the present AAP year), you might want to consider hiring a consultant that specializes in AAP work to help you out. You will pay for that help, but it will be a lot less than the cost of having your federal contracts suspended.

Never fail to deliver all of the documents requested in the Scheduling Letter. When you send them, either hand deliver them or send them by registered mail, return receipt requested so you will have proof they were received by the deadline. When you hand deliver materials, it is a good idea to get a receipt from the OFCCP representative showing what was received, the date, time, and the name of the person accepting them from you.

- ### First phase of the compliance evaluation - the Desk Audit

  You've boxed up all of the documents you have been told to deliver and they have been duly delivered to the Compliance Officer's address. Now the Compliance Officer will open your boxes and begin the process of reviewing all of your documents. This will take some time. Don't expect to hear from the Compliance Officer again for a few weeks. It sometimes takes months. Even though you don't hear from them, they have not forgotten about you.

  During the Desk Audit phase of the review, the Compliance Officer will organize all of your information by extracting certain data and using it to complete a form the agency uses called the SCRR report. More about that in the next section of this chapter.

- ## Second phase of the compliance evaluation - On-Site Visit

    The Compliance Officer will sometimes schedule an on-site visit by telephoning you and making an appointment. Details of the process are described later in this chapter. This visit is usually necessary for gathering information which can't be gotten from the documents you have already sent. There will be interviews with various employees and review of records not sent for the desk audit, such as I-9 Forms and employment posters, plus an inspection of your facilities to be sure there is no segregation of any kind prohibited by EEO laws.

- ## Conclusion of the compliance evaluation

    At the end of the process, you will be told you are either in compliance or you are not. If you are not, the OFCCP will present you with a "settlement agreement" (two possible kinds) that amounts to a contract. In it you will agree to correct any "out-of-compliance" condition.

- ## OFCCP follow up to an out-of-compliance settlement agreement

    The OFCCP will indicate the frequency of follow up visits it plans to make to be sure you follow through with the correction agreement. The period for follow up can last up to two years.

Desk Audit and the SCRR (Rhymes with GURRRRR)

The SCRR (Standard Compliance Evaluation Report) is a tool created by the OFCCP to bring some order to the process of compliance evaluations. Prior to its introduction in 1978, the focus of each audit was based on whatever the Equal Opportunity Specialist (EOS), the Compliance Officer (CO) title at the time, wished to review. Review experiences were inconsistent because they depended totally on the experience and knowledge of the EOS with no consensus about what was important for compliance.

Since the SCRR was introduced, it has brought some semblance of standardization to the process of compliance evaluations. At least it acts as a checklist of subjects that must be covered. And, it has offered an outline for training COs which has not been at all bad either.

A copy of the current SCRR is located in Appendix H. If you look at it you will see that it contains many checklist type pages on which AAP status and completeness can be entered. It also contains pages that are intended for the CO to write a narrative summary of the subject at hand. There is much subjective judgment in this process of determining affirmative action compliance. Descriptive assessments are important to the process. On page 4 of the SCRR you will find a checklist form that is labeled, "Initial Review of AAP and Support Data Submissions." Notice that there are three columns for the CO to enter "yes" or "no" for <u>Included</u>, <u>Reasonable</u>, and <u>Acceptable</u> judgments. If you don't have something in your AAP that should be there it will be marked as not included. That seems fairly straightforward. But as for reasonable and acceptable...those are judgmental calls. There are certain minimum requirements that we have already discussed in previous chapters. The CO will be looking for those minimums to be met as the threshold to reasonableness and acceptability.

On many of the pages, particularly those calling for narrative summaries of information you have sent, you will see small square boxes toward the bottom of the page. These aren't "write-your-complaint-here" boxes. Rather, if checked by the CO, they indicate that additional pages have been added that continue the narrative. It is due to this feature that the original 14 pages of SCRR can expand to dozens, or a hundred or more. There are some optional worksheets that can be added to the SCRR as the CO feels necessary.

The SCRR offers a great deal of value to contractors as a self-evaluation tool. If you wish (and, I strongly recommend that you do), you may use the SCRR yourself and conduct your own internal audit of your AAP program, even before the OFCCP comes knocking on your door, asking to do one of their own.

And, as you already know, the SCRR will be completed in the OFCCP's office, at the desk of the Compliance Officer. That's why it's called the desk audit phase of the compliance evaluation.

The OFCCP also has developed computer software that it makes available to its Compliance Officers. This software will compute IRAs (including standard deviations) and JAARs. All the CO needs to do is enter the raw data. All the formulas are built into the software program. That, too, has been a helpful standardization to the process. Now we don't have COs making arithmetic errors as used to happen. (Unfortunately, the OFCCP formula for calculating standard deviations is flawed.)

If you are interested in reviewing the instructions for the SCRR prepared by the OFCCP, locate a copy of the Compliance Officer's Manual and look in Section 2. It will all be there.

On-Site Visit from Your Compliance Officer

OFCCP is no longer required to make an on-site visit as part of its normal compliance evaluation. If the CO determines that it is necessary for a thorough audit, you will receive a phone call from your CO saying it is time to schedule an on-site visit. I used to think it should go without saying, but have discovered that some contractors don't bother to inspect their own facilities before the arrival of their Compliance Officer. It's in your own best interest to be sure your facility looks its best, and that you make a good impression on the CO. For example, graffiti in the bathrooms can be used as evidence of discrimination and hostile work environment. Look for yourself and get rid of any such problem ahead of the visit by your Compliance Officer. Use the checklist we provide to make sure you are ready for the visit.

You will want to be aware that every 50th audit conducted by OFCCP will involve an on-site visit whether or not there are any "indicators" of a problem. This is a procedure detailed in the agency's Active Case Management Directive which you will find in the Appendix section of this book. It is designed to be a quality control process.

- ### Opening Conference

    This step is often eliminated from the process by the current administration. If the Compliance Officer knows in advance that a site visit will be part of the review, he or she may wish to hold an opening conference with you and your CEO, or senior establishment executive. It is possible to avoid the CEO's presence, but not likely. The CO can insist on having the CEO involved. One of the primary purposes of the conference is to explain the review process, on-site activities and hear the CEO endorse the organization's policies on EEO and AA. That personal endorsement is part of the commitment from senior executives who set examples for other managers and employees to follow. If your CEO cannot look the CO in the eye and proclaim personal endorsement and support for the policies on EEO and AA, watch out.

- ### The CO Working On-Site

    If the Compliance Officer decides that a site visit to your facility is required during the review, follow the suggestions we have for you. In all likelihood you won't have this step in the process either.

    First, give the CO a tour of your facility. Explain the type of work that is done in your establishment. Talk about the working conditions and specific job requirements. Let the CO into all parts of your operation. Nothing should be secret. They have a legal right to view everything.

    I suggest you treat the CO like you would treat a visiting manager. Get him/her a private office in which to work. It should have a telephone, good lighting and good ventilation. It should have a working chair and desk. Provide the CO with paper, pencils, staplers, and any other office supplies that may be needed.

    Then have a heart-to-heart talk with the CO. Explain that you would like to work with some simple ground rules. Here are the ones I suggest you consider:

You are glad to work with the CO to get them any materials or set up interviews they need. All you ask, is that they come to you for those. Ask them not to help themselves to either records or conversations with your employees. (They should NEVER be allowed to wonder through your facility chatting with employees. Information can easily be taken out of context and when it is, you find you have trouble. There are frequently misunderstandings in those situations.)

Explain that you will provide access to any records the CO wishes to see as long as there is a legitimate reason for the CO wanting to look at them. (There are a couple considerations for you here: Some states have privacy laws that can conflict with unlimited access without legitimate business reasons. Involve your employment attorney if you aren't sure about any specific request for documents. Secondly, the CO should be able to articulate a legitimate reason for needing any document requested. If that can't be done, then you should wonder about the legitimacy of the request. Don't respond because you hear something like, "Just because I say so.")

- ## Managing Your Compliance Officer

  Understand that the CO (in official capacity with the OFCCP) has the right to subpoena any records or testimony it wishes in order to fulfill its mission in a compliance evaluation. Getting a subpoena isn't very difficult. However, making a CO go through the process of explaining and justifying why it is necessary will undoubtedly upset them to the point that you will have little or no cooperation from the CO after that.

  Those of us not in government service sometimes tend to see folks who are as bureaucrats. Keep in mind the advice given by the former head of a large state enforcement agency when he said, **"There is only one sin a contractor can commit during a compliance evaluation..."** After a brief pause, he added, **"We call that sin ... contempt of bureaucrat."** We should treat the CO with respect for the job they have to do. And, we should demand respect from them for the same reason. Expect honesty from the CO just as you are expected to be honest with him/her. No covert stuff. No sneaking around. No calling employees at home after working hours to avoid setting up interviews through you.

  Recognize that your relationship with the Compliance Officer will contribute greatly to the type of experience you have during your compliance evaluation. If that relationship is hostile, you will undoubtedly feel you never want to experience such pain again. On the other hand, a good relationship can build a mutual bond in the interest of better management and greater successes with your AAP efforts.

- ## Acceptable and Unacceptable Compliance Officer Behavior

  If, on the off chance, you should have a problem with the Compliance Officer's behavior, what do you do? The answer is, you deal with it just as you would deal with any other management problem. Try to solve the problem directly with the individual involved. If that doesn't work, escalate the issue by calling the District Director to whom the CO reports. District Directors are managers, too. They have budgets and personnel problems just like you and I and every other manager in the world. They want to know if one of their people is misbehaving just as you and I would want to know if it were one of our people causing the problem. If you deal with it in a matter of fact way, rather than in an emotional way, you will probably be well received. If not, take it a step higher and talk with the Regional Director. Inappropriate behavior cannot be tolerated. And you should not. Don't allow anyone to bully you, for any reason. It is not a part of your job. You may not like the idea of taking legal action to protect the rights of your organization, but on rare occasions that is necessary. You should be prepared to do so if that is required.

- ## Intimidation and Interference by Contractor

  In 1997, regulation changes added the following to Chapter 60:

  "(a) The contractor, subcontractor or applicant shall not harass, intimidate, threaten coerce, or discriminate against any individual because the individual has engaged in or may engage in any of the following activities:
  > *(1)   Filing a complaint;*
  > *(2)   Assisting or participating in any manner in an investigation, compliance evaluation, hearing, or any other activity related to the administration of the Order or any other Federal, state or local law requiring equal opportunity;*
  > *(3)   Opposing any act or practice made unlawful by the Order or any other Federal, state or local law requiring equal opportunity; or*
  > *(4)   Exercising any other right protected by the Order.*
  (b) The contractor, subcontractor or applicant shall ensure that all persons under its control do not engage in such harassment, intimidation, threats, coercion or discrimination. The sanctions and penalties contained in this part may be exercised by OFCCP against any contractor, subcontractor or applicant who violates this obligation." (41 CFR 60-1.32)

  Don't be antagonistic to the point of nastiness. If you do, you could be charged with obstruction.

- **Expect Requests for Additional Documentation**

  During the course of the On-Site Visit, your CO will ask to review records which you did not send to the desk audit.

  I-9 Forms - All federal enforcement agencies have been charged with the task of inspecting I-9 forms. You can expect that a request for them will be the first thing out of the Compliance Officer's mouth when you begin the on-site. I-9 Forms are, of course, required of all employers in the country, not just Affirmative Action employers. They are required under *the Immigration Reform and Control Act of 1986*. Employers are required to obtain documented proof of two things for every new employee hired after November 6, 1986. One is proof of identify (that the person is who he/she says), and the other is proof of employment eligibility in this country. Fines go as high as $1,000 for every incorrect or incomplete I-9 Form. Be sure you are using the current version of the I-9 Form. Outdated forms will also earn you a fine.[31] As of this writing, the current revision of the I-9 Form is dated 02/02/09.

  Payroll records - A complete printout of everyone on the payroll in the establishment can be something you expect the Compliance Officer to request. This will be used for several reasons. It will contain compensation information for every individual, sex and ethnic codes, job title, and perhaps some other information such as supervisor's name. If privacy issues are a concern to you, sanitize the report by replacing the employee names with designations such as "Employee #1," etc.

  Job descriptions - Complete and current job descriptions will be reviewed to be sure you have met your obligation to maintain current identification of mental and physical job requirements for every position.

  Interview and hiring records - Documentation on every selection decision made in the establishment during the past two years may be requested. It is a good idea to have these records available in file folders sorted by position opening or requisition. (Remember there is a two-year retention period now.)

  Personnel files - Individual employee personnel folders will be reviewed by the CO. The review will be looking for documentation which should be present and that which should not be present.

  Your AAP support file - All documentation which supports your good faith efforts to implement your AAP.

  Your purchase orders and vender notification letters - Determining that you have fulfilled your obligation to notify vendors and suppliers of their potential for

---

[31] http://www.uscis.gov/files/form/i-9.pdf

AAP responsibilities is one reason. It will also be necessary for the CO to confirm that your purchase orders contain the required EEO clause.

Disability accommodation request files - Showing the request, and the result of your reasonable efforts to make an accommodation.

Employment Posters – State and federal laws require posting certain employment information in a location that can be accessed by each employee every day. The "EEO Is the Law" poster from the EEOC will satisfy OFCCP's requirements. State posters alone will not. You must have federal information posted about how to file a complaint with the EEOC and OFCCP.

Other documents your CO may feel it is necessary to review.

- **Posting of Required Notices**

You will have to show the CO your employee bulletin board on which is displayed your EEO poster. You can use the government issued poster, or you can purchase one from a vendor as long as it contains the required information. You can even make your own, as long as it has the following content:

"(a) Unless alternative notices are prescribed by the Deputy Assistant Secretary, the notices which contractors are required to post by paragraphs (1) and (3) of the equal opportunity clause in Section 60-1.4 will contain the following language and be provided by the contracting or administering agencies:

"Equal Opportunity Is The Law" – Poster Content

Employers Holding Federal Contracts or Subcontracts

Applicants to and employees of companies with a Federal government contract or subcontract are protected under Federal law from discrimination on the following bases:

- ***Race, Color, Religion, Sex, National Origin***
Executive Order 11246, as amended, prohibits job discrimination on the basis of race, color, religion, sex or national origin, and requires affirmative action to ensure equality of opportunity in all aspects of employment.
- ***Individuals with Disabilities***
Section 503 of the Rehabilitation Act of 1973, as amended, protects qualified individuals from discrimination on the basis of disability in hiring, promotion, discharge, pay, fringe benefits, jog training, classification, referral, and other

aspects of employment. Disability discrimination includes not making reasonable accommodation to the known physical or mental limitations of an otherwise qualified individual with a disability who is an applicant or employee, barring undue hardship. Section 503 also requires that Federal contractors take affirmative action to employ and advance in employment qualified individuals with disabilities at all levels of employment, including the executive level.

- **_Disabled, Recently Separated, Other Protected, and Armed Forces Service Medal Veterans_**

The Vietnam Era Veterans' Readjustment Assistance Act of 1974, as amended, 38 U.S.C. 4212, prohibits job discrimination and requires affirmative action to employ and advance in employment disabled veterans, recently separated veterans (within three years of discharge or release from active duty), other protected veterans (veterans who served during a war or in a campaign or expedition for which a campaign badge has been authorized), and Armed Forces service medal veterans (veterans who, while on active duty, participated in a U.S. military operation for which an Armed Forces service medal was awarded).

- **_Retaliation_**

Retaliation is prohibited against a person who files a complaint of discrimination, participates in an OFCCP proceeding, or otherwise opposes discrimination under these Federal laws.

Any person

Who believes a contractor has violated its nondiscrimination or affirmative action obligations under the authorities above should contact immediately:

The Office of Federal Contract Compliance Programs (OFCCP), _U.S. Department of Labor, 200 Constitution Avenue N.W., Washington, DC 20210 1-800-397-6251 (toll-free) or (202) 693-1337 (TTY). OFCCP may also be contacted by e-mail at OFCCP-Public@dol.gov, or by calling an OFCCP regional or district office, listed in most telephone directories under U.S. Government, Department of Labor._

*   *   *   *   *

(41 CFR 60-1.42)

You should give serious consideration to requests from your CO for some documentation. In some cases, you may wish to discuss the request with your employment law specialist before turning over the documents. Specifically, some examples are:

- Medical records on employees.

- ◆ Discrimination complaint investigation files.
- ◆ Security-related files and records.

- **OFCCP Access to Employer Records and Removal of Records**

This is the area of greatest controversy between contractors and enforcement officials. The new 1997 regulation changes say:

"Each contractor shall permit access during normal business hours to its premises for the purpose of conducting on-site compliance evaluations and complaint investigations. Each contractor shall permit the inspecting and copying of such books and accounts and records, including computerized records, and other material as may be relevant to the matter under investigation and pertinent to compliance with the Order, and the rules and regulations promulgated pursuant thereto by the agency, or the Deputy Assistant Secretary. Information obtained in this manner shall be used only in connection with the administration of the Order, the Civil Rights Act of 1964 (as amended), and any other law that is or may be enforced in whole or in part by OFCCP." (41 CFR 60-1.43)

In those few words, the OFCCP has laid claim to any records they wish to see, AND the right to take them off-site if they feel it necessary. Confidentiality was spoken to directly in these 1997 regulation updates:

"(f) Confidentiality and relevancy of information. If the contractor is concerned with the confidentiality of such information as lists of employee names, reasons for termination, or pay data, then alphabetic or numeric coding or the use of an index of pay and pay ranges, consistent with the ranges assigned to each job group, are acceptable for purposes of the compliance evaluation. The contractor must provide full access to all relevant data on-site as required by Section 60-1.43. Where necessary, the compliance officer may take information made available during the on-site evaluation off-site for further analysis. An off-site analysis should be conducted where issues have arisen concerning deficiencies or an apparent violation which, in the judgment of the compliance officer, should be more thoroughly analyzed off-site before a determination of compliance is made. The contractor must provide all data determined by the compliance officer to be necessary for off-site analysis. Such data may only be coded if the contractor makes the key to the code available to the compliance officer. If the contractor believes that particular information which is to be taken off-site is not relevant to compliance with the Executive Order, the contractor may request a ruling by the OFCCP District/Area Director. The OFCCP District/Area Director shall issue a ruling within 10 days. The contractor may appeal that ruling to the OFCCP Regional Director within 10 days. The Regional Director shall issue a final

ruling within 10 days. **Pending a final ruling, the information in question must be made available to the compliance officer off-site,** *but shall be considered a part of the investigatory file and subject to the provisions of paragraph (g) of this section. The agency shall take all necessary precautions to safeguard the confidentiality of such information until a final determination is made. Such information may not be copied by OFCCP and access to the information shall be limited to the compliance officer and personnel involved in the determination of relevancy. Data determined to be not relevant to the investigation will be returned to the contractor immediately.*
(g) Public Access to Information. The disclosure of information obtained from a contractor will be evaluated pursuant to the public inspection and copying provisions of the Freedom of Information Act, 5 U.S.C. 552, and the Department of Labor's implementing regulations at 29 CFR Part 70." (41 CFR 60-1.20)
(Bold face type added for emphasis.)

You can imagine that the contractor community has yelled loudly about this part of the regulatory changes. There was a great deal of input about the question of OFCCP taking records off-site. Contractors expressed concern over "leaks" of sensitive proprietary materials which could damage a competitive advantage in the marketplace, and release of the same sensitive materials through *Freedom of Information Act* requests. The Society for Human Resource Management (SHRM) voiced its opposition to the blanket records access and copying policy as did the Equal Employment Advisory Committee (EEAC), both employer representatives. It was all to no avail, however, because the OFCCP marched over all objections and claimed what it intended from the onset. The only hope for employers faced with a situation they feel is just untenable is to take the issue to court. If you want a good attorney, call me. I'll give you a referral.

This right to remove records from the contractor's worksite has been reinforced in the 2007 regulatory update for Veterans affirmative action. In part it says, *"An analysis and evaluation of the affirmative action program (or any part thereof) and supporting documentation, and other documents related to the contractor's personnel policies and employment actions that may be relevant to a determination of whether the contractor has complied with the requirements of the Executive Order and regulations..."* (41 CFR 60-300.60(a)(2))

It seems there is no choice any longer. One can only negotiate preservation of highly sensitive documents and suggest that the CO review them at the contractor's facility. The CO is under no obligation any more to agree to such a request.

- ### FOIA Requests for Release of Confidential Information

This issue has sometimes spurred heated arguments between OFCCP and contractors.

FOIA Exemption 4 (Confidential Business Information) could give the agency reason for refusing to release compensation data and other sensitive contractor information. The problem lies in expecting agency people to understand what contractors view as sensitive information. For that reason, contractors should adopt an attitude that they will take care of themselves.

OFCCP claims it has never released any document regarding a contractor's compliance evaluation while that audit as still open. They don't make the same claim about post-audit release.

Freedom of Information Act
Exemption #4

The fourth exemption protects from public disclosure two types of information: Trade secrets and confidential business information. A trade secret is a commercially valuable plan, formula, process, or device. This is a narrow category of information. An example of a trade secret is the recipe for a commercial food product.

The second type of protected data is commercial or financial information obtained from a person and privileged or confidential. The courts have held that data qualifies for withholding if disclosure by the government would be likely to harm the competitive position of the person who submitted the information. Detailed information on a company's marketing plans, profits, or costs can qualify as confidential business information. Information may also be withheld if disclosure would be likely to impair the government's ability to obtain similar information in the future.

Only information obtained from a person other than a government agency qualifies under the fourth exemption. A person is an individual, a partnership, or a corporation. Information that an agency created on its own cannot normally be withheld under exemption 4.

Although there is no formal requirement under the FOIA, many agencies will notify a submitter of business information that disclosure of the information is being considered. The submitter then has an opportunity to convince the agency that the information qualifies for withholding. A submitter can also file suit to block disclosure under the FOIA. Such lawsuits are generally referred to as "reverse" FOIA lawsuits because the FOIA is being used in an attempt to prevent rather than to require the disclosure of information. A reverse FOIA lawsuit may be filed when the submitter of documents and the government disagree whether the information is exempt.

It is a good idea to place a "Notice" in the beginning of your AAP binder that tells OFCCP officials the entire document is protected as confidential and private information. In that notice you should also require notification of any FOIA request for release so you will have ample opportunity to respond and resist the release of your confidential data.

TMA INC. AAP

<u>NOTICE</u>

This Equal Opportunity/Affirmative Action Plan is not for use or disclosure outside TMA Inc. except by written approval of the company President or designee. It is intended exclusively for TMA Inc. 's use in internal critical self-analysis and is intended to be protected from discovery or use by parties other than TMA Inc. by the critical self-analysis privilege. The following disclaimers pertain to this Affirmative Action Plan.

❑ This Affirmative Action Plan is not and does not purport to be an agreement between TMA Inc. and any employee, employees, or employee representative.

❑ TMA Inc. reserves the right to unilaterally modify, delete, or add to the guidelines, recommendations, or other language contained herein at any time. Such modifications may be made only with the concurrence of the President or designee.

❑ No statement published by TMA Inc. in this Affirmative Action Plan is intended to grant nor should be construed as granting any employee an employment contract of fixed duration, nor is this Affirmative Action Plan intended to create nor should it be construed as creating an implied contract or express contract of employment. This will serve notice to all employees that nothing in this Affirmative Action Plan is intended to create nor should be construed as creating any contractual or employment relationship that does not otherwise exist.

❑ All information contained herein is intended as general policy statements of guidelines and recommendations and not as a contract or any other commitment.

❑ The guidelines and recommendations set forth herein do not represent or purport to represent terms and conditions of employment applicable to TMA Inc. employees.

❑ Nothing herein should be interpreted as a limitation on the right to discipline or discharge or a limitation on the possible grounds for discipline or discharge.

❑ Nothing herein should be interpreted as establishing hiring quotas or "set asides." This plan establishes voluntary aspirational goals intended to maintain and increase TMA Inc. 's consciousness in recruitment efforts with respect to minorities and females. It is a description of TMA Inc. 's good faith efforts to meet its affirmative action obligations under federal law and regulations.

❑ The materials contained in this Affirmative Action Plan are deemed to constitute trade secrets, operations information, confidential statistical data and other confidential commercial and financial data, within the meaning of the *Freedom of Information Act*, 5 U.S.C. Sec. 552, Title VII of the *Civil Rights Act of 1964* (as amended), 42 U.S.C. Secs. 2000e et seq., the *Trade Secrets Act*, 18 U.S.C. Sec. 1905, and 44 U.S.C. Sec. 3508, the disclosure of which is prohibited by law and would subject the individual making the disclosure to criminal and/or civil sanctions. Any request for information must be handled as described in 29 C.F.R. Sec. 70.26, requiring a pre-disclosure notice to the contractor.   TMA Inc. expects any request for disclosure received by the government, or any of its agencies or offices, will cause immediate written notification to the President and General Manager of TMA Inc. . (<u>E.E.O.C. v. General Telephone Co. of the North</u>

West, 885 F.2d 575, 578 [9th Cir. 1989]; Coates v. Johnson & Johnson, 756 F.2d 524, 551-552 [7th Cir. 1985]). Any release of the information contained in this Affirmative Action Program would be arbitrary and capricious in violation of the *Administration Procedure Act* and not in accordance with the law.

551-552 [7th Cir. 1985]). Any release of the information contained in this Affirmative Action Program would be arbitrary and capricious in violation of the *Administration Procedure Act* and not in accordance with the law.

Retention or disclosure of information relating to identifiable individuals may constitute a violation of the *Privacy Act of 1974.*

- **Employee Interviews**

One key reason for being on-site is for access to employees for the purpose of conducting interviews with them. The CO will ask you to set those up by making arrangements for employees to come in and talk. There are some general guidelines you should follow in this situation.

Given the opportunity, provide a slate of interview candidates to the CO. Include on your suggested list people representing management, non-management, each ethnic group, both males and females, and employees who are disabled and veterans, if you know that. The CO is not obliged to accept your list, and may simply select off the payroll list the individuals to be interviewed. But, I suggest you try. The reason is simple. You can put people on your suggested list who you know to be capable of communicating in a one-on-one situation. The last thing you want is for the CO to interview someone who gets their tongue tangled and can't put a coherent thought together during a conversation.

When managers are interviewed, you should always be present. Management people are legally agents of the organization and anything they say can be legally accepted as the official position of the employer. That being the case, you will want to be present to be sure there are no misunderstandings that the CO might carry out of the interview.

If a non-management person asks for a union representative to be present, let it happen. If a non-management person asks you to be present, agree to the request. Otherwise, I suggest you not be present during interviews with non-management people because you don't want to intimidate them or even give the appearance to the CO that you are trying to intimidate the employee.

For all employees, management and non-management alike, give them the benefit of a short briefing about why they are being asked to talk with the CO. Tell them that they are not in trouble. Explain the compliance evaluation process and help them understand that they will be expected to tell the truth about the things the CO asks them to discuss. Help them relax. People who are relaxed can communicate better.

During these interviews the Compliance Officer will be asking questions like these: Have you ever heard the terms "Equal Employment Opportunity" or "Affirmative Action" around here? Have you ever seen any documents that refer to EEO or AA? Do you know whether or not the organization has any policies that relate to EEO or AA? Have those subjects ever come up in any meetings you have attended? Has there ever been any training offered to employees about EEO and AA?

Employee interviews will be the opportunity for the CO to probe for indications of any discrimination in the workplace. Remember, that uncovering discrimination is one of the key purposes of a compliance evaluation. So, expect to have questions like these asked of your employees: Have you generally been treated fairly in your job? Have you ever seen any behavior in the workplace which you considered unacceptable? If so, tell me about that. Have you ever been discriminated against by your manager? If so, how and in what circumstances?

Be aware that OFCCP has been known to ask for lists of former employees in the establishment being audited. They wish to speak with former employees to ask why they left and if their leaving had anything to do with discriminatory treatment by the employer.

If the Compliance Officer finds a prima facie case of discrimination, an investigation will be opened. Your compliance evaluation will not conclude until that investigation is also ended.

Therein lies the reason that it is hard to judge how long the on-site portion of your compliance evaluation will last. I have known them to take from one-half day to several months. (Isn't that a sobering prospect.)

After all the interviews have been conducted, any complaints have been investigated, and all records have been reviewed, the Compliance Officer will tell you it is time for the Closing Conference.

During the closing conference, you and your CEO will again be present with the CO. It is at this meeting you will be officially told the outcome of your compliance evaluation. As a professional HR Manager, you will know what that outcome is ahead of time, because you will be talking with the CO on a daily basis. You should avoid any surprises in the closing conference by briefing your CEO ahead of time on what type of outcome to expect.

Possible Outcomes from Your Compliance Evaluation

You will receive a piece of written correspondence from OFCCP that tells you the result of your compliance evaluation. However, you should know what it will say from the exit conference you have with your Compliance Officer.

Letter of Compliance and Letter of Commitment

Effective August 5, 1998, OFCCP discontinued the use of "Letters of Compliance" and "Letters of Commitment."

Compliance Evaluation Closure Letter for Minor or No Violations

There is a new "Closure Letter" being used by the agency. Officially, the title of the letter is "Compliance Evaluation Closure Letter for Minor or No Violations." Paragraphs will be inserted or omitted based on whether the contractor was found to have no violations or minor violations. Where contractors used to commonly draft their own letters of commitment for technical violations, the agency has taken over that process with this standardized approach. Under current rules, your letter will not become legally effective until it is accepted by Charles James (national OFCCP director) or 45 days have passed from the date of the letter.

Conciliation Agreement

Most compliance evaluations conclude with a Conciliation Agreement. These are contracts for remedy of the out-of-compliance condition discovered by the CO when those violations are "serious" in nature. These might include such things as:

- Discrimination is found in the establishment.
- AAP submission did not reflect a reasonable effort.
- Contractor failed to demonstrate good faith effort at implementation of AAP or failed to document its implementation activities.
- Failure to comply with a past agreement with OFCCP.

Enforcement Proceedings

If you are not in compliance with the regulations, and you choose not to come into compliance, the OFCCP will begin enforcement against your organization. There are two types of enforcement: administrative and judicial. They will involve either an administrative law judge or the agency can pursue suit against you in federal court.

Each of these enforcement routes will take a considerable amount of time, and the ultimate debarment penalty will be a long time in coming. When it eventually arrives for the unlucky contractor, it means that organization will not be able to participate in federal contracts for up to five years. In fiscal year 1995, there were 5 contractors debarred. Not a lot considering the thousands of contractors across the country. On the other hand, that is a 500% increase over each of the previous four years. Hardly any debarments have occurred in recent years. Remember, the agency is seeking out systemic discrimination because that is where the "pay off" lies in political terms.

OFCCP Follow Up After the Compliance evaluation

If you are in compliance and get a Closure Letter for No Violations, you should have no follow up from the OFCCP for another two years.

If you are out of compliance and receive either a Conciliation Agreement, or a Closure Letter for Minor Violations, you will experience follow up visits from the Compliance Officer at frequencies that will be specified in your agreement. Ordinarily, those occur every six months for up to two years.

If you are out of compliance, and recalcitrant, you can expect to be living with OFCCP representatives until you are debarred as a federal contractor.

While it is not true that good guys finish last, it is true that you have to protect your own back side during a compliance evaluation. You want to have done all of the things you said in your AAP you were planning to do. And, you want to manage the compliance evaluation so it goes as smoothly as you want for it to go.

Violation of Conciliation Agreement or Minor Violations Letter

1997 regulatory changes caused the following to be added to Chapter 60:

"(a)(4) In any proceeding involving an alleged violation of a conciliation agreement OFCCP may seek enforcement of the agreement itself and shall not be required to present proof of the underlying violations resolved by the agreement." (41 CFR 60-1.34)

As it says, if you fail to keep up your agreement under any signed conciliation agreement you will find yourself facing enforcement procedures which will be aimed at removing your government contracting privileges. There is no need for the government to prove any of the violations cited in the prior agreements. That is assumed, now under these latest changes in the regulations.

Unless you are very wealthy, or just don't care about continuing your contract with the government, you would be best advised to follow through with any corrections specified in conciliation agreements.

Records Required During an OFCCP Compliance Evaluation of Affirmative Action Programs

Mandatory Records
Specifically mentioned in the Regulations

Executive Order 11246 (Minorities & Women) [41 CFR 60-1-4, 60-20, 60-30, 60-40, 60-50, 60-60]

- Written AAP for each establishment, updated annually if employer has 50 or more employees <u>and</u> $50,000 or more in federal contracts [41 CFR 60-1.40 (a)(c)]
- Support data [41 CFR 60-2.12 (m)] ... will include but not be limited to ...
  - Progression line charts
  - Seniority rosters
  - Applicant flow data
  - Applicant rejection ratios indicating minority and sex status (one requirement for adverse impact data)
- Analysis of hiring practices, upgrading, transfer, and promotion for past year -- for minority group personnel [41 CFR 60-1.40 (b)(2)] -- (interpreted by OFCCP as a requirement to conduct adverse impact testing)
- Standard Form 100 for past three years (EEO-1, EEO-4, EEO-5 or EEO-6 [41 CFR 60-1.7 (a)(1)]
- EEO Poster [41 CFR 60-1.42]
- Advertising EEO disclaimer [41 CFR 60-1.4 (a)(1)]

- Seven EO clauses in federal sub-contracts [41 CFR 60-1.4 (a-d)]
- Certification of non-segregated facilities [41 CFR 60-1.8 (b)]

Vietnam Era Veterans Readjustment Assistance Act of 1974 (VEVRAA) [41 CFR 60-300]

- Invitation to self-identify
- AAP available for inspection by applicants and employees
- Veterans' EEO Clause in federal contracts and sub-contracts
- Mandatory job listing with State employment service
- VEVRAA poster notice
- Union notification (if appropriate)
- VETS-100A (VETS-100) reports for past 2 years
- Identification of veterans in each category
- Outreach & recruiting for qualified veterans

Rehabilitation Act of 1973, Section 503 [41 CFR 60-741]

- Invitation to self-identify
- AAP available for inspection by applicants and employees
- EEO clauses in federal sub-contracts
- Disability poster notice
- Union notification
- Review of personnel processes including physical and mental requirements of each job in the establishment
- Review of outreach and recruitment practices

Additional Records OFCCP Will Review During Compliance evaluations
(The following records include the current year and past year of dating.)

- Personnel files
- Job descriptions
- <u>All</u> resumes and employment application forms
- <u>All</u> interviewer notes and other recruiting and selection records
- Logs of <u>all</u> database access/searches for candidates
- Applicant definition and applicant tracking/retention procedures
- Training records
- I-9 Forms (work authorization)
- Discrimination charges
- Compensation records
- Performance evaluation records
- Exit interview records
- Sources and backup data for availability analysis (2-factor)
- Employment test validation studies
- Records demonstrating good faith efforts, including: tuition reimbursement programs, employee orientation checklists including EEO/AA subjects/policies, internal audit and review procedures, lists of recruiting sources, recruitment advertising examples targeted to women and minorities or veterans and disabled
- Other posters such as OSHA notice

CHAPTER 12

GLASS CEILING REVIEWS

(CORPORATE MANAGEMENT COMPLIANCE EVALUATION)

Notes

GLASS CEILING REVIEWS
◆◆◆
CORPORATE MANAGEMENT COMPLIANCE EVALUATION

"Glass Ceiling" is a term that was coined to describe the phenomenon of minorities and women climbing to certain levels within a corporate organization, but being blocked by an invisible barrier from attaining truly senior executive positions. "You can see it, but you can't reach it because of that barrier." The original intent of affirmative action programs (outreach and recruiting) worked well to introduce minorities and women, disabled and veterans to entry and mid-levels of contractor organizations, but progress seemed to halt before they achieved senior levels. It is generally agreed that the glass ceiling represents discrimination against minorities and women, albeit not always intentional. (Discrimination doesn't have to be intentional to be "bad.")

On November 14, 1991 the OFCCP issued Chapter 5 of its Federal Contract Compliance Manual. The sole subject of that new chapter is the content and process by which Glass Ceiling reviews will be conducted by the agency. It is an invaluable source of help to contractors who wish to test their own organizations in a self audit, before the real thing happens.

A brief look at the history of this subject takes us back to the late 1980s when Ronald Reagan was President. Ms. Cari Dominguez had been recruited away from her position in San Francisco as the Vice President of EEO/AA for Bank of America to become National Director of the

OFCCP. (This is the same Cari Dominguez who would later become Chair of the Equal Employment Opportunity Commission (EEOC).) Under Secretary of Labor Lynn Martin and later, Secretary Elizabeth Dole, Director Dominguez crafted the glass ceiling project. It began as a study, moved to public comment, and then became a revised standard in the OFCCP's implementation guidelines. With the passage of the Civil Rights Act of 1991, under President George H. W. Bush, money was allocated for further study of the glass ceiling issue. The commission charged with that task made its report to the public late in 1995. Essentially, it confirmed the reality of such discrimination, and that OFCCP review of contractors' programs in executive levels was a good way to contribute to correcting the problem.

OFCCP has conducted 40-45 Corporate Reviews each year for the past several years. Since 1991, **they have never found a case of illegal discrimination they could take to court**.

Outline of Review Process and Content

Officially called Corporate Management Compliance Evaluations, glass ceiling audits are quite different from other compliance reviews done by the OFCCP. First, they will only be conducted in a corporate headquarters establishment. Next, they will focus more on decision making of CEOs and other senior executives, than on job group analysis.

Supply and service contractors with 4,000 or more employees in the organization and more than one reporting subordinate establishment are included in the selection pool for corporate-level reviews. Contractors that have successfully undergone a corporate-level audit within the past 24 months will be excluded.

Functional establishments will be included in the same pool with Corporate Management Compliance Evaluation candidates.[32]

New Regulations on Glass Ceiling Reviews

The December 2000 regulations say: *"(a) Purpose. Corporate Management Compliance Evaluations are designed to ascertain whether individuals are encountering artificial barriers to advancement into mid-level and senior corporate management, i.e., glass*

---

[32] http://www.dol.gov/ofccp/regs/compliance/faqs/cmcefaqs.htm

ceiling. During Corporate Management Compliance Evaluations, special attention is given to those components of the employment process that affect advancement into mid- and senior-level positions.

(b) ***If, during the course of a Corporate Management Compliance Evaluation, it comes to the attention of OFCCP that problems exist at establishments outside the corporate headquarters, OFCCP may expand the compliance evaluation beyond the headquarters establishment.*** *At its discretion, OFCCP may direct its attention to and request relevant data for any and all areas within the corporation to ensure compliance with Executive Order 11246."* (41 CFR 60-2.30) (Bold type added for emphasis.)

As a matter of policy, the OFCCP has laid down these guidelines for glass ceiling reviews:

- Corporate Management Compliance Evaluations will occur only at corporate headquarters establishments.

- A Corporate Management Compliance Evaluation will be done concurrently with an ordinary compliance review in that headquarters establishment. (Two different compliance reviews being done in the same establishment at the same time.)

- A team of OFCCP management will conduct the Corporate Management Compliance Evaluation while a Compliance Officer conducts the normal compliance review.

The subjects addressed in a Corporate Management Compliance Evaluation are normally very sensitive in private sector organizations. And, because they are sensitive, often only the CEO or other senior officials have access to the information that is discussed in one of these reviews.

Due to the nature of those subjects, the OFCCP initially recognized that its credibility would be questioned if it assigned Compliance Officers to conduct such reviews. Compliance Officers, almost universally, have never been CEOs. Most have never been senior officials of any organization. Although, technically, the Compliance Officer job is not entry level, it is close. The OFCCP, for credibility, needed to have people with mid-level and senior-level management experience discussing glass ceiling issues with these senior contractor executives. At first, teams of three agency executives were used to conduct glass ceiling reviews. In the first study, those three reviewers came from the National Director and Region Director levels of the agency. Once it was demonstrated that the process would work, District Directors were trained in the process of glass ceiling reviews and now participate in those review teams, expanding the agency's "capacity" for glass ceiling reviews. In the past several years, we have seen glass ceiling reviews performed by ordinary Compliance Officers with occasional involvement from District Directors.

Focus of Corporate Management Compliance Evaluations

Corporate Management Compliance Evaluations will focus on: *"(a) ...developmental and selection processes and practices for advancement into mid- and upper-level corporate management positions, and (b) treatment in such positions."* *(FCCM, Par 5A03)*

These subject areas will be addressed during a Corporate Management Compliance Evaluation:

- How management jobs are filled, including use of executive search firms and employee referrals.

- Succession planning for internal movement of candidates.

- Promotion and transfer process at these levels.

- Movement across AAP establishments for developmental purposes.

- Movement within headquarters.

- Performance appraisals for executives.

- Developmental assignments for executives including special projects, task forces, corporate committees, special assistants or executive assistants.

- Training offered executive candidates including management skills and executive development.

- Mentoring and networking programs.

- Executive compensation packages including bonuses (cash and stock), stock awards, stock options, and perquisites.

- Recognition programs including awards and honors.

- Termination policies and procedures for executives.

Notice of a Corporate Management Compliance Evaluation

If you are selected as one of the 50 or so glass ceiling reviews each year, you will receive a scheduling letter much like the one issued for normal compliance reviews. How contractors are picked for this "honor" is still much of a mystery. My guess is OFCCP management has 100% discretion in the matter.

You will know you have been selected for a Corporate Management Compliance Evaluation because your scheduling letter will be directed at your headquarters establishment AND it will be signed by a Region Director, not a District Director. Other than that, your Scheduling Letter will look like any other.

Obviously, when the notice arrives, you will want to alert your management attorney and your CEO. Both will be actively involved in the process, or should be. (Unfortunately, when it comes to things like senior executive succession planning and compensation, HR Managers are not always "in the loop" as they say. It is problematic, therefore, whether or not you will participate in the compliance review discussions with the OFCCP and your CEO. You will have to work that one out for yourself with the CEO.)

Briefing your CEO on what to expect from the review is critical. (You could win a friend.) A great deal of time will be spent by your CEO in discussions with the OFCCP. A great deal of time. The CEO needs to understand that and be prepared for it. It will definitely mean some calendar clearing. But, as with so many other things, we shift our priorities, right?

Background Information Gathered by OFCCP

At the same time the agency sends your organization its notice of scheduling, it sends a "Request for Literature Search" to the U.S. Department of Labor Library. This letter requests a search of the following sources of information on your organization:

- Industrial manuals and handbooks, such as <u>Moody's</u>, <u>Hoover's</u>, and <u>Standard and Poor's</u>.

- Publications providing information on company histories and the backgrounds of top officials, such as the <u>International Directory of Company Histories</u>, <u>Reference Book of Corporate Management - America's Corporate Leaders</u>.

- Articles on the corporation within the past two years in business oriented newspapers and periodicals, such as <u>The Wall Street Journal</u>, <u>Forbes</u>, <u>Fortune</u>.

This information will be reviewed and analyzed to identify information in three main areas: *"(1) corporate organization; (2) corporate history and trends; and (3) backgrounds of top corporate officials."* (*FCCM, Par. 5B08*)

The management team assigned to your review will be attempting to answer these questions prior to its first meeting with you: (Questions come directly from FCCM, Par. 5B08)

- What are its major components -- variously called businesses, groups, divisions, etc. -- and subsidiaries, both domestic and foreign?

- What are their major functions or products?

- Where are they located?

- About what percentage of total corporate personnel do they employ? -- e.g., the ADC Products Group accounts for about 40% of total corporate employment.

- When was the corporation founded?

- What was its initial main business? How has this changed over time?

- Has the corporation undergone any recent mergers with or acquisitions of another company?

- What have been its most and least profitable components over the last several years?

- Has the corporation recently undergone or is it projecting substantial growth or cutbacks in particular areas of its business?

- Has it recently been awarded or lost any major contracts? In what business areas?

- What are its long-range projections for areas of business growth?

- To what degree have top corporate officials been appointed from internal vs. external sources?

- What type of background is valued in top management officials?

Then, in addition, the agency will request copies of your company's two most recent Form 10-K reports from the Securities and Exchange Commission (SEC). It will also request copies of your two most recent EEO-1 reports from the Joint Committee on Reporting (of which the OFCCP is a partner with the EEOC). A report will be pulled from the CRIS (Compliance Review Information System) data base managed by the OFCCP. It will detail information about any compliance reviews or complaint investigations conducted in your establishments nationally over the past two years.

The OFCCP will also contact any identified organizations from which you request candidates for management jobs, asking them for their experience with your company concerning the referrals they sent and their impressions of your organization's treatment of minorities and women in management positions. The Regional Director of the Women's' Bureau will also be contacted to determine if the Bureau has any information concerning your corporation's EEO posture toward women in management jobs.

The Desk Audit Phase

All of this background information will be summarized and analyzed. And, all of the materials you have copied and sent in response to the Scheduling Letter will also be summarized and analyzed, just as in a normal compliance review. There may be a Compliance Officer assigned to assist with this part of the process. In this situation, though, there will be an emphasis on determining: (according to FCCM, Par. 5C)

- What is the management level at which there is a marked decline in the participation of minorities and women?

- What type of management jobs exist at that level, both generally and by major functional area (e.g., vice-president, director, senior analyst; finance, legal, sales)?

- What type of jobs held by minorities and/or women below that level are probable feeder groups?

- What information has been provided on developmental and/or selection processes that may apply to jobs around that level?

- What is the amount and type of employment activity in job groups around that level?

There will be an analysis of absences or concentrations of minorities and women in your senior executive/management jobs by department, by function, and by job level. Analysis will be made of differences in representation for "line" and "staff" jobs. For each senior executive title, identification will be made of internal feeder groups, and analysis of minority/female representation in those feeder groups will be completed.

On-Site Review Phase

The initial meeting with your CEO and senior executives on-site will be to clarify information about your corporate organization, general corporate background and to discuss the broad questions of:

- What does the contractor value in candidates for mid- and senior-level positions generally?

- Has the contractor developed any special program(s) designed to help improve the access of minorities and/or women to such positions?
 (FCCM, Par. 5G)

Additional meetings and additional questions will be aimed at identifying what the organization views as its top management titles and how they are filled, internally or externally. If internal supplies are used, questions about candidate pools will be posed. The review team will explore such things as what reward systems you use to retain key personnel at those senior levels.

During interviews of your management people, senior or not, either you or your management attorney (or both) should be present. Exploration of topics in these sessions will usually begin with a discussion about "**corporate culture**." The agency is interested in determining what the company values and how it determines whether or not individuals "fit" into that culture.

Then, discussion will turn to **standards or qualifications for management jobs**. Expect questions such as: (from FCCM, Par. 5G06)

- If advanced and/or specialized degrees are viewed as important, in what fields? For what positions? How important is the specific college or university? Does the company sponsor full-time educational programs for any of its employees?

- How much company service is typical for employees at and above the management level where minority/female participation declines?

- If successful profit and loss responsibility is important, in what areas of the business is one most likely to gain that experience? Least likely? At what management level does one usually gain it? Does that vary from one business area to another? Is the number of profit and loss centers increasing, declining, remaining the same?

- If international assignments are important, at what point in one's career? How are persons chosen?

- If exposure to different facets of the business are important, which business areas should that cover? How does one learn such exposure is important to advancement? How does one obtain such exposure?

You can expect discussion about the process followed by your organization in filling management jobs. Both internal and external search processes will be covered. Some of the questions you will be asked about **external candidate searches** will include:

- Is applicant flow data complete for all management jobs filled in the past year, including those filled by candidates from executive search firms. (*"Note that the decision to seek external candidates for a job can in itself be a selection decision where there are internal candidates with similar qualifications. While filling a job by hire rather than by promotion or transfer (or vice versa) is, in itself, EEO neutral, the [reviewing officers] should be alert to any patterns that correlate with race, sex or another prohibited factor." (FCCM, Par. 5H00))*

- What evidence is there that executive search firms, when used by the company, included qualified minorities, women, individuals with handicaps and covered veterans among those recruited and referred for listed jobs?

- How has the company informed the search firms it uses about its EEO/AA policy?

- Who is responsible for monitoring search firm referrals for EEO/AA?

- Have minorities and women, as well as others, been hired from among search firm referrals? Have they been among the referred? If not, was any effort made to expand the candidate pool?

Employee referrals as a source of candidates for new hires is, in itself, EEO neutral. *"However, where the result of such a reliance effectively excludes minorities/women from the candidate pool for jobs above a certain level and/or in certain fields, the contractor has an obligation to make a good faith effort to broaden its applicant pool -- e.g., by supplementing such employee referrals with sources able to refer qualified minorities/women for the jobs involved. Additionally, such a practice may be discriminatory where there is evidence that the intent behind reliance on employee referrals is to exclude minorities/women from consideration for certain jobs, or where such reliance has a demonstrable and significant disparate impact on minorities/women, and does not serve significant business purposes." (FCCM, Par. 5H03)* Expect questions about your employee referral program to include: (from FCCM, Par.5H)

- To what degree do you rely upon employee referrals for mid- to upper level management jobs? Is this practice formal or informal?

- What is most often the relationship between the employee and the person referred? (e.g., used to work together? went to the same school? met through a professional association? belong to the same club? a neighbor? a relative? a personal friend?)

- Have you received employee referrals of minority/female candidates, as well as others, for jobs at that level? Who were they? Were any hired?

- Have you let employees likely to refer for jobs at that level know that the company is actively interested in referrals of minorities and women as well as others? How did you let them know this?

Once the discussion comes around to the subject of **succession planning**, you know it will get lively. Here are some of the questions you can expect to be raised: (from FCCM, Par. 5I)

- Is there any planning for likely successors if a particular management position were to vacate?

- Down to what management level does any such planning extend?

- Does it include both short-term and long-term planning? -- i.e., persons who are ready now for the position vs. those who may be ready after further developmental experiences?

- Does it include consideration of candidates in intermediate headquarters and other lower-level establishments as well as at corporate headquarters?

- If so, how are such non-headquarters candidates identified? How are headquarters candidates identified?

- Are there any written materials describing the plan and/or offering guidance on selection and development of candidates?

- How often is the plan reviewed? By whom? Does anyone review for EEO aspects? Who is responsible for that EEO review?

- What is the race/sex composition of persons identified as potential permanent successors? How does that compare to the race/sex composition of the total candidate pool for those management jobs?

- Where the proportion of minorities/women identified in the plan is well below their proportion in the general pool, what explanation was found in the EEO audit?

- What kind of developmental experiences may be identified? (training on-site or off-site, rational assignments, special projects) Are there any individual developmental plans?

- Below the level where there may be specific succession planning, does the company have any mechanism for identifying persons with a high potential for advancement?

- Does the company identify promotables separately from a "high potential" group?

Another area of interest to the review team will be **promotions and transfers**. They will give special attention to (1) jobs around the management level where minority/female participation declines, and (2) movement from lower-level establishments to corporate headquarters and vice versa. In this arena, expect questions such as: (from FCCM, Par. 5I)

- Are promotion (transfer) opportunities made known to potential candidates? How? Up to what level? What happens above that level?

- Are openings at corporate headquarters made known to persons in lower-level establishments as well as to persons at headquarters? How?

- Are openings at lower-level establishments made known to persons at corporate headquarters? How?

- Are there any restrictions on cross-establishment moves? Must current manager approve?

- Is willingness to relocate important?

- Are overseas assignments important?

- What happens if someone refuses a job offer requiring relocation? Is the effect on career prospects similar for all?

At some time during the discussion, talk will turn to the issue of **performance appraisals**. Here are some questions from FCCM, Par. 5I dealing with that subject:

- Describe the performance appraisal process for Exempt staff. Is the same appraisal process used for all Exempt staff? Different for Managers vs. Professionals? Different at higher grade levels?

- Is the result of the appraisal a numeric rating? Narrative rating? Both?

- If numeric, what is the highest and lowest score? How are people generally distributed? What score is generally needed for promotion?

- Are there any written guidelines on how to do the appraisal? Is reference made to EEO?

- How often are appraisals done? Who appraises? Who approves? What is the degree of employee input?

- Does the process include any career planning? Short-term, long-term or both?

- Are there any "benchmark" special appraisals -- e.g., career review at 5, 10, 15 years?

- Does the company monitor appraisal results for EEO? If so, how? What have been the results?

- Are raises (bonuses, promotions) based on appraisals? If so, what is the relationship?

The role of **individual visibility** will come up also. Expect the agency to ask: (from FCCM, Par. 5I)

- Does the company make much use of special project teams and/or task forces?

- If so, in what areas of the business? How are people chosen?

- What project teams/task forces are currently operating?

- Does anyone monitor EEO in selections for such teams/task forces? What is the race/sex composition of each?

- Are project teams/task forces viewed as developmental assignments?

Corporate committees and **special assistants/executive assistants** sometimes play a role in development and/or selection of managers for upper level positions. Some of the questions the OFCCP will have for you about these issues include: (from FCCM, Par. 5I)

- How many standing committees are there in the corporation? What is the title and purpose of each?

- Who appoints the members of each committee? Who heads each? Who is on it by race/sex?

- Where membership is discretionary, does anyone audit for EEO?

- Does the company have any special assistant/executive assistant type of positions?

- If so, in what functional areas? How are they filled?

- How long does the incumbent usually stay in such a position? Is the job considered rotational? What is the most likely subsequent type of assignment?

- What is the race/sex of those holding such jobs now? In the past two years?

- Where are past incumbents now? If minorities/women have held such positions in the past, has their subsequent progress been comparable to that of nonminorities/men who have held such positions?

The roles of **training, executive development and mentoring/networking** will be explored during the review meetings. Of course, the agency is interested in seeing if minorities and women have equal access to these programs if they are important to an individual's chances for advancement. Here then, are some questions you can expect in these areas: (from FCCM, Par. 5I)

- What does developmental training consist of? Is it offered in-house or off-site or both?

- Who is eligible for that training?

- Is this training a requirement of the assignment? Have any people been placed into the assignment without that training? What was the race/sex?

- How does one learn of the training? How is one selected for it?

- Who monitors participation in training to ensure EEO?

- What is the race/sex composition of persons participating over the last year?

- How does that compare with the race/sex of those eligible?

- If there is a substantial difference between the proportion of minorities/women eligible and those participating, what cause was found?

- How are persons selected for executive development programs?

- Among managers at the eligible level, who has been sent by race/sex? Have minorities/women participated in the same programs as their peers?

- If minorities/women have not been sent, are there plans to do so? Was their predecessor sent? At what point in his/her career? To what program?

- Does the company have any formal mentoring program? If so, is it described in writing? Who participates?

- How are persons matched with a mentor?

- Does the company have a management club that provides a formal opportunity for managers at a given level to network across division or establishment lines? What level of manager is eligible to join? Have minority/female managers at that level been offered an opportunity to join?

- Does the company subsidize membership fees for its managers with any outside professional associations and/or social clubs? Have minority/female managers been offered an opportunity to participate in that benefit?

One of the most sensitive subjects to private sector companies is **executive compensation**. It is information which employers protect with great care. Now, in your Corporate Management Compliance Evaluation, your senior executives will have the opportunity to discuss this subject with the OFCCP review team. You can expect questions such as these: (from the FCCM, Par. 5J)

- Are bonuses granted to any management people? In what form? Cash? Stock? Both?

- At what level are employees eligible for cash bonuses? Have any bonuses been granted to persons below that level?

- How are decisions on bonus amounts and recipients made? By whom?

- In the last bonus cycle, what proportion of those eligible, by race/sex, received a cash bonus? What was the average cash bonus by race/sex?

- Who monitors for EEO in allocation of cash bonuses?

- Who is eligible for stock bonuses? Have any stock bonuses ever been given to anyone outside this eligible group?

- How are decisions on stock bonuses made? By whom?

- What is the number of shares received and the cash value of those shares for each recipient by race and sex?

- Does the company offer stock options? If so, who is eligible? Any exceptions?

- What standard is applied to determine who receives stock options, and in what amount? Who makes these recommendations? Who approves? Does anyone monitor for EEO?

- Does the company offer perks to any of its management personnel such as: Expense accounts, company cars, paid parking, medical exams, financial counseling, tax preparation, housing expenses, low cost loans, legal support programs?

- At what level are managers eligible for perquisites or "perks?"

- Who has received these types of perks during the past year by sex/race?

"Companies may offer any number of incentive awards or honors, with or without accompanying money. Most often these are for meritorious achievement -- whether individually or as part of a team -- on a particular project at any point during a year. They also, however, can be for superior performance generally, and be granted in conjunction with an annual performance appraisal. In the latter case, when persons have reached the top of the salary range for their jobs, cash awards may be used instead of a permanent increase to base salary to reward high performance." When looking at the issue of **recognition (awards and honors),** the OFCCP will be asking such questions as: (*FCCM, Par. 5J*)

- Does the company have any awards or honors programs?

- Who is eligible to receive an award or honor? Who determines who receives it? What standard is used? Is there any review of the decision to award? By whom?

- If the award or honor is accompanied by money, and the amount of money varies, what standard is used to determine how much money is awarded? Who recommends the amount to be awarded? Who reviews the amount to be rewarded?

- Who monitors the awards and honors program for EEO?

- Over the company's last fiscal year, who, by race/sex and reason has received an award or honor?

- If the award was accompanied by money, and the amount of money varied, what was the average amount received by race/sex?

Finally, the subject of executive **terminations.** The phenomena we see at executive levels is that most terminations are "involuntary" even though the employee is offered the chance to resign. Of course, the OFCCP admits, there are genuine voluntary separations that have to do with "better business opportunity," "leaving to open one's own business," etc. Even those departures, however, may have been influenced by factors such as the perception that advancement prospects are limited. You can expect the review team to look at the distribution of terminations by function and department to identify areas with disproportionate minority/female terminations (both voluntary and involuntary). They will also explore the company's exit interview process and want to review those files. They will want to contact former employees who are minority/female and will attempt to interview them off-site.

At the conclusion of the review, there will be an exit conference. The District Director or Deputy District Director of the OFCCP will meet with the same top corporate officials as attended the opening conference. During the exit conference, there will be feedback on any violation findings and remedies the OFCCP will require be implemented. Standards used to determine whether to use a Closure Letter with Minor Violation or Conciliation Agreement are the same for Corporate Management Compliance Evaluations as for other compliance reviews. Naturally, the best of all outcomes is the Closure Letter with No Violations. We live in hope.

Corporate Reviews as a Gateway to Other Company Establishments

The December 2000 regulatory changes are the first time Corporate Management Compliance Evaluations have been mentioned in the regulations. They, like the Equal Opportunity Survey, are now "codified" in official requirements.

One very important development you should not overlook is the provision of 60-2.30(b). The OFCCP carefully provided for a glass ceiling audit to open the door to audits of other company establishments if problems are identified at the corporate level. This can potentially lead to OFCCP spending more and more time within a company that it believes has affirmative action problems. The closest focus at this writing is on compensation issues. OFCCP is aggressively trying to enforce the *Equal Pay Act*, using "any difference" as the definition of pay discrimination between men and women. They don't stop there. They also proclaim "any difference" in pay between minority and non-minority incumbents as evidence of discrimination.

Once they have gained entry to your company because of a Corporate Management Compliance Evaluation at your headquarters establishment, it is possible for OFCCP to follow your organization from one establishment to another conducting compliance reviews in each of them. The result can be one organization living with auditors for many months or years. Because this provision of the new regulations is yet untested in the courts, I suggest you consult with your management attorney if you discover that you face this possibility.

Suggestions for Employers

If you have been guiding your organization through the AAP process thoughtfully and accurately, making good faith efforts to implement your plan along the way, you will have little, if any, difficulty with your compliance review. Problems arise in Corporate Management Compliance Evaluations when programs that are applied to senior executives are not thoroughly documented or decisions about candidates or candidate development are made without consideration of EEO consequences.

To prepare for a corporate level review, use the questions you know will be asked by the enforcement officials and conduct your own internal review. Determine where your weak spots are and then develop action plans to repair them. Involve your CEO and other executives in the process. Help them understand the sensitivity of the subject matter that will be raised during this "granddaddy of all compliance reviews." Explain the amount of personal time they will have to spend in the process. Help them keep a proper perspective about the enforcement people. Communication is the key to your success. Keep at it... *ad nauseam*.

Expect that there will be follow up visits from the OFCCP if your review ends with an out-of-compliance condition and settlement agreement. They will return, usually at six-month intervals, to verify your implementation of the corrective action plan. And, as with ordinary compliance reviews, when you get a Closure Letter with Minor Violations, you should expect to be "off the hook" for at least two years.

Good luck.

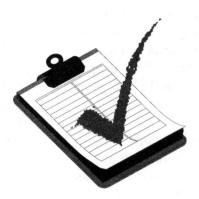

Notes

CHAPTER 13

COMPENSATION ANALYSIS

COMPENSATION
ANALYSIS

The U.S. Department of Labor's Office of Federal Contract Compliance Programs (OFCCP) has been charged with the authority and responsibility to investigate complaints of illegal employment discrimination within organizations run by federal contractors and some other employer groups such as banks. They claim this authority under Executive Order 11246, originally signed by President Johnson and later expanded by President Nixon. That Executive Order requires any employer of a certain size with federal contracts for goods and/or services of $50,000 or more in a 12-month period to develop and implement a written affirmative action plan for Minorities and Women. It insists on evaluation of these affirmative action plans (AAP) by determination if women and minorities are being included in recruitment pools in the same rates as they are present in computed availability demographics. Further, compliance with Title VII of the *Civil Rights Act of 1964* was established as a prerequisite to compliance with the Executive Order.

OFCCP has established its procedures in the Code of Federal Regulations (CFR)[33] and relies on those regulations as the foundation for its enforcement activities, from basic audit evaluation to court challenges attempting to debar contractors from further federal government contract revenue. Enforcement for Minority and Women's Affirmative Action Plans can be found in 41 CFR Chapters 60-1 and 60-2.

Courts have determined, over the years since 1964, that remedies for illegal employment discrimination include

---

[33] 41 CFR 60

such things as back pay, front pay, promotion equivalency, pension contribution, reimbursement for out-of-pocket expenses, and any other monetary reimbursement that would collectively constitute a "make whole" restitution to the victims.

Disparate treatment is one of two forms of illegal discrimination defined as illegal treatment of a protected employee compared to treatment received by a similarly situated employee of a different group. If Black employees are terminated for stealing but White employees are not, that is disparate treatment. This form of discrimination is proven by anecdotal evidence showing comparisons of treatment based on the group membership.

Disparate impact is the other form of illegal discrimination and is defined as illegal treatment of a protected group even though "rules" or "policies" or "procedures" that govern the decision involved appear on their surface to be neutral in their impact. This form of illegal discrimination is proven by statistical analysis. Many years ago, fire departments used to require firefighter job candidates be a certain height and a minimum weight because, they said, those who were not couldn't lift hoses and ladders. Lives were on the line, after all. The U.S. Supreme Court decided[34] that employers should not be using job screening requirements that were not proven to be job requirements. And, since height and weight requirements had a statistically valid disparate impact against Women, Asians and Hispanics, they were judged to be illegal. Now, to legally use height and weight requirements in employment screening employers must demonstrate that they are job requirements and those not meeting such standards cannot perform the work.

The OFCCP shares one of the Chapter 60 regulations with its sister agency, the Equal Employment Opportunity Commission (EEOC). 41 CFR 60-3 is commonly known as the Uniform Guidelines but its official name is the "Uniform Guidelines on Employee Selection Procedures (1978)." These are the rules requiring validation of employment selection devices such as written tests, or height and weight requirements.

---

[34] *Dothard v. Rawlinson*, 433 U.S. 321, 14 EPD Sec 7632 [15 FEP Cases 10] (1977), *Griggs v. Duke Power Co.*, 401 U.S. 424, 3 EPD Sec 8137 [3 FEP Cases 175] (1971)

> Employee compensation programs can be judged by either disparate treatment or disparate impact standards. Unfortunately for enforcement agencies, anything less than a full-blown regression analysis as court evidence was often rejected as invalid.

OFCCP HISTORICAL ENFORCEMENT EFFORTS

Back in the 1990's, one of the OFCCP's Regional Directors, Joseph J. DuBray,[35] suggested that compensation analysis should be based on the employer's own pay grade system. He suggested that all individuals within any given pay grade should be considered cohorts and be treated equally. By doing so, he rejected the U.S. Supreme Court opinion that said statistical significance testing is the only appropriate analysis methodology for systemic discrimination cases.[36]

Equal pay had always been the requirement of EEOC as the enforcement agency for the *Equal Pay Act (EPA)*. Men and women performing the same work are supposed to be paid the same amount.

Mr. DuBray met with a great deal of resistance from the contractor community because the employers claimed pay grades were much too broad to be used in analyzing compensation. There were both technical and administrative professionals (Programmers and Accountants) in the same grade, but they certainly didn't perform the same work. Pay Grades, according to contractors, were a neat and clean way to gather together jobs that were worth about the same in the marketplace. Grades were proclaimed to be an administrative tool only and not a governor of compensation decision.

So, it was back to the drawing board. OFCCP went to the professionals and began hiring statisticians with Ph.D. qualifications to determine how it should proceed with development of a program that would be a valid method for compensation evaluation. Clearly, it has the authority and responsibility to do so.[37]

On June 16, 2006, OFCCP published in the Federal Register two final rules.[38] And, it has not published anywhere the specific three-step analytical process it is now using with contractors during compliance evaluations.

---

[35] DuBray, Joseph H., Regional Director, Region III (Philadelphia), unpublished paper he called *Systemic Compensation Analysis: An Investigatory Approach*, 1997

[36] *Hazelwood School District v. United States* (433 U.S. 299) [309 n. 14] 1997

[37] 41 CFR 60-2.17(b)(3) "At a minimum the contractor must evaluate…Compensation system(s) to determine whether there are gender-, race- or ethnicity-based disparities."

[38] Interpretive standards for systemic compensation discrimination under Executive Order 11246 (Federal Register, Vol 71., No. 116, Page 35124, Friday, June 16, 2006); Final voluntary guidelines for self-

CURRENT OFCCP THREE STEP ANALYSIS PROCESS

Step 1: "1st Pass" ("Tipping Point Analysis" or "Trigger Test")

Test #1: Do women or minorities earn at least 5% less on average than men or non-minorities in the same group?

Test #2: Are there at least 30 negatively impacted women or minorities?

Test #3: Are at least 10% of women or minorities in the establishment negatively impacted?

Test #4: Are women or minorities being negatively impacted at a rate that is at least 3 times the impact rate of the men or non-minorities?

Failing the first pass sequence of tests (reaching the "tipping point" or "pulling the trigger") will result in the Compliance Officer asking you to submit the 12-Item Data File for a Mini-Regression analysis.

If your data does not reach the "tipping point," you will "PASS" this test and nothing further will be asked of you by OFCCP. (This procedure is current as of the date this edition of *Secrets of Affirmative Action Compliance* was prepared. It is subject to change in the future at the discretion of the new OFCCP Director.)

TEST #1

EXAMPLE:

	Average Men Pay	Average Women Pay
Programmers	$10,000.00	$ 8,500.00
Accountants	$ 8,000.00	$ 9,250.00
Sales Agents	$15,000.00	$12,000.00
Facility Admin	$ 8,000.00	$ 7,500.00
Fleet Admin	$ 7,500.00	$ 0.00

	Disadvantage Men	Disadvantage Women
Programmers		$ 1,500.00
Accountants	$ 1,250.00	
Sales Agents		$ 3,000.00
Facility Admin		$ 500.00
Fleet Admin	N/A	N/A

Evaluation of compensation practices for compliance with Executive Order 11246 with respect to systemic compensation discrimination (Federal Register, Vol 71, No. 116, Page 35114, Friday, June 16, 2006)

	% Disadvantage Women
Programmers	17.6%
Accountants	N/A
Sales Agents	25.0%
Facility Admin	6.7%
Fleet Admin	N/A

Programmers, and Sales Agents exceed the 5% level. The other pay categories will be ignored.

TEST #2

	Population of Men	Population of Women
Total Programmers	60	50
Total Sales Agents	10	25

# Women Programmers less than $10,000 annual compensation:	35
# Men Programmers less than $10,000 annual compensation:	11

# Sales Agents less than $15,000 annual compensation:	20

Only Programmers has more than 30 women impacted, earning less than the average earned by men. So we will ignore Sales Agents since they don't "rise to the level" necessary for further investigation.

TEST #3

Are at least 10% of women impacted in the establishment?

If we assume there are a total of 350 employees in the establishment and that 200 of them are women, we ask, "Is the total number of women impacted in Programmers equal to at least 10% of the 200 total women?" Since 35 women programmers earn less than $10,000 annual compensation the answer is, "Yes." OFCCP would continue to the final test.

TEST #4

Are women being impacted at a rate that is at least 3 times the rate of men?

Even though there is a disadvantage to women in the example, OFCCP would not pursue any further investigation of the compensation plan. We know that 35 women programmers are under the threshold of $10,000. There are 11 men under the same threshold. Therefore, there are three times the number of women impacted as there are men impacted in this group.

RESULT: OFCCP will very likely request more data in the form of the 12-item Mini-Regression input file. You should try to get them to limit the focus to Programmers since that is the only group impacted.

So, you "Pass" or "Fail" the Tipping Point test. If you Pass, there is nothing more to be done. If you fail, OFCCP has indicated that it will not issue a Notice of Violation based simply on this test alone. Rather, the failure is an indication that further analysis is required. OFCCP will move to Step 2.

Step 2: Cluster Regression (Mini-Regression Analysis)

OFCCP will request additional data from you if you fail the 1st Pass analysis. The data they want is sometimes called the "12-Item List" and is comprised of these items for each employee:

1. Employee identification number
2. Gender
3. Race
4. Date of Hire or Time With the Company
5. Date of Latest Job Placement or Time in Current Position
6. Date of Latest Educational Degree
7. Current Annual Salary or Hourly Wage Rate (excluding overtime, bonuses and incentives)
8. Full-time or Part-time Status
9. Exempt or Non-Exempt Status
10. Job Title
11. Pay Grade or Salary Band
12. Department or Division Name & Work Location

This data must be delivered in an electronic file. And, don't even think about objecting to the agency taking that data off-site to their office. That battle has been fought and lost.[39]

---

[39] In 1999, OFCCP added Item 11 to its list of data required in an audit submission. That list received Office of Management and Budget (OMB) approval which means it meets the requirements of the

OFCCP will use this data file to "Cluster" your employees and then performs a regression analysis for each cluster. How they build their clusters is discretionary, and can become the foundation of a challenge by you at some later date. Whether or not you'll win is problematic, but you can try.

It is quite possible that these items will be altered over the coming years. Don't be surprised if one or more items are replaced with other factors. There is a pervasive rumor that "age" has been eliminated from the list by OFCCP. You'll just have to wait and learn what they ask for if you get to this point in your audit.

Performing a Cluster Regression Analysis

1. Group employees by job title and compute the average pay of each group.
2. Place employees in order from the job title with the highest average pay to that with the lowest.
3. Form clusters of employees by moving down the ordered list and collecting employees from successive job titles until at least 30 employees are in a cluster and at least 5 are from each comparison group (male and female or minority and non-minority).
4. For each cluster, construct and estimate a regression model that determines whether gender or race has a significant influence on pay rates of employees, after accounting for the influence of a few other independent variables taken from the 12-Item list. Time with the company and age are sometimes chosen.
5. Identify those clusters where the estimated gender or race influence is statistically significant, as indicated by a two-tailed p-value of 5% or less.

Any cluster that does not have at least 5 males and 5 females, for example, must be excluded from the analysis. If a cluster cannot reasonably rise to the total 30 employees requirement then that cluster must be excluded from the analysis also.

One thing the OFCCP has not shared with contractors is the number of clusters that must fail this test for the agency to consider the step "Failed." If you look at the results of this analysis and reasonably conclude that there is a problem, you should probably move on to the next step which is a full regression analysis.

Even if you have several clusters fail this analysis, OFCCP has said it will not issue a Notice of Violation based on this step alone.

Paperwork Reduction Act. And, Item 11 has been interpreted by the OFCCP to mean the list of 12 items it will request if it goes to the Cluster Analysis step in compensation analysis. And, all of this data is delivered to OFCCP by the contractor to be used in analysis done at the OFCCP office. Following the audit, when a determination on compliance has been delivered by the agency to the contractor, all of that data remains in OFCCP custody and is subject to discovery within provisions of the *Freedom of Information Act (FOIA)* (5 U.S.C. 552). OFCCP has repeatedly said it will use FOIA exemptions to prevent release of compensation data, and to date, there are no known cases of the agency violating that promise.

Step 3: Comprehensive Regression Analysis

Chances are that OFCCP will come on site if this step in the compensation analysis process is reached. During their on-site visit, the Compliance Officer (CO) will gather information from your files about job descriptions (or other responsibility level documentation), and any other factor that would or could legitimately influence employee compensation. It is incumbent upon the agency to do this data gathering.

The "final Voluntary Self-Evaluation Guidelines only require a multiple regression analysis for those establishments or AAPs that have 500 or more employees." The agency also says that "a multiple regression analysis is not required under 41 CFR60-2.17(b)(3)."[40]

If you perform a compliant multiple regression analysis on your compensation program you can obtain compliance coordination and the OFCCP will accept your results as proof that you have met the new requirements. We recommend against performing a full regression analysis unless you are involved in a compliance review and the OFCCP is moving to that step in the evaluation process. You will want to know what they will find before they find it. Should you discover problems in your regression analysis results, you can move to remedy them before they are pointed out by the OFCCP. When you do that you stop the clock on remedies under Title VII.   In essence, you are "truncating" your liability.

During the on-site visit, the CO will conduct interviews with both management and non-management employees collecting information about compliance, among other things. If anecdotal evidence of illegal discrimination should surface, the CO will use it to probe further into those issues. Data collection of any sort is possible at that stage.

An integral requirement in the regression data preparation is creation of "Similarly Situated Employee Groups (SSEG)."   According[41] to Marika Litras, Ph.D., Senior OFCCP Statistician, in San Francisco, the agency will do all in its power to amass 30 or more individuals in each SSEG because it acknowledges that fewer people cause the analysis to lose statistical significance. Contractors bristle at this suggestion because it conjures up images of dissimilar jobs being thrown into an SSEG just to reach the headcount minimum. Trust will only come over time following OFCCP's development of a track record on this issue. Officially, the agency says in the Q&A's on its web site, *"Under no circumstances will OFCCP attempt to combine, group, or compare employees who are not similarly situated under these final interpretative standards. If employees are not similarly situated under these final interpretive standards, they will not be included in*

---

[40] Notice of Final Voluntary Guidelines for self-evaluation of compensation practices for compliance with Executive Order 11246 with respect to systemic compensation discrimination, Federal Register, Vol 71, No. 116, Page 35114, Friday, June 16, 2006.

[41] June 12, 2007, Industry Liaison Group (ILG) joint meeting of Northern California ILG, Silicon Valley ILG, and Sacramento ILG at Redwood City, California.

the statistical analysis, regardless of statistical size requirements or OFCCP's general objectives to include a significant majority of employees in the regression analyses."[42]

When Dr. Litras was asked what percentage of Compliance Evaluations (audits) resulted in the need for a Comprehensive Multiple Regression Analysis, she said she didn't know. John Fox, an attorney with Manatt, Phelps & Phillips, LLC in Palo Alto, California indicated that less than two percent (<2%) of audits result in the need for a regression analysis of compensation programs. That means your chances of having to go through this much work are not high…they are actually very low. Yet, it is helpful to understand the process regardless of whether or not you are selected for this final step in the process.

Multiple regression analysis is not something you do with a paper and pencil or even a calculator. It is something that requires computer processing power due to the large numbers of computations necessary. And, running the data file through a regression program is not the most time-consuming part of the process. Getting the data assembled into a file is. Combing files for data and putting that into a file takes a great deal of time. That is why we believe you should conduct a full regression analysis only when you know it is necessary as a tool for your defense. Others will argue with us that our position is irresponsible. They say any right-thinking employer will want to do the right thing by performing a regression analysis just to know its compensation program contains no illegal discrimination. While we think that a valid objective, we question the business value of spending such resources on the process unless it is required.

What to Do If You Fail One of These Steps

If you fail the 1st Pass step, be sure you go to the second step and perform a mini-regression analysis. If you don't have the ability to do that yourself, get the data file to someone who can perform the Cluster Analysis for you. It will take some time to collect all the data, but you really can't afford to avoid this step. Serious problems could be lurking in your compensation program and without further analysis you won't know what they are. We strongly encourage moving to Step 2: Cluster Analysis (Mini-Regression).

If you fail the Cluster Analysis, and there are still indicators of disparate impact in your compensation program, you have a serious decision to make. Are you going to perform a full regression analysis or not. It may be possible to simply take the results of your Cluster Analysis and use those indicators to dig through personnel files, hiring/termination files or promotion records to determine whether or not specific decisions were made with bias or not. At some time in the process, it is usually necessary to review or critique every management decision made in at least some of the employee cases. If you are at this point in the process, you might just as well gather all the files into your conference room, put on a pot of coffee and hunker down for a long weekend of work. Who knows, it might take longer to review every compensation decision made for people in the group (Cluster or SSEG) showing some statistical problems.

---

[42] http://www.dol.gov/esa/regs/compliance/ofccp/faqs/comstrds.htm#Q11

Make notes about reasons for the compensation decisions. If they are non-discriminatory reasons (things other than race, sex, age, etc.) you can build a list of defense items for use in any response you might have to give to OFCCP. After all, anecdotal evidence is an important part of the investigation process.

Unless you decide that you still wish to receive Federal revenues, you have little choice but to spend the time and money needed to go through this process. Times have changed. It costs more these days to be compliant as a federal contractor.

Software to Help Your Compensation Analysis

Until recently, there have been precious few tools available to employers for conducting compensation analysis. There have been programs requiring main-frame computers to process data, but little in the way of analysis tools employers could use themselves on their office PCs.

Biddle Consulting Group's *COMPare 2.0* is a compensation analysis program that allows employers to conduct their own compensation analysis. It offers many forms of analysis from which contractors can choose. It offers legitimate, statistically sound approaches to analysis that will allow you to determine if you have any potential problems of discrimination.

Peopleclick has released an upgraded version of its *PayStat* program that will perform the specific **1st Pass** and **Cluster Test** analyses. It will even do a regression analysis if you have a database populated with all the information necessary. It conforms to the OFCCP guidelines on compensation analysis. (Go to: www.hrwebstore.com)

If you would rather do your regression analysis using Microsoft's Excel® then you can use third-party templates like the one you will find at www.business-spreadsheets.com/summary.asp . Please understand that we are not endorsing this web site or its products. We simply offer it as an example of what might be available if you do a Google search for "Regression Analysis Excel Templates." In this instance a single user license for their excel template will cost you a one-time charge of $14.00 for the download version. If you want the program on CD-ROM, add another $12.50. The program is limited to 10 independent variables. Of course, all this represents information as of the date we published this edition.

Notes

CHAPTER 14

THE FUTURE OF AFFIRMATIVE ACTION

Notes

THE FUTURE
OF AFFIRMATIVE
ACTION

We are 40+ years into the government and social experiment called "Affirmative Action." Where will things go from here?

Glass Ceiling Commission's Recommendations

The *Civil Rights Act of 1991* set aside money and created a group called the "Glass Ceiling Commission." It was charged with conducting a study and preparing recommendations for eliminating "artificial barriers" blocking women and minorities from moving into top executive positions in America's corporations. The commission's study discovered that 97% of all senior managers in *Fortune* 1000 industrial and *Fortune* 500 companies are white and 97% are male.

Of the 21 commission members, 17 voted on the final set of recommendations. All 17 voted to approve the commission's suggestions on November 21, 1995. The commission was disbanded that same day.

In all, there were 12 recommendations in the commission's report, entitled *A Solid Investment: Making Full Use of The Nation's Human Capital*. They were split into two categories: Business and Government.

Glass Ceiling Commission Recommendations for Business

- Demonstrate CEO commitment

    Eliminating the glass ceiling requires that the CEO communicate visible and continuing commitment to workforce diversity throughout the organization. The Commission recommends that all CEOs and boards of directors set companywide policies that actively promote diversity programs and policies that remove artificial barriers at every level.

- <u>Include diversity in all strategic business plans and hold line managers accountable for progress</u>

  Business customarily establishes short-and long-term objectives and measures progress in key business areas. The Commission recommends that all corporations include in their strategic business plans efforts to achieve diversity both at the senior management level and throughout the workforce. Additionally, performance appraisals, compensation incentives and other evaluation measures must reflect a line manager's ability to set a high standard and demonstrate progress toward breaking the glass ceiling.

- <u>Use affirmative action as a tool</u>

  Affirmative action is the deliberate undertaking of positive steps to design and implement employment procedures that ensure the employment system provides equal opportunity to all. The Commission recommends that corporate America use affirmative action as a tool ensuring that all *qualified* individuals have equal access and opportunity to compete based on ability and merit.

- <u>Select, promote and retain qualified individuals</u>

  Traditional prerequisites and qualifications for senior management and board of director positions focus too narrowly on conventional sources of experience. The Commission recommends that organizations expand their vision and seek candidates from non-customary sources, backgrounds and experiences, and that the executive recruiting industry work with business to explore ways to expand the universe of qualified candidates.

- <u>Prepare minorities and women for senior positions</u>

  Too often, minorities and women find themselves channeled into staff positions that provide little access and visibility to corporate decision makers, and removed from strategic business decisions. The Commission recommends that organizations expand access to core areas of the business and to various developmental experiences, and establish formal mentoring programs that provide career guidance and support to prepare minorities and women for senior positions.

- <u>Educate the corporate ranks</u>

  Organizations cannot make members of society blind to differences in color, culture or gender, but they can demand and enforce merit-based practice and behavior internally. The Commission recommends that companies provide formal training at regular intervals on company time to sensitize and familiarize all employees about the strengths and challenges of gender, racial, ethnic and cultural differences.

- <u>Initiate work/life and family friendly policies</u>

  Work/life and family friendly policies, although they benefit all employees, are an important step in an organization's commitment to hiring, retaining and promoting both men and women. The Commission recommends that organizations adopt policies that recognize and accommodate the balance between work and family responsibilities that impact the lifelong career paths of all employees.

- Adopt high performance workplace practices

    There is a positive relationship between corporate financial performance, productivity and the use of high performance workplace practices. The Commission recommends that all companies adopt high performance workplace practices, which fall under the categories of skills and information; participation, organization and partnership; and compensation, security and work environment.

Glass Ceiling Commission's Recommendations for Government

- Lead by example

    Government at all levels must be a leader in the quest to make equal opportunity a reality for minorities and women. The Commission recommends that all government agencies, as employers, increase their efforts to eliminate internal glass ceilings by examining their practices for promoting qualified minorities and women to senior management and decision making positions.

- Strengthen enforcement of anti-discrimination laws

    Workplace discrimination presents a significant glass ceiling barrier for minorities and women. The Commission recommends that Federal enforcement agencies increase their efforts to enforce existing laws by expanding efforts to end systemic discrimination and challenging multiple discrimination. The Commission also recommends evaluating effectiveness and efficiency and strengthening interagency coordination as a way of furthering the effort. Additionally, updating anti-discrimination regulations, strengthening and expanding Corporate Management Compliance Evaluations and improving the complaint processing system play major roles in ending discrimination. Finally, the Commission recommends making sure that enforcement agencies have adequate resources to enforce anti-discrimination laws.

- Improve data collection

    Accurate data on minorities and women can show where progress is or is not being made in breaking glass ceiling barriers. The Commission recommends that relevant government agencies revise the collection of data by refining existing data categories and improving the specificity of data collected. All government agencies that collect data must break it out by race and gender, and avoid double counting of minority women, in order to develop a clear picture of where minorities and women are in the workplace.

- <u>Increase disclosure of diversity data</u>

  Public disclosure of diversity data -- specifically, data on the most senior positions -- is an effective incentive to develop and maintain innovative, effective programs to break glass ceiling barriers. The Commission recommends that both the public and private sectors work toward increased public disclosure of diversity data.

In other recommendations, the commission suggested:

- A confluence of constituencies to take responsibility for implementing the recommendations, influencing others to implement the recommendations, and monitoring the progress and measuring the impact of the recommendations. The constituencies should include business, minority, civil rights, and women's groups.
- A five-to-ten year longitudinal study to determine the "sequence of activities" that would be most effective in dismantling glass ceilings and promoting minorities and women.
- Additional research to quantify the cost of discrimination.
- A national public education campaign designed to dismantle misperceptions, stereotypes, and biases.
- An examination of the role of technology in breaking barriers.
- An examination by state and local governments at what they are doing to break glass ceilings.

Politics as Usual? Maybe Not.

Charles James changed OFCCP substantially during his tenure in office. He eliminated the EO Survey that had no value in helping the agency identify contractors who were discriminating. He published new regulations on the definition of Internet Applicant, which places contractors in a position of having to seek, maintain, and analyze sex and ethnic/race data on all the applicants who respond to the contractor's invitation to self-identify. Then, there are the regulations that updated affirmative action for veterans. We have new definitions for different types of veterans and finally have some consistency between regulations for Disabled and those for Veterans. Mr. James accomplished a great deal after what appeared to be a very slow beginning to his administration.

What the future holds at the OFCCP is once again uncertain with the appointment of Patricia Shiu as Director of the agency. Contractors have been put on notice that additional regulations are coming at the end of 2010 and early 2011 having to do with Veterans, Disabled and Construction Contractors.

In the Final Analysis

Employment affirmative action requirements are not going away, despite all of the political brouhaha in the media. The emotionally charged issues of illegal aliens, welfare reform, health care and equal employment opportunity will ultimately be individually compartmentalized by the average American. Although they will continue to be emotional, politician's efforts to enflame one subject, such as affirmative action, by threatening cataclysmic disaster from other of these issues will generally not last. And the American public will sort them out from one another as issues of importance. That's what has already started to happen in California regarding the so-called "California Initiative" which is designed to eliminate affirmative action in state government. Public polls indicate the residents of California see a difference between "preferential treatment" and "equal treatment."

So, the politicians will continue to argue and put whatever spin enhances their personal positions onto these issues. In the final analysis, the checks and balances of the debate and two party system will lead us to some reasoned conclusions which will form our national social policy for the coming years. It has worked pretty well for the past two hundred and thirty years plus years, and I suspect it will serve us well in this current debate.

In the meantime, don't forget to meet the compliance requirements of affirmative action plan development and implementation if you wish to remain a federal contractor, supplying goods or services to our government.

Where to File EEO-1 Reports

EEO-1 reports are normally mailed to employers with pre-printed employer address information, much as IRS forms are pre-printed. With the pre-printed reporting form will be information indicating where you should mail your completed report. If for some reason that information is missing, send the original and two copies of your completed report to:

> Joint Reporting Committee (EEO-1)
> P.O. Box 779
> Norfolk, VA 23501
> 804-461-1213

EEO-1 reports are due at the government office by September 30th each year. The data you report on this form may be from any one pay period during the third quarter (July, August or September). If you have previously established written approval to use year-end data as of the prior year, you are allowed to do so.

If you wish an extension on the filing deadline, you must make your request in writing and be sure it is postmarked no later than the September 30th filing deadline. Your letter must specify the firm date by which you will file your report. And, be sure to show your "Company Number" (CO=XXXXXX-X) on all your correspondence. Mail your request to:

> EEO-1 Coordinator
> EEOC - Surveys
> 1801 L Street, N.W. - Suite 9222
> Washington, DC 20507
> 804-461-1213

Late in 2005, the EEOC issued new guidelines on the EEO-1 form design. It has added some features and modified others. The changes are effective with the data submission on September 30, 2007. Be sure you are data collection from both employees and applicants comports with the new categories.

CHAPTER 15

COMPARING EEO, AA & DIVERSITY

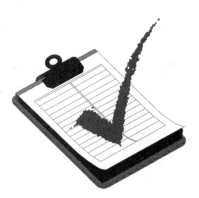

Notes

COMPARING EEO, AA & DIVERSITY

Diversity has been a "hot" topic for consultants and trainers during the past ten years. Many of them have made a great deal of money bringing diversity programs to employers across the country. Learning to live together and learning to value a variety of backgrounds and viewpoints has been the core of much of this training.

Managing diversity has become the common call within our American workplace. Yet, understanding what that means has been difficult to accomplish. Just as some training programs on communication and leadership are outstanding, and others not worth the time they take to sit through them, diversity programs offer the same spectrum of quality. Some diversity training programs are similar to the "sensitivity sessions" we saw proliferate in the mid-60's when EEO was just coming into the corporate world. Some diversity training focuses on management skills and development of an attitude of inclusion. Other diversity training has become theater for bashing white males.

While this text is not intended to be a document about diversity management, suffice it to say that it is possible to treat the subject of diversity in the workplace as a skill-related issue. And, just like communication or leadership or decision making skills, diversity management skills can be taught and practiced.

Some evidence suggests that group decision making can be influenced by a manager skilled in managing diversity. It is interesting to note that decisions reached by homogenous groups (people who are all the same, e.g., all White, all Black, all male or all female) occur fairly quickly. It is easy to get rapid agreement within groups where members all share the same or similar backgrounds and viewpoints. Decisions reached by groups with diverse membership take a great deal longer in the making. There is more time required to air the variety of viewpoints represented.

To me, the most interesting thing to come from these experiments has to do with the quality of the decisions reached. Decision quality increased with an increase in group diversity. Even though it was more difficult to achieve group consensus on a decision, once reached, the decision was of higher quality than one reached quickly by homogenous groups.

The implications of that are clear, I think. Managers of tomorrow will have to work harder. Cultures will have to change within organizations. "Sensitivity" training will likely continue to upset people because it so often pits one group against another, making one group "good" and the other "bad." Such an approach is not helpful. Yet, for those managers who are able to see the value to their organization of higher quality decisions (products, services, problem solving, etc.) achieving a diverse representation among work groups will become a commercial imperative. Those will be the groups that respond best within the marketplace.

Diversity training has existed for a number of years. And, while there are some excellent programs available, some are so bad that their stories have been shared over and over in various employment circles. This has tended to paint all diversity training programs with the same brush, and some organizations are backing away from such programs. There is no legal requirement to implement a diversity training program at any organization in this land.

On the other hand, Equal Opportunity and Affirmative Action are still with us. Both EEO and AA programs are legal requirements. Unfortunately, in some workplaces, managers who didn't have a clue about EEO and AA requirements or processes have decided that implementing diversity training programs would be a way to "put a new spin on affirmative action." Seldom, if ever, does that approach work.

Affirmative Action is a subject that demands management attention, study and understanding. I could liken it to workers' compensation or unemployment insurance in that regard. If managers don't understand the *systems and procedures* involved in workers' compensation, they will be condemned to waste organizational resources doing things which are not necessary, or worse, paying penalties which could have been avoided. The same is true of affirmative action. Smart managers understand the systems and procedures involved. They spend the time required to study and learn. They also gain the organizational benefits associated with their learning and competency. And, in the end they maintain their government revenue stream.

I see the three subjects as a hierarchy. The foundation for everything is Equal Employment Opportunity. That allows equal access for everyone who is qualified to participate in whatever opportunity may exist. On the next layer, Affirmative Action Programs contribute outreach and recruiting in an effort to assure we are actively attempting to include qualified people in each of our employment processes. Finally, the third layer on the stack, is diversity management. It offers us the opportunity to take full advantage of the kaleidoscope of talents and skills our EEO and AA programs have given us.

Take all three together and you have a powerful set of tools for managing your workforce in the 21st century.

COMPARING EEO, AA & DIVERSITY

Employment Action	Equal Opportunity	Affirmative Action	Diversity
Recruitment	Ensure job announcements are accessible to all qualified applicants and employees.	Target outreach in underutilized areas. Encourage minority and female employee referrals.	Diversify candidate pool.
Selection	Select the best qualified candidate based on job requirements and business necessity.	Select the best qualified candidate based on job requirements and business necessity.	Select the best qualified candidate based on job requirements and business necessity.
Promotion, Reclassification & Transfer	Inform all employees about promotion opportunities. Discuss career plans and interests with all employees.	Establish mentorship, internship and apprenticeship programs to prepare employees for requirements of other jobs.	Explore alternative ways to help employees become qualified for such job opportunities.
Training & Career Development	Encourage all employees to discuss their plan for growth. Offer the same training opportunity to all.	Assure all training opportunities are shared by employees from all sex and ethnic groups.	Use employee's own background and skills to help train others.
Education	Educate staff about EEO and non-discrimination policy.	Educate staff about EEO and AAP requirements. Encourage employee participation.	Educate staff in valuing diversity of individual backgrounds, experience and talents.
Layoff & Termination	Determine terminations based on performance standards, fairness, business necessity and seniority.	Determine terminations based on performance standards, fairness, business necessity and seniority.	Determine terminations based on performance standards, fairness, business necessity and seniority.
Complaint Resolution & Handling Harassment	Maintain fairness. Manage conflict effectively by using internal resolution process.	Maintain fairness. Manage conflict effectively by using internal resolution process.	Maintain fairness. Manage conflict effectively by using internal resolution process.

CHAPTER 16

OFCCP DIRECTIVES
(Some key policy decisions that affect Federal Contractors)

Notes

OFCCP DIRECTIVES

The OFCCP has created a system for issuing directives on policy issues and staff instructions. Some key policy positions related to Federal Contractors are included here.

Introduction

The OFCCP's Division of Program Policy has responsibility for operation of the agency's directives system. Each directive, when issues, is signed by the current director of the agency.

There are different categories of directives. The two most common categories which attract attention of Federal Contractors are Orders and Notices.

Notices are temporary instructions or announcements to be retained no longer than three months. Information requested from the OFCCP on a one-time basis will be issued as a notice.

Orders establish official "policies, procedures, instructions, definitions of functions and organizational structure, delegations of authority, assignments of responsibility, and other continuing instructions essential to OFCCP employees." Orders are permanent instructions to staff that remain in effect until canceled.

Orders can indirectly revise or supplement the Federal Contract Compliance Manual. "Policies, procedures, instructions, etc. which may eventually, in whole or in part, be incorporated into the Contract Compliance Manual will be issued as Orders rather than Notices. At such time as this information is incorporated into the Manual, the affected portion of this Order may be changed by issuance of a revised Order, deleting the affected portion." (Order No. 110a2)

Reinsurance Companies Covered by Government Contracts

Order No. 610a1   Dated: 2-16-77
From: A. Diane Graham, Acting Director, OFCCP

"Insurance companies are ... covered if they provide coverage to the government, or if they are subcontractors providing necessary coverage to government contractors. Since reinsurance is necessary protection for insurance companies to help spread their own risks, it is essentially a subcontract of insurance to insurance companies.

"Therefore, if a reinsurance company has a contract of reinsurance with a government contractor for protection exceeding $10,000, it is a service subcontractor, and is covered.

Under Executive Order 11246 the existence of mutual contractual obligations necessary for performance of the government contract is sufficient to establish coverage irrespective of whether the contract will result in employment opportunities.

Please note that the affirmative action clause must be included in all reinsurance contracts entered into by government contracts or subcontracts."

Background: Question arose as to whether reinsurers of the Federal Employees Group Life Insurance Program hold subcontracts with the Metropolitan Life Insurance Company within the meaning of Executive Order 11246, as amended.

Suppliers of Workers' Compensation Insurance to Federal Contractors

Order No. 940b2   Dated: 3-26-82
From: John C. Fox, for Director OFCCP

"OFCCP will no longer assert Executive Order coverage over insurance companies because of a contract to supply workers' compensation insurance to a Federal contractor. Accordingly, all complaints or compliance reviews involving the workers' compensation jurisdictional issue should be closed immediately."

Background: *Liberty Mutual Insurance Company v. Friedman,* 639 F. 2d 164 (4th Cir. 1980). The case raised the issue of whether there is authority under Executive Order 11246 for OFCCP to assert jurisdiction over an insurance company subcontractor (Liberty Mutual) which supplied workers' compensation insurance to a prime Federal contractor. The court held that the application of the Executive Order to Liberty Mutual exceeded OFCCP's authority. Accordingly, OFCCP does not have the authority to entertain complaints or conduct compliance reviews of insurance companies who have no other nexus with the Federal procurement system than to supply workers' compensation insurance to other Federal contractors.

Indefinite Quantity Contracts

Order No. 610a3   Dated: 3-15-85
From: Susan R. Meisinger, Acting Director, OFCCP

"OFCCP policy continues to be that an indefinite quantity contract is a single contract and not a series of separate contracts. The contractor will be subject to the requirements of Section 503 if 'the contracting agency has reason to believe that the amount to be ordered in any year' under such an indefinite quantity contract will be more than $2,500. The contractor will be subject to the requirements of 38 U.S.C. Sec. 2012 if 'the contracting agency has reason to believe that the amount to be ordered in any year' under such an indefinite quantity contract will be $10,000 or more. The contractor will be subject to the equal opportunity clause of Executive Order 11246, as amended, if (1) 'the purchaser has reason to believe that the amount to be ordered in any year' under an indefinite quantity contract will exceed $10,000, or (2) contracts or subcontracts in any 12-month period have an aggregate total value exceeding $10,000.

"In all three program areas, once the specified dollar volume is reached and the equal opportunity or affirmative action clause(s) become applicable, the contractor is subject to the clause(s) for the duration of the contract regardless of the amount ordered, or reasonably expected to be ordered, in any succeeding year.

"Finally, a contractor will be subject to the written AAP requirements under 38 U.S.C. Sec. 2012, Section 503 and the Executive Order, if the contracting agency has reason to believe that 'in any year' the amount to be ordered under an indefinite quantity contract will be $50,000 or more and the contractor has 50 or more employees. Thereafter, the written AAP requirements apply for the duration of the contract."

Background: The total dollar value of a Government contract is important because it is one of the criteria used in determining a Government contractor's obligations under the programs administered by the OFCCP.

The indefinite quantity contract is one type of contract which the Government uses. This type of contract takes different forms and has different names, but, typically, it is a master agreement under which the contractor agrees to sell, and the Government agrees to buy, supplies or services, as required. The master agreement contemplates the placing of one or more orders under the agreement and it specifies significant terms under which the orders will be made. However, terms such as the actual number of goods or services, and the total contract price, might not be specified.

Referenced cases include:
- *OFCCP v. Star Machinery Company,* 83-OFCCP-4 (September 21, 1983)
- *United Biscuit Company v. Wirtz,* 359 F. 2d 206 (D.C.C. 1966)
- *United States v. Thurston Motor Lines,* 4th Cir., No. 76-2230 (April 4, 1978)

Federal Reserve Banks

Order No. 610a4   Dated: 2-26-85
From: Susan R. Meisinger, Acting Director, OFCCP

"Federal Reserve Banks will not be scheduled for compliance reviews. Federal Reserve Banks listings on current EEDS should be disregarded until they can be omitted from the next EEDS issuance."

Background: The question of the status of Federal Reserve Banks arose because several Federal Reserve Banks appear on OFCCP EEDS listings, and, in one instance, a compliance review of a Federal Reserve Bank was scheduled. The Federal Reserve Bank asserted that OFCCP lacked jurisdiction because the Bank is an instrumentality of the United States Government.

For purposes of programs administered by OFCCP, Federal Reserve Banks are to be treated as Federal entities and thus not Federal contractors. This determination is limited to OFCCP and is not intended to be conclusive as to the status of the Federal Reserve Banks under any other civil rights statutes.

The majority of Federal and state courts in which the status of the Federal Reserve Banks has been raised have been persuaded that the governmental functions performed by the banks make them Federal entities.

Health Care Contractors Accepting Medicare and Medicaid

Order No. ADM 93-1/JUR   Dated: 12-16-93
From: Leonard J. Biermann, Acting Director, OFCCP

"OFCCP will not assert jurisdiction over a health care entity solely on the basis of its receiving reimbursement for services to Medicare or Medicaid beneficiaries.

"OFCCP jurisdiction may be found if a health care entity holds a Federal contract or subcontract of the requisite amount. Therefore, staff should carefully examine such a possibility whenever coverage of a health care entity is in question."

Background: Health care entities enter into provider agreements with the U.S. Department of Health and Human Services (HHS) pursuant to Section 1866 of the Medicare statute (42 U.S.C. 1395 et seq.). The agreement authorizes the health care provider to receive reimbursement for services rendered to Medicare eligible beneficiaries. Providers may also receive reimbursement for services to Medicaid beneficiaries pursuant to a provider agreement between a state and the health care entity.

In *United States v. Baylor University Medical Center*, 564 F. Supp. 1495 (N.D. Tex. 1983), the district court concluded that Medicare and Medicaid are Federal financial assistance programs. As a result of this case, OFCCP considers health care institutions that provide services to Medicare and Medicaid beneficiaries as recipients of Federal financial assistance and not as contractors.

Corporate-level Selection Decisions

Order No. 830a1   Dated: 6-14-88
From: Jerry D. Blakemore, Director, OFCCP

"Equal Opportunity Specialists conducting a compliance review of a multi-establishment contractor's corporate office or intermediate level office must investigate and otherwise ensure that the affirmative action program of that office includes in its workforce analysis, utilization analysis and goal setting, ..., all those positions located in subordinate and/or lower-level establishments for which the selection decisions are made at the establishment under review. Similarly, Equal Opportunity Specialists conducting a compliance review of a contractor's establishment which is subordinate to a higher level establishment in the contractor's organization will ensure that all positions in the work force of this lower-level establishment for which the selection decisions are made at a higher corporate level are excluded from the utilization analysis and goal setting of the establishment under review, although such positions must still be shown in the establishment's workforce analysis, ..., in order that the complete work force structure of the establishment under review is readily apparent.

"In those cases where because of informal or fluctuating managerial appointment authorities, the appropriate level for job title placement cannot be clearly or consistently defined, managerial and other appropriate titles should be placed in the AAP of the highest organizational level where ultimate approval authority may reside. As a result, there may be instances when the majority of mid- and upper-level management and other titles should appropriately be placed in the corporate headquarters' AAP, notwithstanding personnel responsibility at intermediate organizational levels. Management should be given substantial discretion in determining proper organizational levels for job title placement provided such placement is not inconsistent with the purpose of this directive."

Background: In the case of multi-establishment contractors, it is not unusual for selection decisions regarding certain positions to be made at the corporate level or at an intermediate level, rather than at the subordinate establishment where the position is located. This is particularly true for example, in the case of plant manager positions, but it also may apply to other positions such as professional and technical jobs. In such cases, it is not appropriate for affirmative action goals for such positions to be established in the subordinate establishment's AAP because that decision to select regarding such positions is not within the control of that establishment. On the other hand, the inclusion of such positions in the AAP of the contractor's corporate or intermediate level offices would provide for utilization analysis and goal setting for those positions to be accomplished at the same level at which the selection decisions are made. OFCCP's practice of encouraging contractors to treat such positions in this fashion is long-standing.

Functional Affirmative Action Plans (AAPs)

Directive No. 254   Dated: 3-21-2002
From: Charles E. James, Sr., Deputy Assistant Secretary for Federal Contract Compliance

"Any multi-establishment supply and service contractor subject to AAP requirements may request an agreement that would allow for the development and use of AAPs based on functional or business units."

"A functional AAP agreement must cover the contractor's entire workforce. However this does not mean that the entire workforce must be covered by functional AAP(s). In some cases it may be appropriate for a contractor to use both functional AAP(s) and establishment-based AAP(s)."

Procedures to be used in seeking OFCCP approval of a Functional AAP.

- Contractor must submit a written request to the Deputy Assistant Secretary (DAS) explaining why use of a functional AAP would be most appropriate for its particular corporate structure. The contractor must also designate a contact person who has the authority, resources, and support of top management to ensure effective implementation of the functional AAP.
- The request for a functional AAP must be submitted at least 120 calendar days prior to the expiration of the current corporate headquarters AAP.
- OFCCP will provide written acknowledgement of the request within two weeks of receipt.
- OFCCP may schedule a meeting or conference call with the contractor to discuss the request. The contractor must give OFCCP a list of meeting participants in advance of the meeting.
- Contractor must be prepared to discuss with OFCCP the following:
  - Location of facilities where employees perform their duties.
  - How the company is organized within each functional or business unit.
  - The reporting hierarchy within each functional or business unit.
  - Total number of employees within the contractor's workforce.
  - Total number of employees within each functional or business unit and the identification of the managing official of each functional or business unit.
  - Total number of employees not covered by functional AAP(s) that are covered in establishment-based AAP(s).
  - A description of the personnel processes (including recruitment, hiring and promotion) as they apply to each unit.
  - Any other information the contractor believes would further assist OFCCP in understanding its corporate structure, procedures and need for a functional AAP(s).
  - Preparation of the mandatory components, e.g., job group construction and the appropriate methodology for determining availability.
- OFCCP may request additional information following the initial meeting or conference call.
- OFCCP will create a Coordination Support Team (CST) to work with the contractor's designated representatives to coordinate the development of an acceptable functional AAP agreement. Members of the CST may come from the OFCCP's Division of Program Operations, the Division of Policy, Planning and Program Development, and the Regional Office in which the contractor's corporate headquarters is located.

- Once agreement is reached, the functional AAP agreement will be sent to the DAS for approval. Once final approval is received, a copy of the agreement will be sent to the contractor.

"Until the functional AAP agreement is approved, the contractor must continue to develop and maintain AAPs for each establishment."

Either party may terminate the functional AAP agreement upon 90 calendar days written notice. The notice must provide a brief explanation of the reason(s) for the termination, and the effective date of the termination.

Functional AAP agreements will expire five years after the date of approval. The contractor may request that the agreement be renewed for another five-year term. The renewal request is to be submitted to the DAS at least 120 calendar days prior to the expiration of the functional AAP agreement. "The request from the contractor that the agreement be renewed for another five-year term will be deemed accepted by OFCCP unless rejected in writing within 60 calendar days of receipt."

"After 120 calendar days from OFCCP's confirmed receipt of the contractor's request, if OFCCP has neither approved nor disapproved the contractor's request for a functional AAP agreement, the request will be deemed approved by the DAS and may be implemented 120 calendar days after the date OFCCP received the written request."

Functional AAPs will be included in the Corporate Management Compliance Evaluation pool for selection of audit candidates.

Online Application Selection System

Directive No. 281   Dated: 7-10-2008
From: Charles E. James, Sr., Deputy Assistant Secretary for Federal Contract Compliance

In response to changing technologies, many contractors have moved towards using an online application system as their primary, if not exclusive, method for accepting applications for employment. While some of these systems may be accessible to individuals with disabilities, others may be completely inaccessible or only partially accessible due to technological limitations. Irrespective of the level of accessibility of the online application system, federal contractors and subcontractors must ensure that qualified individuals with disabilities and disabled veterans have an equal opportunity for employment.[43]

Section 503 and its implementing regulations at 41 CFR Part 60-741, and VEVRAA and its implementing regulations at Parts 60-250 and 60-300, require that contractors provide equal opportunity to qualified individuals with disabilities and disabled veterans. In addition, under 60-741.5, 60-250.5, and 60-300.5, the contractor agrees to take affirmative action to employ and advance these individuals, including, but not limited to, "recruitment, advertising, and job application procedures." These job application procedures include online application systems.

---

[43] http://www.dol.gov/ofccp/regs/compliance/directives/dir281.htm

POLICY: *Effective immediately, all compliance evaluations shall include a review of the contractor's online application systems to ensure that the contractor is providing equal opportunity to qualified individuals with disabilities and disabled veterans. The review should include whether the contractor is providing reasonable accommodation, when requested, unless such accommodation would cause an undue hardship. In this directive, the term "online system" shall include, but not be limited to, all electronic or web-based systems that the contractor uses in all of its personnel activities.*

See page 85 for more information about how to accomplish this requirement.

Preserving Employment and Personnel Records in Electronic Format[44]

Directive No. 279   Dated: 5-14-2008
From: Charles E. James, Sr., Deputy Assistant Secretary for Federal Contract Compliance

Section 60-1.12 (a) of the regulations implementing Executive Order 11246 currently requires any personnel or employment record that is made or kept by the contractor to be "preserved" by the contractor for a minimum of two years. However, if the contractor has fewer than 150 employees or does not have a contract of at least $150, 000, § 60-1.12 (a) provides that the record retention period is a minimum of one year. The regulations implementing the Vietnam Era Veterans' Readjustment Assistance Act of 1974, as amended, 38 U.S.C. 4212, and Section 503 of the Rehabilitation Act of 1973, as amended, contain record retention provisions that are similar to § 60-1.12. See 41 CFR 60 250.80, 41 CFR 60 300.80, and 41 CFR 60 741.80. The current regulations also require that contractors permit access to their premises so that the OFCCP may inspect and copy their books and records, including computerized records. See 41 CFR 60-1.43, 60-250.81, 60-300.81, and 60-741.81.

Contractors and consultants have asked whether the OFCCP record retention regulations permit the destruction of the paper originals of employment and personnel records when such records are otherwise retained electronically.

The OFCCP has interpreted the term "preserve" as having its ordinary dictionary meaning, "to keep safe from harm, injury, or destruction." Webster's Ninth New Collegiate Dictionary, p. 931 (1984). Historically, the OFCCP has required that records be retained in their original form, and precluded a contractor from destroying the original paper records before the retention period has expired. However, the regulations do not prescribe a particular format in which the records must be preserved.

The OFCCP record retention provisions contain language similar to that found in the Equal Employment Opportunity Commission's (EEOC) regulations. Significantly, the EEOC addressed whether electronic recordkeeping would satisfy the recordkeeping requirements under Title VII, the ADA, and the ADEA in an Informal Discussion Letter. See www.eeoc.gov/foia/letters/2006/titlevii_ada_adea_recordkeeping.html. The Informal Discussion

---

[44] http://www.dol.gov/ofccp/regs/compliance/directives/dir279.htm

letter states in part "nothing in 29 CFR § 1602.14 (Title VII and ADA record keeping) requires preservation of records in paper, rather than electronic, form. However, please make sure that any system adopted by your clients captures and retains all information contained in documents. This would ensure that documents are properly 'preserved' as required by 29 CFR § 1602.14."

In addition, several Government agencies have issued regulations on the use of electronic recordkeeping systems. See e.g., DOL's Employee Benefits Security Administration's(EBSA) regulation at 29 CFR 2520.107-1; the Pension Benefit Guaranty Corporation's (PBGC) regulations at 29 CFR 4000.53 and 4000.54; the Securities and Exchange Commission's regulations at 17 CFR 31.a-2 and 17 CFR 275.204-2; and the Commodities Futures Trading Commission's regulation at 17 CFR 1.31. Generally, these regulations allow paper or non-electronic records to be stored in electronic formats provided certain safeguards are in place to ensure that the electronic storage system is reliable and records stored electronically are complete, accurate, and accessible.

In light of the increasing use of electronic media in all aspects of business administration, and the advances made in the technology used for converting paper documents into electronic formats, the OFCCP believes that it is appropriate to reexamine whether it is permissible for contractors to preserve in an electronic format those personnel and employment records originally created in paper form, and dispose of the paper originals.

POLICY: *The OFCCP regulations at 41 CFR 60-1.12, 60-250.80, 60 300.80 and 60-741.80 require that contractors preserve complete and accurate personnel records. The regulations at 41 CFR 60-1.43, 60-250.81, 60-300.81 and 60-741.81 also require contractors to permit the OFCCP access to their records, including computerized records, for inspection and copying. See also 41 CFR 60-1.4(a)(5) and 60-1.20(f). These obligations continue. Contractors may use an electronic recordkeeping system to comply with the record retention requirements. However, if records are maintained electronically, contractors must take care to ensure that the electronic records comply with the record retention and access regulations, i.e., the electronic records are accurate, complete, and accessible to the OFCCP.*

A contractor may transfer original paper records to its electronic recordkeeping system, if the medium used accurately reproduces the paper original and would constitute a duplicate or substitute copy of the original paper record under Federal law. In addition, a contractor may dispose of the original paper records any time after they are transferred to its electronic recordkeeping system, except that the original paper record may not be disposed of if the electronic copy would not accurately reproduce the original record. During a compliance evaluation, compliance officers may ask that paper originals stored in electronic format be converted into legible and readable paper copies and provided to OFCCP.

The use of an electronic recordkeeping system does not in any way alter the longstanding requirement that the contractor allow OFCCP to inspect and copy records at the contractor's premises during a compliance evaluation or complaint investigation. Thus, all of the contractor's electronic records must be made readily available for review, and must be readable and capable of being copied by OFCCP.

Compliance officers should consider electronic recordkeeping systems with the following characteristics as complying with record retention regulations:

- *the system has reasonable controls to ensure the integrity, accuracy, authenticity, and reliability of the records kept in electronic form;*
- *the electronic records are maintained in such a manner that they may be readily inspected and/or copied by the OFCCP, as required under the regulations at 41 CFR 60-1.43, 60-250.81, 60-300.81 and 60-741.81 (for example, the recordkeeping system should be capable of retaining, preserving, retrieving and reproducing the electronic records);*
- *paper originals stored in electronic format are readily convertible into legible and readable paper copy; and*
- *adequate records management practices are established and implemented (for example, such practices might include labeling electronically maintained or retained records, providing a secure storage environment, creating back-up electronic copies, observing a quality assurance program evidenced by regular evaluations of the electronic recordkeeping system, and retaining paper copies of records that cannot be clearly, accurately or completely transferred to an electronic recordkeeping system).*

Procedures for Inspection of the Form I-9 While Conducting the Onsite Phase of a Compliance Evaluation[45]

Directive No. 284   Dated: 9-5-2008
From: Charles E. James, Sr., Deputy Assistant Secretary for Federal Contract Compliance

When reviewing the new Form I-9 during an on-site review, the Compliance Officer should pay special attention to the following points:

    a. Contractors must use the new Form I-9, labeled (Rev. 06/05/07)N, for all employees hired, rehired, or reverified after November 7, 2007.

    b. The CO (Compliance Officer) must make certain that any electronically reproduced or retrieved Form I-9 is legible and has no evidence of inserts or changes made to the name, content, or sequence of the data elements.

    c. The CO may request that the contractor retrieve and reproduce Form I-9 and supporting documentation that are electronically stored. To ensure that retrieved and reproduced documents are free of tampering, the inspecting CO may ask for the associated audit trails that show who has access to the computer system and the actions performed within or on the computer system during a given period of time.

    d. The CO may also request that the contractor provide appropriate hardware and software, personnel, and documentation necessary to locate, retrieve, read, and reproduce any electronically stored Form I-9, supporting documents, and their associated audit trails, reports, and other data used to maintain the authenticity, integrity and reliability of the records.

    e. Contractors are obligated to provide, if requested, any reasonably available or obtainable electronic summary file(s), such as a spreadsheet containing all the information fields on all the electronically stored Form I-9. The CO should request such summary file(s) and

---

[45] http://www.dol.gov/ofccp/regs/compliance/directives/dir284.htm

use them to select specific Form I-9 when they inspect the electronically retained documents.

Active Case Management

Directive No. 285   Dated: 9-17-2008
From: Charles E. James, Sr., Deputy Assistant Secretary for Federal Contract Compliance

This Directive implements the "Tiered Compliance Review" process authorized in regulatory changes. It spells out the search for systemic discrimination and how that pursuit shall be conducted.

See a copy of the directive at page 512 or at
http://www.dol.gov/ofccp/regs/compliance/directives/dir285.pdf

 # Notes

CHAPTER 17

AFFIRMATIVE ACTION PROGRAMS
FOR CONSTRUCTION CONTRACTORS
(If you build roads, bridges or space ports for the government, this is for you.)

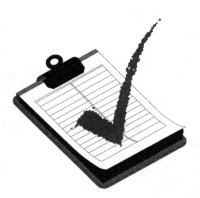

Notes

INTRODUCTION TO CONSTRUCTION AFFIRMATIVE ACTION PLANS

Any employer who is involved in federal construction projects, rather than selling goods and services, is subject to a separate set of requirements dealing with affirmative action. The "look and feel" of construction-related AAPs is quite different from that of the AAPs we have discussed up to this point.

Introduction

Federal construction projects account for billions of dollars each year. They include all sorts of work including highway construction, paving, trenching, bridge construction, and building construction. These projects can be for civilian applications or for the military. As a matter of fact, the military spends a great deal of money on construction projects.

Any employer who wishes to secure construction contracts from federal sources must understand and abide by the rules relating to affirmative action plan requirements for that segment of the federal contractor population.

It's not just the huge companies that must abide by these rules, either. If you have any federal or federally assisted construction contract in excess of $10,000, you must comply with these requirements. Shoot, today you can hardly pave a driveway for $10,000. Consequently, almost every construction contractor who is doing business with the federal government must meet these requirements.

Federal Regulations for Construction Contractors

Construction contractors are still subject to Executive Order 11246 (EO 11246) just as are contractors for goods and services. However, construction contractors have been given a different type of obligation. It is spelled out in 41 CFR 60-4 of the regulations. It is also based on the presumption of equal employment opportunity.

Federal Regulations say, *"...applies to all contractors and subcontractors which hold any Federal or federally assisted construction contract in excess of $10,000..."*

"...[This part is] applicable to all of a construction contractor's or subcontractor's construction employees who are engaged in on site construction including those construction employees who work on a non-Federal or nonfederally assisted construction site."

"In addition, this part applies to construction work performed by construction contractors and subcontractors for Federal nonconstruction contractors and subcontractors if the construction work is necessary in whole or in part to the performance of a nonconstruction contract or subcontract." [41 CFR 60-4.1]

So, now you know. Chances are pretty good that you are covered if you do construction work for any federal agency, the military, or a private organization that has its own contracts with the government and your work is vital to their completion of their government work.

If Construction Contractors Prepare an AAP for 60-4, Do They Also Have to Prepare an AAP for 60-2?

To answer this question, determine if the construction contractor is working on a federally assisted construction project, or if it has a direct contract or subcontract for goods and services to a specific government agency.

For example, a contract with the Army Corps of Engineers to construct specific flood control measures can capture the company as a federal contractor and require a 60-2 AAP along with AAPs for Disabled and Veterans. If, however, the company is working on a road construction project that has federally assisted funding, it will be subject to requirements for Construction Contractors in 60-4 and need only to develop a 16-step program for trade employees.

The 16-step program outlined in 60-4 applies only to trade employees. Construction contractors do not have to develop affirmative action programs covering administrative workers or other job categories outside the trades as long as they are not a prime- or first-tier subcontractor for goods or services.

AAP Content Requirements

As you might expect, there are several requirements for construction AAPs. Here is a checklist for your use. We will explain each of the requirements following the list.

Sixteen Items Required in a Construction AAP File

Item	Requirement	Regulatory Section
1	EEO Policy Statement.	41 CFR 60-4.3(a)(7)(a)
2	List of current minority and female recruitment sources with proof of written notification about EEO policy and job opening announcements with record of responses from each source.	41 CFR 60-4.3(a)(7)(b)
3	List of names and address of all walk-in applicants and all union and other referrals with sex and ethnic identification of each.	41 CFR 60-4.3(a)(7)(c)
4	Report to OFCCP instances of union failure to refer female or minority job candidates the contractor has sent to the union for processing.	41 CFR 60-4.3(a)(7)(d)
5	Develop on-the-job training opportunities or participate in apprenticeship programs which expressly include minorities and women so they can upgrade their skills to meet contractor's employment needs.	41 CFR 60-4.3(a)(7)(e)
6	Distribute copies of contractor's EEO Policy Statement to all relevant unions and include a copy in all employee handbooks. Ensure that all the policy is posted where all employees can see it.	41 CFR 60-4.3(a)(7)(f)
7	Annually, train all supervisors and managers who are involved in hiring & firing decision-making about the EEO Policy and the contractor's obligations under the affirmative action requirements of 41 CFR 60-4.3.	41 CFR 60-4.3(a)(7)(g)
8	Send copies of EEO Policy to all other contractors and subcontractors with whom the contractor does business, or anticipates doing business.	41 CFR 60-4.3(a)(7)(h)
9	Notify in writing all recruiting sources, including schools, minority, female and community organizations about job openings and openings in apprenticeship programs.	41 CFR 60-4.3(a)(7)(i)

Item	Requirement	Regulatory Section
10	Encourage female and minority employees to recruit other females and minorities into consideration for job openings with the contractor.	41 CFR 60-4.3(a)(7)(j)
11	Validate all tests and other selection requirements as required under Uniform Guidelines to Employee Selection.	41 CFR 60-4.3(a)(7)(k) 41 CFR 60-3
12	Conduct an annual evaluation of all minorities and females in the workforce to determine if they should be considered for promotion, and to encourage these employees to seek promotion or training to prepare themselves for promotion.	41 CFR 60-4.3(a)(7)(l)
13	Continually monitor seniority practices, job classifications, work assignments and other personnel practices to assure they meet requirements of the EEO Policy.	41 CFR 60-4.3(a)(7)(m)
14	Audit company facilities and activities to assure they are nonsegregated aside from privacy requirements in toilet facilities.	41 CFR 60-4.3(a)(7)(n)
15	Maintain records of all solicitations or offers of subcontracts from minority or female construction contractors and suppliers, including any solicitations initiated by your organization.	41 CFR 60-4.3(a)(7)(o)
16	Conduct an annual review of all supervisors' adherence to and performance under the EEO Policy and contractor's AAP obligations.	41 CFR 60-4.3(a)(7)(p)

Collectively these 16 items are considered affirmative action obligations of federal construction contractors. There are other requirements, however, in addition to these.

Checklist of Additional Activities Required of Construction Contractors

Item	Requirement	Regulatory Section
A	Place the "Notice of Requirement" in all solicitations for offers and bids on all Federal and federally assisted construction contracts or subcontracts in excess of $10,000.	41 CFR 60-4.2(d)
B	Include the "Equal Opportunity Clause" (See pages 38 to 40) in all contracts, subcontracts and purchase orders relating to the work done with other organizations.	41 CFR 60-4.3(a)

C	Include the specifications shown beginning on page 363 in all Federal and federally assisted construction contracts in excess of $10,000 to be performed in the geographical areas designated by the Director of OFCCP.	41 CFR 60-4.3(a)
D	Beck Poster Requirements Notice to union members that they may direct that none of their dues go to political support.	Executive Order 13201

STANDARD FEDERAL EQUAL EMPLOYMENT OPPORTUNITY CONSTRUCTION CONTRACT SPECIFICATIONS (EXECUTIVE ORDER 11246)

1. As used in these specifications:
   a. "Covered area" means the geographical area described in the solicitation from which this contract resulted;
   b. "Director" means Director, Office of Federal Contract Compliance Programs, United States Department of Labor, or any person to whom the Director delegates authority;
   c. "Employer Identification Number" means the Federal Social Security number used on the Employer's Quarterly Federal Tax Return, U.S. Treasury Department Form 941.
   d. "Minority" includes:
      i. Black (all persons having origins in any of the Black African racial groups not of Hispanic origin);
      ii. Hispanic (all persons of Mexican, Puerto Rican, Cuban, Central or South American or other Spanish Culture or origin, regardless of race);
      iii. Asian and Pacific Islander (all persons having origins in any of the original peoples of the Far East, Southeast Asia, the Indian Subcontinent, or the Pacific Islands); and
      iv. American Indian or Alaskan Native (all persons having origins in any of the original peoples of North America and maintaining identifiable tribal affiliations through membership and participation or community identification).

1. Whenever the Contractor, or any Subcontractor at any tier, subcontracts a portion of the work involving any construction trade, it shall physically include in each subcontract in excess of $10,000 the provisions of these specifications and the Notice which contains the applicable goals for minority and female participation and which is set forth in the solicitations from which this contract resulted.

2. If the Contractor is participating (pursuant to 41 CFR 60-4.5) in a Hometown Plan approved by the U.S. Department of Labor in the covered area either individually or through an association, its affirmative action obligations on all work in the Plan area (including goals and timetables) shall be in accordance with that Plan for those trades which have unions participating in the Plan. Contractors must be able to demonstrate their participation in and compliance with the provisions of any such Hometown Plan. Each Contractor or Subcontractor participating in an approved Plan is individually required to comply with its obligations under the EEO clause, and to make a good faith effort to achieve each goal under the Plan in each trade in which it has employees. The overall good faith performance by other Contractors or Subcontractors toward a goal in an approved Plan does not excuse any

covered Contractor's or Subcontractor's failure to take good faith efforts to achieve the Plan goals and timetables.

3. The Contractor shall implement the specific affirmative action standards provided in paragraphs 7 a through p of these specifications. The goals set forth in the solicitation from which this contract resulted are expressed as percentages of the total hours of employment and training of minority and female utilization the Contractor should reasonably be able to achieve in each construction trade in which it has employees in the covered area. Covered Construction contractors performing construction work in geographical areas where they do not have a Federal or federally assisted construction contract shall apply the minority and female goals established for the geographical area where the work is being performed. Goals are published periodically in the Federal Register in notice form, and such notices may be obtained from any Office of Federal Contract Compliance Programs office or from Federal procurement contracting officers. The Contractor is expected to make substantially uniform progress in meeting its goals in each craft during the period specified.

4. Neither the provisions of any collective bargaining agreement, nor the failure by a union with whom the Contractor has a collective bargaining agreement, to refer either minorities or women shall excuse the Contractor's obligations under these specifications, Executive Order 11246, or the regulations promulgated pursuant thereto.

5. In order for the nonworking training hours of apprentices and trainees to be counted in meeting the goals, such apprentices and trainees must be employed by the Contractor during the training period, and the Contractor must have made a commitment to employ the apprentices and trainees at the completion of their training, subject to the availability of employment opportunities. Trainees must be trained pursuant to training programs approved by the U.S. Department of Labor.

6. The Contractor shall take specific affirmative actions to ensure equal employment opportunity. The evaluation of the Contractor's compliance with these specifications shall be based upon its effort to achieve maximum results from its actions. The Contractor shall document these efforts fully, and shall implement affirmative action steps at least as extensive as the following:
    a. Ensure and maintain a working environment free of harassment, intimidation, and coercion at all sites, and in all facilities at which the Contractor's employees are assigned to work. The Contractor, where possible, will assign two or more women to each construction project. The Contractor shall specifically ensure that all foremen, superintendents, and other on-site supervisory personnel are aware of and carry out the Contractor's obligation to maintain such a working environment, with specific attention to minority or female individuals working at such sites or in such facilities.
    b. Establish and maintain a current list of minority and female recruitment sources, provide written notification to minority and female recruitment sources and to community organizations when the Contractor or its unions have employment opportunities available, and maintain a record of the organizations' responses.
    c. Maintain a current file of the names, addresses and telephone numbers of each minority and female off-the-street applicant and minority or female referral from a union, a recruitment source or community organization and of what action was taken with respect to each such individual. If such individual was sent to the union hiring hall for referral and was not referred back to the Contractor by the union or, if referred, not employed by the Contractor, this shall be documented in the file with the reason therefore, along with whatever additional actions the Contractor may have taken.
    d. Provide immediate written notification to the Director when the union or unions with which the Contractor has a collective bargaining agreement has not referred to the Contractor a minority person or woman sent by the Contractor, or when the

Contractor has other information that the union referral process has impeded the Contractor's efforts to meet its obligations.

e. Develop on-the-job training opportunities and/or participate in training programs for the area which expressly include minorities and women, including upgrading programs and apprenticeship and trainee programs relevant to the Contractor's employment needs, especially those programs funded or approved by the Department of Labor. The Contractor shall provide notice of these programs to the sources compiled under 7b above.

f. Disseminate the Contractor's EEO policy by providing notice of the policy to unions and training programs and requesting their cooperation in assisting the Contractor in meeting its EEO obligations; by including it in any policy manual and collective bargaining agreement; by publicizing it in the company newspaper, annual report, etc.; by specific review of the policy with all management personnel and with all minority and female employees at least once a year; and by posting the company EEO policy on bulletin boards accessible to all employees at each location where construction work is performed.

g. Review, at least annually, the company's EEO policy and affirmative action obligations under these specifications with all employees having any responsibility for hiring, assignment, layoff, termination or other employment decisions, including specific review of these items with onsite supervisory personnel such as Superintendents, General Foreman, etc., prior to the initiation of construction work at any job site. A written record shall be made and maintained identifying the time and place of these meetings, persons attending, subject matter discussed, and disposition of the subject matter.

h. Disseminate the Contractor's EEO policy externally by including it in any advertising in the news media, specifically including minority and female news media, and providing written notification to and discussing the Contractor's EEO policy with other Contractors and Subcontractors with whom the Contractor does or anticipates doing business.

i. Direct its recruitment efforts, both oral and written, to minority, female and community organizations, to schools with minority and female students and to minority and female recruitment and training organizations serving the Contractor's recruitment area and employment needs. Not later than one month prior to the date for the acceptance of applications for apprenticeship or other training by any recruitment source, the Contractor shall send written notification to organizations such as the above, describing the openings, screening procedures, and tests to be used in the selection process.

j. Encourage present minority and female employees to recruit other minority persons and women and, where reasonable, provide after school, summer and vacation employment to minority and female youth both on the site and in other areas of a Contractor's work force.

k. Validate all tests and other selection requirements where there is an obligation to do so under 41 CFR Part 60-3.

l. Conduct, at least annually, an inventory and evaluation at least of all minority and female personnel for promotional opportunities and encourage these employees to seek or to prepare for, through appropriate training, etc., such opportunities.

m. Ensure that seniority practices, job classifications, work assignments and other personnel practices, do not have a discriminatory effect by continually monitoring all personnel and employment related activities to ensure that the EEO policy and the Contractor's obligations under these specifications are being carried out.

n. Ensure that all facilities and company activities are nonsegregated except that separate or single-user toilet and necessary changing facilities shall be provided to assure privacy between the sexes.

o. Document and maintain a record of all solicitations of offers for subcontracts from minority and female construction contractors and suppliers, including circulation of solitations to minority and female contractor associations and other business associations.

p. Conduct a review, at least annually, of all supervisors' adherence to and performance under the Contractor's EEO policies and affirmative action obligations.

7. Contractors are encouraged to participate in voluntary associations which assist in fulfilling one or more of their affirmative action obligations (7a through p). The efforts of a contractor association, joint contractor-union, contractor-community, or other similar group of which the contractor is a member and participant, may be asserted as fulfilling any one or more of its obligations under 7a through p of these Specifications provided that the contractor actively participates in the group, makes every effort to assure that the group has a positive impact on the employment of minorities and women in the industry, ensures that the concrete benefits of the program are reflected in the Contractor's minority and female workforce participation, makes a good faith effort to meet its individual goals and timetables, and can provide access to documentation which demonstrates the effectiveness of actions taken on behalf of the Contractor. The obligation to comply, however, is the Contractor's and failure of such a group to fulfill an obligation shall not be a defense for the Contractor's noncompliance.

8. A single goal for minorities and a separate single goal for women have been established. The Contractor, however, is required to provide equal employment opportunity and to take affirmative action for all minority groups, both male and female, and all women, both minority and non-minority. Consequently, the Contractor may be in violation of the Executive Order if a particular group is employed in a substantially disparate manner (for example, even though the Contractor has achieved its goals for women generally, the Contractor may be in violation of the Executive Order if a specific minority group of women is underutilized).

9. The Contractor shall not use the goals and timetables or affirmative action standards to discriminate against any person because of race, color, religion, sex, or national origin.

10. The Contractor shall not enter into any Subcontract with any person or firm debarred from Government contracts pursuant to Executive Order 11246.

11. The Contractor shall carry out such sanctions and penalties for violation of these specifications and of the Equal Opportunity Clause, including suspension, termination and cancellation of existing subcontracts as may be imposed or ordered pursuant to Executive Order 11246, as amended, and its implementing regulations, by the Office of Federal Contract Compliance Programs. Any Contractor who fails to carry out such sanctions and penalties shall be in violation of these specifications and Executive Order 11246, as amended.

12. The Contractor, in fulfilling its obligations under these specifications shall implement specific affirmative action steps, at least as extensive as those standards prescribed in paragraph 7 of these specifications, so as to achieve maximum results from its efforts to ensure equal employment opportunity. If the Contractor fails to comply with the requirements of the Executive Order, the implementing regulations, or these specifications, the Director shall proceed in accordance with 41 CFR 60-4.8.

13. The Contractor shall designate a responsible official to monitor all employment related activity to ensure that the company EEO policy is being carried out, to submit reports relating to the provisions hereof as may be required by the Government and to keep records. Records shall at least include for each employee the name, address, telephone numbers, construction trade, union affiliation if any, employee identification number when assigned, social security number, race, sex, status (e.g., mechanic, apprentice trainee, helper, or laborer), dates of changes in status, hours worked per week in the indicated trade, rate of pay, and locations at which the work was performed. Records shall be maintained in an easily understandable and

retrievable form; however, to the degree that existing records satisfy this requirement, contractors shall not be required to maintain separate records.

14. Nothing herein provided shall be construed as a limitation upon the application of other laws which establish different standards of compliance or upon the application of requirements for the hiring of local or other area residents (e.g., those under the Public Works Employment Act of 1977 and the Community Development Block Grant Program).

Recordkeeping Requirements

Every construction contractor who is subject to these requirements must maintain detailed records of employees, recruiting efforts, recruiting results, applicants produced from these efforts, and project-related hiring.

As long as the construction contractor is not a contractor or subcontractor for goods or services under specific contracts, the administrative support groups in the company will not be subject to scrutiny by the OFCCP. It will only be the trade groups that OFCCP concerns itself with.

Recordkeeping Requirements

Records Required	Citation
Employee Information • Name • Address • Telephone numbers • Construction trade • Union affiliation • Employee identification number (if used) • Social Security Number • Race • Sex • Status (mechanic, apprentice trainee, helper, laborer, etc.) • Dates of changes in status • Hours worked per week in the indicated trade • Rate of pay • Locations at which the work was performed	41 CFR 60-4.3(a)(14)
Industrial Association Membership & Participation Activities • Voluntary associations • Joint Contractor-Union groups • Joint Contractor-Community groups • Contractor Associations	41 CFR 60-4.3(a)(8)

Secrets of Affirmative Action Compliance

Records Required	Citation
Recruitment Sources • List of current minority & female recruitment sources • List of current community recruitment organizations • List of recruitment sources notified when job openings occur • Copy of each notification sent to recruitment sources	41 CFR 60-4.3(a)(7)(b)

Job Applicants
• Off-the-street minority & female applicants
  o Name
  o Address
  o Telephone numbers
• Minority & female applicants referred from union, community organization or other recruitment source
  o Name
  o Address
  o Telephone numbers
• Minority & female applicants sent by Contractor to union
  o Name
  o Address
  o Telephone numbers
  o Referred back to contractor or not?
  o Reason for not employing applicant if referred
  o Other actions taken by contractor on applicant
	41 CFR 60-4.3(a)(7)(c)

Notice of Union's Failure to Refer • Copy of notice sent to OFCCP Director when a minority or female candidate sent to the union is not referred back to the contractor as a candidate	41 CFR 60-4.3(a)(7)(d)
Female Work Assignments • Record of each work site operation to prove two or more females were assigned to each site	41 CFR 60-4.3(a)(7)(a)

Supervisor Training
• Record of EEO/Affirmative Action training provided to all supervisors, superintendents, job site supervisors and others having employee management responsibilities
  o Trainee name
  o Trainee title
  o Trainee work assignment
  o Date of training
  o Subjects covered or training agenda
	41 CFR 60-4.3(a)(7)(a)
	41 CFR 60-4.3(a)(7)(g)

Records Required	Citation

On-the-Job Training
• List of training programs that include minorities & women including skill development/upgrade programs, & apprenticeship programs
• List of individuals participating in each training program including:
   o Trainee name
   o Trainee title
   o Trainee work assignment
   o Trainee sex & race/ethnicity
	41 CFR 60-4.3(a)(7)(e)

Policy Dissemination • List of all work locations where EEO policy is posted • List of all recruitment sources and community organizations to which a copy of the EEO policy is sent • List of all unions to which a copy of the EEO policy is sent • Copy of each advertisement for job openings showing EEO "tag line" • List of all minority/female publications in which job opening advertisements are placed	41 CFR 60-4.3(a)(7)(f) 41 CFR 60-4.3(a)(7)(h)
Employee Recruitment • Description of methods used to encourage present minority and female employees to recruit other minority persons and women • Description of employment programs offered by contractor to minorities and women after school and during summer and other school vacations	41 CFR 60-4.3(a)(7)(j)
Promotional Inventory • Annual inventory of all minority and female employees and their qualifications for promotional opportunities	41 CFR 60-4.3(a)(7)(l)
Disparate Impact Testing • Document that seniority practices, job classifications, work assignments and other personnel practices do not have a disparate impact on minorities or women • Validate all tests and other selection requirements where required under the Uniform Guidelines for Employee Selection	41 CFR 60-4.3(a)(7)(k) 41 CFR 60-4.3(a)(7)(m) 41 CFR 60-3

Records Required	Citation
Subcontractor Solicitations • Documentation of all solicitations of offers for subcontracts from minority and female construction contractors and suppliers • List of all solicitations sent to minority or female construction contractors and suppliers	41 CFR 60-4.3(a)(7)(o)
Management & Supervisor Performance Evaluation • Documentation of annual review of each supervisor's and manager's job performance related to requirements of EEO policy and affirmative action obligations	41 CFR 60-4.3(a)(7)(p)

Formatting an AAP for Construction Contractors

Putting your AAP to paper is fairly easy. There are going to be two sections to the plan.

AAP Section 1: EEO Policy

Place your EEO Policy in the document as the first item. This is your expression of commitment to nondiscrimination. I suggest you include each of the protected categories you want your management/supervisory staff to understand so they don't inadvertently make an employment decision based on a protected category. Include all of the additional categories your state may protect over and above those protected by federal legislation.

Your policy statement can be made in a single paragraph.

AAP Section 2: List of 16 Steps Required in Regulations

List each of the requirements listed in Section 7 of the Specification Standards for construction contractors (41 CFR 60-4.3). Number or letter your list so it is easy to refer to later. That can also help you avoid omitting something you are obliged to include.

CEO Signature & Date:

Finally, your CEO or senior executive should sign and date the document. This needs to be done each year to reflect a current-year date.

Your entire AAP document can be printed on two or three pages of paper. Tracking all of the data and records you must keep to support it is another matter.

Hometown Plans – Goals for Minority Workers

The Department of Labor has approved certain geographical areas in the country to be designated as Hometown Plan areas. Construction contractors that are participating in an approved Hometown Plan are required to comply with the goals of the Hometown Plan with regard to construction work they perform in the area covered by the Hometown Plan.

For all other work construction contractors perform, they are required to comply with applicable SMSA or Economic Area goals contained in 46 FR 7533, effective January 23, 1981.

If the company is a signatory to a Hometown Plan, it is obligated to use the goals for minority workers contained in that plan. If it ceases to be a signatory to the Hometown Plan, goals are established from the list of Economic Areas specified in Federal Regulations. You will find them listed beginning on the next page.

Goals for Female Workers

The following goals and timetables for female utilization shall be included in all Federal and federally assisted construction contracts and subcontracts in excess of $10,000. The goals are applicable to the contractor's aggregate on-site construction workforce whether or not part of that workforce is performing work on a Federal or federally assisted construction contract or subcontract.

Area covered: Goals for Women apply nationwide.

Goals and Timetables

Timetable	Goals (Percent)
From 4/1/78 until 3/31/79	*3.1*
From 4/1/79 until 3/31/80	*5.0*
From 4/1/80 until notice from DOL	*6.9*

(45 FR 85750, effective December 30, 1980)

So, clearly, **the goal for females in on-site trade jobs is 6.9%** regardless of the construction contractor's location in the country.

Economic Area – Goals for Minority Workers[46]

45 FR 85750, Appendix B-80, as amended by 46 FR 7533, became effective January 23, 1981. It specifies, by location in the country, the percentage of minority workers that should be on-site in trade jobs at construction sites. Contractors who are subject to these goals because they work on projects funded with federal money are also obliged to maintain the same goals at locations where there may be no federal funding involved. Captured by the regulations in only one site-specific job, the contractor is then obligated to apply the goals at all work locations, regardless of their involvement in federally funded efforts.

If the contractor has work sites at more than one of the designated Economic Areas, it is expected to meet the goals at each site according to the Economic Area goals specified in the Federal Register.

Contractors working under an approved Hometown Plan should use the goals established in the Hometown Plan. All others should use the goals for Economic Areas shown beginning on the next page.

---

[46] The Ninth Circuit Court [*Western States Paving Co., Inc. v. Washington State Department of Transportation*, 9th Cir No. 03-35783, May 9, 2005] has called state Disadvantaged Business Enterprise Programs (DBE) into question. It has said in its review, "…each of the principal minority groups benefited by Washington's DBE program – Black Americans, Hispanic Americans, Native Americans, Asian-Pacific Americans, Subcontinent Asian Americans, and women – must have suffered discrimination within the State. If that is not the case, then the DBE program provides minorities who have not encountered discriminatory barriers with an unconstitutional competitive advantage at the expense of both non-minorities and any minority groups that have actually been targeted for discrimination." Further, "…claims of general societal discrimination – and even generalized assertions about discrimination in an entire industry – cannot be used to justify race-conscious remedial measures." In conclusion, the Court said about this case, "The record is therefore devoid of any evidence suggesting that minorities currently suffer – or have ever suffered – discrimination in the Washington transportation contracting industry. We must therefore conclude that Washington's application of TEA-21 conflicts with the guarantees of equal protection because the State's DBE program is not narrowly tailored to further Congress's remedial objective. The 'exact connection' between means and ends that is a prerequisite to the use of racial classifications is demonstrably absent from Washington's DBE program." We will just have to wait to see what other U.S. Circuit Courts have to say about this issue. Perhaps a case such as this one will reach the U.S. Supreme Court one day and we will have more input about the construction and application of DBE programs.

Economic Area Percentage Goals for Minorities in Trades
Construction Contractors
Effective January 23, 1981 – 46 FR 7533

Alabama:

047 Mobile, AL:
SMSA Counties:
5160 Mobile, AL...25.9
AL Baldwin; AL Mobile.
6025 Pascagoula-Moss Point, MS.................16.9
MS Jackson.
Non-SMSA Counties......................................26.4
AL Choctaw; AL Clarke; AL Conecuh; AL
Escambia; AL Monroe; AL Washington; AL Wilcox;
MS George; MS Greene.

048 Montgomery, AL:
SMSA Counties:
5240 Montgomery, AL...............................29.9
AL Autauga; AL Elmore; AL Montgomery.
Non-SMSA Counties:
AL Barbour; AL Bullock; AL Butler; AL Coffee; AL
Coosa; AL Covington; AL Crenshaw; AL Dale; AL
Dallas; AL Geneva; AL Henry; AL Houston; AL
Lowndes; AL Macon; AL Perry; AL Pike; AL
Tallapoosa.

049 Birmingham, AL:
SMSA Counties:
0450 Anniston, AL....................................14.3
AL Calhoun.
1000 Birmingham, AL...............................24.9
AL Jefferson; AL St. Clair; AL Shelby; AL Walker;
AL Etowah.
8600 Tuscaloosa, AL.................................20.6
AL Tuscaloosa.
Non-SMSA Counties..................................20.7
AL Bibb; AL Blount; AL Cherokee; AL Chilton;
AL Clay; AL Cleburne; AL Cullman; AL Fayette; AL
Greene; AL Hale; AL Lamar; AL Marion; AL
Pickens; AL Randolph; AL Sumter; AL Talladega;
AL Winston.

050 Huntsville-Florence, AL:
SMSA Counties:
2650 Florence, AL....................................11.9
AL Colvert; AL Lauderdale.
3440 Huntsville, AL..................................12.0
AL Limestone; AL Madison; AL Marshall.
Non-SMSA Counties..................................11.2
AL Franklin; AL Lawrence; AL Morgan; TN
Lincoln.

Alaska:

182 Anchorage, AK:
SMSA Counties:
0380 Anchorage, AK.................................8.7
AK Anchorage Division.
Non-SMSA Counties.................................15.1
AK Aleutian Islands Division; AK Angoon
Division; AK Barrow–North Slope Division; AK
Bethel Division; AK Bristol Bay Borough; AK Bristol
Bay Division; AK Cordova McCarthy Division; AK
Fairbanks Division; AK Haines Division; AK Juneau
Division; AK Kenai–Cook Inlet Division; AK
Ketchikan Division; AK Kobuk Division; AK Kodiak
Division; AK Kwskikwim Division; AK
Mantansuska–Susitna Division; AK Nome Division;
AK Outer Ketchikan Division; AK Prince of Wales
Division; AK Seward Division; AK Sitka Division;
AK Skagaway-Yakutat Division; AK Southeast
Fairbanks Division; AK Upper Yukon Division; AK
Valdez-Citina-Whittier Division; AK Wade Hampton
Division; AK Wrangell-Petersburg Division; AK
Yokon-Koyukuk Division.

Arkansas:

109 Fayetteville, AR:
Non-SMSA Counties..................................3.3
AR Baxter; AR Benton; AR Boone; AR Carroll; AR
Madison; AR Marion; AR Newton; AR Searcy; AR
Washington; OK Adair; OK Delaware.

110 Fort Smith, AR
SMSA Counties:
2720 Fort Smith, AR-OK...........................5.6
AR Crawford; AR Sebastian; OK LeFlore; OK
Sequoyah.
Non-SMSA Counties..................................6.6
AR Franklin; AR Logan; AR Polk; AR Scott; OK
Choctaw; OK Haskell; OK Latimer; OK McCurtain;
OK Pittsburg; OK Pushmataha.

111 Little Rock – North Little Rock, AR:
SMSA Counties:
4400 Little Rock-North Little Rock, AR...........15.7
AR Pulaski; AR Saline.
6240 Pine Bluff, AR.................................31.2
AR Jefferson.
Non-SMSA Counties..................................16.4
AR Arkansas; AR Ashley; AR Bradley; AR
Calhoun; AR Chicot; AR Clark; AR Cleburne; AR
Cleveland; AR Conway; AR Dallas; AR Desha; AR
Drew; AR Faulkner; AR Fulton; AR Garland; AR
Grant; AR Hot Springs; AR Independence; AR Izard;

AR Jackson; AR Johnson; AR Lincoln; AR Lonoke; AR Monroe; AR Montgomery; AR Ouachita; AR Perry; AR Pope; AR Prairie; AR Sharp; AR Stone; AR Union; AR Van Buren; AR White; AR Woodruff; AR Yell.

Arizona:
161 Tuscon, AZ:
 SMSA counties:
  8520 Tuscon, AZ.....................................24.1
  AZ Pima.
 Non-SMSA counties....................................27.0
  AZ Cochise; AZ Graham; AZ Greenlee; AZ Santa Cruz.

162 Phoenix, AZ:
 SMSA Counties:
  6200 Phoenix, AZ...................................15.8
  AZ Maricopa.
 Non-SMSA Counties.................................19.6
  AZ Appache; AZ Coconino; AZ Gila; AZ Mohave; AZ Navajo; AZ Pinal; AZ Yavapai; AZ Yuma.

California:
174 Redding, CA:
 Non-SMSA Counties.....................................6.8
  CA Lassen; CA Modoc; CA Plumas; CA Shasta; CA Siskiyou; CA Tehama.

175 Eureka, CA:
 Non-SMSA Counties...................................6.6
  CA Del Norte; CA Humboldt; CA Trinity.

176 San Francisco-Oakland-San Jose, CA:
 SMSA Counties:
  7120 Salinas-Seaside-Monterey, CA...............28.9
  CA Monterey.
  7360 San Francisco-Oakland, CA..................25.6
  CA Alameda; CA Contra Costa; CA Marin; CA San Francisco; CA San Mateo.
  7400 San Jose, CA...................................19.6
  CA Santa Clara.
  7485 Santa Cruz, CA................................14.9
  CA Santa Cruz.
  7500 Santa Rosa, CA.................................9.1
  CA Sonoma.
  8720 Vallejo-Fairfield-Napa, CA..................17.1
  CA Napa; CA Solano.
 Non-SMSA Counties.................................23.2
  CA Lake; CA Mendocino; CA San Benito.

177 Sacramento, CA:
 SMSA Counties:
  6920 Sacramento, CA................................16.1
  CA Placer, CA Sacramento, CA Yolo.
 Non-SMSA Counties.................................14.3
  CA Butte; CA Colusa; CA El Dorado; CA Glenn; CA Nevada; CA Sierra; CA Sutter; CA Yuba.

178 Stockton-Modesto, CA:
 SMSA Counties:
  5170 Modesto, CA...................................12.3

  CA Stanislaus.
  8120 Stockton, CA..................................24.3
  CA San Joaquin.
 Non-SMSA Counties.................................19.8
  CA Alpine; CA Amador; CA Calaveras; CA Mariposa; CA Merced; CA Tuolumne.

179 Fresno-Bakersfield, CA
 SMSA Counties:
  0680 Bakersfield, CA................................19.1
  CA Kern.
  2840 Fresno, CA....................................26.1
  CA Fresno.
 Non-SMSA Counties.................................23.6
  CA Kings; CA Madera; CA Tulare.

180 Los Angeles, CA:
 SMSA Counties:
  0360 Anaheim-Santa Ana-Garden Grove, CA....11.9
  CA Orange.
  4480 Los Angeles-Long Beach, CA..............28.3
  CA Los Angeles.
  6000 Oxnard-Simi Valley-Ventura, CA..........21.5
  CA Ventura.
  6780 Riverside-San Bernardino-Ontario, CA.....19.0
  CA Riverside; CA San Bernardino.
  7480 Santa Barbara-Santa Maria-Lompoc, CA....19.7
  CA Santa Barbara.
 Non-SMSA Counties.................................24.6
  CA Inyo; CA Mono; CA San Luis Obispo.

181 San Diego, CA:
 SMSA Counties:
  7320 San Diego, CA................................16.9
  CA San Diego.
 Non-SMSA Counties.................................18.2
  CA Imperial.

Colorado:
157 Denver, CO:
 SMSA Counties:
  2080 Denver-Boulder, CO..........................13.8
  CO Adams; CO Arapahoe; CO Boulder; CO Denver; CO Douglas; CO Gilpin; CO Jefferson.
  2670 Fort Collins, CO...............................6.9
  CO Larimer.
  3060 Greeley, CO...................................13.1
  CO Weld.
 Non-SMSA Counties.................................12.8
  CO Cheyenne; CO Clear Creek; CO Elbert; CO Grand; CO Kit Carson; CO Logan; CO Morgan; CO Park; CO Phillips; CO Sedgwick; CO Summit; CO Washington; CO Yuma.

158 Colorado Springs-Pueblo, CO:
 SMSA Counties:
  1720 Colorado Springs, CO........................10.9
  CO El Paso; CO Teller.
  6560 Pueblo, CO....................................27.5
  CO Pueblo.
 Non-SMSA Counties.................................19.0

CO Alamosa; CO Baca; CO Bent; CO Chaffee; CO Conejos; CO Costilla; CO Crowley; CO Custer; CO Fremont; CO Huerfano; CO Kiowa; CO Lake; CO Las Animas; CO Lincoln; CO Mineral; CO Otero; CO Prowers; CO Rio Grande; CO Saguache.

159 Grand Junction, CO:
Non-SMSA Counties..................................10.2
CO Archuleta; CO Delta; CO Dolores; CO Eagle; CO Garfield; CO Gunnison; CO Hinsdale; CO LaPlata; CO Mesa; CO Moffat; CO Montezuma; CO Montrose; CO Ouray; CO Pitkin; CO Rio Blanco; CO Routt; CO San Juan; CO San Miguel; UT Grand; UT San Juan.

Connecticut (Mass):
006 Hartford-New Haven-Springfield, CT-MA:
SMSA Counties:
3283 Hartford-New Britain-Bristol, CT.............6.9
CT Hartford; CT Middlesex; CT Tolland.
5483 New Haven-Waterbury-Meriden, CT..........9.0
CT New Haven.
5523 New London-Norwich, CT.....................4.5
CT New London.
6323 Pittsfield, MA.................................1.6
MA Berkshire.
8003 Springfield-Chicopee-Holyoke, MA-CT......4.8
MA Hampden; MA Hampshire.
Non-SMSA Counties.................................5.9
CT Litchfield; CT Windham; MA Franklin; NH Cheshire; VT Windham.

Florida:
041 Jacksonville, FL:
SMSA Counties:
2900 Gainesville, FL..............................20.6
FL Alachua.
3600 Jacksonville, FL.............................21.8
FL Baker; FL Clay; FL Deval; FL Nassau; FL St. Johns.
Non-SMSA Counties................................22.2
FL Bradford; FL Columbia; FL Dixie; FL Gilchrist; FL Hamilton; FL LaFayette; FL Levy; FL Marion; FL Putnam; FL Suwannee; FL Union; GA Brantley; GA Camden; GA Charlton; GA Glynn; GA Pierce; GA Ware.

042 Orlando-Melbourne-Daytona Beach, FL:
SMSA Counties:
2020 Daytona Beach, FL...........................15.7
FL Volusia.
4900 Melbourne-Titusville-Coca, FL..............10.7
FL Brevard.

5960 Orlando, FL...................................15.5
FL Orange; FL Oseceola; FL Seminole.
Non-SMSA Counties................................14.9
FL Flagler; FL Lake; FL Sumter.

043 Miami-Fort Lauderdale, FL:
SMSA Counties:
2680 Fort Lauderdale-Hollywood, FL..............15.5

FL Broward.
5000 Miami, FL....................................39.5
FL Dade.
8960 West Palm Beach-Boca Raton, FL...........22.4
FL Palm Beach.
Non-SMSA Counties................................30.4
FL Glades; FL Hendry; FL Indian River; FL Martin; FL Monroe; FL Okeechobee; FL St. Lucie.

044 Tampa-St. Petersburg, FL:
SMSA Counties:
1140 Bradenton, FL................................15.9
FL Manatee.
2700 Fort Myers, FL...............................15.3
FL Lee.
3980 Lakeland-Winter Haven, FL..................18.0
FL Polk.
7510 Sarasota, FL.................................10.5
FL Sarasota.
8280 Tampa-St Petersburg, FL.....................17.9
FL Hillsborough; FL Pasco; FL Pipellas.
Non-SMSA Counties................................17.1
FL Charlotte; FL Citrus; FL Collier; FL Desoto; FL Hardee; FL Hernando; FL Highlands.

045 Tallahassee, FL:
SMSA Counties:
8240 Tallahassee, FL..............................24.3
FL Leon; FL Wakulla.
Non-SMSA Counties................................29.5
FL Calhoun; FL Franklin; FL Gladsden; FL Jackson; FL Jefferson; FL Liberty; FL Madison; FL Taylor.

046 Pensacola-Panama City, FL:
SMSA Counties:
6015 Panama City, FL..............................14.1
FL Bay.
6080 Pensacola, FL................................18.3
FL Escambia; FL Santa Rosa.
Non-SMSA Counties................................15.4
FL Gulf; FL Holmes; FL Okaloosa; FL Walton; FL Washington.

Georgia:
035 Augusta, GA:
SMSA Counties:
0600 Augusta, GA-SC...............................27.2
GA Columbia; GA Richmond; SC Aiken.
Non-SMSA Counties................................32.8
GA Burke; GA Emanuel; GA Glascock; GA Jefferson; GA Jenkins; GA Lincoln; GA McDuffie; GA Taliaferro; GA Warren; GA Wilkes; SC Allendale; SC Bamberg; SC Barnwell; SC Edgefield; SC McCormick.

036 Atlanta, GA:
SMSA Counties:
0520 Atlanta, GA..................................21.2
GA Butts; GA Cherokee; GA Clayton; GA Cobb; GA Dekalb; GA Douglas; GA Fayette; GA Forsyth; GA Fulton; GA Winett; GA Henry; GA Newton; GA Paulding; GA Rockdale; GA Walton.

Non-SMSA Counties…………………...……..19.5
    GA Banks; GA Barrow; GA Bartow; GA Carroll;
GA Clarke; GA Coweta; GA Dawson; GA Elbert; GA
Fannin; GA Floyd; GA Franklin; GA Gilmer; GA
Gordon; GA Greene; GA Habersham; GA Hall; GA
Haralson; GA Hart; GA Heard; GA Jackson; GA
Jasper; GA Lamar; GA Lumpkin; GA Madison; GA
Morgan; GA Oconee; GA Oglethorpe; GA Pickens;
GA Pike; GA Polk; GA Rabun, GA Spalding; GA
Stephens; GA Towns; GA Union; GA Upson; GA
White.

037 Columbus, GA:
  SMSA Counties:
    1800 Columbus, GA-AL………..…………….29.6
    Al Russell; GA Chattahoochee; GA Columbus.
  Non-SMSA Counties……………….…………..31.6
    AL Chambers; AL Lee; GA Harris; GA Marion; GA
Meriwether; GA Quitman; GA Schley; GA Stewart;
GA Sumter; GA Talbot; GA Troup; GA Webster.

038 Macon, GA:
  SMSA Counties:
    4680 Macon, GA………………….……………..27.5
    GA Bibb; BA Houston; GA Jones; GA Twiggs.
  Non-SMSA Counties…………………………….31.7
    GA Baldwin; GA Bleckley; GA Crawford; GA
Crisp; GA Dodge; GA Dooly; GA Hancock; GA
Johnson; GA Laurens; GA Macon; GA Monroe; GA
Peach; GA Pulaski; GA Putnam; GA Taylor; GA
Telfair; GA Treulen; GA Washington; GA Wheeler;
GA Wilcox; GA Wilkinson.

039 Savannah, GA:
  SMSA Counties:
    7520 Savannah, GA……………….…………..30.6
    GA Bryan; GA Chatham; GA Effingham.
  Non-SMSA Counties…………….……………..29.8
    GA Appling; GA Atkinson; GA Bacon; GA
Bulloch; GA Candler; GA Coffee; GA Evans; GA Jeff
Davis; GA Liberty; GA Long; GA McIntosh; GA
Montgomery; GA Screven; GA Tattnall; GA Toombs;
GA Wayne; SC Beaufort; SC Hampton; SC Jasper.

040 Albany, GA:
  SMSA Counties:
    0120 Albany, GA……………….……………..32.1
    GA Dougherty, GA Lee.
  Non-SMSA Counties…………….……………..31.1
    GA Baker; GA Ben Hill; GA Barrien; GA Brooks;
GA Calhoun; GA Clay; GA Clinch; GA Colquitt; GA
Cook; GA Decatur; GA Early; GA Echois; GA Grady;
GA Irwin; GA Lanier; GA Lowndes; GA Miller; GA
Mitchell; GA Randolph; GA Seminole; GA Terrell;
GA Thomas; GA Tift; GA Turner; TA Worth.

Hawaii:
183 Honolulu, HI:
  SMSA Counties:
    3320 Honolulu, HI…………………………....…..69.1
    HI Honolulu.
  Non-SMSA Counties…………….……………..70.4

HI Hawaii; HI Kauai; HI Maui and Kalowao.

Idaho:
166 Pocatello-Idaho Falls, ID:
  Non-SMSA Counties………………...………….…..4.0
    ID Bannock; ID Bingham; ID Baline; ID
Bonneville; ID Butte; ID Camas; ID Caribou; ID
Cassia; ID Clark; ID Custer; ID Fremont; ID Gooding;
ID Jefferson; ID Jerome; ID Lemhi; ID Lincoln; ID
Madison; ID Minidoka; ID Power; ID Teton; ID Twin
Falls; WY Teton.

167 Boise City, ID:
  SMSA Counties:
    1080 Boise City, ID……………………………..2.3
    ID Ada.
  Non-SMSA Counties………………….…………..4.4
    ID Adams; ID Boise; ID Canyon; ID Elmore; ID
Gem; ID Owyhee; ID Payette; ID Valley; ID
Washington; OR Haney; OR Malheur.

Illinois:
083 Chicago, IL:
  SMSA Counties:
    1600 Chicago, IL…………………………….19.6
    IL Cook; IL Du Page; IL Kane; IL Lake; IL
McHenry; IL Will.
    2960 Gray-Hammond-East Chicago, IN………..20.9
    IN Lake; IN Porter.
    3740 Kankakee, IL………………………………..9.1
    IL Kankakee.
    3800 Kenosha, WI………………………………..3.0
    WI Kenosha.
  Non-SMSA Counties…………………………..18.4
    IL Bureau; IL De Kalb; IL Grundy; IL Iroquois; IL
Kendall; IL La Salle; IL Livingston; IL Putnam; IL
Jasper; IN Laporte; IN Newton; IN Pulaski; IN Starke.

084 Champaign-Urbana, IL:
  SMSA Counties:
    1400 Champaign-Urbana-Rantoul, IL……………7.8
    IL Champaign.
  Non-SMSA Counties………………….…………..4.8
    IL Cotes; IL Cumberland; IL Douglas; IL Edgar; IL
Ford; IL Piatt; IL Vermilion.

085 Springfield-Decatur, IL:
  SMSA Counties:
    2040 Decatur, IL…………………….…………..7.6
    IL Macon.
    7880 Springfield, IL……………………………..4.5
    IL Menard; IL Sangamon.
  Non-SMSA Counties……………………………..4.0
    IL Cass; IL Christian; IL De Witt; IL Logan; IL
Morgan; IL Moultrie; IL Scott; IL Shelby.

086 Quincy, IL:
  Non-SMSA Counties……………………………..3.1
    IL Adams; IL Brown; IL Pike; MO Lewis; MO
Marion; MO Pike; MO Ralls.

087 Peoria, IL:

SMSA Counties:
  1040 Bloomington-Normal, IL......................2.5
  IL McLean.
  6120 Peoria, IL.......................................4.4
  IL Peoria; IL Tazewell; IL Woodford.
Non-SMSA Counties.....................................3.3
  IL Fulton; IL Knox; IL McDonough; IL Marshall;
IL Mason; IL Schuyler; IL Stark; IL Warren.

088 Rockford, IL:
SMSA Counties:
  6880 Rockford, IL....................................6.3
  IL Boone; IL Winegago.
  3620 Janesville-Beloit, WI.........................3.1
  Rock Co.
Non-SMSA Counties.....................................4.6
  IL Lee; IL Ogle; IL Stephenson.

Indiana:
075 South Bend, IN:
SMSA Counties:
  7800 South Bend, IN.................................7.1
  IN Marshall; IN St. Joseph.
  2330 Elkhart, IN....................................4.0
  IN Elkhart.
Non-SMSA Counties.....................................6.2
  IN Fulton; IN Kosciusko; IN Lagrange; MI Berrien;
MI Cass; MI St. Joseph.

076 Fort Wayne, IN:
Non-SMSA Counties.....................................4.4
  IN Allen; IN Dekalb; IN Wells; IN Huntington; IN
Noble; IN Steuben; IN Whitley; OH Defiance; OH
Paulding; OH Williams.

077 Kokomo-Marion, IN:
SMSA Counties:
  3850 Kokomo, IN....................................4.4
  IN Howard; IN Tipton.
Non-SMSA Counties.....................................3.7
  IN Cass; IN Grant; IN Miami; IN Wabash.

078 Anderson-Muncie, IN:
SMSA Counties:
  0400 Anderson, IN..................................4.9
  IN Madison.
  5280 Muncie, IN....................................5.3
  IN Delaware.
Non-SMSA Counties.....................................3.9
  IN Blackford; IN Fayette; IN Henry; IN Jay; IN
Randolph; IN Union; IN Wayne.

079 Indianapolis, IN:
SMSA Counties:
  1020 Bloomington, IN...............................3.1
  IN Monroe.
  3480 Indianapolis, IN.............................12.5
  IN Boone; IN Hamilton; IN Hendricks; IN Johnson;
IN Marion; IN Morgan; IN Shelby.
Non-SMSA Counties.....................................9.7

IN Bartholomew; IN Brown; IN Daviess; IN
Decatur; IN Greene; IN Jackson; IN Jennings; IN
Lawrence; IN Martin; IN Owen; IN Putnam; IN Rush.

080 Evansville, IN:
SMSA Counties:
  2440 Evansville, IN-KY.............................4.8
  IN Gibson; IN Posey; IN Vanderburgh; IN Warrick;
KY Henderson.
  5990 Owensboro, KY................................4.7
  KY Daviess.
Non-SMSA Counties.....................................3.5
  IL Edwards; IL Gallatin; IL Hamilton; IL Lawrence;
IL Saline; IL Wabash; IL White; IN Dubois; IN Knox;
IN Perry; IN Pike; IN Spencer; KY Hancock; KY
Hopkins; KY McLean; KY Muhlenberg; KY Ohio;
KY Union; KY Webster.

081 Terre Haute, IN:
SMSA Counties:
  8320 Terre Haute, IN...............................3.1
  IN Clay; IN Sullivan; IN Vermillion; IN Vigo.
Non-SMSA Counties.....................................2.5
  IL Clark; IL Crawford; IN Parke.

082 Lafayette, IN:
SMSA Counties:
  3920 Lafayette-West Lafayette, IN.................2.7
  IN Tippecanoe.
Non-SMSA Counties.....................................1.5
  IN Benton; IN Carroll; IN Clinton; IN Fountain; IN
Montgomery; IN Warren; IN White.

Iowa:
098 Dubuque, IA:
SMSA Counties:
  2200 Dubuque, IA...................................0.6
  IA Dubuque.
Non-SMSA Counties.....................................0.5
  IL Jo Daviess; IA Allamakee; IA Clayton; IA
Delaware; IA Jackson; IA Winneshiek; WI Crawford;
WI Grant; WI Lafayette.

099 Davenport Rock Island Moline, IA-IL:
SMSA Counties:
  1960 Davenport Rock Island Moline, IA-IL......4.6
  IL Henry; IL Rock Island; IA Scott.
Non-SMSA Counties.....................................3.4
  IL Carroll; IL Handcock; IL Henderson; IL Mercer;
IL Whiteside; IA Clinton; IA Des Moines; IA Henry;
IA Lee; IA Louisa; IA Muscatine; MO Clark.

100 Cedar Rapids, IA:
SMSA Counties:
  1360 Cedar Rapids, IA.............................1.7
  IA Linn.
Non-SMSA Counties.....................................1.5
  IA Benton; IA Cedar; IA Iowa; IA Johnson; IA
Jones; IA Washington.

101 Waterloo, IA:
SMSA Counties:
  8920 Waterloo-Cedar Falls, IA.......................4.7
  IA Black Hawk.
Non-SMSA Counties.......................................2.0
  IA Bremer; IA Buchanan; IA Butler; IA Cerro
Gordo; IA Chickasaw; IA Fayette; IA Floyd; IA
Franklin; IA Grundy; IA Hancock; IA Hardin; IA
Howard; IA Mitchell; IAWinebago; IA Worth.

102 Fort Dodge, IA:
Non-SMSA Counties.......................................0.4
  IA Buena Vista; IA Calhoun; IA Carroll; IA Clay;
IA Dickinson; IA Emmet; IA Greene; IA Hamilton;
IA Humboldt; IA Kossuth; IA Palo Alto; IA
Pocahontas; IA Sac; IA Webster; IA Wright.

103 Sioux City, IA:
SMSA Counties:
  7720 Sioux City, IA-NE.............................1.9
  IA Woodbury; NE Dakota.
Non-SMSA Counties.......................................1.2
  IA Cherokee; IA Crawford; IA Ida; IA Monona; IA
O'Brien; IA Plymouth; IA Sioux; NE Antelope; NE
Cedar; NE Cuming; NE Dixon; NE Knox; NE
Madison; NE Pierce; NE Stanton; NE Thurston; NE
Wayne; SD Bon Homme; SD Clay; SD Union; SD
Yankton.

104 Des Moines, IA:
SMSA Counties:
  2120 Des Moines, IA...............................4.5
  IA Polk; IA Warren.
Non-SMSA Counties.......................................2.4
  IA Adair; IA Appanoose; IA Boone; IA Clarke; IA
Dallas; IA Davis; IA Decatur; IA Guthrie; IA Jasper;
IA Jefferson; IA Keokuk; IA Lucas; IA Madison; IA
Mahaska; IA Marion; IA Marshall; IA Monroe; IA
Poweshiek; IA Ringgold; IA Story; IA Tama; IA
Union; IA Van Buren; IA Wapello; IA Wayne.

Kansas:
139 Wichita, KS:
SMSA Counties:
  9040 Wichita, KS..................................7.9
  KS Butler; KS Sedgwick.
Non-SMSA Counties......................................5.7
  KS Barber, KS Barton; KS Chase; KS Chautauqua;
KS Clark; KS Comanche; KS Cowley; KS Edwards;
KS Elk; KS Finney; KS Ford; KS Grant; KS Gray; KS
Greeley; KS Greenwood; KS Hamilton; KS Harper;
KS Harvey; KS Haskell; KS Hodgeman; KS Kerny;
KS Kingman; KS Kiowa; KS Lane; KS McPherson;
KS Marion; KS Meade; KS Morton; KS Ness; KS
Pawnee; KS Pratt; KS Reno; KS Rice; KS Rush; KS
Scott; KS Seward; KS Stafford; KS Stanton; KS
Stevens; KS Sumner; KS Wichita.

140 Salina, KS:
Non-SMSA Counties.......................................1.5

KS Cheyenne; KS Cloud; KS Decatur; KS
Dickinson; KS Ellis; KS Ellsworth; KS Gove; KS
Graham; KS Jewell; KS Lincoln; KS Logan; KS
Mitchell; KS Norton; KS Osborne; KS Ottawa; KS
Phillips; KS Rawlins; KS Republic; KS Rooks; KS
Russell; KS Saline; KS Sheridan; KS Sherman; KS
Smith; KS Thomas; KS Trego; KS Wallace.

141 Topeka, KS:
SMSA Counties:
  8440 Topeka, KS...................................9.0
  KS Jefferson; KS Osage; KS Shawnee.
Non-SMSA Counties.......................................6.5
  KS Clay; KS Coffey; KS Geary; KS Jackson; KS
Lyon; KS Marshall; KS Morris; KSS Nemaha; KS
Pottawatomie; KS Riley; KS Wabaunsee; KS
Washington.

Kentucky:
056 Paducah, KY:
Non-SMSA Counties.......................................5.2
  IL Hardin, IL Massac; IL Pope; KY Ballard; KY
Caldwell; KY Calloway; KY Carlisle; KY Crittenden;
KY Fulton; KY Graves; KY Hickman; KY
Livingston; KY Lyon; KY McCracken; KY Marshall.

057 Louisville, KY:
SMSA Counties:
  4520 Louisville, KY-IN............................11.2
  IN Clark; IN Floyd; KY Bullitt; KY Jefferson; KY
Oldham.
Non-SMSA Counties......................................9.6
  IN Crawford; IN Harrison; IN Jefferson; IN Orange;
IN Scott; IN Washington; KY Breckinridge; KY
Grayson; KY Hardin; KY Hart; KY Henry; KY Larue;
KY Marion; KY Meade; KY Nelson; KY Shelby; KY
Spencer; KY Trimble; KY Washington.

058 Lexington, KY:
SMSA Counties:
  4280 Lexington-Fayette, KY........................10.8
  KY Bourbon; KY Clark; KY Fayette; KY
Jassamine; KY Scott; KY Woodford.
Non-SMSA Counties......................................7.0
  KY Adair; KY Anderson; KY Bath; KY Boyle; KY
Breathitt; KY Casey; KY Clay; KY Estill; KY
Franklin; KY Garrard; KY Green; KY Harrison; KY
Jackson; KY Knott; KY Lee; KY Leslie; KY Letaher;
KY Lincoln; KY Madison; KY Magoffin; KY
Menifee; KY Mercer; KY Montgomery; KY Morgan;
KY Nicholas; KY Owsley; KY Perry; KY Powell; KY
Pulaski; KY Rockcastle; KY Russell; KY Taylor; KY
Wolfe.

Louisiana:
113 New Orleans, LA:
SMSA Counties:
  0920 Biloxi-Gulfport, MS..........................19.2
  MS Hancock; MS Harrison; MS Stone.
  5560 New Orleans, LA..............................31.0
  LA Jefferson, LA Orleans; LA St. Bernard; LA St.
Tammany.

Non-SMSA Counties..................................27.7
LA Assumption; LA Lafourche; LA Plaquemines; LA St. Charles; LA St. James; LA St. John the Baptist; LA Tangipahoa; LA Terrebonne; LA Washington; MS Forrest; MS Lamar; MS Marion; MS Pearl River; MS Perry; MS Pike; MS Walthall.

114 Baton Rouge, LA:
SMSA Counties:
 0760 Baton Rouge, LA.......................26.1
LA Ascension; LA East Baton Rouge; LA Livingston; LA West Baton Rouge.
 Non-SMSA Counties.........................30.4
LA Concordia; LA E. Feliciana; LA Iberville; LA Pointe Coupee; LA St. Helena; LA West Feliciana; MS Adams; MS Amite; MS Wilkinson.

115 Lafayette, LA:
SMSA Counties:
 3880 Lafayette, LA...........................20.6
LA Lafayette.
 Non-SMSA Counties.........................24.1
LA Acadia; LA Evangeline; LA Iberia; LA St. Landry; LA St. Martin; LA St. Mary; LA Vermilion.

116 Lake Charles, LA:
SMSA Counties:
 3960 Lake Charles, LA.......................19.3
LA Calcasieu.
 Non-SMSA Counties.........................17.8
LA Allen; LA Beauregard; LA Cameron; LA Jefferson Davis; LA Vernon.

117 Shreveport, LA:
SMSA Counties:
 0220 Alexandria, LA..........................25.7
LA Grant; LA Rapides.
 7680 Shreveport, LA..........................29.3
LA Bossier; LA Caddo; LA Webster.
 Non-SMSA Counties.........................29.3
LA Avoyelles; LA Bienville; LA Clairborne; LA De Soto; LA Natchitoches; LA Red River; LA Sabine; LA Winn.

118 Monroe, LA:
SMSA Counties:
 5200 Monroe, LA.............................22.8
LA Ouachita.
 Non-SMSA Counties.........................27.9
LA Caldwell; LA Catahoula; LA East Carroll; LA Franklin; LA Jackson; LA La Salle; LA Lincoln; LA Madison; LA Morehouse; LA Richland; LA Tensas; LA Union; LA West Carroll.

Maine:
001 Bangor, ME:
 Non-SMSA Counties..........................0.8
ME Aroostook; ME Hancock; ME Penobscot; ME Piscataquis; ME Waldo; ME Washington.

002 Portland-Lewiston, ME:
SMSA Counties:

 4243 Lewiston-Auburn, ME...................0.5
ME Androscoggin.
 6403 Portland, ME.............................0.6
ME Cumberland; ME Sagadahoc.
 Non-SMSA Counties..........................0.5
ME Franklin; ME Kennebec; ME Knox; ME Lincoln; ME Oxford; ME Somserset; ME York.

Maryland:
019 Baltimore, MD:
SMSA Counties:
 0720 Baltimore, MD..........................23.0
MD Anne Arundel; MD Baltimore; MD Carroll; MD Hartford; MD Howard; MD Baltimore City.
 Non-SMSA Counties.........................23.6
MD Caroline; MD Dorchester; MD Kent; MD Queen Annes; MD Somerset; MD Talbot; MD Wicomico; MD Worcester; VA Accomack; VA Northampton.

Massachusetts:
004 Boston, MA:
SMSA Counties:
 1123 Boston-Lowell-Brockton-Lawrence-Haverhill, MA-NH......................................4.0
MA Essex; MA Middlesex; MA Norfolk; MA Plymouth; MA Suffolk; NH Rockingham.
 4763 Manchester-Nashua, NH................0.7
NH Hillsborough.
 5403 Fall River-New Bedford, MA...........1.6
MA Bristol.
 9243 Worcester-Fitchburg-Leominster, MA....1.6
MA Worcester.
 Non-SMSA Counties.........................3.6
MA Barnstable; MA Dukes; MA Nantucket; NH Belnap; NH Carroll; NH Merrimack; NH Strafford.

Michigan:
071 Detroit, MI:
SMSA Counties:
 0440 Ann Arbor, MI..........................8.5
MI Washtenaw.
 2160 Detroit, MI.............................17.7
MI Lapeer; MI Livingston; MI Macomb; MI Oakland; MI St. Clair; MI Wayne.
 2640 Flint, MI...............................12.6
MI Genesee; MI Shiawassee.
 Non-SMSA Counties.........................16.7
MI Sanilac.

072 Saginaw, MI:
SMSA Counties:
 0800 Bay City, MI............................2.2
MI Bay.
 6960 Saginaw, MI............................14.3
MI Saginaw.
 Non-SMSA Counties.........................5.2
MI Alcona; MI Alpena; MI Arenac; MI Cheboygan; MI Chippewa; MI Clare; MI Crawford; MI Gladwin; MI Gratiot; MI Huron; MI Iosco; MI Isabella; MI Luce; MI Mackinac; MI Midland; MI Montmorency;

MI Ogemaw; MI Oscoda; MI Otsego; MI Presque Isle; MI Roscommon; MI Tuscola.

073 Grand Rapids, MI:
SMSA Counties:
  3000 Grand Rapids, MI…………..……….5.2
    MI Kent; MI Ottawa.
  5320 Muskegon-North Shores-Muskegon Heights, MI……………………………………..9.7
    MI Muskegon; MI Oceana.
  Non-SMSA Counties………………..…………4.9
    MI Allegan; MI Antrim; MI Benzie; MI Charlevoix; MI Emmet; MI Grand Traverse; MI Kalkaska; MI Lake; MI Leelanau; MI Manistee; MI Mason; MI Mecosta; MI Missaukee; MI Montcalm; MI Newaygo; MI Osecola; MI Wexford.

074 Lansing-Kalamazoo, MI:
SMSA Counties:
  0780 Battle Creek, MI…………………..…….7.2
    MI Barry; MI Calhoun.
  3520 Jackson, MI…………………..…………5.1
    MI Jackson.
  3720 Kalamazoo-Portage, MI……………….5.9
    MI Kalamazoo; MI Van Buren.
  4040 Lansing-East Lansing, MI……………….5.5
    MI Clinton; MI Eaton; MI Ingham; MI Iona.
  Non-SMSA Counties……………………………5.5
    MI Branch; MI Hillsdale.

Minnesota:
096 Minneapolis-St. Paul, MN:
SMSA Counties:
  5120 Minneapolis-St. Paul, MN-WI……………..2.9
    MN Anoka; MN Carver; MN Chisago; MN Dakota; MN Hennepin; MN Ramsey; MN Scott; MN Washington; MN Wright; MN St. Croix.
  6980 St. Cloud, MN……………………………...0.5
    MN Benton; MN Sherburne; MN Stearns.
  Non-SMSA Counties………………..……………2.2
    MN Aitkin; MN Big Stone; MN Blue Earth; MN Brown; MN Cass; MN Chippewa; MN Crow Wing; MN Douglas; MN Fairbault; MN Goodhue; MN Grant; MN Isanti; MN Kanabec; MN Kandiyohi; MN Lac Qui Parle; MN Le Sueur; MN McLeod; MN Martin; MN Meeker; MN Mille Lacs; MN Morrison; MN Nicollet; MN Pine; MN Pope; MN Renville; MN Rice; MN Sibley; MN Stevens; MN Swift; MN Todd; MN Traverse; MN Wadena; MN Waseca; MN Watonwan; MN Yellow Medicine; WI Burnett; WI Pierce; WI Polk.

097 Rochester, MN:
SMSA Counties:
  6820 Rochester, MN………………..…………1.4
    MN Olmsted.
  Non-SMSA Counties…………………..…………0.9
    MN Dodge; MN Fillmore; MN Freeborn; MN Mower; MN Steele; MN Wabasha.

Mississippi:
112 Jackson, MS:

SMSA Counties:
  3560 Jackson, MS……………...……………30.3
    MS Hinds; MS Rankin.
  Non-SMSA Counties…………..……………32.0
    MS Attala; MS Choctaw; MS Claiborne; MS Clarke; MS Copiah; MS Covington; MS Franklin; MS Holmes; MS Humphreys; MS Issaquena; MS Jasper; MS Jefferson; MS Jefferson Davis; MS Jones; MS Kemper; MS Lauderdale; MS Lawrence; MS Leake; MS Lincoln; MS Lowndes; MS Madison; MS Neshoba; MS Newton; MS Noxubee; MS Oktibbeha; MS Scott; MS Sharkey; MS Simpson; MS Smith; MS Warren; MS Wayne; MS Winston; MS Yazoo.

Missouri:
105 Kansas City, MO:
SMSA Counties:
  3760 Kansas City, MO-KS………..…………12.7
    KS Johnson; KS Wayandotte; MO Cass; MO Clay; MO Jackson; MO Platte; MO Ray.
  4150 Lawrence, KS……………….……………7.2
    KS Lawrence.
  7000 St. Joseph, MO……………..……………3.2
    MO Andrew; MO Buchanan.
  Non-SMSA Counties…………………………10.0
    KS Anderson; KS Atchison; KS Brown; KS Doniphan; KS Franklin; KS Leavenworth; KS Linn; KS Miami; MO Atchison; MO Bates; MO Benton; MO Caldwell; MO Caroll; MO Clinton; MO Daviess; MO Dekalb; MO Gentry; MO Grundy; MO Harrison; MO Henry; MO Holt; MO Johnson; MO Lafayette; MO Livingston; MO Mercer; MO Nodaway; MO Pettis; MO Saline; MO Worth.

106 Columbia, MO
SMSA Counties:
  1740 Columbia, MO………………..……………6.3
    MO Boone.
  Non-SMSA Counties………………..………...4.0
    MO Adair; MO Audrain; MO Callaway; MO Camden; MO Chariton; MO Cole; MO Cooper; MO Howard; MO Knox; MO Linn; MO Macon; MO Miller; MO Moniteau; MO Monroe; MO Morgan; MO Osage; MO Putnam; MO Randolph; MO Schuyler; MO Scotland; MO Shelby; MO Sullivan.

107 St. Louis, MO:
SMSA Counties:
  7040 St. Louis, MO-IL…………………..…….14.7
    IL Clinton; IL Madison; IL Monroe; IL St. Clair; MO Franklin; MO Jefferson; MO St. Charles; MO ST. Louis; MO St. Louis City.
  Non-SMSA Counties………………………….11.4
    IL Alexander; IL Bond; IL Calhoun; IL Clay; IL Effingham; IL Fayette; IL Franklin; IL Greene; IL Jackson; IL Jasper; IL Jefferson; IL Jersey; IL Johnson; IL Macoupin; IL Marion; IL Montgomery; IL Perry; IL Pulaski; IL Randolph; IL Richland; IL Union; IL Washington; IL Wayne; IL Williamson; MO Bollinger; MO Butler; MO Cape Girardeau; MO Carter; MO Crawford; MO Dent; MO Gasconade; MO Iron; MO Lincoln; MO Madison; MO Maries; MO

Mississippi; MO Montgomery; MO Perry; MO Phelps; MO Reynolds; MO Ripley; MO St. Francois; MO Ste. Genevieve; MO Scott; MO Stoddard; MO Warren; MO Washington; MO Wayne.

108 Springfield, MO:
SMSA Counties:
  7920 Springfield, MO…………….....…………..2.0
  MO Christian; MO Greene.
Non-SMSA Counties……………………...……….2.3
  KS Allen; KS Bourbon; KS Cherokee; KS Crawford; KS Labette; KS Montgomery; KS Neosho; KS Wilson; KS Woodson; MO Barry; MO Barton; MO Cedar; MO Dade; MO Dallas; MO Douglas; MO Hickory; MO Howell; MO Jasper; MO Laclede; MO Lawrence; MO McDonald; MO Newton; MO Oregon; MO Ozark; MO Polk; MO Pulaski; MO St. Clair; MO Shannon; MO Stone; MO Taney; MO Texas; MO Vernon; MO Webster; MO Wright; OK Craig; OK Ottawa.

Montana:
153 Greeat Falls, MT:
SMSA Counties:
  3040 Great Falls, MT…………….…..…………3.2
  MT Cascade.
Non-SMSA Counties…………….....……………4.1
  MT Blaine; MT Broadwater; MT Chouteau; MT Fergus; MT Glacier; MT Hill; MT Jefferson; MT Judity Basin; MT Lewis and Clark; MT Liberty; MT Meagher; MT Petroleum; MT Phillips; MT Pondera; MT Teton; MT Toole; MT Valley; MT Wheatland.

154 Missoula, MT:
Non-SMSA Counties……………………..……...2.7
  MT Beaverhead; MT Deer Lodge; MT Flathead; MT Granite; MT Lincoln; MT Madison; MT Mineral; MT Missoula; MT Powell; MT Ravalli; MT Sanders; MT Silver Bow; MT Lake.

155 Billings, MT:
SMSA Counties:
  0880 Billings, MT…………………..………..3.3
  MT Yellowstone.
Non-SMSA Counties…………………………….3.3
  MT Big Horn; MT Carbon; MT Carter; MT Custer; MT Dawson; MT Fallon; MT Gallatin; MT Garfield; MT Golden Valley; MT McCone; MT Musselshell; MT Park; MT Powder River; MT Prairie; MT Rosebud; MT Stillwater; MT Sweet Grass; MT Treasure; MT Wilbaux; MT Yellowstone Park & Part; WY Big Horn; WY Hot Springs; WY Park; WY Sheridan; WY Washakie.

156 Cheyenee-Casper, WY:
Non-SMSA Counties……………………………7.5
  CO Jackson; WY Albany; WY Campbell; WY Carbon; WY Converse; WY Fremont; WY Johnson; WY Laramie; WY Natrona; WY Platte.

Nebraska:
142 Lincoln, NE:
SMSA Counties:
  4360 Lincoln, NE………………...………………2.8
  NE Lancaster.
Non-SMSA Counties………………...…………….1.9
  NE Butler; NE Fillmore; NE Cage; NE Jefferson; NE Johnson; NE Nemaha; NE Otoe; NE Pawnee; NE Polk; NE Richardson; NE Saline; NE Seward; NE Thayer; NE York.

143 Omaha, NE:
SMSA Counties:
  5920 Omaha, NE-IA……………….…………….7.6
  IA Pottawattamie; NE Douglas; NE Sarpy.
Non-SMSA Counties………………….………….5.3
  IA Adams; IA Audubon; IA Cass; IA Fremont; IA Harrison; IA Mills; IA Montgomery; IA Page; IA Shelby; IA Taylor; NE Burt; NE Cass; NE Colfax; NE Dodge; NE Platte; NE Saunders; NE Washington.

144 Grand Island, NE:
Non-SMSA Counties……………………………1.4
  NE Adams; NE Aurther; NE Blaine; NE Boone; NE Boyd; NE Brown; NE Buffalo; NE Chase; NE Cherry; NE Clay; NE Custer; NE Dawson; NE Dundy; NE Franklin; NE Frontier; NE Furnas; NE Garfield; NE Gosper; NE Grant; NE Greeley; NE Hall; NE Hamilton; NE Harlan; NE Hayes; NE Hitchcock; NE Holt; NE Hooker; NE Howard; NE Kearney; NE Keith; NE Keya Paha; NE Lincoln; NE Logan; NE Loup; NE McPherson; NE Merick; NE Nance; NE Nuckolls; NE Perkins; NE Phelps; NE Red Willow; NE Rock; NE Sherman; NE Thomas; NE Valley; NE Webster; NE Wheeler.

145 Scottsbluff, NE:
Non-SMSA Counties………………....………….5.3
  NE Banner; NE Box Butte; NE Cheyenne; NE Dawes; NE Deuel; NE Garden; NE Kimball; NE Morrill; NE Scotts Buff; NE Sheridan; NE Sioux; NE Goshen.

Nevada:
163 Las Vegas, NV:
SMSA Counties:
  4120 Las Vegas, NV…………………………….13.9
  NV Clark.
Non-SMSA Counties……………………………12.6
  NV Esmeralda; NV Lincoln; NV Nye; UT Beaver; UT Garfield; UT Iron; UT Kane; UT Washington.

164 Reno, NV:
SMSA Counties:
  6720 Reno, NV………………...……………….8.2
  NV Washoe.
Non-SMSA Counties………………………..9.2
  NV Churchill; NV Douglas; NV Elko; NV Eureka; NV Humboldt; NV Lander; NV Lyon; NV Mineral;

NV Pershing; NV Storey; NV White Pine; NV Carson City.

New Mexico:
160 Albuquerque, NM:
 SMSA Counties:
  0200 Albuquerque, NM............……..……..38.3
  NM Bernalillo; NM Sandoval.
  Non-SMSA Counties...............................45.9
  NM Catron; NM Colfax/ NM de Baca; NM Guadalupe; NM Lincoln; NM Los Alamos; NM McKinley; NM Mora; NM Rio Arriba; NM San Juan; NM San Miguel; NM Santa Fe; NM Socorro; NM Taos; NM Torrance; NM Valencia.

New York:
007 Albany-Schnectady-Troy, NY:
 SMSA Counties:
  0160 Albany-Schenectady-Troy, NY................3.2
  NY Albany; NY Montgomery; NY Rensselaer; NY Saratoga; NY Schenectady.
  Non-SMSA Counties...……...................2.6
  NY Clinton; NY Columbia; NY Essex; NY Fulton; NY Greene; NY Hamilton; NY Schoharie; NY Warren; NY Washington; VT Bennington.

008 Syracuse-Utica, NY:
 SMSA Counties:
  8160 Syracuse, NY...3.8
  NY Madison; NY Onondaga; NY Oswego.
  8680 Utica-Rome, NY................................….2.1
  NY Herkimer; NY Oneida.
  Non-SMSA Counties..........................……...2.5
  NY Cayuga; NY Cortland; NY Franklin; NY Jefferson; NY Lewis; NY St. Lawrence.

009 Rochester, NY:
 SMSA Counties:
  6840 Rochester, NY.......................................5.3
  NY Livingston; NY Monroe; NY Ontario; NY Orleans; NY Wayne.
  Non-SMSA Counties..............…...................5.9
  NY Genesee; NY Seneca; NY Yates.

010 Buffalo, NY:
 SMSA Counties:
  1280 Buffalo, NY…...........……................7.7
  NY Erie; NY Niagara.
  Non-SMSA Counties..............……...........6.3
  NY Allegany; NY Cattaraugus; NY Chautauqua; NY Wyoming; PA McKean; PA Potter.

011 Binghamton-Elmira, NY:
 SMSA Counties:
  0960 Binghamton, NY-PA...............…...........1.1
  NY Broome; NY Tioga; PA Susquehanna.
  2335 Elmira, NY.......................................….....2.2
  NY Chumung.
  Non-SMSA Counties.......................…….......1.2
  NY Chenango; NY Delaware; NY Otsego; NY Schuyler; NY Steuben; NY Tompkins; PA Bradford; PA Tioga.

012 New York, NY:
 SMSA Counties:
  1163 Bridgeport-Stamford-Norwalk-Danbury, CT..……..........10.2
   CT Fairfield.
  3460 Jersey City, NJ..................................12.8
   NJ Hudson.
  4410 Long Brancy-Asbury Park, NJ.................9.5
   NJ Monmouth
  5360 Nassau-Suffolk, NY…….....................5.8
   NY Nassau; NY Suffolk.
  5460 New Brunswick-Perty Amboy-Sayreville, NJ..……..............5.8
   NJ Middlesex.
  5600 New York, NY, NJ...........................22.6
   NJ Bergen; NY Putnam; NY Rockland; NY Westchester
  (The following goal ranges are applicable to the indicated trades in the Counties of Bronx, Kings, New York, Queens and Richmond.)

Electricians...................................…......9.0 to 10.2
Carpenters..............................…..............27.6 to 32.0
Steam fitters...............…........................12.2 to 13.5
Metal lathers...24.6 to 25.6
Painters..28.6 to 26.0
Operating engineers...................................25.6 to 26.0
Plumbers...12.0 to 14.5
Iron workers (struct)...........................…....25.9 to 32.0
Elevator constructors............................…....5.5 to 6.5
Bricklayers.....................…........................13.4 to 15.5
Asbestos workers.................….................22.8 to 28.0
Roofers..……........6.3 to 7.5
Iron workers (ornamental)....................…...22.4 to 23.0
Cement masons.............….........................23.0 to 27.0
Glaziers..…...16.0 to 20.0
Plasters................…...................................15.8 to 18.0
Teamsters..22.0 to 22.5
Boilermakers.................................…..........13.0 to 15.5
All others..…..........16.4 to 17.5

  5460 Newark, NJ....................................17.3
  NJ Essex; NJ Morris; NJ Somerset; NJ Union.
  6040 Paterson-Clinton-Passaic, NJ................12.9
  NJ Passaic.
  6460 Poughkeepsie, NY.............................6.4
  NY Duchess
  Non-SMSA Counties................................17.0
  NJ Hunterdon; NJ Ocean; NJ Sussex; NY Orange; NY Sullivan; NY Ulster; PA Pike.

North Carolina:
024 Rocky Mount-Wilson-Greenville, NC:
 Non-SMSA Counties................................31.7
  NC Beaufort; NC Carteret; NC Craven; NC Dare; NC Edgecombe; NC Greene; NC Halifax; NC Hyde; NC Jones; NC Lenoir; NC Martin; NC Nash; NC Northampton; NC Pamlico; NC Pitt; NC Tyrrell; NC Washington; NC Wayne; NC Wilson.

025 Wilmington, NC:
 SMSA Counties:

9200 Wilmington, NC.............................20.7
NC Brunswick; NC New Hanover.
Non-SMSA Counties................................23.5
NC Columbus; NC Duplin; NC Onslow; NC Pender.

026 Fayetteville, NC:
SMSA Counties:
 2560 Fayetteville, NC.............................26.2
 NC Cumberland.
 Non-SMSA Counties................................33.5
NC Bladen; NC Hoke; NC Richmond; NC Robeson;
NC Sampson; NC Scotland.

027 Raleigh-Durham, NC:
SMSA Counties:
 6640 Raleigh-Durham, NC.......................22.8
 NC Durham; NC Orange; NC Wake.
 Non-SMSA Counties...............................24.7
 NC Chatham; NC Franklin; NC Granville; NC
Hamlett; NC Johnston; NC Lee; NC Person; NC
Vance; NC Warren.

028 Greensboro-Winston Salem-High Pont, NC:
SMSA Counties:
 1300 Burlington, NC..............................16.2
 NC Alamance.
 3120 Greensboro-Winston Salem-High Point,
NC..16.4
 NC Davidson; NC Forsyth; NC Guilford; NC
Randolf; NC Stokes; NC Yadkin.
 Non-SMSA Counties................................15.5
 NC Alleghany; NC Ashe; NC Caswell; NC Davie;
NC Montgomery; NC Moore; NC Rockingham; NC
Surry; NC Watauga; NC Wilkes.

029 Charlotte, NC:
SMSA Counties:
 1520 Charlotte-Gastonia, NC....................18.5
 NC Gaston; NC Mecklenburg; NC Union.
 Non-SMSA Counties................................15.7
 NC Alexander; NC Anson; NC Burke; NC Cabarrus;
NC Caldwell; NC Catawba; NC Cleveland; NC
Iredell; NC Lincoln; NC Rowan; NC Rutherford; NC
Stanley; SC Chester; SC Lancaster; SC York.

030 Asheville, NC:
SMSA Counties:
 0480 Asheville, NC................................8.5
 NC Buncombe; NC Madison.
 Non-SMSA Counties................................6.3
 NC Avery; NC Cherokee; NC Clay; NC Graham;
NC Haywood; NC Henderson; NC Jackson; NC
McDowell; NC Macon; NC Mitchell; NC Swain; NC
Transylvania; NC Yancey.

North Dakota:
149 Fargo-Moorhead, ND-MN:
 Non-SMSA Counties................................0.7
 MN Becker; MN Clay; MN Cass; MN Wilkin; ND
Barnes; ND Dickey; ND Eddy; ND Foster; ND
Griggs; ND LaMoure; ND Logan; ND McIntosh; ND

Ransom; ND Richland; ND Sargent; ND Steele; ND
Stutsman; ND Traill.

150 Grand Forks, ND:
SMSA Counties:
 2985 Grand Forks, ND-MN.........................1.2
 MN Polk; ND Grand Forks.
 Non-SMSA Counties................................2.0
 MN Bletrami; MN Clearwater; MN Hubbard; MN
Kittson; MN Lake of the Woods; MN Mahnomen;
MN Marshall; MN Norman; MN Pennington; MN
Red Lake; MN Roseau; MN Benson; ND Cavalier;
ND Nelson; ND Pembina; ND Ramsey; ND Towner;
ND Walsh.

151 Bismarck, ND:
SMSA Counties:
 1010 Bismarck,
ND..................................0.4
 ND Burleigh; ND Morton.
 Non-SMSA Counties................................1.3
 ND Adams; ND Billings; ND Bowman; ND Dunn;
ND Emmons; ND Golden Valley; ND Grant; ND
Hettinger; ND Kidder; ND Mercer; ND Oliver; ND
Sheridan; ND Sioux; ND Slope; ND Stark; ND Wells.

152 Minot, ND:
 Non-SMSA Counties................................4.4
 MT Daniels; MT Richland; MT Roosevelt; MT
Sheridan; ND Bottineau; ND Burke; ND Divide; ND
McHenry; ND McKenzie; ND McLean; ND
Mountrail; ND Pierce; ND Renville; ND Rolette; ND
Ward; ND Williams.

Ohio:
064 Youngstown-Warren, OH:
SMSA Counties:
 9320 Youngstown-Warren, OH......................9.4
 OH Mahoning; OH Trumbull.
 Non-SMSA Counties................................6.7
 OH Columbiana; PA Lawrence; PA Mercer.

065 Cleveland, OH:
SMSA Counties:
 0080 Akron, OH...................................7.8
 OH Portage; OH Summit.
 1320 Canton, OH..................................6.1
 OH Carroll; OH Stark.
 1680 Cleveland, OH...............................16.1
 OH Cuyahoga; OH Geauga; OH Lake; OH Medina.
 4440 Lorain-Elyria, OH...........................9.3
 OH Lorain.
 4800 Mansfield, OH...............................6.3
 OH Richland.
 Non-SMSA Counties................................11.3
 OH Ashland; OH Ashtabula; OH Coshocton; OH
Crawford; OH Erie; OH Holmes; OH Huron; OH
Tuscarawas; OH Wayne.
066 Columbus, OH:
SMSA Counties:
 1840 Columbus, OH................................10.6

OH Delaware; OH Fairfield; OH Franklin; OH Madison; OH Pickaway.
Non-SMSA Counties...................................7.3
OH Athens; OH Fayette; OH Guernsey; OH Hocking; OH Jackson; OH Knox; OH Licking; OH Marion; OH Meigs; OH Morgan; OH Morrow; OH Muskingum; OH Noble; OH Perry; OH Pike; OH Ross; OH Scioto; OH Union; OH Vinton.

067 Cincinnati, OH:
SMSA Counties:
1640 Cincinnati, OH-KY-IN.....................11.0
IN Dearborn; KY Boone; KY Campbell; KY Kenton; OH Clemont; OH Hamilton; OH Warren.
3200 Hamilton-Middletown, OH....................5.0
OH Butler.
Non-SMSA Counties..................................9.2
IN Franklin; IN Ohio; IN Ripley; IN Switzerland; KY Bracken; KY Carroll; KY Fleming; KY Gallatin; KY Brant; KY Lewis; KY Mason; KY Owen; KY Pendleton; KY Robertson; OH Adams; OH Brown; OH Clinton; OH Highland.

068 Dayton, OH:
SMSA Counties:
2000 Dayton, OH......................................11.5
OH Greene; OH Miami; OH Montgomery; OH Preble.
7960 Springfield, OH................................7.8
OH Champaign; OH Clark.
Non-SMSA Counties..................................9.9
OH Darke; OH Logan; OH Shelby.

069 Lima, OH:
SMSA Counties:
4320 Lima, OH.......................................4.4
OH Allen; OH Auglaize; OH Putnam; OH Van Wert.
Non-SMSA Counties..................................3.5
OH Hardin; OH Mercer.

070 Toledo, OH:
SMSA Counties:
8400 Toledo, OH-MI...............................8.8
MI Monroe; OH Fulton; OH Lucas; OH Ottawa; OH Wood.
Non-SMSA Counties..................................7.3
MI Lenawee; OH Hancock; OH Henry; OH Sandusky; OH Seneca; OH Wyandot.

Oklahoma:
136 Lawton, OK:
SMSA Counties:
4200 Lawton, OK....................................14.8
OK Comanche.
Non-SMSA Counties................................10.8
OK Cotton; OK Greer; OK Harmon; OK Jackson; OK Jefferson; OK Kiowa; OK Stephens; OK Tillman.

137 Oklahoma City, OK:
SMSA Counties:

5880 Oklahoma City, OK.............................10.2
OK Canadian; OK Cleveland; OK McClain; OK Oklahoma; OK Pottawatomie.
Non-SMSA Counties..................................9.0
OK Alfalfa; OK Atoka; OK Beckham; OK Blaine; OK Caddo; OK Carter; OK Coal; OK Custer; OK Dewey; OK Ellis; OK Garfield; OK Garvin; OK Grady; OK Grant; OK Harper; OK Hughes; OK Johnston; OK Kingfisher; OK Lincoln; OK Logan; OK Love; OK Major; OK Marshall; OK Murray; OK Okfuskee; OK Pontotoc; OK Roger Mills; OK Seminole; OK Washita; OK Woods; OK Woodward.

138 Tulsa, OK:
SMSA Counties:
8560 Tulsa, OK.......................................10.2
OK Creek; OK Mayes; OK Osage; OK Rogers; OK Tulsa; OK Wagoner.
Non-SMSA Counties................................10.0
OK Cherokee; OK Key; OK McIntosh; OK Muskogee; OK Noble; OK Nowata; OK Okmulgee; OK Pawnee; OK Payne; OK Washington.

Oregon:
172 Portland, OR:
SMSA Counties:
6440 Portland, OR-WA.............................4.5
OR Clackamas; OR Multnomah; OR Washington; WA Clark.
7080 Salem, OR......................................2.9
OR Marion; OR Polk.
Non-SMSA Counties..................................3.8
OR Benton; OR Clatsop; OR Columbia; OR Crook; OR Deschutes; OR Hood River; OR Jefferson; OR Lincoln; OR Linn; OR Sherman; OR Tillamook; OR Wasco; OR Yamhill; WA Cowlitz; WA Klickitat; WA Skamania; WA Wahkiakum.

173 Eugene, OR:
SMSA Counties:
2400 Eugene-Springfield, OR.......................2.4
OR Lane.
Non-SMSA Counties..................................2.4
OR Coos; OR Curry; OR Douglas; OR Jackson; OR Josephine; OR Klamath; OR lake.

Pennsylvania:
013 Scranton-Wilkes-Barre, PA:
SMSA Counties:
5745 Northeast Pennsylvania.........................0.6
PA Lackawanna; PA Luzerne; PA Monroe.
Non-SMSA Counties..................................0.5
PA Columbia; PA Wayne; PA Wyoming.

014 Williamsport, PA:
SMSA Counties:
9140 Williamsport, PA...............................1.0
PA Lycoming.
Non-SMSA Counties..................................0.7
PA Cameron; PA Centre; PA Clearfield; PA Clinton; PA Elik; PA Jefferson; PA Montour; PA Northumberland; PA Snyder; PA Sullivan; PA Union.

015 Erie, PA:
 SMSA Counties:
  2360 Erie, PA………………………………..2.8
  PA Erie.
 Non-SMSA Counties………………………..1.8
  PA Clarion; PA Crawford; PA Forest; PA Venango; PA Warren.

016 Pittsburg, PA:
 SMSA Counties:
  0280 Altoona, PA…………………………...1.0
  PA Blair.
  3680 Johnson, PA…………………………..1.3
  PA Cambria; PA Somerset.
  6280 Pittsburgh, PA………………………..6.3
  PA Allegheny; PA Beaver; PA Washington; PA Westmoreland.
 Non-SMSA Counties……………...…………4.6
  MD Allegany; MD Garrett; PA Armstrong; PA Bedford; PA Butler; PA Fayette; Pa Greene; PA Indiana; WV Mineral.

017 Harrisburg-York-Lancaster, PA:
 SMSA Counties:
  3240 Harrisburg, PA………………………..6.2
  PA Cumberland; PA Dauphin; PA Perry.
  4000 Lancaster, PA…………………..……..2.0
  PA Lancaster.
  9280 York, PA………………..……………..2.2
  PA Adams; PA York.
 Non-SMSA Counties………...………………3.1
  PA Franklin; PA Fulton; PA Huntington; PA Juniata; PA Lebanon; PA Mifflin.

018 Philadelphia, PA:
 SMSA Counties:
  0240 Allentown-Bethlehem-Easton, PA-NJ……...1.6
  NJ Warren; PA Carbon; PA Lehigh; PA Northampton.
  0560 Atlantic City, NJ……………….……..18.2
  NJ Atlantic.
  6160 Philadelphia, PA-NJ………………...…..17.3
  NJ Burlington; NJ Camden; NJ Gloucester; PA Bucks; PA Chester; PA Delaware; PA Montgomery; PA Philadelphia.
  6680 Reading, PA………………………….....2.5
  PA Berks.
  8480 Trenton, NJ…………………………….16.4
  NJ Mercer.
  8760 Vineland-Millville- Bridgeton, NJ………..16.0
  NJ Cumberland
  9160 Wilmington, DE-NJ-MD………………….12.3
  DE New Castle; MD Cecil; NJ Salem.
 Non-SMSA Counties……………...………….14.5
  DE Kent; DE Sussex; NJ Cape May; PA Schuylkill.

Rhode Island:
005 Providence-Warwick-Pawtucket, RI:
 SMSA Counties:
  6483 Providence-Warwick-Pawtucket, RI……….3.0

RI Bristol; RI Kent; RI Providence; RI Washington.
 Non-SMSA Counties……………………..………3.1
 RI Newport.

South Carolina:
031 Greenville-Spartanburg, SC:
 SMSA Counties:
  3160 Greenville-Spartanburg, SC……………….16.0
  SC Greenville; SC Pickens; SC Spartanburg.
 Non-SMSA Counties…………………………...…17.8
  SC Polk; SC Abbeville; SC Anderson; SC Cherokee; SC Greenwood; SC Laurens; SC Oconee; SC Union.

032 Columbia, SC:
 SMSA Counties:
  1760 Columbia, SC……………………………..23.4
  SC Lexington, SC Richland.
 Non-SMSA Counties…………………………….32.0
  SC Calhoun; SC Clarendon; SC Fairfield; SC Kershaw; SC Lee; SC Newberry; SC Orangeburg; SC Saluda; SC Sumter.

033 Florence, SC:
 Non-SMSA Counties………………………..33.0
  SC Chesterfield; SC Darlington; SC Dillon; SC Florence; SC Georgetown; SC Horry; SC Marion; SC Marlboro; SC Williamsburg.

034 Charleston-North Charleston, SC:
 SMSA Counties:
  1440 Charleston- North Charleston, SC………....30.0
  SC Berkeley; SC Charleston; SC Dorchester.
 Non-SMSA Counties…………………………….30.7
  SC Collection.

South Dakota:
146 Rapid City, SD:
 SMSA Counties:
  6660 Rapid City, SD………………………...…..3.4
  SD Pennington; SD Meade.
 Non-SMSA Counties……………………….......7.9
  SD Bennett; SD Buffalo; SD Butte; SD Campbell; SD Corson; SD Custer; SD Dewey (Armstrong); SD Fall River; SD Haakon; SD Harding; SD Hughes; SD Hyde; SD Jackson; SD Jones; SD Lawrence; SD Lyman; SD Mellette; SD Perkins; SD Potter; SD Shannon (Washington); SD Stanley; SD Sully; SD Todd; SD Tripp; SD Walworth; SD Washabaugh; SD Ziebach; WY Crook; WY Niobrara; WY Weston.

147 Sioux Falls, SD:
 SMSA Counties:
  7760 Sioux Falls, SD……………………………1.2
  SD Minnehaha.
 Non-SMSA Counties……………………..……..0.8
  IA Lyon; IA Osceola; MN Cottonwood; MN Jackson; MN Lincoln; MN Lyon; MN Murray; MN Nobles; MN Pipestone; MN Redwood; MN Rock; SD Aurora; SD Beadle; SD Brookings; SD Brule; SD Charles Mix; SD Davison; SD Douglas; SD Gregory;

SD Hand; SD Hanson; SD Hutchinson; SD Jerauld; SD Kingsbury; SD Lake; SD Lincoln; SD Mc Cook; SD Miner; SD Moody; SD Sanborn; SD Turner.

148 Aberdeen, SD:
  Non-SMSA Counties.....................................1.3
    SD Brown; SD Clark; SD Codington; SD Day; SD Deuel; SD Edmunds; SD Faulk; SD Grant; SD Hamlin; SD McPherson; SD Marshall; SD Roberts; SD Spink.

Tennessee:
051 Chattanooga, TN:
  SMSA Counties:
    1560 Chattanooga, TN-GA........................12.5
    GA Catoosa; GA Dade; GA Walker; TN Hamilton; TN Marion; TN Sequatchie.
  Non-SMSA Counties.....................................8.6
    AL De Kalb; AL Jackson; GA Chattooga; GA Murray; GA Whitfield; TN Bledsoe; TN Bradley; TN Grundy; TN McMinn; TN Meigs; TN Monroe; TN Polk; TN Rhea.

052 Johnson City-Kingsport-Bristol, TN-VA:
  SMSA Counties:
    3660 Johnson City-Kingsport-Bristol, TN-VA.....2.6
    TN Carter; TN Hawkins; TN Sullivan; TN Unicoi; TN Washington; VA Scott; VA Washington; VA Bristol.
  Non-SMSA Counties.........................3.2
    TN Greene; TN Hancock; TN Johnson; VA Buchanan; VA Dickenson; VA Lee; VA Russell; VA Smyth; VA Tazewell; VA Wise; VA Norton; WV McDowell; WV Mercer.

053 Knoxville, TN:
  SMSA Counties:
    3840 Knoxville, TN.........................6.6
    TN Anderson; TN Blount; TN Knox; TN Union.
  Non-SMSA Counties.........................4.5
    KY Bell; KY Harlan; KY Knox; KY Laurel; KY McCreary; KY Wayne; KY Whitley; TN Campbell; TN Claiborne; TN Cocke; TN Cumberland; TN Fentress; TN Grainger; TN Hamblen; TN Jefferson; TN Loudon; TN Morgan; TN Roane; TN Scott; TN Sevier.

054 Nashville, TN:
  SMSA Counties:
    1660 Clarksville-Hopkinsville, TN-KY...........18.2
    KY Christian; TN Montgomery.
    5360 Nashville-Davidson, TN......................15.8
    TN Cheatham; TN Davidson; TN Dickson; TN Robertson; TN Rutherford; TN Sumner; TN Williamson; TN Wilson.
  Non-SMSA Counties.................................12.0
    KY Allen; KY Barren; KY Butler; KY Clinton; KY Cumberland; KY Edmonson; KY Logan; KY Metcalfe; KY Monroe; KY Simpson; KY Todd; KY Trigg; KY Warren; TN Bedford; TN Cannon; TN Clay; TN Coffee; TN DeCalb; TN Franklin; TN Giles; TN Hickman; TN Houston; TN Humphreys; TN

Jackson; TN Lawrence; TN Lewis; TN Macon; TN Marshall; TN Maury; TN Moore; TN Overton; TN Perry; TN Pickett; TN Putnam; TN Smith; TN Stewart; TN Trousdale; TN Van Buren; TN Warren; TN Wayne; TN White.

055 Memphis, TN:
  SMSA Counties:
    4920 Memphis, TN-AR-MS.........................32.3
    AR Crittenden; MS De Soto; TN Shelby; TN Tipton.
  Non-SMSA Counties.................................26.5
    AR Clay; AR Craighead; AR Cross; AR Greene; AR Lawrence; AR Lee; AR Mississippi; AR Phillips; AR Poinsett; AR Randolph; AR St. Francis; MS Alcom; MS Benton; MS Bolivar; MS Calhoun; MS Carroll; MS Chickasaw; MS Clay; MS Coahoma; MS Grenada; MS Itawamba; MS Lafayette; MS Lee; MS Leflore; MS Marshall; MS Monroe; MS Montgomery; MS Panola; MS Pontotoc; MS Prentiss; MS Quitman; MS Sunflower; MS Tallahatchie; MS Tate; MS Tippah; MS Tishomingo; MS Union; MS Washington; MS Webster; MS Yalobusha; MO Dunkin; MO New Madrid; MO Pemiscot; TN Benton; TN Carroll; TN Chester; TN Crockett; TN Decatur; TN Dyer; TN Fayette; TN Gibson; TN Hardeman; TN Hardin; TN Haywood; TN Henderson; TN Henry; TN Lake; TN Lauderdale; TN McNairy; TN Madison; TN Obion; TN Weakley.

Texas:
119 Texarkana, TX:
  SMSA Counties:
    8360 Texarkana, TX-Texarkana, AR...............19.7
    AR Little River, AR Miller; TX Bowie.
  Non-SMSA Counties.................................20.2
    AR Columbia; AR Hempstead; AR Howard; AR Lafayette; AR Nevada; AR Pike; AR Sevier; TX Camp; TX Cass; TX Lamar; TX Morris; TX Red River; TX Titus.

120 Tyler-Longview, TX:
  SMSA Counties:
    4420 Longview, TX..............................22.8
    TX Gregg, TX Harrison.
    8640 Tyler, TX.................................23.5
    TX Smith.
  Non-SMSA Counties.................................22.5
    TX Anderson; TX Angelina; TX Cherokee; TX Henderson; TX Houston; TX Marion; TX Nacogdoches; TX Panola; TX Rusk; TX San Augustine; TX Shelby; TX Upshur; TX Wood.

121 Beaumont-Port Arthur, TX:
  SMSA Counties:
    0840 Beaumont-Port Arthur-Orange, TX..........22.6
    TX Hardine; TX Jefferson; TX Orange.
  Non-SMSA Counties.................................22.6
    TX Jasper, TX Newton; TX Sabine; TX Tyler.

122 Houston, TX:
  SMSA Counties:
    1260 Bryan-College Station, TX...................23.7

TX Brazos.
2920 Galveston-Texas City, TX.................28.9
TX Galveston.
3360 Houston, TX.................................27.3
TX Brazoria; TX Fort Bend; TX Harris; TX Liberty;
TX Montgomery; TX Waller.
Non-SMSA Counties...............................27.4
TX Austin; TX Burleson; TX Calhoun; TX
Chambers; TX Colorado; TX De Witt; TX Fayette;
TX Goliad; TX Grimes; TX Jackson; TX Lavaca; TX
Leon; TX Madison; TX Matagorda; TX Polk; TX
Robertson; TX San Jacinto; TX Trinity; TX Victoria;
TX Walker; TX Washington; TX Wharton.

123 Austin, TX:
 SMSA Counties:
  0640 Austin, TX............................24.1
   TX Hays; TX Travis; TX Williamson.
 Non-SMSA Counties...............................24.2
   TX Bastrop; TX Blanco; TX Burnet; TX Caldwell;
TX Lee; TX Llano.

124 Waco-Killeen-Temple, TX:
 SMSA Counties:
  3810 Killeen-Temple, TX.....................16.4
   TX Bell; TX Coryell.
  8800 Waco, TX...............................20.7
   TX McLennan.
 Non-SMSA Counties.............................18.6
   TX Bosque; TX Falls; TX Freestone; TX Hamilton;
TX Hill; TX Lampasas; TX Limestone; TX Milam;
TX Mills.

125 Dallas-Fort Worth, TX:
 SMSA Counties:
  1920 Dallas-Fort Worth, TX....................18.2
   TX Collin; TX Dallas; TX Denton; TX Ellis; TX
Hood; TX Johnson; TX Kaufman; TX Parker; TX
Rockwall; TX Tarrant; TX Wise.
  7640 Sherman-Denison, TX.....................9.4
   TX Grayson.
 Non-SMSA Counties.............................17.2
   OK Bryan; TX Cooke; TX Delta; TX Erath; TX
Fannin; TX Franklin; TX Hopkins; TX Hunt; TX
Jack; TX Montague; TX Navarro; TX Palo Pinto; TX
Rains; TX Sommervell; TX Van Zandt.

126 Wichita Falls, TX:
 SMSA Counties:
  9080 Wichita Falls, TX.......................12.4
   TX Clay; TX Wichita.
 Non-SMSA Counties.............................11.0
   TX Archer; TX Baylor; TX Cottle; TX Foard; TX
Hardeman; TX Wilbarger; TX Young.

127 Abilene, TX:
 SMSA Counties:
  0040 Abilene, TX.............................11.6
   TX Callahan; TX Jones; TX Taylor.
 Non-SMSA Counties.............................10.9

TX Brown; TX Coleman; TX Comanche; TX
Eastland; TX Fisher; TX Haskell; TX Kent; TX Knox;
TX Mitchell; TX Nolan; TX Scurry; TX Shakelford;
TX Stephens; TX Stonewall; TX Throckmorton.

128 San Angelo, TX:
 SMSA Counties:
  7200 San Angelo, TX.........................19.2
   TX Tom Green.
 Non-SMSA Counties.............................20.0
   TX Coke; TX Concho; TX Crockett; TX Irion; TX
Kimble; TX McCulloch; TX Mason; TX Menard; TX
Reagan; TX Runnels; TX San Saba; TX Schleicher;
TX Sterling; TX Sutton; TX Terrell.

129 San Antonio, TX:
 SMSA Counties:
  4080 Laredo, TX..............................87.3
   TX Webb.
  7240 San Antonio, TX........................47.8
   TX Bexar; TX Comal; TX Guadalupe.
 Non-SMSA Counties.............................49.4
   TX Atascosa; TX Bandera; TX Dimmit; TX
Edwards; TX Frio; TX Gillespie; TX Gonzales; TX
Jim Hogg; TX Karnes; TX Kendall; TX Kerr; TX
Kinney; TX La Salle; TX McMullen; TX Maverick;
TX Medina; TX Real; TX Uvalde; TX Vale Verde;
TX Wilson; TX Zapata; TX Zavala.

130 Corpus Christi, TX:
 SMSA Counties:
  1880 Corpus Christie, TX....................41.7
   TX Nueces; TX San Patricio.
 Non-SMSA Counties.............................44.2
   TX Arkansas; TX Bee; TX Brooks; TX Duval; TX
Jim Wells; TX Kennedy; TX Kyberg; TX Live Oak;
TX Refugio.

131 Brownsville-McAllen-Harligen, TX:
 SMSA Counties:
  1240 Brownsville-Harlingen-San Benito, TX....71.0
   TX Cameron
  4880 McAllen-Pharr-Edinburg, TX..............72.8
   TX Hidalga.
 Non-SMSA Counties.............................72.9
   TX Starr; TX Willacy;

132 Odessa-Midland, TX:
 SMSA Counties:
  5040 Midland, TX............................19.1
   TX Midland.
  5800 Odessa, TX.............................15.1
   TX Ector.
 Non-SMSA Counties.............................18.9
   TX Andrews; TX Crane; TX Glassock; TX Howard;
TX Loving; TX Martil; TX Pecos; TX Reeves; TX
Upton; TX Ward; TX Winkler.

133 El Paso, TX:
 SMSA Counties:
  2320 El Paso, TX.............................57.8

TX El Paso.
Non-SMSA Counties.................................49.0
NM Chaves; NM Dona Ana; NM Eddy; NM Grant;
NM Hidalgo; NM Luna; NM Otero; NM Sierra; TX
Brewster; TX Culbertson; TX Hudspeth; TX Jef
Davis; TX Presidio.

134 Lubbock, TX:
 SMSA Counties:
  4600 Lubbock, TX.................................19.6
  TX Lubbock.
 Non-SMSA Counties.................................19.5
  NM Lea; NM Roosevelt; TX Bailey; TX Borden;
TX Cochran; TX Crosby; TX Dawson; TX Dickens;
TX Floyd; TX Gaines; TX Garza; TX Hale; TX
Hockley; TX King; TX Lamb; TX Lynn; TX Motley;
TX Terry; TX Yoakum.

135 Amarillo, TX:
 SMSA Counties:
  0320 Amarillo, TX.................................9.3
  TX Potter; TX Randall.
 Non-SMSA Counties...............................11.0
  NM Curry; NM Harding; NM Quay; NM Union;
OK Beaver; OK Cimarron; OK Texas; TX Armstrong;
TX Briscoe; TX Carson; TX Castro; TX Childress;
TX Collingsworth; TX Dallam; TX Deaf Smith; TX
Donley; TX Gray; TX Hall; TX Hansford; TX
Hartley; TX Hemphill; TX Hutchinson; TX Lipscomb;
TX Moore; TX Ochiltree; TX Oldham; TX Parmer;
TX Roberts; TX Sherman; TX Swisher; TX Wheeler.

Utah:
165 Salt Lake City-Ogden, UT:
 SMSA Counties:
  6520 Provo-Orem, UT..............................2.4
  UT Utah.
  7160 Salt Lake City-Ogden, UT.....................6.0
  UT Davis; UT Salt Lake; UT Toole; UT Weber.
 Non-SMSA Counties.................................5.1
  ID Bear Lake; ID Franklin; ID Oneida; UT Box
Elder; UT Cache; UT Carbon; UT Daggett; UT
Duchesne; UT Emery; UT Juab; UT Millard; UT
Morgan; UT Piute; UT Rich; UT Sanpete; UT Servier;
UT Summit; UT Uintah; UT Wasatch; UT Wayne;
WY Lincoln; WY Sublette; WY Sweetwater; WY
Unita.

Vermont:
003 Burlington, VT:
 Non-SMSA Counties...................................0.8
  NH Coos; NH Grafton; NH Sullivan; VT Addison;
VT Caledonia; VT Chittenden; VT Essex; VT
Franklin; VT Grand Isle; VT Lamoille; VT Orange;
VT Orleans; VT Ruthland; VT Washington; VT
Windsor.

Virginia:
021 Roanoke-Lynchburg, VA:
 SMSA Counties:
  4640 Lynchburg, VA...............................19.3

VA Amherst; VA Appomattox; VA Campbell; VA
Lynchburg.
  6800 Roanoke, VA...................................10.2
  VA Botetourt; VA Craig; VA Roanoke; VA
Roanoke City; VA Salem.
 Non-SMSA Counties.................................12.0
  VA Alleghany; VA Augusta; VA Bath; VA
Bedford; VA Bland; VA Carroll; VA Floyd; VA
Franklin; VA Giles; VA Grayson; VA Henry; VA
Highland; VA Montgomery; VA Nelson; VA Patrick;
VA Pittsylvania; VA Pulaski; VA Rockbridge; VA
Rockingham; VA Wythe; VA Bedford City; VA
Buena Vista; VA Clifton Forge; VA Covington; VA
Danville; VA Galex; VA Harrisonburg; VA
Lexington; VA Martinsville; VA Radford; VA
Staunton; VA Waynesboro; WV Pendleton.

022 Richmond, VA:
 SMSA Counties:
  6140 Petersburg-Colonial Heights-Hopewell,
VA...30.6
  VA Dinwiddie; VA Prince George; VA Colonial
Heights; VA Hopewell; VA Petersburg.
  6760 Richmond, VA.................................24.9
  VA Charles City; VA Chesterfield; VA Goochland;
VA Hanover; VA Henrico; VA New Kent; VA
Powhatan; VA Richmond.
 Non-SMSA Counties.................................27.9
  VA Albemarle; VA Amelia; VA Brunswick; VA
Buckingham; VA Caroline; VA Charlotte; VA
Cumberland; VA Essex; VA Fluvanna; VA Greene;
VA Greensville; VA Halifax; VA King and Queen;
VA King William; VA Lancaster; VA Louisa; VA
Lunenberg; VA Madison; VA Mecklenburg; VA
Northumberland; VA Nottoway; VA Orange; VA
Prince Edward; VA Richmond; VA Sussex; VA
Charlottesville; VA Emporia; VA South Boston.

023 Norfolk-Virginia Beach-Newport News, VA:
 SMSA Counties:
  5680 Newport News-Hampton, VA.............27.1
  VA Gloucester; VA James City; VA York; VA
Hampton; VA Newport News; VA Williamsburg.
  5720 Norfolk-Virginia Beach-Portsmouth, VA-
NC..26.6
  NC Currituck; VA Chesapeake; VA Norfolk; VA
Portsmouth; VA Suffolk; VA Virginia Beach.
 Non-SMSA Counties.................................29.7
  NC Bertie; NC Camden; NC Chowan; NC Gates;
NC Hertford; NC Pasquotank; NC Perquimans; VA
Isle of Wright; VA Matthews; VA Middlesex; VA
Southampton; VA Surry; VA Franklin.

Washington:
168 Spokane, WA:
 SMSA Counties:
  7840 Spokane, WA.................................2.8
  WA Spokane.
 Non-SMSA Counties.................................3.0
  ID Benewah; ID Bonner; ID Boundary; ID
Clearwater; ID Idaho; ID Kootenai; ID Latah; ID
Lewis; ID Nez Perce; ID Shoshone; WA Adams; WA

Asotin; WA Columbia; WA Ferry; WA Garfield; WA Lincoln; WA Pend Oreille; WA Stevens; WA Whitman.

169 Richland, WA:
 SMSA Counties:
  6740 Richland-Kennewick, WA.................5.4
  WA Benton; WA Franklin.
 Non-SMSA Counties...................3.6
  OR Baker; OR Gilliam; OR Grant; OR Morrow; OR Umatilla; OR Union; OR Wallowa; OR Wheeler; WA Walla Walla.

170 Yakima, WA:
 SMSA Counties:
  9260 Yakima, WA.................9.7
  WA Yakima.
 Non-SMSA Counties...................7.2
  WA Chelan; WA Douglas; WA Grant; WA Kittitas; WA Okanogan.

171 Seattle, WA:
 SMSA Counties:
  7600 Seattle-Everett, WA.................7.2
  WA King; WA Snohomish.
  8200 Tacoma, WA.................6.2
  WA Pierce.
 Non-SMSA Counties...................6.1
  WA Callam; WA Grays Harbor; WA Island; WA Jefferson; WA Kitsap; WA Lewis; WA Mason; WA Pacific; WA San Juan; WA Skagit; WA Thurston; WA Whatcom.

Washington, DC:
020 Washington, DC:
 SMSA Counties:
  8840 Washington, DC-MD-VA.................28.0
  DC District of Columbia; MD Charles; MD Montgomery; MD Prince Georges; VA Arlington; VA Fairfax; VA Loudoun; VA Prince William; VA Alexandria; VA Fairfax City; VA Falls Church.
 Non-SMSA Counties.................25.2
  MD Calvert; MD Frederick; MD St. Marys; MD Washington; VA Clarke; VA Culpeper; VA Fauquire; VA Frederick; VA King George; VA Page; VA Rapahannock; VA Shenandoah; VA Spottsylvania; VA Stafford; VA Warren; VA Westmoreland; VA Fredericksburg; VA Winchester; WV Berkley; WV Grant; WV Hampshire; WV Hardy; WV Jefferson; WV Morgan.

West Virginia:
059 Huntington, WV:
 SMSA Counties:
  3400 Huntington-Ashland, WV-KY-OH.....2.9
  KY Boyd; KY Greenup; OH Lawrence; WV Cabell; WV Wayne.
 Non-SMSA Counties.................2.5
  KY Carter; KY Elliott; KY Floyd; KY Johnson; KY Lawrence; KY Martin; KY Pike; KY Rowan; OH Gallia; WV Lincoln; WV Logan; WV Mason; WV Mingo.

060 Charleston, WV:
 SMSA Counties:
  1480 Charleston, WV.................4.9
  WV Kanawha; WV Putnam.
 Non-SMSA Counties.................4.2
  WV Boone; WV Braxton; WV Calhoun; WV Clay; WV Fayette; WV Gilmer; WV Greenbrier; WV Jackson; WV Monroe; WV Nicholas; WV Pocahontas; WV Raleigh; WV Roane; WV Summers; WV Webster; WV Wyoming.

061 Morgantown-Fairmont, WV:
 Non-SMSA Counties.................2.1
  WV Barbour; WV Doddridge; WV Harrison; WV Lewis; WV Marion; WV Monogalia; WV Preston; WV Randolph; WV Taylor; WV Tucker; WV Upshur.

062 Parkersburg, WV:
 SMSA Counties:
  6020 Parkersburg-Marietta, WV-OH.................1.1
  OH Washington; WV Wirt; WV Wood.
 Non-SMSA Counties.................1.2
  WV Pleasants; WV Ritchie.

063 Wheeling-Steubenville-Wierton, WV-OH:
 SMSA Counties:
  8080 Steubenville-Wierton, OH-WV.................4.3
  OH Jefferson; WV Brooke; WV Hancock.
  9000 Wheeling, WV-OH.................2.4
  OH Belmont; WV Marshall; WV Ohio.
 Non-SMSA Counties.................3.0
  OH Harrison; OH Monroe; WV Tyler; WV Wetzel.

Wisconsin:
089 Milwaukee, WI:
 SMSA Counties:
  5080 Milwaukee, WI.................8.0
  WI Milwaukee; WI Ozaukee; WI Washington; WI Waukesha.
  6600 Racine, WI.................8.4
  WI Racine.
 Non-SMSA Counties.................7.0
  WI Dodge; WI Jefferson; WI Sheboygan; WI Walworth.

090 Madison, WI:
 SMSA Counties:
  4720 Madison, WI.................2.2
  WI Dane.
 Non-SMSA Counties.................1.7
  WI Adams; WI Columbia; WI Green; WI Iowa; WI Marquette; WI Richland; WI Sauk.

091 La Crosse, WI:
 SMSA Counties:
  3870 La Crosse, WI.................0.9
  WI La Crosse.
 Non-SMSA Counties.................0.6

MN Houston; MN Winona; WI Buffalo; WI Jackson; WI Juneau; WI Monroe; WI Trempealeau; WI Vernon.

092 Eau Claire, WI:
 SMSA Counties:
  2290 Eau Claire, WI…………………………..0.5
  WI Chippewa; WI Eau Claire.
 Non-SMSA Counties……………………………0.6
  WI Barron; WI Dunn; WI Pepin; WI Rusk; WI Sawyer; WI Washburn.

093 Wausau, WI:
 Non-SMSA Counties……………………………0.6
  WI Clark; WI Langlade; WI Lincoln; WI Marathon; WI Oneida; WI Portage; WI Price; WI Taylor; WI Vilas; WI Wood.

094 Appleton-Green Bay-Oshkosh, WI:
 SMSA Counties:
  0460 Appleton-Oshkosh, WI………..…………0.9
  WI Calumet; WI Outagamie; WI Winebago.
  3080 Green Bay, WI……………...……………1.3

WI Brown.
 Non-SMSA Counties…………………..…………1.0
  MI Alger; MI Baraga; MI Delta; MI Dickinson; MI Houghton; MI Iron; MI Keweenaw; MI Marquette; MI Menominee; MI Schoolcraft; WI Door; WI Florence; WI Ford Du Lac; WI Forest; WI Green Lake; WI Kewaunee; WI Manitowoc; WI Marinette; WI Menominee; WI Oconto; WI Shawano; WI Waupaca; WI Waushara.

095 Duluth, MN:
 SMSA Counties:
  2240 Duluth-Superior, MN-WI……..…………1.0
  MN St. Louis; WI Douglas.
 Non-SMSA Counties……………………..……..1.2
  MI Gogebic; MI Ononagon; MN Carlton; MN Cook; MN Itasca; MN Koochiching; MN Lake; WI Ashland; WI Bayfield; WI Iron.

Compliance Audits & Scheduling Letter

Audits of construction contractors are quite different from those of other contractors. First of all, they take much less time. If the contractor has all relevant data available for the auditor's arrival the only variable tends to be the number of employee interviews the Compliance Officer wants to conduct.

Remember, every audit will be used as an opportunity for the government to check your file of I-9 Forms. Be sure you have them in order. And, be sure you have reviewed each form to be sure there is no missing information and that there are no missing forms. Each error can cost you $1,000. The total increases dramatically in short order.

A sample scheduling letter, explaining your audit requirements, can be found on in Appendix H.

Notes

Appendix A

Chart of State EEO Protections

A Note About Appendix A Tables

On the following pages are tables which reflect, state by state, fair employment practices protections offered to employees by state laws. These are IN ADDITION TO those offered by federal legislation. All states are subject to federal employee protections. Some choose to go beyond the federal levels of protection and embrace additional categories. It is particularly important, if you are a multi-state employer, that you be aware of ALL the legal protections offered your employees by the various jurisdictions in which you operate.

You might want to consider making a master list of protected categories for the states in which you operate. If you use that list in your EEO/AA policy statement, you will be able to have your policy statement apply in each of your various state locations. Such an approach will simplify your management training and implementation of your AAP.

Federal laws offer employees protection against discrimination based on:

- Age
- Race
- National Origin
- Religion
- Color
- Sex
- Disability (Physical & Mental)
- Pregnancy
- Veteran Status
- Equal Pay
- Denial of Family Care Leave
- Harassment (Sexual, Racial, Religious)
- Genetic Information
- Retaliation for Protected Activity (complaint)

INDIVIDUAL STATE EEO PROTECTIONS
IN ADDITION TO FEDERAL PROTECTIONS

State	Protection	State Laws/Regulations
AL		None
AK	Retaliation, Parenthood	Alaska Stat. Sec.18.80.220.
AZ	Retaliation	Ariz. Rev. Stat. Ann. Sec. 41-1461...1464.
AR	Retaliation	Ark. Code Ann. Sec. 16-123-101, 102, 107, 108
CA	Family Care Leave, National Guard service, HIV, AIDS, Gender Identity, Political Orientation, Retaliation	Cal. Govt. Code. Sec. 12920, 12926, 12940, 12945.2, 12949, 19700...19703. Labor Code Sec. 230, 232, 1101, 1102, 1171.5
CO	Marriage to another employee, Gender Identity, Retaliation	Colo. Rev. Stat Sec. 24-34-301, 401, 402, 402.5
CT	Status as parent or potential parent, History of mental illness, Arrest records, Retaliation	Conn. Gen. Stat. Ann. Sec. 46a-51, 60, 61, 81c
DE	Genetic Information, Retaliation	Del. Code Ann. Tit. 19, Sec. 711
DC	Personal appearance, Gender Identity, Family responsibilities, Genetic Information, Source of Income	D.C. Code Ann. Sec. 2-1401, 1402
FL	Marital Status, AIDS, HIV, Sickle-cell Trait, Retaliation	Fla. Stat. Ann. Sec. 448.075, 448.076, 760.10, 760.50
GA	Retaliation	Ga. Code Ann. Sec. 45-19-1
HI	Sexual Orientation, Marital Status, Genetic Information, Breast Feeding, Retaliation	HI Rev Stat. Sec. 378-1, 2
ID	Sexual Orientation, Marital Status, Association with disabled person, Retaliation	Idaho Code Sec. 67-5901, 67-5902, 5909, 5911
IL	Sexual Orientation, Gender Identity, Marital Status, Citizenship Status, Retaliation	IL Comp. Stat. Ann. 5/1-101
IN	Rehabilitated drug user or someone currently enrolled in a rehabilitation program, Retaliation	Indiana Code Ann. Sec. 22-9-1-2, 3, 6, 13, 22-9-5-6, 13
IA	Sexual Orientation, Gender Identity, Retaliation	Iowa Code Ann Sec. 216.2, .5, .6, .11, .21

Secrets of Affirmative Action Compliance

INDIVIDUAL STATE EEO PROTECTIONS
IN ADDITION TO FEDERAL PROTECTIONS

State	Protection	State Laws/Regulations
KS	Political Affiliation (public employees only), Genetic Information, Retaliation	KS Stat. Ann. Sec. 44-1002, 1009, 75-2941
KY	Political Orientation (public employees only), Familial status, AIDS, HIV, Retaliation	KY Rev Stat. Ann. Sec. 18A.140, 207.135, 344.010, .020, .040
LA	Sickle-cell Trait, Genetic Information, Retaliation	Louisiana Rev Stat Ann. Sec. 23:301, 961, 962, 964-966, 1361
ME	Sexual Orientation, Marital Status (public employees only), Gender Identity, Retaliation	ME Rev. Stat. Ann. Title 5 Sec 4553, 4572, 7051
MD	Sexual Orientation, Marital Status, Genetic Information, Retaliation	MD Ann. Code Art. 49B, Sec 7, 14, 16
MA	Sexual Orientation, Genetic Information, Retaliation	Mass Gen Laws Ann. Ch 151B Sec 4
MI	Marital Status, Height and Weight, Genetic Information, Retaliation	Mich. Comp. Laws Ann. Sec 37.1202, .2201, .2202, .2205a, .2701
MN	Sexual Orientation, Marital Status, Gender Identity, Retaliation	Minn. Stat. Ann. Sec. 363A.08, 363A.19, 364.04
MS	Political Orientation, Retaliation (public employees only)	Miss Code Ann. Sec 25-9-149, 173, 303
MO	Rehabilitated drug users, AIDS, Retaliation	MO Rev. Stat. Sec 191.665, 213.010, .055, .070
MT	Marital Status, Political Orientation, Retaliation	Mont Code Ann. Sec. 49-1-102, 49-2-301, 303, 308, 405, 49-3-201, 209
NE	Marital Status, Political Orientation, HIV, Retaliation (Excludes members of communist organizations)	NE Rev. Stat. Ann. Sec. 20-160-20-162, 20-167, 48-236, 48-1101-48-1104
NV	Sexual Orientation, Political Orientation (public employees only), Genetic Information, Use of Service animal, Retaliation	Nev. Rev. Stat. Ann. Sec. 281.370, 613.040, .310, .330, .333, .340, .345
NH	Sexual Orientation, Marital Status, Retaliation	NH Rev. Stat. Ann. Sec. 155, 275:37-a
NJ	Sexual Orientation, Marital Status, Gender identity, Civil union status, Domestic partnership status, Atypical hereditary cellular or blood trait, Use of service dog, Retaliation	NJ Stat. Ann. Sec. 10:5-3, -4, -5

410

INDIVIDUAL STATE EEO PROTECTIONS
IN ADDITION TO FEDERAL PROTECTIONS

State	Protection	State Laws/Regulations
NM	Sexual Orientation, Spousal Affiliation, Political Orientation (state employees only), Gender Identity, Retaliation	NM Stat. Ann. Sec. 10-9-21, 28-1-2, -7
NY	Sexual Orientation, Marital Status, Political Orientation (civil service employees), Genetic Predisposition, Sicle-cell Trait, Tay-Sachs Syndrome, Cooley's Anemia, AIDS, Use of Service Dog	NY Civil Rights Law Sec. 40-c, 47-b, 48
NC	Political Orientation, Retaliation	NC Gen Stat. Sec. 126-13, -16, -17, -36, -80, -85
ND	Marital Status, Retaliation	ND Cent. Code Sec. 14-02
OH	Retaliation	OH Rev. Code Ann. Sec. 4112.01, .02, OH Admin Code Sec 4112-5-02, -08
OK	Retaliation	OK Stat. Ann. Title 25, Sec. 1302-1306, Title 74 Sec. 840-2.9, 954
OR	Sexual Orientation, Marital Status, Gender Identity, Domestic Partnership Status, Retaliation	OR Rev. Stat. Sec. 236.380, 659A
PA	Use of Guide Dogs or Support Animals, Retaliation	43 PA Cons. Stat. Sec. 952-955
RI	Sexual Orientation, Gender Identity, Retaliation	RI Gen. Laws Sec. 28-5-3, 28-5-5-28-5-7
SC	Retaliation	SC Code Ann. Sec. 1-13-20
SD	Political Orientation (public employees only), Genetic Information, Retaliation	SD Cod. Laws Sec. 3-6A-15, 20-13-10
TN	Retaliation	TN Code Ann. Sec. 4-21-102, -301, -401
TX	Genetic Information, Refusing a Genetic Test, Retaliation	TX Lab. Code Ann. Sec. 21.002, .051, .105, .124, .402
UT	Political Orientation (public employees only), Genetic Information, Retaliation	UT Code Ann. Sec. 34A-5-102, -106, 62A-5b-105, 67-19-4, -19
VT	Sexual Orientation, Political Orientation (public employees only), Place of Birth, HIV, Gender Identity, Retaliation	VT Stat. Ann. Title 3 Sec. 961, Title 21, Sec. 495, 497, 1726
VA	Marital Status, Retaliation	VA Code Ann.Sec. 2.2-3900 to 3902

Secrets of Affirmative Action Compliance

**INDIVIDUAL STATE EEO PROTECTIONS
IN ADDITION TO FEDERAL PROTECTIONS**

State	Protection	State Laws/Regulations
WA	Sexual Orientation, Marital Status, Gender Identity, AIDS, Hepatitis C Infection, Use of Service Animal, Retaliation	WA Rev. Code Ann. Sec. 49.60.172, .180, .210, 71A.10.040
WV	Political Orientation (state employees only), Familial Status, Retaliation	WV Code Sec 5-11-3, -9, 29-6-4, -20
WI	Sexual Orientation, Marital Status, Political Orientation (public employees only), Height and Weight, Genetic Testing, Retaliation	WI Stat. Ann. Sec. 111.31 – 372, 230.18-.20
WY	Retaliation	WY Stat. Ann. Sec. 27-9-105

Appendix B

Organizations and Recruiting Sources

ORGANIZATIONS AND
RECRUITING SOURCES

American Indian Science/Engineering Society
2305 Renard SE, Ste 200
Albuquerque, NM 87106
505-765-1052
www.aises.org

American Indian Lawyer Training Pgm
319 MacArthur Blvd.
Oakland, CA 94610
510-834-9333

Consortium of United Indian Nations
1320 Webster Street
Oakland, CA 94612
510-763-3410

American Indian Training Institute
4221 Northgate Blvd, Ste 2
Sacramento, CA 95834
916-920-0731
www.aitiincl.org

California Indian Manpower Consortium, Inc.
738 North Market Blvd.
Sacramento, CA 95834
916-920-0285
www.dcn.davis.ca.us/YoloLINK/programs/pCali
foIndianManpow-4378.html

Chinese for Affirmative Action
17 Walter U. Lum Place
San Francisco, CA 94108
415-274-6750
www.caasf.org

Asian American Architects/Engineers
8230 Lincoln Blvd #8
Los Angeles, CA 90045
213-896-9270
www.aaaesc.com

Korean Center Inc.
1362 Post Street
San Francisco, CA 94109
415-441-1881
www.koreannet.org/about/contact.html

100 Black Men of America, Inc.
141 Auburn Ave
Atlanta, GA 30303
404-688-5100
www.100blackmen.org/

Black Data Processing Associates
6301 Ivy Lane, Suite 700
Greenbelt, MD 20770
800-727-2372
www.bdpa.org

National Society of Black Engineers
1454 Duke Street
Alexandria, VA 22314
703-549-2207
www.nsbe.org

National Black MBA Association
180 N. Michigan, Ste 1400
Chicago, IL 60601
312-236-2622
www.nbmbaa.org

Forty Plus
(Check the White Pages of your local phone
directory)

Goodwill Industries International, Inc.
15810 Indianola Dr.
Rockville, MD 20855
800-741-0186
www.goodwill.org

Hispanic Alliance for Career Enhancement
25 East Washington, Ste 1500
Chicago, IL 60602
312-435-0498
www.hace-usa.org

National Association of Multicultural
Engineering Program Advocates, Inc.
1133 W. Morse Blvd., Suite 201
Winter Park, FL 32789
407-647-8839
www.namepa.org/

California Office of Small and Disadvantaged
Businesses
707 3rd Street

West Sacramento, CA 95605
916-375-4400
www.pd.dgs.ca.gov/contact/default.htm

PROFESSIONAL ASSOCIATIONS

American Business Women's Association
800-228-0007
www.abwa.org

American Medical Women's Association
www.amwa-doc.org

Association of Black Psychologists
202-722-0808
www.abpsi.org

Chi Eta Phi Sorority (Black nurses organization)
317-278-2206
www.chietaphi.com/

National Association of Insurance Women
800-766-6249
www.naiw.org

National Federation of Press Women
800-780-2715
www.nfpw.org

National Action Council for Minorities in
Engineering
914-539-4032
www.nacme.org

National Newspaper Publishers Association
202-588-8764
www.nnpa.org

National Alliance of Black School Educators
202-608-6310
www.nabse.org

National Council of Black Engineers &
Scientists
212-279-2626
www.ncbes.org

National Association of Black Journalists
301-445-7100
www.nabj.org

National Association of Women in Construction
817-877-5551
www.nawic.org

National Association of Black Accountants
301-474-6222
www.nabainc.org

National Association of Women Lawyers
312-988-6186
www.abanet.org/nawl

National Association for Advancement of
Colored People
410-521-4939
www.naacp.org

National Coalition of Black Meeting Planners
202-628-3952
www.ncbmp.com

National Urban League
212-558-5300
www.nul.org

National Black Nurses Association
301-589-3200
www.nbna.org

National Minority Supplier Development
Council
212-944-2430
www.nmsdc.org

National Association of Minority Contractors
202-347-8259
www.namcline.org/

National Organization of Minority Architects
202-686-2780
www.noma.net/local/

National Association of Negro Business &
Professional Women's Clubs
202-483-4206
www.nanbpwc.org

National Organization for Women
www.now.org

National Society of Hispanic MBAs
877-467-4622
www.nshmba.org

Society of Women Engineers
312-596-5223
www.swe.org

YOU ARE INVITED

You are invited to send us additional recruiting resource contact information. We would like to include your suggestions in future editions of this reference list.

Please send your comments and suggestions to:

AAP@management-advantage.com

Thank you for your help. Your colleagues in other organizations will also appreciate having your information about reliable resources you have used to fulfill your recruiting obligations within your affirmative action plan.

Internet Recruiting Sites

Internet Address	Accepts Job Listing?	Approximate $/Ad
www.alljobsearch.com	Yes	?
www.career.com	Yes	$60 to $250
www.careerbuilder.com	Yes	$150
www.careercity.com	Yes	$500/yr
www.careers.org	Yes	?
www.execunet.com	Yes	Free
www.jobster.com	Yes	?
www.monster.com	Yes	?
www.thejobspider.com	Yes	Free
www.veteranemployment.com/	Yes	?
www.vetjobs.com/	Yes	?
www.militaryhire.com/	Yes	?
www.recruitmilitary.com/	Yes	?
www.militaryexits.com/	Yes	?
www.hireveterans.com/jobs-for-military-veterans.htm	Yes	?

PLEASE NOTE: Internet resources change every day. You may find that these addresses no longer work. One way to find current resources is to use Google.com or other search engines to locate the types of sites you have in mind. While this information was current as of publication, it may become outdated rapidly. We ask that you verify every resource you intend to use.

Notes

Appendix C

EEO-1 Form

On the following pages you will find the EEO-1 Form finalized by the EEOC and published in the Federal Register on November 28, 2005. The revised content was implemented for reports which are due on and after September 30, 2007.

EEO-1 JOINT REPORTING COMMITTEE

- Equal Employment Opportunity Commission
- Office of Federal Contract Compliance Programs

O.M.B. No. 3046-0007
Approval Expires 1/2009

EQUAL EMPLOYMENT
OPPORTUNITY COMMISSION

WASHINGTON, D.C. 20507

EQUAL EMPLOYMENT OPPORTUNITY

STANDARD FORM 100, REV. January 2006, EMPLOYER INFORMATION REPORT
EEO-1

INSTRUCTION BOOKLET

The Employer Information EEO-1 survey is conducted annually under the authority of Title VII of the Civil Rights Act of 1964, 42 U.S.C. 2000e, et. seq., as amended. All employers with 15 or more employees are covered by Title VII and are required to keep employment records as specified by Commission regulations. Based on the number of employees and federal contract activities, certain large employers are required to file an EEO-1 report on an annual basis.

See the Appendix for the applicable provisions of the law, Section 709(c) of Title VII, and the applicable regulations, Sections 1602.7-1602.14, Chapter XIV, Title 29 of the Code of Federal Regulations. State and local governments, school systems and educational institutions are covered by other employment surveys and are excluded from Standard Form 100, Employer Information Report EEO-1.

In the interests of consistency, uniformity and economy, Standard Form 100 has been jointly developed by the Equal Employment Opportunity Commission and the Office of Federal Contract Compliance Programs of the U. S. Department of Labor, as a single form which meets the statistical needs of both programs. In addition, this form should be a valuable tool for companies to use in evaluating their own internal programs for insuring equal employment opportunity.

As stated above, the filing of Standard Form 100 is required by law; *it is not voluntary*. Under section 709(c) of Title VII, the Equal Employment Opportunity Commission may compel an employer to file this form by obtaining an order from the United States District Court.

Under Section 209(a) of Executive Order 11246, the penalties for failure by a federal contractor or subcontractor to comply may include termination of the federal government contract and debarment from future federal contracts.

\1. WHO MUST FILE

Standard Form 100 must be filed by --

(A) All private employers who are: (1) subject to Title VII of the Civil Rights Act of 1964, as amended, with 100 or more employees **EXCLUDING** State and local governments, primary and secondary school systems, institutions of higher education, Indian tribes and tax-exempt private membership clubs other than labor organizations; OR (2) subject to Title VII who have fewer than 100 employees if the company is owned or affiliated with another company, or there is centralized ownership, control or management (such as central control of personnel policies and labor relations) so that the group legally constitutes a single enterprise, and the entire enterprise employs a total of 100 or more employees.

(B) All federal contractors (private employers), who: (1) are not exempt as provided for by 41 CFR 60-1.5; (2) have 50 or more employees; **and** (a) are prime contractors or first-tier subcontractors, and have a contract, subcontract, or purchase order amounting to $50,000 or more; or (b) serve as a depository of government funds in any amount, or (c) is a financial institution which is an issuing and paying agent for U.S. Savings Bonds and Notes.

Only those establishments located in the District of Columbia and the 50 states are required to submit Standard Form 100. No reports should be filed for establishments in Puerto Rico, the Virgin Islands or other American Protectorates.

2. HOW TO FILE

Note: Submission of EEO-1 data through the *EEO-1 Online Filing System* or as an electronically transmitted data file is <u>strongly</u> <u>preferred.</u> See paragraph 6, EEO-1 Alternate Reporting Formats.

Single-establishment employers, i.e., employers doing business at only one establishment in one location must complete a single EEO-1 online data record or submit a single EEO-1 paper report.

Multi-establishment employers, i.e., employers doing business at more than one establishment, must complete online: (1) a report covering the principal or headquarters office; (2) a separate report for <u>EACH</u> establishment employing 50 or more persons; and (3) a separate report (Type 8 record) for each establishment employing fewer than 50 employees, OR an Establishment List (Type 6 record), showing the name, address, and total employment for each establishment employing fewer than 50 persons, including a Type 6 employment data grid that combines all employees working at establishments employing fewer than 50 employees by race, sex, and job category. For the EEO-1 online application, keyed employment data automatically transfers to the overall Consolidated Report.

The total number of employees indicated on the headquarters report, **PLUS** the establishment reports, **PLUS** the list of establishments employing fewer than 50 employees, **MUST** equal the total number of employees shown on the Consolidated Report.

Employment data for multi-establishment companies, including parent corporations and their subsidiary holdings, must report all employees working at each company establishment or subsidiary establishment. For the purposes of this report, the term **parent corporation** refers to any corporation which owns all or the majority stock of another corporation so that the latter relates to it as a subsidiary.

3. WHEN TO FILE

This annual report must be filed not later than September 30. Employment figures from any pay period in July through September may be used.

4. WHERE TO FILE [Paper EEO-1 form(s) ONLY]

Mail one copy to the address indicated in the annual survey mail out memorandum.

5. REQUESTS FOR INFORMATION AND SPECIAL PROCEDURES

An employer who claims that preparation or the filing of Standard Form 100 would create undue hardship may apply to the Commission for a special reporting procedure. In such cases, the employer must submit **in writing** a detailed alternative proposal for compiling and reporting information to: **The EEO-1 Coordinator, EEOC-Survey Division, 1801 L Street, NW, Washington, DC 20507.**

Only those special procedures approved **in writing** by the Commission are authorized. Such authorizations remain in effect until notification of cancellation is given. All requests for information should be sent to the address above.

6. EEO-1 ALTERNATE REPORTING FORMATS

EEO-1 reporting is an electronic, online application. Pursuant to the Government Paperwork Elimination Act of 1998, we **STRONGLY** recommend that EEO-1 reports be submitted via the *EEO-1 Online Filing System*, or as an electronically transmitted data file. A copy of the **prescribed** EEO-1 data file format is available at the website address in the survey mail out memorandum; or by calling the telephone number or writing to the address in the survey mail out memorandum. *Paper EEO-1 forms will be generated on request only, in extreme cases where Internet access is not available to the employer.* An EEO-1 report submitted on paper must be prepared following the directions in paragraph 2, HOW TO FILE.

7. CONFIDENTIALITY

All reports and information from individual reports will be kept confidential, as required by Section 709(e) of Title VII. Only data aggregating information by industry or area, in such a way as not to reveal any particular employers statistics, will be made public. The prohibition against disclosure mandated by Section 709(e) does not apply to the Office of Federal Contract Compliance Programs and contracting agencies of the federal government which require submission of SF 100 pursuant to Executive Order 11246. Reports from prime contractors and subcontractors doing business with the federal government may not be confidential under Executive Order 11246.

8. ESTIMATE OF BURDEN

Public reporting burden for this collection of information is estimated to average three and five tenths (3.5) hours per response, including the time for reviewing instructions, searching existing data sources, gathering and maintaining the data needed and completing and reviewing the collection of information. A response is defined as one survey form. Send comments regarding this burden estimate or any other aspect of this collection of information, including suggestions for reducing this burden to:

> The EEOC Clearance Officer
> Office of the Chief Financial Officer and Administrative Services -- Room 2100
> 1801 L Street, N.W.
> Washington, D.C. 20507

AND

> Paperwork Reduction Project (3046-0007)
> Office of Management and Budget
> Washington, D.C. 20503

The full text of the OMB regulations may be found at 5 CFR Part 1320. **PLEASE DO NOT SEND YOUR COMPLETED REPORT TO EITHER OF THESE ADDRESSES.**

EEO-1 Terms Applicable To All Reporting Formats

Type of Report (Status Code)

1 Single-establishment company

Multi-establishment company

2 Consolidated Report (Required)

3 Headquarters Report (Required)

4 Establishment Report (50 or more employees)

6 Establishment List (Option 1)

8 Establishment Report (less than 50 employees) (Option 2)

Company Identification

Refers to the company name and address of the headquarters office of the multi-establishment company (Report Types 2 and 3); or the establishment name and address.

Employers Who Are Required To File

Questions 1, 2 and 3 **MUST** be answered by all employers. If the answer to Question C-3 is Yes, please enter the company's Dun and Bradstreet identification number if the company has one. If the answer is Yes to question 1, 2, or 3, complete the entire form. Otherwise skip to Section G.

Employment Data

Employment data must include **ALL** full-time and part-time employees who were employed during the selected payroll period, except those employees specifically excluded as indicated in the Appendix. Employees must be counted by sex and race or ethnic category for each of the ten occupational categories and subcategories. See Appendix for detailed explanation of job categories and race and ethnic identification.

Every employee must be accounted for in one and **ONLY** one of the categories in Columns A thru N.

Occupational Data Employment data must be reported by job category. Report each employee in only one job category. In order to simplify and standardize the method of reporting, all jobs are considered as belonging in one of the broad occupations shown in the table. To assist you in determining where to place your jobs within the occupational categories, a description of job categories is in the *EEO-1 Job Classification Guide* or you may consult the EEO-1-Census Codes Cross Walk on the Commission's web site. For further clarification, you may wish to consult the Alphabetical and Classified Indices of Industries and Occupations (2000 Census) published by the U.S. Department of Commerce, Census Bureau.

Establishment Information

The major activity should be sufficiently descriptive to identify the industry and product produced or service provided. If an establishment is engaged in more than one activity, describe the activity at which the **greatest** number of employees work.

The description of the major activity indicated on the Headquarters Report (Type 3) must reflect the dominant economic activity of the company in which the greatest number of employees are engaged.

Remarks

Include in this section any remarks, explanations, or other pertinent information regarding this report.

Certification

If all reports have been completed at headquarters, the authorized official should check Item 1 and sign the Consolidated Report only. If the reports have been completed by the individual establishments, the authorized official should check Item 2 and sign the establishment report.

APPENDIX

1. DEFINITIONS APPLICABLE TO ALL EMPLOYERS

a. "Commission" refers to the Equal Employment Opportunity Commission.

b. "OFCCP" refers to the Office of Federal Contract Compliance Programs, U.S. Department of Labor, established to implement Executive Order 11246, as amended.

c. "Joint Reporting Committee" is the committee representing the Commission and OFCCP for the purpose of administering this report system.

d. "Employer" under Section 701(b), Title VII of the Civil Rights Act of 1964, as amended, means a person engaged in an industry affecting commerce who has fifteen or more employees for each working day in each of twenty or more calendar weeks in the current or preceding calendar year, and any agent of such a person, but such term does not include the United States, a corporation wholly owned by the government of the United States, an Indian tribe, or any department or agency of the District of Columbia subject by statute to procedures of the competitive service (as defined in section 2102 of Title 5 of the United States Code), or a bona fide private membership club (other than a labor organization) which is exempt from taxation under Section 501(c) of the Internal Revenue Code of 1954; OR any person or entity subject to Executive Order 11246 who is a federal government prime contractor or subcontractor at any tier (including a bank or other establishment serving as a depository of federal government funds, or an issuing and paying agent of U.S. Savings Bonds and Notes, or a holder of a federal government bill of lading) or a federally-assisted construction prime contractor or subcontractor at any tier.

e. "Employee" means any individual on the payroll of an employer who is an employee for purposes of the employers withholding of Social Security taxes except insurance sales agents who are considered to be employees for such purposes solely because of the provisions of 26 USC 3121 (d) (3) (B) (the Internal Revenue Code). Leased employees are included in this definition. Leased Employee means a permanent employee provided by an employment agency for a fee to an outside company for which the employment agency handles all personnel tasks including payroll, staffing, benefit payments and compliance reporting. The employment agency shall, therefore, include leased employees in its EEO-1 report. The term employee SHALL NOT include persons who are hired on a casual basis for a specified time, or for the duration of a specified job (for example, persons at a construction site whose employment relationship is expected to terminate with the end of the employees work at the site); persons temporarily employed in any industry other than construction, such as temporary office workers, mariners, stevedores, lumber yard workers, etc., who are hired through a hiring hall or other referral arrangement, through an employee contractor or agent, or by some individual hiring arrangement, or persons **(EXCEPT** leased employees) on the payroll of an employment agency who are referred by such agency for work to be performed on the premises of another employer under that employers direction and control.

It is the opinion of the General Counsel of the Commission that Section 702, Title VII of the Civil Rights Act of 1964, as amended, does not authorize a complete exemption of religious organizations from the coverage of the Act or of the reporting requirements of the Commission. The exemption for religious organizations applies to discrimination on the basis of religion. Therefore, since the Standard Form 100 does not provide for information as to the religion of employees, religious organizations must report all information required by this form.

f. "Commerce" means trade, traffic, commerce, transportation, transmission, or communication among the several States; or between a State and any place outside thereof; or within the District of Columbia, or a possession of the United States; or between points in the same State but through a point outside thereof.

g. "Industry Affecting Commerce" means any activity, business or industry in commerce or in which a labor dispute would hinder or obstruct commerce or the free flow of commerce and includes any activity or industry affecting commerce within the meaning of the Labor Management Reporting and Disclosure Act of 1959. Any employer of 15 or more persons is presumed to be in an industry affecting commerce.

h. "Establishment" is an economic unit which produces goods or services, such as a factory, office, store, or mine. In most instances, the establishment is at a single physical location and is engaged in one, or predominantly one, type of economic activity. (definition adapted from the **North American Industry Classification System, 2002**).

Units at different physical locations, even though engaged in the same kind of business operation, must be reported as separate establishments. For locations involving construction, transportation, communications, electric, gas, and sanitary services, oil and gas fields, and similar types of physically dispersed industrial activities, however, it is not necessary to list separately each individual site, project, field, line, etc., unless it is treated by you as a separate legal entity. For these types of activities, list as establishments only those relatively permanent main or branch offices, terminals, stations etc., which are either: (a) directly responsible for supervising such dispersed activities; or (b) the base from which personnel and equipment operate to carry out these activities. (Where these dispersed activities cross State lines, at least one such establishment should be listed for each State involved.)

i. "Major Activity" means the major product or group of products produced or handled, or services rendered by the reporting unit (e.g., manufacturing airplane parts, retail sales of office furniture) in terms of the activity at which the greatest number of all employees work. The description includes the type of product manufactured or sold or the type of service provided.

2. DEFINITIONS APPLICABLE ONLY TO GOVERNMENT CONTRACTORS SUBJECT TO EXECUTIVE ORDER 11246

a. "Order" means Executive Order 11246, as amended.

b. "Contract" means any government contract or any federally-assisted construction contract.

c. "Prime Contractor" means any employer having a government contract or any federally-assisted construction contract, or any employer serving as a depository of federal >government funds.

d. "Subcontractor" means any employer having a contract with a prime contractor or another subcontractor calling for supplies or services required for the performance of a government contract or federally assisted construction contract.

e. "Contracting Agency" means any department, agency and establishment in the executive branch of the government, including any wholly-owned government corporation, which enters into contracts.

f. "Administering Agency" means any department, agency and establishment in the executive branch of the government, including any wholly-owned government corporation, which administers a program involving federally-assisted construction contracts.

3. RESPONSIBILITIES OF PRIME CONTRACTORS

a. At the time of an award of a subcontract subject to these reporting requirements, the prime contractor shall inform the subcontractor of its responsibility to submit annual EEO-1 employment data in accordance with these instructions.

b. If prime contractors are required by their Contracting Officer or subcontractors by their prime contractors, to submit notification of filing, they shall do so by ordinary correspondence. However, such notification is not required by and should not be sent to the Joint Reporting Committee.

4. RACE AND ETHNIC IDENTIFICATION

Self-identification is the preferred method of identifying the race and ethnic information necessary for the EEO-1 report. Employers are required to attempt to allow employees to use self-identification to complete the EEO-1 report. If an employee declines to self-identify, employment records or observer identification may be used.

Where records are maintained, it is recommended that they be kept separately from the employees basic personnel file or other records available to those responsible for personnel decisions.

Race and ethnic designations as used by the Equal Employment Opportunity Commission do not denote scientific definitions of anthropological origins. Definitions of the race and ethnicity categories are as follows:

Hispanic or Latino - A person of Cuban, Mexican, Puerto Rican, South or Central American, or other Spanish culture or origin regardless of race.

White (Not Hispanic or Latino) - A person having origins in any of the original peoples of Europe, the Middle East, or North Africa.

Black or African American (Not Hispanic or Latino) - A person having origins in any of the black racial groups of Africa.

Native Hawaiian or Other Pacific Islander (Not Hispanic or Latino) - A person having origins in any of the peoples of Hawaii, Guam, Samoa, or other Pacific Islands.

Asian (Not Hispanic or Latino) - A person having origins in any of the original peoples of the Far East, Southeast Asia, or the Indian Subcontinent, including, for example, Cambodia, China, India, Japan, Korea, Malaysia, Pakistan, the Philippine Islands, Thailand, and Vietnam.

American Indian or Alaska Native (Not Hispanic or Latino) - A person having origins in any of the original peoples of North and South America (including Central America), and who maintain tribal affiliation or community attachment.

Two or More Races (Not Hispanic or Latino) - All persons who identify with more than one of the above five races.

Instructions for assigning employees into the race/ethnic categories:

Hispanic or Latino - Include all employees who answer YES to the question, Are you Hispanic or Latino. Report all Hispanic males in Column A and Hispanic females in Column B.

White (Not Hispanic or Latino) - Include all employees who identify as White males in Column C and as White females in Column I.

Black or African American (Not Hispanic or Latino)- Include all employees who identify as Black males in Column D and as Black females in Column J.

Native Hawaiian or Other Pacific Islander (Not Hispanic or Latino) - Include all employees who identify as Native Hawaiian or Other Pacific Islander males in Column E and as Native Hawaiian or Other Pacific Islander females in Column K.

Asian (Not Hispanic or Latino) - Include all employees who identify as Asian males in Column F and as Asian females in Column L.

American Indian or Alaska Native (Not Hispanic or Latino) - Include all employees who identify as American Indian or Alaska Native males in Column G and as American Indian or Alaska Native females in Column M.

Two or More Races (Not Hispanic or Latino) - Report all male employees who identify with more than one of the above five races in Column H and all female employees who identify with more than one of the above five races in Column N.

As to the method of collecting data, the basic principles for ethnic and racial self-identification for purposes of the EEO-1 report are:

(1) Offer employees the opportunity to self- identify

(2) Provide a statement about the voluntary nature of this inquiry for employees. For example, language such as the following may be used (employers may adapt this language):

"The employer is subject to certain governmental recordkeeping and reporting requirements for the administration of civil rights laws and regulations. In order to comply with these laws, the employer invites employees to voluntarily self-identify their race or ethnicity. Submission of this information is voluntary and refusal to provide it will not subject you to any adverse treatment. The information obtained will be kept confidential and may only be used in accordance with the provisions of applicable laws, executive orders, and regulations, including those that require the information to be summarized and reported to the federal government for civil rights enforcement. When reported, data will not identify any specific individual."

5. DESCRIPTION OF JOB CATEGORIES

The major job categories are listed below, including a brief description of the skills and training required for occupations in that category and examples of the job titles that fit each category. The examples shown below are illustrative and not intended to be exhaustive of all job titles in a job category. These job categories are primarily based on the average skill level, knowledge, and responsibility involved in each occupation within the job category.

The Officials and Managers category as a whole is to be divided into the following two subcategories: Executive/Senior Level Officials and Managers and First/Mid Level Officials and Managers. These subcategories are intended to mirror the employers own well established hierarchy of management positions. Small employers who may not have two well-defined hierarchical steps of management should report their management employees in the appropriate categories.

Executive/Senior Level Officials and Managers. Individuals who plan, direct and formulate policies, set strategy and provide the overall direction of enterprises/organizations for the development and delivery of products or services, within the parameters approved by boards of directors or other governing bodies. Residing in the highest levels of organizations, these executives plan, direct or coordinate activities with the support of subordinate executives and staff managers. They include, in larger organizations, those individuals within two reporting levels of the CEO, whose responsibilities require frequent interaction with the CEO. Examples of these kinds of managers are: chief executive officers, chief operating officers, chief financial officers, line of business heads, presidents or executive vice presidents of functional areas or operating groups, chief information officers, chief human resources officers, chief marketing officers, chief legal officers, management directors and managing partners.

First/Mid Level Officials and Managers. Individuals who serve as managers, other than those who serve as Executive/Senior Level Officials and Managers, including those who oversee and direct the delivery of products, services or functions at group, regional or divisional levels of organizations. These managers receive directions from the

Executive/Senior Level management and typically lead major business units. They implement policies, programs and directives of executive/senior management through subordinate managers and within the parameters set by Executive/Senior Level management. Examples of these kinds of managers are: vice presidents and directors, group, regional or divisional controllers; treasurers; human resources, information systems, marketing, and operations managers. The First/Mid Level Officials and Managers subcategory also includes those who report directly to middle managers. These individuals serve at functional, line of business segment or branch levels and are responsible for directing and executing the day-to-day operational objectives of enterprises/organizations, conveying the directions of higher level officials and managers to subordinate personnel and, in some instances, directly supervising the activities of exempt and non-exempt personnel. Examples of these kinds of managers are: first-line managers; team managers; unit managers; operations and production mangers; branch managers; administrative services managers; purchasing and transportation managers; storage and distribution managers; call center or customer service managers; technical support managers; and brand or product mangers.

Professionals. Most jobs in this category require bachelor and graduate degrees, and/or professional certification. In some instances, comparable experience may establish a person's qualifications. Examples of these kinds of positions include: accountants and auditors; airplane pilots and flight engineers; architects; artists; chemists; computer programmers; designers; dieticians; editors; engineers; lawyers; librarians; mathematical scientists; natural scientists; registered nurses; physical scientists; physicians and surgeons; social scientists; teachers; and surveyors.

Technicians. Jobs in this category include activities that require applied scientific skills, usually obtained by post secondary education of varying lengths, depending on the particular occupation, recognizing that in some instances additional training, certification, or comparable experience is required. Examples of these types of positions include: drafters; emergency medical technicians; chemical technicians; and broadcast and sound engineering technicians.

Sales Workers. These jobs include non-managerial activities that wholly and primarily involve direct sales. Examples of these types of positions include: advertising sales agents; insurance sales agents; real estate brokers and sales agents; wholesale sales representatives; securities, commodities, and financial services sales agents; telemarketers; demonstrators; retail salespersons; counter and rental clerks; and cashiers.

Administrative Support Workers. These jobs involve non-managerial tasks providing administrative and support assistance, primarily in office settings. Examples of these types of positions include: office and administrative support workers; bookkeeping; accounting and auditing clerks; cargo and freight agents; dispatchers; couriers; data entry keyers; computer operators; shipping, receiving and traffic clerks; word processors and typists; proofreaders; desktop publishers; and general office clerks.

Craft Workers(formerly Craft Workers (Skilled)). Most jobs in this category includes higher skilled occupations in construction (building trades craft workers and their formal apprentices) and natural resource extraction workers. Examples of these types of positions include: boilermakers; brick and stone masons; carpenters; electricians;

painters (both construction and maintenance); glaziers; pipe layers, plumbers, pipefitters and steamfitters; plasterers; roofers; elevator installers; earth drillers; derrick operators; oil and gas rotary drill operators; and blasters and explosive workers. This category also includes occupations related to the installation, maintenance and part replacement of equipment, machines and tools, such as: automotive mechanics; aircraft mechanics; and electric and electronic equipment repairers. This category also includes some production occupations that are distinguished by the high degree of skill and precision required to perform them, based on clearly defined task specifications, such as: millwrights; etchers and engravers; tool and die makers; and pattern makers.

Operatives (formerly Operatives (Semi-skilled)). Most jobs in this category include intermediate skilled occupations and include workers who operate machines or factory-related processing equipment. Most of these occupations do not usually require more than several months of training. Examples include: textile machine workers; laundry and dry cleaning workers; photographic process workers; weaving machine operators; electrical and electronic equipment assemblers; semiconductor processors; testers, graders and sorters; bakers; and butchers and other meat, poultry and fish processing workers. This category also includes occupations of generally intermediate skill levels that are concerned with operating and controlling equipment to facilitate the movement of people or materials, such as: bridge and lock tenders; truck, bus or taxi drivers; industrial truck and tractor (forklift) operators; parking lot attendants; sailors; conveyor operators; and hand packers and packagers.

Laborers and Helpers (formerly Laborers (Unskilled)). Jobs in this category include workers with more limited skills who require only brief training to perform tasks that require little or no independent judgment. Examples include: production and construction worker helpers; vehicle and equipment cleaners; laborers; freight, stock and material movers; service station attendants; construction laborers; refuse and recyclable materials collectors; septic tank servicers; and sewer pipe cleaners.

Service Workers. Jobs in this category include food service, cleaning service, personal service, and protective service activities. Skill may be acquired through formal training, job-related training or direct experience. Examples of food service positions include: cooks; bartenders; and other food service workers. Examples of personal service positions include: medical assistants and other healthcare support positions; hairdressers; ushers; and transportation attendants. Examples of cleaning service positions include: cleaners; janitors; and porters. Examples of protective service positions include: transit and railroad police and fire fighters; guards; private detectives and investigators.

6. LEGAL BASIS FOR REQUIREMENTS

SECTION 709(c), TITLE VII, CIVIL RIGHTS ACT OF 1964, AS AMENDED

Recordkeeping; reports

Every employer, employment agency, and labor organization subject to this title shall (1) make and keep such records relevant to the determinations of whether unlawful employment practices have been or are being committed, (2) preserve such records for such periods, and (3) make such reports there from as the Commission shall prescribe by regulation or order, after public hearing, as reasonable, necessary, or appropriate for the enforcement of this title or the regulations or orders there under. The Commission shall, by regulation, require each employer, labor organization, and joint labor-management committee subject to this title which controls an apprenticeship or other training program to maintain such records as are reasonably necessary to carry out the purposes of this title, including, but not limited to, a list of applicants who wish to participate in such program, including the chronological order in which applications were received, and to furnish to the Commission upon request, a detailed description of the manner in which persons are selected to participate in the apprenticeship or other training program. Any employer, employment agency, labor organization, or joint labor-management committee which believes that the application to it of any regulation or order issued under this section would result in undue hardship may apply to the Commission for an exemption from the application of such regulation or order, and, if such application for an exemption is denied, bring a civil action in the United States District Court for the district where such records are kept. If the Commission or the court, as the case may be, finds that the application of the regulation or order to the employer, employment agency, or labor organization in question would impose an undue hardship, the Commission or the court, as the case may be, may grant appropriate relief. If any person required to comply with the provisions of this subsection fails or refuses to do so, the United States District Court for the district in which such person is found, resides, or transacts business, shall, upon application of the Commission, or the Attorney General in a case involving a government, governmental agency or political subdivision, have jurisdiction to issue to such person an order requiring him to comply.

TITLE 29, CHAPTER XIV CODE OF FEDERAL REGULATIONS

NOTE: A few aspects of the following regulations will need to be revised to conform with the EEO-1 Report to be used beginning with the 2007 reporting period.

Subpart B -- Employer Information Report

§1602.7 Requirement for filing of report.

On or before September 30 of each year, every employer that is subject to Title VII of the Civil Rights Act of 1964, as amended, and that has 100 or more employees, shall file with the Commission or its delegate executed copies of Standard Form 100, as revised (otherwise known as "Employer Information Report EEO-1"), in conformity with the directions set forth in the form and accompanying instructions. Notwithstanding the provisions of §1602.14, every such employer shall retain at all times at each reporting unit, or at company or divisional headquarters, a copy of the most recent report filed for each such unit and shall make the same available if requested by an officer, agent, or employee of the Commission under the authority of section 710 of Title VII. Appropriate copies of Standard Form 100 in blank will be supplied to every employer known to the Commission to be subject to the reporting requirements, but it is the responsibility of all such employers to obtain necessary supplies of the form from the Commission or its delegate prior to the filing date.

§1602.8 Penalty for making of willfully false statements on report.

The making of willfully false statements on Report EEO-1 is a violation of the United States Code, Title 18, section 1001, and is punishable by fine or imprisonment as set forth therein.

§1602.9 Commissions remedy for employers failure to file report.

Any employer failing or refusing to file Report EEO-1 when required to do so may be compelled to file by order of a U.S. District Court, upon application of the Commission.

§1602.10 Employers exemption from reporting requirements.

If an employer claims that the preparation or filing of the report would create undue hardship, the employer may apply to the Commission for an exemption from the requirements set forth in this part, according to instruction 5. If an employer is engaged in activities for which the reporting unit criteria described in section 5 of the instructions are not readily adaptable, special reporting procedures may be required. If an employer seeks to change the date for filing its Standard Form 100 or seeks to change the period for which data are reported, an alternative reporting date or period may be permitted. In such instances, the employer should so advise the Commission by submitting to the Commission or its delegate a specific written proposal for an alternative reporting system prior to the date on which the report is due.

§1602.11 Additional reporting requirements.

The Commission reserves the right to require reports, other than that designated as the Employer Information Report EEO-1, about the employment practices of individual employers or groups of employers whenever, in its judgment, special or supplemental reports are necessary to accomplish the purposes of Title VII or the Americans with Disabilities Act (ADA). Any system for the requirement of such reports will be established in accordance with the procedures referred to in section 709(c) of Title VII or section 107 of the ADA and as otherwise prescribed by law.

Subpart C--Recordkeeping by Employers

§1602.12 Records to be made or kept.

The Commission has not adopted any requirement, generally applicable to employers, that records be made or kept. It reserves the right to impose recordkeeping requirements upon individual employers or groups of employers subject to its jurisdiction whenever, in its judgment, such records (a) are necessary for the effective operation of the EEO-1 reporting system or of any special or supplemental reporting system as described above; or (b) are further required to accomplish the purposes of Title VII or the ADA. Such recordkeeping requirements will be adopted in accordance with the procedures referred to in section 709(c) of Title VII, or section 107 of the ADA, and otherwise prescribed by law.

§1602.13 Records as to racial or ethnic identity of employees.

Employers may acquire the information necessary for completion of items 5 and 6 of Report EEO-1 either by visual surveys of the work force, or at their option, by the maintenance of post-employment records as to the identity of employees where the same is permitted by State law. In the latter case, however, the Commission recommends the maintenance of a permanent record as to the racial or ethnic identity of an individual for purpose of completing the report form only where the employer keeps such records separately from the employees basic personnel form or other records available to those responsible for personnel decisions, e.g., as part of an automatic data processing system in the payroll department.

§1602.14 Preservation of records made or kept.

Any personnel or employment record made or kept by an employer (including but not necessarily limited to requests for reasonable accommodation, application forms submitted by applicants and other records having to do with hiring, promotion, demotion, transfer, lay-off or termination, rates of pay or other terms of compensation, and selection for training or apprenticeship) shall be preserved by the employer for a period of one year from the date of the making of the record or the personnel action involved, whichever occurs later. In the case of involuntary termination of an employee, the personnel records of the individual terminated shall be kept for a period of one year from the date of termination. Where a charge of discrimination has been filed, or an action brought by the Commission or the Attorney General, against an employer under Title VII or the ADA, the respondent employer shall preserve all personnel records relevant to the charge or action until final disposition of the charge or the action. The term personnel records relevant to the charge, for example, would include personnel or employment records relating to the aggrieved person and to all other employees holding positions similar to that held or sought by the aggrieved person and application forms or test papers completed by an unsuccessful applicant and by all other candidates for the same position as that for which the aggrieved person applied and was rejected. The date of *final disposition of the charge or the action* means the date of expiration of the statutory period within which the aggrieved person may bring an action in a U. S. District Court or, where an action is brought against an employer either by the aggrieved person, the Commission, or by the Attorney General, the date on which such litigation is terminated.

Joint Reporting Committee
- Equal Employment Opportunity Commission
- Office of Federal Contract Compliance Programs (Labor)

EQUAL EMPLOYMENT OPPORTUNITY

EMPLOYER INFORMATION REPORT EEO—1

Standard Form 100
REV. 01/2006

O.M.B. No. 3046-0007
EXPIRES 01/2009
100-214

Section A—TYPE OF REPORT
Refer to instructions for number and types of reports to be filed.

1. Indicate by marking in the appropriate box the type of reporting unit for which this copy of the form is submitted (MARK ONLY ONE BOX).

(1) ☐ Single-establishment Employer Report

Multi-establishment Employer:
(2) ☐ Consolidated Report (Required)
(3) ☐ Headquarters Unit Report (Required)
(4) ☐ Individual Establishment Report (submit one for each establishment with 50 or more employees)
(5) ☐ Special Report

---

2. Total number of reports being filed by this Company (Answer on Consolidated Report only) _____

Section B—COMPANY IDENTIFICATION (To be answered by all employers)

OFFICE USE ONLY

1. Parent Company

a. Name of parent company (owns or controls establishment in item 2) omit if same as label

a.

Address (Number and street)

b.

City or town	State	ZIP code

c.

2. Establishment for which this report is filed. (Omit if same as label)

a. Name of establishment

d.

Address (Number and street)	City or Town	County	State	ZIP code

e.

b. Employer identification No. (IRS 9-DIGIT TAX NUMBER)

f.

c. Was an EEO–1 report filed for this establishment last year? ☐ Yes ☐ No

Section C—EMPLOYERS WHO ARE REQUIRED TO FILE (To be answered by all employers)

☐ Yes ☐ No	1.	Does the entire company have at least 100 employees in the payroll period for which you are reporting?
☐ Yes ☐ No	2.	Is your company affiliated through common ownership and/or centralized management with other entities in an enterprise with a total employment of 100 or more?
☐ Yes ☐ No	3.	Does the company or any of its establishments (a) have 50 or more employees AND (b) is not exempt as provided by 41 CFR 60–1.5, AND either (1) is a prime government contractor or first-tier subcontractor, and has a contract, subcontract, or purchase order amounting to $50,000 or more, or (2) serves as a depository of Government funds in any amount or is a financial institution which is an issuing and paying agent for U.S. Savings Bonds and Savings Notes?

If the response to question C–3 is yes, please enter your Dun and Bradstreet identification number (if you have one): ▢▢▢▢▢▢▢▢▢

NOTE: If the answer is yes to questions 1, 2, or 3, complete the entire form, otherwise skip to Section G.

Employment at this establishment – Report all permanent full- and part-time employees including apprentices and on-the-job trainees unless specifically excluded as set forth in the instructions. Enter the appropriate figures on all lines and in all columns. Blank spaces will be considered as zeros.

Section D–EMPLOYMENT DATA
(Report employees in only one category)

Number of Employees

Job Categories	Hispanic or Latino		Not-Hispanic or Latino													
	Male	Female	Male						Female							Total Col A–N
			White	Black or African American	Native Hawaiian or Other Pacific Islander	Asian	American Indian or Alaska Native	Two or more races	White	Black or African American	Native Hawaiian or Other Pacific Islander	Asian	American Indian or Alaska Native	Two or more races		
	A	B	C	D	E	F	G	H	I	J	K	L	M	N		O
Executive/Senior Level Officials and Managers 1.1																
First/Mid-Level Officials and Managers 1.2																
Professionals 2																
Technicians 3																
Sales Workers 4																
Administrative Support Workers 5																
Craft Workers 6																
Operatives 7																
Laborers and Helpers 8																
Service Workers 9																
TOTAL 10																
PREVIOUS YEAR TOTAL 11																

1. Date(s) of payroll period used:

(Omit on the Consolidated Report.)

Section E – ESTABLISHMENT INFORMATION (Omit on the Consolidated Report)

1. What is the major activity of this establishment? (Be specific, i.e., manufacturing steel castings, retail grocer, wholesale plumbing supplies, title insurance, etc. Include the specific type of product or type of service provided, as well as the principal business or industrial activity)

Section F - REMARKS

Use this item to give any identification data appearing on the last EEO-1 report which differs from that given above, explain major changes in composition of reporting units and other pertinent information.

Section G - CERTIFICATION

Check one
1 ☐ All reports are accurate and were prepared in accordance with the instructions. (Check on Consolidated Report only.)
2 ☐ This report is accurate and was prepared in accordance with the instructions.

Name of Certifying Official	Title	Signature	Date
Name of person to contact regarding this report	Title	Address (Number and Street)	
City and State	Zip Code	Telephone No. (including Area Code and Extension)	Email Address

All reports and information obtained from individual reports will be kept confidential as required by Section 709(e) of Title VII.
WILLFULLY FALSE STATEMENTS ON THIS REPORT ARE PUNISHABLE BY LAW, U.S. CODE, TITLE 18, SECTION 1001

SF 100 – Page 2

Appendix D

EEO-4 Form

Even though the EEO-1 Form has been changed, there is no indication that changes will be made to the EEO-4 Form. Public entities that must file an EEO-4 will continue using the form they have become used to seeing. That may create a recordkeeping problem for some organizations. How much of a problem will depend on their tracking of race/ethnicity.

Depending on geography, cities and counties are prone to tracking race by populations contained within their borders. Such a decision is often political. So, we find San Francisco, California tracking Asian categories such as Vietnamese, Chinese, and Japanese. They also separate Pacific Islanders into sub-groups such as Indonesia, Philippines, etc.

To complicate matters, the U.S. Census accepts "2 or More Races" as a valid response to the race question.

Yet, when reporting on the EEO-4 spreadsheet, public agencies must consolidate these various race options into those that are officially acceptable. It can be a nightmare in arithmetic if computer systems can't do it automatically. And, politicians don't much care how difficult the HR Manager's life is because of this reporting difficulty. I guess, in the end, you just have to get a box of pencils, a quiet room, all the reports you can generate, and a pot of black coffee. When you are through tallying, you can report on the document formats shown in the next few pages.

EQUAL EMPLOYMENT
OPPORTUNITY COMMISSION
WASHINGTON, D.C.

State and Local Reporting Committee
1801 L Street, N.W.
Washington, D.C. 20507

Approved by OMB
No. 3046-0008
Expires 7/31/2003

EEOC FORM 164, STATE AND LOCAL GOVERNMENT INFORMATION (EEO-4)

INSTRUCTION BOOKLET

[Please Read This Booklet Before Completing Enclosed Report]

Under Public Law 88-352, Title VII of the Civil Rights Act of 1964, as amended by the Equal Employment Opportunity Act of 1972, all State and local governments that have 15 or more employees are required to keep records and to make such reports to the Equal Employment Opportunity Commission as are specified in the regulations of the Commission. The applicable provisions of the law, Section 709(c) of Title VII, and the regulations issued by the Commission are printed in full in the Appendix (4) of these instructions. School systems and educational institutions are covered by other employment surveys and are excluded from EEO-4.

In the interests of consistency, uniformity and economy, State and Local Government Report EEO-4 is being utilized by Federal government agencies that have responsibilities with respect to equal employment opportunity. A joint State and Local Reporting Committee, with which this report must be filed, represents those various Federal agencies. In addition, this report should bring about uniformity in State and local government recordkeeping and reporting and should serve as a valuable tool for use by the political jurisdictions in evaluating their own internal programs for ensuring equal employment opportunity.

As stated above, the filing of Report EEO-4 is required by law; it *is not voluntary*. Under Section 709(c) of Title VII, the Attorney General of the United States may compel a jurisdiction to file this report by obtaining an order from a United States District Court.

1. WHO MUST FILE

Beginning with the 1993 survey year and biennially (every odd-numbered year) thereafter, those who must file this report include: (1) all States; (2) all other political jurisdictions which have 100 or more employees; and (3) a sample of those political jurisdictions which have 15-99 employees. The sample is rotated biennially, so that none of the smaller jurisdictions will be required to file in consecutive survey years, but all will be required to file in their turn. Sampled jurisdictions will be informed by receipt of the forms that they have been selected to report in a particular survey year.

2. WHO MUST KEEP RECORDS

Every political jurisdiction with 15 or more employees must make and keep records and statistics which would be necessary for the completion of Report EEO-4, as set forth in these instructions. Records must be kept for a period of 3 years. See regulations 1602.30 and 1602.31 in the Appendix (4).

Although the EEO-4 report requires the combining of agency data to complete the report, separate data for each agency must be maintained either by the agency itself or by the office responsible for preparing the EEO-4 report, and should be available upon request to representatives of Federal agencies.

3. HOW TO FILE

State and local governments must file EEO-4 reports according to the number of full-time employees on the payroll as follows:

A. FEWER THAN 1,000 FULL-TIME EMPLOYEES

(1) File one (1) report which includes all employees in functions performed with fewer than 100 employees.

(2) In addition to (1), file a separate report for each function which has 100 or more employees.

(3) Check each box in Section C which represents a function performed by the jurisdiction.

(4) Include a list of any agencies not included in the report with the complete address for those agencies.

B. MORE THAN 999 FULL-TIME EMPLOYEES

File one form for each function listed on page 1 of the form (if that function is performed), for a maximum of 15 forms. Jurisdictions should report only persons on the jurisdiction's payroll.

Blank forms will be sent to a central office for the political jurisdiction. In those jurisdictions where all data are available at a single location, forms may be completed by the central office. Where data are not available centrally, figures should be obtained by the central office from all agencies and aggregated onto the proper forms by functions.

If you file forms for more than one function, a Summary Sheet will be included with your forms. On the Summary Sheet you are requested to check those functions for which you are submitting completed reports; functions for which you are not reporting; and functions for which you will be reporting at a later date. This will facilitate our own record-keeping, and minimize unnecessary follow-up correspondence. Full-time employment must also be reported on the Summary Sheet.

The Summary Sheet provides for one certification statement as to the accuracy and completeness of the entire report from the jurisdiction. If such certification can be and is made by one official, a separate signature on every form will not be required.

The fact that a branch or agency of a government has separately elected officials, or is autonomous or semi-autonomous in its operations does not affect the legal status of the jurisdiction, nor the requirement that EEO-4 cover the entire jurisdiction. To the extent feasible, the report should cover all branches of the government. In any cases where that is not feasible, and data are not available to the central office of the government, *a list of agencies and addresses not included should accompany the report.*

Where interstate, intercounty, etc., boards, agencies, commissions, or other type special district governments exist, **ONE FORM** should be submitted by the headquarters of the special district.

In conclusion, the submitted report must contain the following, submitted in one (1) package:

(1) One (1) SUMMARY SHEET.
(2) The original and one (1) copy of up to 15 reports based on the number of functions performed.
(3) A list of agencies not included in the report but which should have been included in the report, with the complete address for any agency listed.

4. WHEN TO FILE

This biennial report must be filed with the Equal Employment Opportunity Commission no later than the date printed in the accompanying cover letter. Full-time and part-time employment figures should cover the payroll period which includes June 30 of the survey year. New hires data is for the entire fiscal year which ends on June 30.

5. WHERE TO FILE

The original and one (1) copy of the completed reports (in duplicate) should be forwarded to the address indicated on the EEO-4 form. All requests for additional information and report forms should also be directed to that address.

6. SPECIAL REPORTING PROCEDURES

An employer who claims that preparation or the filing of Report EEO-4 would create undue hardships may apply to the Commission for a special reporting procedure. In such cases, the employer must submit in writing a proposal for compiling and reporting information to:

The EEO-4 Coordinator
EEOC-Surveys
1801 L Street, N.W.
Washington, D.C. 20507

Only those special procedures approved in writing by the Commission are authorized. Such authorizations remain in effect until notification of cancellation is given or EEOC publishes a change to the survey form.

A computer printout, magnetic tape or diskette is also a special reporting procedure. Only the report formats for those media which are designed and approved by EEOC will be accepted. A copy of those formats with an explanatory memorandum may be acquired from the EEO-4 Coordinator at the above address.

7. ELECTED AND APPOINTED OFFICIALS

Section 701(f) of the Equal Employment Opportunity Act of 1972 contains an exemption for elected and certain appointed officials that is set forth in the definition of "employee" in Appendix (1). Based on the legislative history of Section 701(f), the General Counsel of the Commission has ruled that this exemption was intended by the Congress to be construed narrowly. This ruling concluded that only the following persons would be included in the exemption:

(1) State and local elected officials.
(2) Such official's immediate secretary, administrative, legislative, or other immediate or first-line aide.
(3) Such official's legal advisor.
(4) Appointed cabinet officials in the case of a Governor, or heads of executive departments in the case of a Mayor or County Council.

No other persons appointed by an elected official are exempt under this interpretation. In no case is any person exempt who is appointed by an appointed official, whether or not the latter is exempt. Furthermore, as specified in Section 701(f), the exemption does not include employees subject to the civil service laws of a State government, governmental agency or political subdivision.

8. CONFIDENTIALITY

All reports and information from individual reports are subject to the confidentiality provisions of Section 709(e) of Title VII, and may not be made public by EEOC

2

prior to the institution of any proceeding under Title VII. However, aggregate data may be made public in a manner so as not to reveal any particular jurisdiction's statistics. Barring prohibitive State or local legislation, a political jurisdiction may make its EEO-4 Report public at any time.

9. ESTIMATE OF BURDEN

Public reporting burden for this collection of information is estimated to vary from one (1) to five (5) hours per response, including the time for reviewing instructions, searching existing data sources, gathering and maintaining the data needed and completing and reviewing the collection of information. A response is defined as one survey form. Send comments regarding this burden estimate or any other aspect of this collection of information, including suggestions for reducing this burden to:

The EEOC Clearance Officer
Office of Financial and Resource Management
1801 L Street, N.W.
Washington, D.C. 20507

Unless the collection displays a currently valid Office of Management and Budget (OMB) control number, respondents are not required to fill out this form.

The full text of the new OMB regulations may be found at 5 CFR Part 1320, or Federal Register, vol. 60, no. 167, Tuesday, August 29, 1995, page 44978.

PLEASE DO NOT SEND YOUR COMPLETED REPORT TO THE ABOVE ADDRESS.

INSTRUCTIONS ON HOW TO PREPARE INFORMATION REPORTS

Definitions of Terms and Categories are
Located in the Appendix

SECTION A—TYPE OF GOVERNMENT

Check one box indicating type of government.

SECTION B—IDENTIFICATION

Indicate the name and central mailing address of the governmental jurisdiction if different from address label in top margin.

SECTION C—FUNCTION

Jurisdiction with fewer than 1,000 full-time employees are initially mailed only one form. Report all jurisdiction employees on this form unless you are filing a separate report for a function which has 100 or more employees, in which case a request for additional form(s) must be made. Indicate in Section C of the form which functions are performed by your jurisdiction. On page 4 of the form, list the departments or agencies included on the form by activity function.

Jurisdictions with more than 999 full-time employees are mailed up to 15 forms. Please use a separate form for each function for which you are reporting in accordance with the instructions provided in part 3 of this booklet.

The data should be aggregated for all agencies performing in a particular function. This also applies to unspecified functions which are to be combined in one report for Function 15, "Other". State education agencies, both agencies covering elementary and secondary schools and those covering higher education, should be included in Function 15.

Where the political jurisdiction is unable to separate data, the agency should be reported under the function that represents its dominant activity. For example, if a transportation department includes among other functions, streets and highways, and two-thirds of the employees of the department are engaged in street and highway activities, those employees should be separated out and reported separately if feasible. If not, the entire department should be reported separately in Function 2, Streets and Highways. On page 4 of each function report, list the departments or agencies included in this function. For instance, Function 1 might include: Office of the Tax Collector, Office of the Mayor, Office of the District Attorney, etc.

SECTION D—EMPLOYMENT DATA AS OF JUNE 30

For purposes of this report, a person is an employee of a political jurisdiction if he or she is on the payroll of that jurisdiction, regardless of the source of the funds by which the person is paid.

1. FULL-TIME EMPLOYEES

(For detailed explanation of job categories and race/ethnic identification, see Appendix.)

Employment data should include total full-time employment except those elected and appointed officials specified in Section 7 above of these instructions. Where employees receive separate salaries or payments from two or more jurisdictions, but work full-time for one jurisdiction, they should be counted as full-time employees by that jurisdiction, and to the extent possible their annual salary should reflect their total earnings from all jurisdictions from which they are paid. Also, where a person is a full-time employee of a jurisdiction, but is employed in more than one function, he or she should be reported for the function which accounts for most of the worktime. Trainees should be counted in appropriate columns by job, salary, race/ethnic group, and sex. Every employee must be accounted for in one and only one of the categories. Definitions are included in the Appendix (2).

a. Race/Sex Data—Columns B through K must reflect employment for the categories indicated. The line totals for columns B through K are entered in Column A.

b. Occupational Data—Employment data should be reported by annual salary within job category. Report each employee in *only one* job/salary category. In order to simplify and standardize the method of reporting, all jobs are considered as belonging in one of the broad occupations shown in the table. To assist you in determining how to place your jobs within the occupational groups, a description of job categories with examples follows in the Appendix (3). The list of examples is in no way exhaustive.

3

*Total Lines—Report *total employment for this matrix,* as well as row totals.

c. **Annual Salary**—Where employees are paid on an other than annual basis, their regular earnings in the payroll period which includes June 30 should be expanded and expressed in terms of an annual income. All special increments of an employee's annual earnings which are regular and recurrent should be included. Overtime pay should not be included.

2. OTHER THAN FULL-TIME EMPLOYEES

Employment data should include all employees not included in a full-time matrix. except those specifically exempted (see Section 7, Elected and Appointed Officials.) Where employees are working part-time for different jurisdictions, and are on separate payrolls of different jurisdictions, they should be reported as part-time employees of the separate jurisdictions. Persons on the payroll of the jurisdiction for a specified temporary appointment, such as a public employment program, should be included in this category.

*Total Lines—Report *total employment for this matrix,* as well as row totals.

3. NEW HIRES DURING FISCAL YEAR (A FISCAL YEAR COVERS THE PERIOD JULY 1-JUNE 30)

Include those employees who were hired during the fiscal year into permanent full-time positions whether or not they terminated employment prior to the end of the fiscal year. New Hires are included in Section D-1 if they were full-time employees at the end of the fiscal year. Total Lines—Report *total employment for this matrix,* as well as row totals.

REMARKS

Include in this section: (1) the list of your government agencies included in this report, and (2) any remarks, explanations, or other pertinent information regarding this report.

NOTE: List here the National Crime Information Center (NCIC) numbers assigned by the U.S. Department of Justice to any criminal justice agencies whose data are included.

CERTIFICATION

Each form must be certified and signed by an official responsible for the information, unless a Summary Sheet has been certified and signed and submitted with the completed forms.

APPENDIX

1. DEFINITION APPLICABLE TO ALL EMPLOYERS

a. **"Commission"** refers to the Equal Employment Opportunity Commission established under Title VII of the Civil Rights Act of 1964.

b. **"Employee"** means an individual employed by a political jurisdiction, who is on the payroll of that jurisdiction, regardless of the source of the funds by which the worker is paid. The following is an exception from the definition, subject to the interpretation in Section 7 above of these instruc-

tions. The term "employee" shall not include any person elected to public office in any State or political subdivision of any State by the qualified voters thereof, or any person chosen by such officer to be on such officer's personal staff, or an appointee on the policy making level or an immediate adviser with respect to the exercise of the constitutional or legal powers of the office. The exception set forth in the preceding sentence shall *not* include employees subject to the civil service laws of a State government, governmental agency or political subdivision.

c. **"Full-time Employees"**—Persons employed during this pay period to work the number of hours per week that represent regular full-time employment (excluding temporaries and intermittents).

d. **"Other Than Full-time Employees"**—Persons employed during this pay period on a part-time basis. Include those daily or hourly employees usually engaged for less than the regular full-time work week, temporaries working on a seasonal basis (whether part-time or full-time) or hired for the duration of a particular job or operation, including public employment programs, and intermittents.

e. **"New Hires During Fiscal Year"**—Persons both with and without previous experience and transfers who were hired for the first time in this jurisdiction or rehired after a break in service for permanent full-time employment.

2. RACE/ETHNIC IDENTIFICATION

An employer may acquire the race/ethnic information necessary for this section either by visual surveys of the work force, or from post-employment records as to the identity of employees. Since visual surveys are permitted, and the fact that race/ethnic identifications are not present on agency records is not an excuse for failure to provide the data called for. However, although the Commission does not encourage direct inquiry as a method of determining racial or ethnic identity, this method is not prohibited in cases where it has been used in the past, or where other methods are not practical, provided it is not used for purposes of discrimination.

Moreover, the fact that employees may be located at different addresses does not provide an acceptable reason for failure to comply with the reporting requirements. In such cases, it is recommended that visual surveys be conducted for the employer by persons such as supervisors who are responsible for the work of the employees or to whom the employees report for instruction or otherwise.

Please note that the General Counsel of the Commission has ruled, on the basis of court decisions, that the Commission has the authority to require the racial and ethnic identification of employees, regardless of any possible conflicting state or local laws.

The concept of race as used by the Equal Employment Opportunity Commission does *not* denote clearcut scientific definitions of anthropological origins. For the purposes of this report, an employee may be included in the group to which he or she appears to belong, identifies with, or is regarded in the community as belonging. However, no person may be counted in more than one race/ethnic category.

4

NOTE: The category "HISPANIC", while not a race identification, is included as a separate race/ethnic category because of the employment discrimination often encountered by this group; for this reason do not include HISPANIC under either "white" or "black".

For the purposes of the report, the following race/ethnic categories will be used:

a. **White (not of Hispanic origin):** All persons having origins in any of the original peoples of Europe, North Africa, or the Middle East.

b. **Black (not of Hispanic origin):** All persons having origins in any of the Black racial groups of Africa.

c. **Hispanic:** All persons of Mexican, Puerto Rican, Cuban, Central or South American, or other Spanish culture or origin, regardless of race.

d. **Asian or Pacific Islander:** All persons having origins in any of the original peoples of the Far East, Southeast Asia, the Indian Subcontinent, or the Pacific Islands. This area includes, for example, China, India, Japan, Korea, the Philippine Islands, and Samoa.

e. **American Indian or Alaskan Native:** All persons having origins in any of the original peoples of North America, and who maintain cultural identification through tribal affiliation or community recognition.

3. DESCRIPTION OF JOB CATEGORIES

a. **Officials and Administrators:** Occupations in which employees set broad policies, exercise overall responsibility for execution of these policies, or direct individual departments or special phases of the agency's operations, or provide specialized consultation on a regional, district or area basis. Includes: department heads, bureau chiefs, division chiefs, directors, deputy directors, controllers, wardens, superintendents, sheriffs, police and fire chiefs and inspectors, examiners (bank, hearing, motor vehicle, warehouse), inspectors (construction, building, safety, rent-and-housing, fire, A.B.C. Board, license, dairy, livestock, transportation), assessors, tax appraisers and investigators, coroners, farm managers, and kindred workers.

b. **Professionals:** Occupations which require specialized and theoretical knowledge which is usually acquired through college training or through work experience and other training which provides comparable knowledge. Includes: personnel and labor relations workers, social workers, doctors, psychologists, registered nurses, economists, dietitians, lawyers, systems analysts, accountants, engineers, employment and vocational rehabilitation counselors, teachers or instructors, police and fire captains and lieutenants, librarians, management analysts, airplane pilots and navigators, surveyors and mapping scientists, and kindred workers.

c. **Technicians:** Occupations which require a combination of basic scientific or technical knowledge and manual skill which can be obtained through specialized post-secondary school education or through equivalent on-the-job training. Includes: computer programmers, drafters, survey and map-

ping technicians, licensed practical nurses, photographers, radio operators, technical illustrators, highway technicians, technicians (medical, dental, electronic, physical sciences), police and fire sergeants, inspectors (production or processing inspectors, testers and weighers), and kindred workers.

d. **Protective Service Workers:** Occupations in which workers are entrusted with public safety, security and protection from destructive forces. Includes: police patrol officers, firefighters, guards, deputy sheriffs, bailiffs, correctional officers, detectives, marshals, harbor patrol officers, game and fish wardens, park rangers (except maintenance), and kindred workers.

e. **Paraprofessionals:** Occupations in which workers perform some of the duties of a professional or technician in a supportive role, which usually require less formal training and/or experience normally required for professional or technical status. Such positions may fall within an identified pattern of staff development and promotion under a "New Careers" concept. Included: research assistants, medical aides, child support workers, policy auxiliary welfare service aides, recreation assistants, homemakers aides, home health aides, library assistants and clerks, ambulance drivers and attendants, and kindred workers.

f. **Administrative Support (Including Clerical and Sales):** Occupations in which workers are responsible for internal and external communication, recording and retrieval of data and/or information and other paperwork required in an office. Includes: bookkeepers, messengers, clerk-typists, stenographers, court transcribers, hearing reporters, statistical clerks, dispatchers, license distributors, payroll clerks, office machine and computer operators, telephone operators, legal assistants, sales workers, cashiers, toll collectors, and kindred workers.

g. **Skilled Craft Workers:** Occupations in which workers perform jobs which require special manual skill and a thorough and comprehensive knowledge of the processes involved in the work which is acquired through on-the-job training and experience or through apprenticeship or other formal training programs. Includes: mechanics and repairers, electricians, heavy equipment operators, stationary engineers, skilled machining occupations, carpenters, compositors and typesetters, power plant operators, water and sewage treatment plant operators, and kindred workers.

h. **Service-Maintenance:** Occupations in which workers perform duties which result in or contribute to the comfort, convenience, hygiene or safety of the general public or which contribute to the upkeep and care of buildings, facilities or grounds of public property. Workers in this group may operate machinery. Includes: chauffeurs, laundry and dry cleaning operatives, truck drivers, bus drivers, garage laborers, custodial employees, gardeners and groundkeepers, refuse collectors, construction laborers, park rangers (maintenance), farm workers (except managers), craft apprentices/trainees/helpers, and kindred workers.

5

4. LEGAL BASIS FOR REQUIREMENTS

Section 709(c), Title VII, Civil Rights Act of 1964

(As Amended by the Equal Employment
Opportunity Act of 1972)

Recordkeeping: reports

Every employer, employment agency, and labor organization subject to this title shall (1) make and keep such records relevant to the determinations of whether unlawful employment practices have been or are being committed, (2) preserve such records for such periods, and (3) make such reports therefrom as the Commission shall prescribe by regulation or order, after public hearing, as reasonable, necessary, or appropriate for the enforcement of this title or the regulations or orders thereunder. The Commission shall, by regulation, require each employer, labor organization, and joint labor-management committee subject to this title which controls an apprenticeship or other training program to maintain such records as are reasonably necessary to carry out the purposes of this title, including, but not limited to, a list of applicants who wish to participate in such programs, including the chronological order in which applications were received, and to furnish to the Commission upon request, a detailed description of the manner in which persons are selected to participate in the apprenticeship or other training program. Any employer, employment agency, labor organization, or joint labor-management committee which believes that the application to it of any regulation or order issued under this section would result in undue hardship may apply to the Commission for an exemption from the application of such regulation or order, and, if such application for an exemption is denied, bring a civil action in the United States district court for the district where such records are kept. If the Commission or the court, as the case may be, finds that the application of the regulation or order to the employer, employment agency, or labor organization in question would impose an undue hardship, the Commission or the court, as the case may be, may grant appropriate relief. If any person required to comply with the provisions of this subsection fails or refuses to do so, the United States district court for the district in which such person is found, resides, or transacts business, shall, upon application of the Commission, or the Attorney General in a case involving a government, governmental agency or political subdivision, have jurisdiction to issue to such person an order requiring him to comply.

Title 29, Chapter XIV, Code of Federal Regulations

Subpart I—State and Local Governments Recordkeeping

§ 1602.30 Records to be made or kept.

On or before September 30, 1974, and annually thereafter, every political jurisdiction with 15 or more employees is required to make or keep records and the information there-

from which are or would be necessary for the completion of report EEO-4 under the circumstances set forth in the instructions thereto, whether or not the political jurisdiction is required to file such report under § 1602.32 of the regulations in this part. The instructions are specifically incorporated therein by reference and have the same force and effect as other sections of this part.[1] Such records and the information therefrom shall be retained at all times for a period of 3 years at the central office of the political jurisdiction and shall be made available if requested by an officer, agent, or employee of the Commission under Section 710 of Title VII, as amended. Although agency data are aggregated by functions for purposes of reporting, separate data for each agency must be maintained either by the agency itself or by the office of the political jurisdiction responsible for preparing the EEO-4 form. It is the responsibility of every political jurisdiction to obtain from the Commission or its delegate necessary instructions in order to comply with the requirements of this section.

§ 1602.31 Preservation of records made or kept.

(a) Any personnel or employment record made or kept by a political jurisdiction (including but not necessarily limited to application forms submitted by applicants and other records having to do with hiring, promotion, demotion, transfer, layoff or termination, rates of pay or other terms of compensation, and selection of training or apprenticeship) shall be preserved by the political jurisdiction for a period of 2 years from the date of the making of the record or the personnel action involved, whichever occurs later. In the case of involuntary termination of an employee, the personnel records of the individual terminated shall be kept for a period of 2 years from the date of termination. Where a charge of discrimination has been filed, or an action brought by the Attorney General against a political jurisdiction under Title VII, the respondent political jurisdiction shall preserve all personnel records relevant to the charge or action until final disposition of the charge or the action. The term "personnel record relevant to the charge," for example, would include personnel or employment records relating to the person claiming to be aggrieved and to all other employees holding positions similar to that held or sought by the person claiming to be aggrieved; and application forms or test papers completed by an unsuccessful applicant and by all other candidates for the same position as that for which the person claiming to be aggrieved applied and was rejected. The date of final disposition of the charge or the action means the date of expiration of the statutory period within which a person claiming to be aggrieved may bring an action in a U.S. district court, or where an action is brought against a political jurisdiction either by a person claiming to be aggrieved or by the Attorney General, the date on which such litigation is terminated.

(b) The requirements of this section shall not apply to application forms and other preemployment records of applicants for positions known to applicants to be of a temporary or seasonal nature.

---

[1] Note.—Instructions were published as an appendix to the proposed regulations on Mar. 2, 1973 (38 FR 5662).

6

Subpart J—State and Local Government Information Report

§ 1602.32 Requirement for filing and preserving copy of report.

On or before September 30, 1993 and biennially thereafter certain political jurisdictions subject to Title VII of the Civil Rights Act of 1964, as amended, shall file with the Commission or its delegate executed copies of "State and Local Government Information Report EEO-4" in conformity with the directions set forth in the form and accompanying instructions. The political jurisdictions covered by this section are (a) Those which have 100 or more employees, and (b) Those other political jurisdictions which have 15 or more employees from whom the Commission requests the filing of reports.

Every such political jurisdiction shall retain at all times a copy of the most recently filed EEO-4 at the central office of the political jurisdiction for a period of 3 years and shall make the same available if requested by an officer, agent, or employee of the Commission under the authority of Section 710 of Title VII, as amended.

§ 1602.33 Penalty for making of willfully false statements on report.

The making of willfully false statements on report EEO-4, is a violation of the United States Code, Title 18, Section 1001, and is punishable by fine or imprisonment as set forth therein.

§ 1602.34 Commission's remedy for political jurisdiction's failure to file report.

Any political jurisdiction failing or refusing to file report EEO-4 when required to do so may be compelled to file by order of a U.S. district court, upon application of the Attorney General.

§ 1602.35 Political jurisdiction's exemption from reporting requirements.

If it is claimed the preparation or filing of the report would create undue hardship, the political jurisdiction may apply to the Commission for an exemption from the requirements set forth in this part by submitting to the Commission or its delegate a specific proposal for an alternative reporting system prior to the date on which the report is due.

§ 1602.36 Schools exemption.

The recordkeeping and report-filing requirements of subparts I and J shall not apply to State or local educational institutions or to school districts or school systems or any other educational functions. The previous sentence of this section shall not act to bar jurisdiction which otherwise would attach under §1602.30.

§ 1602.37 Additional reporting requirements.

The Commission reserves the right to require reports, other than that designated as the "State and Local Government Information Report EEO-4," about the employment practices of individual political jurisdictions or group of political jurisdictions whenever, in its judgment, special supplemental reports are necessary to accomplish the purposes of Title VII. Any system for the requirement of such reports will be established in accordance with the procedures referred to in section 709(c) of Title VII and as otherwise prescribed by law.

Subpart K—Records and Inquiries as to Race, Color, National Origin, or Sex

§ 1602.38 Applicability of State or Local Law.

The requirements imposed by the Equal Employment Opportunity Commission in these regulations, subparts I and J, supersede any provisions of State or local law which may conflict with them.

EEO-4 BK (6/97) Previous Editions are Obsolete.

*U.S. Government Printing Office: 1999 – 455-377/16764

EQUAL EMPLOYMENT OPPORTUNITY COMMISSION	APPROVED BY OMB 3046-0008
STATE AND LOCAL GOVERNMENT INFORMATION (EEO-4)	EXPIRES 12/31/2005
EXCLUDE SCHOOL SYSTEMS AND EDUCATIONAL INSTITUTIONS (Read attached instructions prior to completing this form)	

DO NOT ALTER INFORMATION PRINTED IN THIS BOX	MAIL COMPLETED FORM TO:
	State & Local Reporting Committee (EEO-4) PO Box 62229 Virginia Beach, VA 23466-2229

A. TYPE OF GOVERNMENT (Check one box only)

☐ 1. State   ☐ 2. County   ☐ 3. City   ☐ 4. Township   ☐ 5. Special District

☐ 6. Other (Specify)_____

B. IDENTIFICATION

1. NAME OF POLITICAL JURISDICTION (If same as label, skip to Item C)

2. Address--Number and Street	CITY/TOWN	COUNTY	STATE/ZIP	EEOC USE ONLY A
				B

C. FUNCTION

(Check one box to indicate the function(s) for which this form is being submitted. Data should be reported for all departments and agencies in your government covered by the function(s) indicated. If you cannot supply the data for every agency within the function(s) attach a list showing name and address of agencies whose data are not included.)

	1.Financial Administration. Tax billing and collection, budgeting, purchasing, central accounting and similar financial administration carried on by a treasurer's, auditor's or comptroller's office and GENERAL CONTROL. Duties usually performed by boards of supervisors or commissioners, central administration offices and agencies, central personnel or planning agencies, all judicial offices and employees (judges, magistrates, bailiffs, etc.)		8. HEALTH. Provision of public health services, out-patient clinics, visiting nurses, food and sanitary inspections, mental health, alcohol rehabilitation service, etc. 9. HOUSING. Code enforcement, low rent public housing, fair housing ordinance enforcement, housing for elderly, housing rehabilitation, rent control.
	2. STREETS AND HIGHWAYS. Maintenance, repair, construction and administration of streets, alleys, sidewalks, roads, highways and bridges.		10. COMMUNITY DEVELOPMENT. Planning, zoning, land development, open space, beautification, preservation.
	3. PUBLIC WELFARE. Maintenance of homes and other institutions for the needy; administration of public assistance. (Hospitals and sanatoriums should be reported as item7.)		11. CORRECTIONS. Jails, reformatories, detention homes, half-way houses, prisons, parole and probation activities
	4. POLICE PROTECTION. Duties of a police department sheriff's, constable's, coroner's office, etc., including technical and clerical employees engaged in police activities.		12. UTILITIES AND TRANSPORTATION. Includes water supply, electric power, transit, gas, airports, water transportation and terminals.
	5. FIRE PROTECTION. Duties of the uniformed fire force and clerical employees. (Report any forest fire protection activities as item 6.)		13. SANITATION AND SEWAGE. Street cleaning, garbage and refuse collection and disposal. Provision, maintenance and operation of sanitary and storm sewer systems and sewage disposal plants.
	6. NATURAL RESOURCES. Agriculture, forestry, forest fire protection, irrigation drainage, flood control, etc., and PARKS AND RECREATION. Provision, maintenance and operation of parks, playgrounds, swimming pools, auditoriums, museums, marinas, zoos, etc.		14. EMPLOYMENT SECURITY STATE GOVERNMENTS ONLY
	7. HOSPITALS AND SANATORIUMS. Operation and maintenance of institutions for inpatient medical care.		15. OTHER (Specify on Page Four)

EEOC FORM 164 FEB 97 (Previous Editions are Obsolete)   PAGE 1

D. EMPLOYMENT DATA AS OF JUNE 30
(Do not include elected/appointed officials. Blanks will be counted as zero)

1. FULL-TIME EMPLOYEES (Temporary employees are not included)

JOB CATEGORIES	ANNUAL SALARY (In thousands 000)	MALE						FEMALE				
		TOTAL (COLUMNS B-K)	NON-HISPANIC ORIGIN		HISPANIC	ASIAN OR PACIFIC ISLANDER	AMERICAN INDIAN OR ALASKAN NATIVE	NON-HISPANIC ORIGIN		HISPANIC	ASIAN OR PACIFIC ISLANDER	AMERICAN INDIAN OR ALASKAN NATIVE
			WHITE	Black				White	Black			
		A	B	C	D	E	F	G	H	I	J	K
OFFICIALS ADMINISTRATORS	1. $0.1-15.9											
	2. 16.0-19.9											
	3. 20.0-24.9											
	4. 25.0-32.9											
	5. 33.0-42.9											
	6. 43.0-54.9											
	7. 55.0-69.9											
	8. 70.0 PLUS											
PROFESSIONALS	9. $0.1-15.9											
	10. 16.0-19.9											
	11. 20.0-24.9											
	12. 25.0-32.9											
	13. 33.0-42.9											
	14. 43.0-54.9											
	15. 55.0-69.9											
	16. 70.0 PLUS											
TECHNICIANS	17. $0.1-15.9											
	18. 16.0-19.9											
	19. 20.0-24.9											
	20. 25.0-32.9											
	21. 33.0-42.9											
	22. 43.0-54.9											
	23. 55.0-69.9											
	24. 70.0 PLUS											
PROTECTIVE SERVICE	25. $0.1-15.9											
	26. 16.0-19.9											
	27. 20.0-24.9											
	28. 25.0-32.9											
	29. 33.0-42.9											
	30. 43.0-54.9											
	31. 55.0-69.9											
	32. 70.0 PLUS											
PARA-PROFESSIONALS	33. $0.1-15.9											
	34. 16.0-19.9											
	35. 20.0-24.9											
	36. 25.0-32.9											
	37. 33.0-42.9											
	38. 43.0-54.9											
	39. 55.0-69.9											
	40. 70.0 PLUS											
ADMINISTRATIVE SUPPORT	41. $0.1-15.9											
	42. 16.0-19.9											
	43. 20.0-24.9											
	44. 25.0-32.9											
	45. 33.0-42.9											
	46. 43.0-54.9											
	47. 55.0-69.9											
	48. 70.0 PLUS											

D. EMPLOYMENT DATA AS OF JUNE 30 (Cont.)

(Do not include elected/appointed officials. Blanks will be counted as zero)

1. FULL-TIME EMPLOYEES (Temporary employees are not included)

JOB CATEGORIES	ANNUAL SALARY (In thousands 000)	TOTAL (COLUMNS B-K)	MALE NON-HISPANIC ORIGIN WHITE	Black	HISPANIC	ASIAN OR PACIFIC ISLANDER	AMERICAN INDIAN OR ALASKAN NATIVE	FEMALE NON-HISPANIC ORIGIN White	Black	HISPANIC	ASIAN OR PACIFIC ISLANDER	AMERICAN INDIAN OR ALASKAN NATIVE
		A	B	C	D	E	F	G	H	I	J	K
SKILLED CRAFT	49. $0.1-15.9											
	50. 16.0-19.9											
	51. 20.0-24.9											
	52. 25.0-32.9											
	53. 33.0-42.9											
	54. 43.0-54.9											
	55. 55.0-69.9											
	56. 70.0 PLUS											
SERVICE MAINTENANCE	57. $0.1-15.9											
	58. 16.0-19.9											
	59. 20.0-24.9											
	60. 25.0-32.9											
	61. 33.0-42.9											
	62. 43.0-54.9											
	63. 55.0-69.9											
	64. 70.0 PLUS											
65. TOTAL FULL TIME (LINES 1 – 64)												

2. OTHER THAN FULL-TIME EMPLOYEES (Including temporary employees

	A	B	C	D	E	F	G	H	I	J	K
66. OFFICIALS/ADMIN											
67. PROFESSIONALS											
68. TECHNICIANS											
69. PROTECTIVE SERVICE											
70. PARA-PROFESSIONAL											
71. ADMIN. SUPPORT											
72. SKILLED CRAFT											
73. SERVICE/MAINTENANCE											
74. TOTAL OTHER THAN FULL TIME (LINES 66 – 73)											

3. NEW HIRES DURING FISCAL YEAR - Permanent full time only JULY 1 – JUNE 30

	A	B	C	D	E	F	G	H	I	J	K
75. OFFICIALS/ADMIN											
76. PROFESSIONALS											
77. TECHNICIANS											
78. PROTECTIVE SERVICE											
79. PARA-PROFESSIONAL											
80. ADMIN. SUPPORT											
81. SKILLED CRAFT											
82. SERVICE/MAINTENANCE											
83. TOTAL NEW HIRES (LINES 75 – 82)											

EEOC FORM 164, FEB 97 (Previous Editions are Obsolete) PAGE 3

REMARKS (List National Crime Information Center (NCIC) number assigned to any Criminal Justice Agencies whose data are included in this report)

LIST AGENCIES INCLUDED ON THIS FORM

CERTIFICATION. I certify that the information given in this report is correct and true to the best of my knowledge and was reported in accordance with accompanying instructions. (Willfully false statements on this report are punishable by law, US Code, Title 18, Section 1001.)

NAME OF PERSON TO CONTACT REGARDING THIS FORM	TITLE	
ADDRESS (Number and Street, City, State, Zip Code)	TELEPHONE NUMBER extension: FAX NUMBER	
DATE E-MAIL	TYPED NAME/TITLE OF AUTHORIZED OFFICIAL	SIGNATURE

EEOC FORM 164, FEB 97 (Previous Editions Obsolete)   PAGE 4

Appendix E

VETS-100A Form

Federal Contractor Veterans' Employment Report
VETS-100A Form
EEO Category Matching

The VETS-100A Form uses EEO-1 categories for reporting. That's OK for the private commercial sector, but public sector employers, elementary and secondary schools, and higher education employers will have to make a translation in order to report their data. Here, then is the translation table you can use to realign your data to the EEO-1 categories used in the VETS-100 report.

STATE AND LOCAL GOVERNMENT TRANSLATION

EEO-4 CATEGORY	VETS-100A CATEGORY
Officials and Administrators	Officials and Managers – Senior Executives OR Supervisor/Mid Level
Professionals	Professionals
Technicians	Technicians
Protective Services	Service Workers
Paraprofessionals	Professionals
Administrative Support	Office and Clerical
Skilled Crafts	Craft Workers (Skilled)
Service/Maintenance Workers	Service Workers

ELEMENTARY AND SECONDARY SCHOOLS TRANSLATION

EE0-5 CATEGORY	VETS-100A CATEGORY
Officials, Administrators and Managers	Officials and Managers – Senior Executives OR Supervisor/Mid Level
Principals	Officials and Managers – Senior Executives OR Supervisor/Mid Level
Assistant Principals (Teaching)	Professionals
Assistant Principals (Non-Teaching)	Professionals
Elementary Classroom Teachers	Professionals
Secondary Classroom Teachers	Professionals
Other Classroom Teachers	Professionals
Guidance	Professionals
Psychological	Professionals
Librarians and Audio-Visual	Professionals
Consultants/Supv. Instructions	Professionals
Other Professional Staff	Professionals
Teacher Aides	Technicians
Technicians	Technicians
Clerical and Secretarial Staff	Office and Clerical
Service Workers	Service Workers
Skilled Craft Workers	Craft Workers (Skilled)
Laborers (Unskilled)	Laborers (Unskilled)

HIGHER EDUCATION TRANSLATION

EEO-6 CATEGORY	VETS-100A CATEGORY
Executive, Administrative, Managerial	Officials and Managers – Senior Executives OR Supervisor/Mid Level
Professional Non-Faculty	Professionals
Faculty (All Categories)	Professionals
Secretarial and Clerical	Office and Clerical
Technical and Paraprofessional	Technicians
Skilled Craft Workers	Craft Workers (Skilled)
Service and Maintenance Workers	Service Workers

What Are the Differences Between the VETS-100 and the VETS-100A Reports?

The most obvious difference is the categories of veterans included on each report.[47]

The VETS-100 Report reflects the categories of veterans covered under the affirmative action provisions of VEVRAA prior to the *Jobs for Veterans Act (JVA)* amendments. Accordingly, the VETS-100 Report calls for Federal contractors and subcontractors to report the number of employees and new hires during the reporting period who are:

(1) Special disabled veterans;

(2) Veterans of the Vietnam era;

(3) Other protected veterans (veterans who served on active duty in the U.S. military during a war or in a campaign or expedition for which a campaign badge is awarded); and

(4) Recently separated veterans (veterans within 12 months from discharge or release from active duty).

The JVA amendments eliminated the coverage category of "Vietnam era veterans" and added the category "Armed Forces service medal veterans." In addition, the JVA amendments expanded the coverage of "recently separated veterans" from one year after discharge or release from active duty to three years. Finally, the JVA amendments expanded the coverage of veterans with disabilities to include all veterans with service connected disabilities.

The VETS-100A Report reflects the categories of veterans covered under the JVA amendments and requests that Federal contractors and subcontractors report the number of employees and new hires during the reporting period belonging to the following categories:

(1) Disabled veterans;

(2) Other protected veterans (veterans who served on active duty in the U.S. military during a war or in a campaign or expedition for which a campaign badge is awarded);

(3) Armed Forces service medal veterans (veterans who, while serving on active duty in the Armed Forces, participated in a United States military operation for which an Armed Forces service medal was awarded pursuant to Executive Order 12985); and

(4) Recently separated veterans (veterans within 36 months from discharge or release from active duty).

---

[47] http://www.dol.gov/vets/contractor/main.htm

The other significant difference between the VETS-100 and VETS-100A Report forms is in the job categories. The job categories on the Veterans' Employment Report forms are consistent with the job categories used on the EEO-1 Report. EEOC revised the EEO-1 Report in 2005, (November 28, 2005, 70 FR 71294), and the revisions included dividing the Officials and Managers category into two subgroups - Executives/ Senior Level Officials and Managers and First/Mid Level Officials and Managers. The VETS-100A Report adopts the job categories used on the revised EEO-1 Report, while the VETS-100 Report has a single Officials and Managers job category.

Currently, nothing is being done with the data submitted on the VETS-100 and VETS-100A reports. That may change in the future, depending on the regulatory changes proposed by OFCCP at the end of 2010. We'll just have to wait and see what develops.

The difficulty with this data is that it is voluntary and consequently it is unreliable. By definition it is incomplete and the definitions are sometimes said to be "confusing." People don't understand why contractors are required to invite them to identify themselves as veterans. Sometimes, being a veteran is perceived as a negative in the employment process, as it was following the return of warriors from the Viet Nam Era war.

These days, the government and employers alike are more inclined to give veterans the credit they are due for their contribution on behalf of the country. We expect that there will be more emphasis placed on the hiring of veterans. If we can only get them to self-identify it will be easier to take credit for their job placement.

FEDERAL CONTRACTOR VETERANS' EMPLOYMENT REPORT VETS-100A
(For covered contracts entered into or modified on or after December 1, 2003.)

OMB NO: 1293-0005
Expires:

Persons are not required to respond to this collection of information unless it displays a valid OMB number

RETURN COMPLETED REPORT TO:
U.S. DEPARTMENT OF LABOR
VETERANS' EMPLOYMENT AND TRAINING SERVICE
VETS-100 Reporting Office
4200 Forbes Blvd., Suite 202
Lanham, Maryland 20706

ATTN: Human Resource/EEO Department

TYPE OF REPORTING ORGANIZATION (Check one or both, as applicable)
☐ Prime Contractor
☐ Subcontractor

TYPE OF FORM (Check only one)
☐ Single Establishment
☐ Multiple Establishment-Headquarte
☐ Multiple Establishment-Hiring Locat
☐ Multiple Establishment-State Cons
(specify number of locations) _____

COMPANY IDENTIFICATION INFORMATION (Omit items preprinted above-ADD Company Contact Information Below)

COMPANY No:	TWELVE MONTH PERIOD ENDING			2	
NAME OF PARENT COMPANY:	ADDRESS (NUMBER AND STREET):
CITY:	COUNTY:	STATE:	ZIP COD
NAME OF COMPANY CONTACT:	TELEPHONE FOR CONTACT:	EMAIL:
NAME OF HIRING LOCATION:	ADDRESS (NUMBER AND STREET):
CITY:	COUNTY:	STATE:	ZIP COD

NAICS: DUNS: -   -   EMPLOYER ID (IRS TAX No.) -

INFORMATION ON EMPLOYEES

REPORT ALL PERMANENT FULL-TIME OR PART-TIME EMPLOYEES AND NEW HIRES WHO ARE VETERANS, AS DEFINED ON REVERSE. DATA ON NUMBER O EMPLOYEES IS TO BE ENTERED IN COLUMNS L, M, N, O, AND P, LINES 1-10. DATA ON NEW HIRES IS TO BE ENTERED IN COLUMNS Q, R, S, T, AND U. ENTE THE MAXIMUM AND MINIMUM NUMBER OF EMPLOYEES. INSTRUCTIONS ARE FOUND ON THE REVERSE OF THIS FORM.

JOB CATEGORIES	DISABLED VETERANS (L)	OTHER PROTECTED VETERANS (M)	ARMED FORCES SERVICE MEDAL VETERANS (N)	RECENTLY SEPARATED VETERANS (O)	TOTAL EMPLOYEES, BOTH VETERANS AND NON-VETERANS (P)	DISABLED VETERANS (Q)	OTHER PROTECED VETERANS (R)	ARMED FORCES SERVICE MEDAL VETERANS (S)	RECENTLY SEPARATED VETERANS (T)	TOTAL BOTH VE NON-\
EXECUTIVE/SENIOR LEVEL OFFICIALS AND MANAGERS 1										
FIRST/MID LEVEL OFFICIALS AND MANAGERS 2										
PROFESSIONALS 3										
TECHNICIANS 4										
SALES WORKERS 5										
ADMINISTRATIVE SUPPORT WORKERS 6										
CRAFT WORKERS 7										
OPERATIVES 8										
LABORERS/HELPERS 9										
SERVICE WORKERS 10										
TOTAL 11										

Report the total maximum and minimum number of permanent employees during the period covered by this report.

Maximum Number   Minimum Number

WHO MUST FILE

This VETS-100A Report is to be completed by each federal contractor or subcontractor with a contract or subcontract entered into or modified on or after December 1, 2003, in the amount of $100,000 or more with any department or agency of the United States for the procurement of personal property and non-personal services (including construction). Entering into a covered federal contract or subcontract during a given calendar year establishes the requirement to file a VETS-100A Report during the following calendar year. A VETS-100 Report is to be completed by each federal contractor or subcontractor with a contract or subcontract of $25,000 or more entered into before December 1, 2003 with any department or agency of the United States for the procurement of personal property and non-personal services (including construction) and which did not become subject to 41 CFR part 61-300 through contract modification.

WHEN/WHERE TO FILE

This annual report must be filed no later than September 30. Mail to the address pre-printed on the front of the form.

LEGAL BASIS FOR REQUIREMENTS

Title 38, United States Code, Section 4212(d), as amended by the Jobs for Veterans Act (PL 107-288) enacted in 2002, requires federal contractors covered under the Act's affirmative action provisions in Section 4212(a) to report at least annually the numbers of employees in the workforce by job category and hiring location, and the number of such employees, by job category and hiring location, who are qualified covered veterans. Federal contractors must report the total number of new hires during the period covered by the report and the number of such employees who are qualified covered veterans. Additionally, federal contractors must report on the maximum and minimum number of employees during the period covered by the report. The Department of Labor has promulgated regulations to implement the requirements of 38 U.S.C. 4212, as amended by the Jobs for Veterans Act. The regulations at 41 CFR Part 61-300 require the submission of this VETS-100A Report to comply with the requirements of 38 U.S.C. 4212(d), as amended.

HOW TO SUBMIT THE VETS-100A REPORT

Single-establishment employers must file one completed VETS-100A Report. All multi-establishment employers, i.e., those doing business at more than one hiring location, must file (A) one VETS-100A Report covering the principal or headquarters office: (B) a separate VETS-100A Report for each hiring location employing 50 or more persons: and (C) EITHER, (i) a separate VETS-100A Report for each hiring location employing fewer than 50 persons, OR (ii) consolidated reports that cover hiring locations within one State that have fewer than 50 employees. Each state consolidated report must also list the name and address of the hiring locations covered by the report. Company consolidated reports such as those required by EEO-1 reporting procedures are NOT required for the VETS-100A Report. Completed reports for the headquarters location and all other hiring locations for each company should be mailed in one package to the address indicated on the front of the form. Employers may submit their reports via the Internet at http://vets.dol.gov/vets100/ . A company number is required in order to use this method of submission. This number is provided to employers on the VETS-100A Report mailed annually to those employers listed in the VETS-100 Report database. Other employers may obtain a company number by e-mailing their request to http://vets.dol.gov/vets100/vets100login.htm .

Employers that submit computer-generated output for more than 10 hiring locations to satisfy their VETS-100A reporting obligations must submit the output in the form of an electronic file. This file must comply with current DOL specifications for the layout of these records, along with any other specifications established by the Department for the applicable reporting year. Employers that submit VETS-100A Reports for ten locations or less are exempt from this requirement, but are strongly encouraged to submit an electronic file. In these cases, state consolidated reports count as one location each.

RECORD KEEPING
Employers must keep copies of the completed annual VETS-100A Report submitted to DOL for a period of one year.

HOW TO PREPARE THE FORMS

Multi-establishment employers submitting hard copy reports should produce facsimile copies of the headquarters form for reporting data on each location.

Type of Reporting Organization Indicate the type of contractual relationship (prime contractor or subcontractor) that the organization has with the Federal Government. If the organization serves as both a prime contractor and a subcontractor on various federal contracts, check both boxes.

Type of Form If a reporting organization only has a covered contract that was entered into or modified on or after December 1, 2003, it then must use a VETS-100A Report. If a reporting organization only has a covered contract that was entered before December 1, 2003, (and did not become subject to 41 CFR part 61-300 through contract modification) it must use a VETS-100 Report. If a reporting organization has a covered contract entered both before and on or after December 1, 2003, it then must use both a VETS-100 and a VETS-100A Report.

If a reporting organization submits only one VETS-100A Report for a single location, check the Single Establishment box. If the reporting organization submits more than one form, only one form should be checked as Multiple Establishment-Headquarters. The remaining forms should be checked as either Multiple Establishment-Hiring Location or Multiple Establishment-State Consolidated. For state consolidated forms, the number of hiring locations included in that report should be entered in the space provided. For each form, only one box should be checked within this block.

455

COMPANY IDENTIFICATION INFORMATION:

Company Number Do not change the Company Number that is printed on the form. If there are any questions regarding your Company Number, please call the VETS-100 staff at (703) 461-2460 or e-mail HELPDESK@VETS100.COM.

Twelve Month Period Ending Enter the end date for the twelve month reporting period used as the basis for filing the VETS-100A Report. To determine this period, select a date in the current year between July 1 and August 31 that represents the end of a payroll period. The selected date will be the basis for reporting Number of Employees, as described below. The twelve-month period preceding that date will be your twelve-month period covered. This period is the basis for reporting New Hires, as described below. Any federal contractor or subcontractor who has written approval from the Equal Employment Opportunity Commission to use December 31 as the ending date for the EEO-1 Report may also use that date as the ending date for the payroll period selected for the VETS-100A Report.

Name and Address for Single Establishment Employers COMPLETE the identifying information under the Parent Company name and address section. LEAVE BLANK all of the identifying information for the Hiring Location.

Name and Address for Multi Establishment Employers **For parent company headquarters location,** COMPLETE the name and address for the parent company headquarters, LEAVE BLANK the name and address of the Hiring Location. **For hiring locations of a parent company,** COMPLETE the name and address for the Parent Company location, COMPLETE the name and address for the Hiring Location.

NAICS Code, DUNS Number, and Employer ID Number Single Establishment and Multi Establishment Employers must COMPLETE the Employer ID Number, NAICS Code, DUNS Number, if available, as described below.

NAICS Code Enter the six (6) digit NAICS Code applicable to the hiring location for which the report is filed. If there is not a separate NAICS Code for the hiring location, enter the NAICS Code for the parent company.

Dun and Bradstreet I.D. Number (DUNS) If the company or any of its establishments has a Dun and Bradstreet Identification Number, please enter the nine (9) digit number in the space provided. If there is a specific DUNS Number applicable to the hiring location for which the report is filed, enter that DUNS Number. Otherwise, enter the DUNS number for the parent company.

Employer I.D. Number (EIN) Enter the nine (9) digit number assigned by the I.R.S. to the contractor. If there is a specific EIN applicable to the hiring location for which the report is filed, enter that EIN. Otherwise, enter the EIN for the parent company.

INFORMATION ON EMPLOYEES

<u>Counting Veterans</u>. Some veterans will fall into more than one of the qualified covered veteran categories. For example, a veteran may be both a disabled veteran and an other protected veteran. In such cases the veteran must be counted in each category.

<u>Number of Employees</u>. Provide all data for regular full-time and part-time employees who were disabled veterans, other protected veterans, Armed Forces service medal veterans, or recently separated veterans employed as of the ending date of the selected payroll period. Do not include employees specifically excluded as indicated in 41 CFR 61-300.2(b)(2). Employees must be counted by qualified covered veteran status for each of the 10 occupational categories (Lines 1-10) in columns L, M, N, and O. Column P must count all employees, including qualified covered veterans, in each of the 10 occupational categories (Lines 1-10). Blank spaces will be considered zeros.

<u>New Hires</u>. Report the number of regular full-time and part-time employees who were hired, both veterans and non-veterans, as well as those who were hired by veteran category, and who were included in the payroll for the first time during the 12-month period preceding the ending date of the selected payroll period. The total line in columns Q, R, S, T, and U (Line 11) is required. Enter all applicable numbers, including zeros.

<u>Maximum/Minimum Employees</u>. Report the maximum and minimum number of regular employees on board during the twelve-month period covered by this report, as indicated by 41 CFR 61-300.10(a)(3).

DEFINITIONS:

'Hiring location' means an establishment as defined at 41 CFR 61-300.2(b)(1).

'Job Categories' means any of the following: Officials and Managers (Executive/Senior Level Officials and Managers and First/Mid Level Officials and Managers), Professionals, Technicians, Sales Workers, Administrative Support Workers, Craft Workers, Operatives, Laborers and Helpers, and Service Workers and are defined in 41 CFR 61-300.2(b)(3).

'Disabled Veteran' means (i) a veteran of the U.S. military, ground, naval or air service who is entitled to compensation (or who but for the receipt of military retired pay would be entitled to compensation) under laws administered by the Secretary of Veterans Affairs, or (ii) a person who was discharged or released from active duty because of a service-connected disability.

'Other Protected Veteran' means a veteran who served on active duty in the U.S. military, ground, naval, or air service during a war or in a campaign or expedition for which a campaign badge has been authorized. For those with Internet access, the information required to make this determination is available at http://www.opm.gov/veterans/html/vgmedal2.htm. A replica of that list is enclosed with the annual VETS-100A mailing. A copy of the list also may be obtained by sending an e-mail to OtherVets@vets100.com or by calling (703) 461-2460 and requesting that a copy be mailed to you.

'Armed Forces Service Medal Veteran' means a veteran who, while serving on active duty in the U.S. military, ground, naval or air service, participated in a United States military operation for which an Armed Forces service medal was awarded pursuant to Executive Order 12985 (61 Fed. Reg. 1209) at http://www.opm.gov/veterans/html/vgmedal2.asp

'Recently Separated Veteran' means a veteran during the three-year period beginning on the date of such veteran's discharge or release from active duty in the U.S. military, ground, naval or air service,

'Covered Veteran' means a veteran as defined in the four veteran categories above.

A copy of 41 CFR part 61-300 can be found at http://www.dol.gov/dol/allcfr/vets/Title_41/Chapter_61.htm.

Public reporting burden for this collection is estimated to average 60 minutes per paper response, and 30 minutes per electronic response, including the time for reviewing instructions, searching existing data source, gathering and maintaining the data needed, and completing and reviewing the collection of information. Send comments regarding this burden estimate or any other aspect of this collection of information, including suggestions for reducing the burden to the Department of Labor, Office of Information Management, Room N-1301, 200 Constitution Avenue, NW, Washington D.C. 20210 or electronically transmitted to www.vets100.cudenver.edu. All completed VETS-100A Reports should be sent to the address indicated on the front of the form.

Appendix F

OFCCP and EEOC Offices

OFCCP	EEOC

National Office

Office of Federal Contract Comp Programs
Employment Standards Administration
U.S. Department of Labor
200 Constitution Ave. NW, Rm C3310
Washington, DC 20210
202-693-0101

Northeast Regional Office
OFCCP/DOL
201 Varick St., Rm 750
New York, NY 10014
646-264-3170

Boston District Office
JFK Federal Bldg, Rm E325
Boston, MA 02203
617-624-6780

Hartford District Office
219 William R. Cotter Federal Bldg.
135 High St.
Hartford, CT 06103
860-240-4277

New York District Office
26 Federal Plaza, Rm 36-116
New York, NY 10278
212-264-7743

Mountainside District Office
200 Sheffield St., Rm 102
Mountainside, NJ 07092
908-317-6969

Buffalo Area Office
130 S. Elmwood, Rm 536
Buffalo, NY 14202
716-842-2979

National Office

Equal Employment Opportunity Commission
131 M St NE, Ste 100
Washington, DC 20507
202-663-4900

Boston Area Office
475 Government Center
Boston, MA 02203
617-565-3200

New York District Office
33 Whitehall St.
New York, NY 10004
212-336-3620

Newark Area Office
1 Newark Center, 21st Flr
Newark, NJ 07102
973-645-6383

Buffalo Local Office
6 Fountain Plaza, Ste 350
Buffalo, NY 14202
716-551-4441

OFCCP	EEOC
Caribbean Field Station 1202 Plaza Las Americas 525 Franklin D. Roosevelt Ave. San Juan, PR 00918 212-264-7743	San Juan Local Office 525 Franklin D. Roosevelt Ave., Ste 1202 San Juan, PR 00918 787-771-1464
Mid-Atlantic Regional Office OFCCP/DOL Curtis Center, Suite 750 West 170 S. Independence Mall W Philadelphia, PA 19106 215-861-5765	Norfolk Local Office 200 Granby Street, Ste 739 Norfolk, VA 23510 757-441-3470
Baltimore District Office Appraisers' Stores Bldg 103 S. Gay St., Rm 202 Baltimore, MD 21203 410-962-3572	Baltimore Field Office 10 S. Howard St., 3rd Flr Baltimore, MD 21201 410-962-3932
Richmond District Office 400 N. Eighth St., Rm 552 Richmond, VA 23240 804-771-2136	Richmond Local Office 830 E. Main St., 6th Flr Richmond, VA 23219 804-771-2200
Philadelphia District Office Robert Nix Sr. Federal Bldg. Ninth and Market Streets, Ste 311 Philadelphia, PA 19107 215-597-4121	Philadelphia District Office 801 Market St, Ste 1300 Philadelphia, PA 19107 215-440-2600
Pittsburgh District Office Federal Bldg., Rm 1132 1000 Liberty Ave. Pittsburgh, PA 15222 412-395-6330	Pittsburgh Area Office 1001 Liberty Ave., Rm 1112 Pittsburgh, PA 15222 412-644-3444
Washington District Office 680 MetroPlex II 8201 Corporate Dr. Landover, MD 20785 301-429-2190	Washington, DC Field Office 131 M St NE, Ste 4NW02F Washington, DC 20507 202-419-0700
Southeast Regional Office OFCCP/DOL Atlanta Federal Center, Rm 7B75 61 Forsyth St. SW Atlanta, GA 30303 404-893-4545	Savannah Local Office 410 Mall Blvd., Ste G Savannah, GA 31406 912-652-4234

OFCCP	EEOC
Atlanta District Office 61 Forsyth St. SW, Rm 7B65 Atlanta, GA 30303 404-893-4575	Atlanta District Office 100 Alabama St. SW, Ste 4R30 Atlanta, GA 30303 404-562-6800
Birmingham District Office Medical Forum Bldg 950 22nd St. North, Ste 660 Birmingham, AL 35203 205-731-0820	Birmingham District Office 1130 22nd Street S., Ste 2000 Birmingham, AL 35205 205-212-2100
Jackson Area Office 100 W. Capitol St., Rm 721 Jackson, MS 39269 601-965-4668	Jackson Area Office Dr. A. H. McCoy Federal Building 100 West Capitol St., Ste 207 Jackson, MS 39269 601-948-8400
Jacksonville Area Office 400 W. Bay St., Ste 939 Jacksonville, FL 32202 904-351-0551	Greensboro Local Office 2303 W. Meadowview Rd., Ste 201 Greensboro, NC 27407 336-547-4188
Miami Area Office 909 SE First Ave., Ste 722 Miami, FL 33131 305-536-5670	Miami District Office Two S. Biscayne Blvd. Ste 2700 Miami, FL 33131 305-808-1740
Orlando District Office 1001 Executive Building, Ste 100 Orlando, FL 32803 407-648-6181	Tampa Field Office 501 E. Polk St., Ste 1000 Tampa, FL 33602 813-228-2310
Charlotte District Office Mart Office Bldg. 3800 Arco Corp Dr, Ste 465 Charlotte, NC 28273 704-749-3380	Charlotte District Office 129 W. Trade St., Ste 400 Charlotte, NC 28202 704-344-6682
Columbia Area Office 1835 Assembly St., Ste 608 Columbia, SC 29201 803-765-5244	Greenville Local Office 301 N. Main St., Ste 1402 Greenville, SC 29601 864-241-4400
Raleigh Area Office 4407 Bland Rd, Ste 270 Raleigh, NC 27601 919-790-8248	Raleigh Area Office 1309 Annapolis Drive Raleigh, NC 27608 919-856-4064

OFCCP	EEOC

Nashville District Office
1321 Murfreesboro Rd, Ste 301
Nashville, TN 37217
615-781-5395

Nashville Area Office
50 Vantage Way, Ste 202
Nashville, TN 37228
615-736-5820

Memphis Area Office
167 N. Main St., Ste 101
Memphis, TN 38103
901-544-3458

Memphis District Office
1407 Union Ave., 9th Flr
Memphis, TN 38104
901-544-0115

Louisville Area Office
601 W. Broadway
Louisville, KY 40202
502-582-6275

Louisville Area Office
600 Martin Luther King Jr. Pl., Ste 268
Louisville, KY 40202
502-582-6082

Mobile Local Office
63 S. Royal St., Ste 504
Mobile, AL 36602
251-690-2590

Midwest Regional Office
OFCCP/DOL
Kluczynski Federal Bldg., Rm 570
230 S. Dearborn St.
Chicago, IL 60604
312-596-7010

Chicago District Office
230 S. Dearborn St., Rm 434
Chicago, IL 60604
312-596-7045

Chicago District Office
500 W. Madison St., Ste 2000
Chicago, IL 60661
312-353-2713

Cleveland Field Office
1240 E. 9th St., Ste 3001
Cleveland, OH 44199
216-522-2003

Indianapolis District Office
46 E. Ohio St., Rm 419
Indianapolis, IN 46204
317-226-5860

Indianapolis District Office
101 W. Ohio St., Ste 1900
Indianapolis, IN 46204
317-226-7212

Columbus District Office
200 N. High St., Rm 409
Columbus, OH 43215
614-469-5831

Cincinnati Area Office
550 Main St., 10th Flr
Cincinnati, OH 45202
513-684-2851

Detroit District Office
211 W. Fort St., Rm 1320
Detroit, MI 48226
313-442-3360

Detroit Field Office
477 Michigan Ave., Rm 865
Detroit, MI 48226
313-226-4600

OFCCP	EEOC

Grand Rapids Area Office
Suite 300-HUD
50 Louis Street NW
Grand Rapids, MI 49503
616-456-2144

Milwaukee District Office
310 W. Wisconsin Ave., Ste 1115
Milwaukee, WI 53203
414-297-3822

Milwaukee Area Office
310 W. Wisconsin Ave., Ste 800
Milwaukee, WI 53203
414-297-1111

Minneapolis Area Office
900 Second Ave. S, Ste 480
Minneapolis, MN 55402
612-370-3177

Minneapolis Area Office
330 S. Second Ave., Ste 720
Minneapolis, MN 55401
612-335-4040

Kansas City District Office
2300 Main St, Ste 1030
Kansas City, MO 64105
816-502-0370

Kansas City Area Office
400 State Ave. 9th Flr
Kansas City, MO 66101
913-551-5655

St. Louis District Office
Robert A. Young Bldg.
1222 Spruce St., Rm 10.207
St. Louis, MO 63103
314-539-6394

St. Louis District Office
1222 Spruce St., Rm 8.100
St. Louis, MO 63103
314-539-7800

Omaha District Office
111 S. 18th Plaza, Ste 2231
Omaha, NE 68102
402-221-3381

Southwest and Rock Mountain Regional Office
OFCCP/DOL
Federal Bldg., Rm 840
525 S. Griffin St.
Dallas, TX 75202
972-850-2550

El Paso Area Office
300 E. Main St., Ste 500
El Paso, TX 79901
915-534-6700

Houston District Office
2320 La Branch, Rm 1103
Houston, TX 77004
713-718-3800

Houston District Office
1919 Smith St., 6th Flr
Houston, TX 77002
713-209-3320

New Orleans Area Office
701 Loyola Ave, Rm 13029
New Orleans, LA 70113
504-589-6575

New Orleans Field Office
1555 Poydras St., Ste 1900
New Orleans, LA 70112
504-589-2825

Dallas District Office
525 S. Griffin St., Rm 512
Dallas, TX 75202
972-850-2650

Dallas District Office
207 S. Houston St., 3rd Flr
Dallas, TX 75202
214-253-2700

OFCCP	EEOC
San Antonio District Office 800 Dolorosa St., Ste 200 San Antonio, TX 78216 210-472-5835	San Antonio Field Office 5410 Fredericksburg Rd., Ste 200 San Antonio, TX 78229 210-281-7600
Tulsa Area Office 5110 S. Yale Ave., Rm 304 Tulsa, OK 74135 918-496-6772	Oklahoma Area Office 215 Dean A. McGee Ave., 5th Flr Oklahoma City, OK 73102 405-231-4911
Albuquerque Area Office 500 Fourth St. NW, Ste 402 Albuquerque, NM 87102 505-245-2108	Albuquerque Area Office 505 Marquette NW, Ste 900 Albuquerque, NM 87102 505-248-5201
	Little Rock Area Office 820 Louisiana St., Ste 200 Little Rock, AR 72201 501-324-5060
Salt Lake City Area Office 150 E. Social Hall Ave., Ste 685 Salt Lake City, UT 84111 801-524-4470	
Denver District Office 1999 Broadway, Ste 1177 Denver, CO 80202 720-264-3200	Denver Field Office 303 E. 17th St., Ste 510 Denver, CO 80203 303-866-1300

Pacific Regional Office
OFCCP/DOL
90 7th St., Ste 18-300
San Francisco, CA 94103
415-625-7800

OFCCP	EEOC
SF Bay Area District Office 90 7th St, Ste 11-100 San Francisco, CA 94105 415-625-7828	San Francisco District Office 350 The Embarcadero, Ste 500 San Francisco, CA 94105 415-625-5600
Los Angeles District Office 11000 Wilshire Blvd., Ste 8130 Los Angeles, CA 90024 310-235-6800	Los Angeles District Office 255 E. Temple, 4th Flr Los Angeles, CA 90012 213-894-1000

Secrets of Affirmative Action Compliance

OFCCP	EEOC
	Fresno Local Office 2300 Tulare St, Ste 215 Fresno, CA 93721 559-487-5793
San Jose District Office 60 S. Market St., Ste 410 San Jose, CA 95113 408-291-7384	San Jose Local Office 96 N. Third St., Ste 250 San Jose, CA 95112 408-291-7352
San Diego District Office 5675 Ruffin Rd., Ste 320 San Diego, CA 92123 619-557-6489	San Diego Local Office 555 W Beech St, Ste 504 San Diego, CA 92101 619-557-7235
Phoenix District Office 230 N. First Ave., Ste 503 Phoenix, AZ 85003 602-514-7033	Phoenix District Office 3300 N. Central Ave., Ste 690 Phoenix, AZ 85012 602-640-5000
	Honolulu Local Office 300 Ala Moana Blvd., Ste 7-127 Honolulu, HI 96850 808-541-3120
Seattle District Office 1111 Third Ave., Ste 745 Seattle, WA 98101 206-398-8000	Seattle Field Office Federal Office Bldg. 909 First Ave., Ste 400 Seattle, WA 98104 206-220-6883
Portland Area Office 620 SW Main St., Ste 410 Portland, OR 97201 503-326-4112	Las Vegas Local Office 333 Las Vegas Blvd., Ste 8112 Las Vegas, NV 89101 702-388-5099

Appendix G

OFCCP Documents

- **Corporate Scheduling Announcement Letter (CSAL) (As of 11/2009)**

- **Compliance Evaluation Scheduling Letter (Approved by OMB through 9/30/2011)**

- **Construction Contractor Scheduling Letter**

- **Conciliation Agreement**

- **Show Cause Notice**

- **SCRR Form**

- **Active Case Management Directive (#285, 9/17/2008)**

OFCCP Corporate Scheduling Announcement Letter (CSAL)

The following three pages constitute the CSAL letter sent out in the Fall of 2009 by OFCCP Director Patricia Shiu.

U.S. Department of Labor

Office of Federal Contract
Compliance Programs
200 Constitution Avenue, N.W.
Washington, D.C. 20210

November 2009

Chief Executive Officer
Federal Contractor Establishment
123 Main
Anytown, USA 12345

Dear Federal Contractor:

The Office of Federal Contract Compliance Programs (OFCCP) of the Department of Labor is sending this letter to you as a courtesy to advise you that at least two of your establishments have been identified for possible scheduling of a compliance evaluation during this scheduling cycle. This letter is intended to facilitate your complete, accurate and timely production of materials and information should your company receive a scheduling letter and be selected for an evaluation. It is not required by law. As you know, as a condition of receiving a federal contract, employers have an ongoing duty to develop, implement and maintain an affirmative action program annually and to maintain any personnel or employment records that they make or keep, generally for two years, regardless of whether they are subject to an evaluation. In order to facilitate communication within your organization, please transmit this letter to the appropriate Human Resource Department at your company.

The establishments on the enclosed list were selected through OFCCP's Federal Contractor Selection System (FCSS). The FCSS is an administratively neutral selection system that identifies Federal contractor establishments for evaluation through multiple information sources and analytical procedures, including the use of EEO-1 Reports; development of threshold requirements, such as establishment size; random sampling; analysis of external Federal contract databases to better establish jurisdictional coverage; and the use of a mathematical model that ranks Federal contractor establishments based on an indicator of potential workplace discrimination. Establishments on the FCSS are released to OFCCP field offices for scheduling one name at a time in a pre-determined specific order.

The enclosed list is not all-inclusive; therefore, it is possible that other establishments within your company will be selected for a compliance evaluation during this scheduling cycle. For example, company establishments that are not clearly associated with your parent organization through currently available EEO-1 Reports, such as those that have been acquired through recent mergers, are not included in this list. In addition, the enclosed list does not include any establishment of your company that has been selected for evaluation because of a contract award notice, a directed review, as a result of conciliation agreement monitoring or an individual complaint, or as part of the agency's Corporate Management Compliance Evaluation (CMCE), Functional Affirmative Action Program (FAAP), or American Recovery and Reinvestment Act of 2009 (ARRA) initiatives. Finally, there will be no limit on the number of new compliance evaluations of your company's facilities that OFCCP will conduct during a fiscal year. OFCCP will also schedule compliance evaluations as a result of the agency's CMCE or FAAP initiatives.

-2-

contract award notices, directed reviews, conciliation agreement monitoring, or credible reports of an alleged violation of a law or regulation, including complaints.

I encourage you to take advantage of OFCCP's Compliance Assistance which can be found at its Internet website http://www.dol.gov/ofccp/index.htm which hosts a wealth of technical assistance materials, including information about OFCCP's regulations, policy directives, and answers to frequently asked questions. The website also has information about free compliance assistance seminars in your area. Please take advantage of these services as they will enable a smooth, timely and efficient completion of evaluations.

If you have any other questions about the compliance evaluation process or would like individualized compliance assistance, please contact the nearest OFCCP regional office. You can find a list of OFCCP regional offices at http://www.dol.gov/ofccp/contacs/ofcpkeyp.htm. Our regional offices will be happy to provide compliance assistance at the corporate level for establishments covered by this letter and any other facilities you may wish to include.

Sincerely,

PATRICIA A. SHIU
Director
Office of Federal Contract Compliance Programs

Enclosure

-3-

ESTABLISHMENTS IDENTIFIED FOR POTENTIAL SCHEDULING
Fall 2009

Federal Contractor Headquarters
123 Main
Anytown, USA 12345

Establishment EEO-1#	Establishment

Sample
Compliance Evaluation Scheduling Letter

OMB NO. 1215-0072
Expires 09/30/2011

VIA CERTIFIED MAIL
(NUMBER)
RETURN RECEIPT REQUESTED

(Name of CEO)
(Title of CEO)
(Establishment Name)
(Street Address)
(City, State, Zip Code)

Dear (Name of contractor official):

The U.S. Department of Labor, Office of Federal Contract Compliance Programs (OFCCP) has selected your establishment located at _____ for a compliance review under Executive Order 11246, as amended, Section 503 of the Rehabilitation Act of 1973, as amended, and the Vietnam Era Veterans' Readjustment Assistance Act of 1974, as amended, 38 U.S.C. 4212, and their implementing regulations at 41 CFR Chapter 60. In addition, the review will include an examination of your establishment's compliance with the Federal Contractor Veterans' Employment Report (VETS-100) requirements (38 U.S.C. 4212(d)) and the Employment Eligibility Verification (I-9) Report requirements of the Immigration Reform and Control Act of 1986.

OFCCP will conduct the compliance review as described in the regulations at 41 CFR 60-1.20(a)(1) and 60-250.60(a)(1), 60-300.60, and 60-741.60, which outline the three possible phases of the process. These phases may include a desk audit, an onsite review, and an offsite analysis.

For the desk audit, please submit the following information: (1) a copy of your Executive Order Affirmative Action Program (AAP) prepared according to the requirements of 41 CFR 60-1.40 and 60-2.1 through 60-2.17*; (2) a copy of your Section 503/38 U.S.C. 4212 AAP(s) prepared according to the requirements of 41 CFR Parts 60-741 and 41 CFR Parts 60-250 and/or 60-300, respectively; and (3) the support data specified in the enclosed Itemized Listing.

OFCCP will treat the information you submit in response to this letter as sensitive and confidential to the maximum extent permitted under the Freedom of Information Act.

The findings OFCCP makes during the desk audit generally will determine whether an onsite review will be necessary, and if so, whether the onsite review will focus on one, two, or several issues. If an onsite review is necessary, we will notify you.

-2-

You should note that 41 CFR 60-2.2 authorizes the initiation of enforcement proceedings if the materials you submit for desk audit do not represent a reasonable effort* to meet the requirements of the regulations.

Please submit your AAPs and the support data specified in the enclosed Itemized Listing to the address listed on page one of this letter as soon as possible, but no later than 30 days from the date of your receipt of this letter. We encourage you to submit as much information as possible in electronic format as doing so may reduce the amount of time it takes to complete our review.

If an onsite review is necessary, we will need to have available for inspection copies of your I-9 forms. Employers must retain completed I-9s for three years after the date of hire OR one year after the date employment ends, whichever is later. We will also need documentation (e.g., payroll records) sufficient to identify all employees for whom I-9 forms are required. This letter provides you with three business days advance notice of the I-9 inspection, as required by law.

If you have any questions concerning the compliance review, please feel free to contact _____.

Sincerely,

(Name of District Director)
District Director

Enclosure: Itemized Listing

*See Itemized Listing, "NOTE 1."

NOTE: The authority for requesting the following information is Executive Order (EO) 11246, as amended; Section 503 of the Rehabilitation Act of 1973, as amended; and the Vietnam Era Veterans' Readjustment Assistance Act of 1974 (VEVRAA), as amended, 38 U.S.C. 4212. The information will be used in the compliance evaluation process. Furnishing the requested information is required. Failure to furnish the requested information may constitute noncompliance with the contractor's obligations per the above authorities.

According to the Paperwork Reduction Act of 1995, an agency may not conduct or sponsor, and a person is not required to respond to, a collection of information unless it displays a valid OMB control number. The valid OMB control number for this information collection is 1215-0072. The time required to complete this information collection is estimated to average

-3-

28.35 hours per response, including the time for reviewing instructions, searching existing data sources, gathering and maintaining the data needed, and completing and reviewing the collection of information. Send any comments concerning this burden estimate or any other aspect of this collection of information, including suggestions for reducing the burden, to the Office of Federal Contract Compliance Programs, Room C-3325, 200 Constitution Avenue, N.W., Washington, D.C. 20210.

ITEMIZED LISTING

NOTE 1: The Executive Order AAP submission must demonstrate a reasonable effort to comply with 41 CFR Part 60-2. To do so, at a minimum, you must submit the following elements.

Both the AAP and support data are essential to conduct the desk audit phase of the compliance review. If any of the following information is computerized, you may submit it in an electronic format.

Executive Order AAP:

1. An organizational profile prepared according to 41 CFR 60-2.11.

2. The formation of job groups (covering all jobs) consistent with criteria given in 41 CFR 60-2.12;

3. For each job group, a statement of the percentage of minority and female incumbents, as described in 41 CFR 60-2.13;

4. For each job group, a determination of minority and female availability that considers the factors given in 41 CFR 60-2.14(c)(1) and (2);

5. For each job group, the comparison of incumbency to availability, as explained in 41 CFR 60-2.15.

6. Placement goals for each job group in which the percentage of minorities or women employed is less than would be reasonably expected given their availability, consistent with 41 CFR 60-2.16.

Support Data

7. A copy of your Employer Information Report EEO-1 (Standard Form 100 Rev., see 41 CFR 60-1.7) for the last three years.

8. A copy of your collective bargaining agreement(s), if applicable. Please also include any other information you have already prepared that would assist us in understanding your employee mobility system(s), e.g., promotion, etc.

9. Information on your affirmative action goals for the preceding AAP year and, where applicable (see below), progress on your goals for the current AAP year. See 41 CFR 60-1.12(b), -2.1(c) and -2.16.

ITEMIZED LISTING (continued)

- 2 -

For the preceding AAP year, this report must include information that reflects:

(a) job group representation at the start of the AAP year, (i.e., total incumbents, total minority incumbents, and total female incumbents);

(b) the percentage placement rates (% goals) established for minorities and/or women at the start of the AAP year; and

(c) the actual number of placements (hires plus promotions) made during the AAP year into each job group with goals (i.e., total placements, total minority placements, and total female placements). For goals not attained, describe the specific good faith efforts made to achieve them.

If you are six months or more into your AAP year on the date you receive this listing, please also submit information that reflects progress on goals established in your current AAP, and describe your implementation of action-oriented programs designed to achieve these goals (see 41 CFR 60-2.17(c)).

10. Data on your employment activity (applicants, hires, promotions, and terminations) for the preceding AAP year and, if you are six months or more into your current AAP year when you receive this listing, for the current AAP year. These data must be presented either by job group (as defined in your AAP) or by job title (see 41 CFR 60-3.4 and 3.15).

a. Applicants and Hires: The regulations at 41 CFR 60-2.17(b) and (d) require an analysis of your selection process, including whether the process eliminates a significantly higher percentage of minorities or women than nonminorities or men.

For each job group or job title, this analysis must consist of the total number of applicants and the total number of hires, as well as the number of minority and the number of female applicants and hires.

However, if some of your job groups or titles (most commonly, entry-level) are filled from the same applicant pool, you may consolidate your applicant data (but not hiring data) for those job groups or titles.

For example, where applicants expressly apply for or would qualify for a broad spectrum of jobs (such as "Production," "Office," etc.) that includes several job groups, you may consolidate applicant data.

ITEMIZED LISTING (continued)

- 3 -

b. <u>Promotions</u>: The regulations at 41 CFR 60-2.17(b) and (d) require an analysis of your promotion practices to determine if upward mobility of minority or female employees is occurring at a lesser rate (compared to workforce mix) than nonminority or male employees.

For each job group or job title, this analysis must consist of the total number of promotions, as well as the number of minority and the number of female promotions.

Please note that:
(1) If you present promotions by <u>job group</u>, indicate how your company defines promotions and the basis on which the data were compiled (<u>e.g.</u>, promotions to the job group, from and/or within the job group, etc.), or
(2) If you present promotions by job <u>title</u>, include the department and job group from which and to which the person(s) was promoted.

c. <u>Terminations</u>: The regulations at 41 CFR 60-2.17(b) and (d) require an evaluation of the degree to which nondiscrimination policy is carried out with respect to employee terminations.

For each job group or job title, this analysis must consist of the total number of employee terminations, as well as the number of minority and the number of female terminations.

Please note that if you present terminations by job <u>title</u>, include the department and job group from which the person(s) terminated.

11. Please provide annualized compensation data (wages, salaries, commissions, and bonuses) by either salary range, rate, grade, or level showing total number of employees** by race and gender and total compensation by race and gender. Present these data in the manner most consistent with your current compensation system. If you maintain the information in electronic format, please submit in that format. <u>See</u> 41 CFR 60-1.4(a)(1). You may also include any other information you have already prepared that would assist us in understanding your compensation system(s). Alternatively, under the voluntary guidelines for self-evaluation of compensation practices, 71 Fed. Reg. 35114 (June 16, 2006), you have the option of seeking compliance coordination. If you so choose, you need not submit the annualized compensation data outlined in Item 11. However, you must notify OFCCP that you "seek compliance coordination under the voluntary OFCCP compensation self-evaluation guidelines."

**For this purpose, the method used to determine employee totals by the contractor should be the same as that used to determine employee totals in the organizational profile for the AAP.

Sample
Scheduling Letter
Construction Contractor Compliance Review

CERTIFIED MAIL
RETURN RECEIPT REQUESTED

REPLICA

[Name of Establishment CEO]
[Title of CEO]
[Establishment Name]
[Street Address]
[City, State, Zip Code]

OMB NO.
Expires

Dear [Name of CEO]:

The _____Company has been selected for an equal employment opportunity (EEO) compliance review. As discussed with your office, the review will commence on

_____.

The purpose of this review is to determine if your firm is in compliance with its EEO obligations, and what affirmative action steps are being taken to provide equal opportunity in each trade used on the construction projects in the _____
Standard Metropolitan Statistical Area (SMSA) under the provisions of the Federal regulations.

To assist in the conduct of the review, you are requested to have the following records and information available:

1. A copy of your EEO Policy Statement.

2. Records of EEO notices to subcontractors, if any, regarding their EEO obligations, monthly reporting.

3. A list of all ongoing Federal and non-Federal construction projects (by name and location) in the _____SMSA. For Federally funded projects, also indicate the funding agency, amount of contract and date of award.

3. A list of subcontractors by name, address, telephone number, project working on, dollar amount of contract, estimated starting and ending date, and geographical area that the subcontract is being performed.

4. A list of trade organization affiliations.

5. Any pertinent documentation which will evidence the implementation of each of the specific affirmative action standards required by 41 CFR 60-4.3 and compliance with the requirements of 41 CFR 60-4.3(a).

6. Correspondence and communications with unions and community organizations which concern the company's EEO obligations and recruitment efforts to hire women and minorities.

_____ Company

7. A current employee listing indicating name, race, sex, date of hire, and job classification in trade.

   The review period will cover _____, through _____. In order to facilitate the review, please have the following information available for inspection:

8. Total number of apprentices, minority apprentices, and female apprentices during the review period.

9. The total work hours, minority work hours, and female work hours in each trade on all projects in the _____ SMSA. Please provide a summary of work hours for each trade during the review period using the format in Attachment A.

10. The total overtime work hours, minority overtime hours, and female overtime hours in each trade on all projects in the _____SMSA. Please provide a summary of work hours for each trade during the review period using the format in Attachment A.

11. Payroll records for validation of hours worked during the review period.

12. Total number of new hires, minority new hires, and female new hires by trade during the review period.

13. A list of all employees who were laid off during the review period by name, race, sex, trade, and job classification.

14. A list of all employees who were recalled during the review period by race, sex, trade, and job classification.

REPLICA

15. The review will also include an examination of your Immigration and Naturalization Service (INS) I-9 Forms. Accordingly, please have available a list of all of your employees hired after November 7, 1986, or since the last inspection of the I-9 Forms for which you were found to be in compliance.

16. That list should include the termination dates of the aforementioned hires that are no longer employed at your establishment.

   This list may be a seniority list or a copy of a list used for other government agencies (e.g., a workers' compensation list, list used to make quarterly social security payments to the IRS). We also request that you provide information on when the last I-9 inspection was performed (if any), and by which government agency. This letter provides you the advance notice required by law (three business days) of our intent to inspect your completed I-9 Forms.

   It is requested that your company have a responsible official available to answer questions and discuss company policies and practices. It is also requested that you provide sufficient working space for the Compliance Officer. The Compliance Officer may also visit at least one project site and conduct employee interviews.

REPLICA

_____ Company
Page 3

Should you have any questions, please contact _____, Compliance Officer at
_____/

Sincerely,

District Director

Enclosure: Sample Work Hour Reporting Sheet

REPLICA

CONCILIATION AGREEMENT

BETWEEN

U.S. DEPARTMENT OF LABOR
OFFICE OF FEDERAL CONTRACT COMPLIANCE PROGRAMS

AND

[ESTABLISHMENT NAME]
[STREET ADDRESS]
[CITY, STATE, ZIP CODE]

PART I: GENERAL PROVISIONS

1.   This Agreement is between the Office of Federal Contract Compliance Programs (hereinafter OFCCP) and [Name of Establishment] (hereinafter _____).

2.   The violations identified in this Agreement were found during a compliance review of [Name of Establishment] which began on _____ and they were specified in a Notice of Violation issued on _____. OFCCP alleges that [Name of Establishment] has violated Executive Order 11246, as amended, Section 503 of the Rehabilitation Act of 1973, as amended, and/or the Vietnam Era Veterans' Readjustment Assistance Act of 1974, as amended, 38 U.S.C. 4212 (formerly 2012), and the implementing regulations at 41 CFR Chapter 60 due to the specific violations cited in PART II below.

3.   This Agreement does not constitute an admission by [Name of Establishment] of any violation of Executive Order 11246, as amended, Section 503 of the Rehabilitation Act of 1973, as amended, and/or the Vietnam Era Veteran's Readjustment Assistance Act of 1974, as amended, 38 U.S.C. 4212 (formerly 2012), and implementing regulations.

4.   The provisions of this Agreement will become part of [Name of Establishment]'s AAP. Subject to the performance by [Name of Establishment] of all promises and representations contained herein and in its Affirmative Action Program, all named violations in regard to the compliance of [Name of Establishment] with the OFCCP programs will be deemed resolved. However, [Name of Establishment] is advised that the commitments contained in this Agreement do not preclude future determinations of noncompliance based on a finding that the commitments are not sufficient to achieve compliance.

5.   [Name of Establishment] agrees that OFCCP may review compliance with this Agreement. As part of such review, OFCCP may require written reports, inspect the premises, interview witnesses, and examine and copy documents, as may be relevant to the matter under investigation and pertinent to [Name of Establishment]'s compliance. [Name of Establishment] shall permit access to its premises during normal business hours for these purposes.

6.   Nothing herein is intended to relieve [Name of Establishment] from the obligation to comply with the requirements of Executive Order 11246, as amended, Section 503 of the Rehabilitation Act of 1973, as amended, and/or the Vietnam Era Veterans' Readjustment Assistance Act of 1974, as amended, 38 U.S.C. 4212 (formerly 2012), and implementing regulations, or any other equal employment statute or executive order or its implementing regulations.

7.   [Name of Establishment] agrees that there will be no retaliation of any kind against any beneficiary of this Agreement or against any person who has provided information or assistance, or who files a complaint, or who participates in any manner in any proceeding under Executive Order 11246, as

amended, Section 503 of the Rehabilitation Act of 1973, as amended, and/or the Vietnam Era Veterans' Readjustment Assistance Act of 1974, as amended, 38 U.S.C. 4212 (formerly 2012).

8.   This Agreement will be deemed to have been accepted by the Government on the date of signature by the District Director for OFCCP, unless the Regional Director or Director, OFCCP indicates otherwise within 45 days of the District Director's signature of this Agreement.

9.   If at any time in the future, OFCCP believes that [Name of Establishment] has violated any portion of the Agreement during the term of this Agreement, [Name of Establishment] will be promptly notified of the fact in writing. This notification will include a statement of the facts and circumstances relied upon in forming that belief. In addition, the notification will provide [Name of Establishment] with 15 days from receipt of the notification to respond in writing, except where OFCCP alleges that such delay would result in irreparable injury.

Enforcement proceedings for violation of this Agreement may be initiated at any time after the 15-day period has elapsed (or sooner, if irreparable injury is alleged) without issuing a Show Cause Notice.

Where OFCCP believes that [Name of Establishment] has violated this Conciliation Agreement, evidence regarding the entire scope of [Name of Establishment]'s alleged noncompliance which gave rise to the Notice of Violations from which this Conciliation Agreement resulted, in addition to the evidence regarding [Name of Establishment]'s alleged violation of the Conciliation Agreement, may be introduced at enforcement proceedings.

Liability for violations of this Agreement may subject [Name of Establishment] to sanctions set forth in Section 209 of the Executive Order, 41 CFR 60-250.28, 41 CFR 60-300.63 and/or 41 CFR 60-741.28 and/or other appropriate relief.

PART II: SPECIFIC PROVISIONS

1.   Violation: [Description of specific violation.]

     Remedy: [Description of specific remedy.]
     [Name of Establishment] commits that this violation will not recur.

2.   Violation: [Description of specific violation.]

     Remedy: [Description of specific remedy.]
     [Name of Establishment] commits that this violation will not recur.

3.   Violation: [Description of specific violation.]

     Remedy: [Description of specific remedy.]
     [Name of Establishment] commits that this violation will not recur.

REPLICA

4.   Violation: [Description of specific violation.]

     Remedy: [Description of specific remedy.]
     [Name of Establishment] commits that this violation will not recur.

5.   Violation: [Description of specific violation.]

     Remedy: [Description of specific remedy.]
     [Name of Establishment] commits that this violation will not recur.

6.   Violation: [Description of specific violation.]

        Remedy: [Description of specific remedy.]
        [Name of Establishment] commits that this violation will not recur.

REPLICA

PART III: REPORTING

[Name of Establishment] agrees to furnish the OFCCP, _____ District Office, [OFCCP Street Address], [OFCCP City, State, Zip Code], with the following reports, due on _____.

1.   [Report #1 required from contractor.]

2.   [Report #2 required from contractor.]

3.   [Report #3 required from contractor.]

4.   [Report #4 required from contractor.]

This Conciliation Agreement will remain in effect for one (1) year from the date of OFCCP's approval.

PART IV: SIGNATURES

This Conciliation Agreement is hereby executed by and between the Office of Federal Contract Compliance Programs and [Name of Establishment], [Establishment City], [Establishment State].

DATE:_____   DATE:_____

_____   _____
[Name & Title of Establishment CEO]   [Name of Compliance Officer]
[Name of Establishment]   Compliance Officer
[Street Address]   Office of Federal Contract Compliance
[City, State, Zip Code]   Programs
                                                  _____ District Office

DATE:_____   DATE:_____

_____   _____
[Name of Asst. District Director]   [Name of District Director]
Assistant District Director   District Director
Office of Federal Contract Compliance   Office of Federal Contract Compliance
Programs   Programs
_____ District Office   _____ District Office

Sample
Show Cause Notice

CERTIFIED MAIL
RETURN RECEIPT REQUESTED

REPLICA

[Name of Establishment CEO]
[Title of CEO]
[Establishment Name]
[Street Address]
[City, State, Zip Code]

Dear [Name of CEO]:

In our letter of [date], you were requested to submit to this office within 30 days a copy of your establishment's Affirmative Action Programs (AAPs) and supporting documentation prepared in accordance with our regulations implementing:

- Executive Order 11246, as amended (41 CFR Part 60-2),
- Section 503 of the Rehabilitation Act of 1973, as amended (41 CFR Part 60-741), and
- the Vietnam Era Veterans' Readjustment Assistance Act of 1974, as amended, 38 U.S.C. 2012 (41 CFR Part 60-300).

To date, your Executive Order [Section 503 and/or 38 U.S.C. 2012] AAP[s] has [have] not been received.

Due to your firm's failure to submit an Executive Order AAP, we are now issuing this Notice to Show Cause, within 30 calendar days of your receipt of this Notice, why enforcement proceedings should not be initiated pursuant to Sections 208 and 209(a) of the Executive Order, as implemented by 41 CFR 60-1.26. Due to your firm's additional failure to submit a Section 503 and/or 38 U.S.C. 2012 AAP(s), we offer you a concurrent 30-day period to show why enforcement proceedings should not also be initiated pursuant to 41 CFR 60-741.28 and/or 41 CFR 60-300.28.

You are required to submit this [these] AAPs and the support data specified in our original request (copy enclosed) within 30 calendar days of your receipt of this Notice, or we shall recommend that enforcement proceedings be initiated in accordance with 41 CFR 60-1.26, 60-741.28 and/or 60-300.28. In those proceedings you would have an opportunity to request a hearing before any sanctions are imposed.

The submission of this [these] AAPs and support data does not preclude the identification of further violations, based either upon a finding during the desk audit or subsequent onsite review, that your AAPs do not meet the requirements of 41 CFR Part 60-2, Part 60-741 and/or Part 60-300 or that your establishment is not in compliance or has failed to comply in the past with the requirements of the Executive Order, Section 503 and/or 38 U.S.C. 2012 and their implementing regulations. We shall not withdraw this Notice to Show Cause until all deficiencies cited in this Notice (or subsequently identified in an Amended Show Cause Notice incorporating any additional violations found during the desk audit or onsite review) have been fully and satisfactorily resolved in a written Conciliation Agreement.

We wish to avoid enforcement proceedings if at all possible. Therefore, it is suggested that you meet with [Compliance Officer's Name], Compliance Officer at [time] on [date], at this office to conciliate a resolution of these violations. Please contact [Compliance Officer's Name] or [his/her] supervisor, [Supervisor's Name], at [telephone number] to confirm this meeting or to arrange another mutually acceptable time or date.

Sincerely,

REPLICA

[Regional/District Director]

Enclosure

cc: [Name of Corporate CEO]
       [Name of properly designated representative]

Standardized Compliance Review Report (SCRR)

This is the document your Compliance Officer will fill out during your desk audit.

The following 15 pages represent a blank SCRR document.

Special Thanks to John C. Fox of Fox, Wang & Morgan PC for securing this copy of the SCRR for us.

Secrets of Affirmative Action Compliance

REVIEW SUMMARY		DESK AUDIT ONLY	

1. ESTABLISHMENT NAME AND ADDRESS

2. PARENT NAME AND ADDRESS

3. LABOR AREA: SCTO County

% Fem.	% Min.	% Black.	% Hisp.	% A/PI.	% AI/AN
%	%	%	%	%	%

184. COMPLAINTS INVESTIGATED DURING REVIEW:
( ) = resolved
#_____ ( )   #_____ ( )

5. CONTRACT ESTABLISHING OFCCP JURISDICTION:
Case file location of required contract information (see instructions): EEO Survey

6. COMPANT CONTACTS:

		NAME	TITLE	PHONE
Establishment	CEO			
	EEO/AA			
Corporate	CEO			
	EEO/AA			

7. EEDS Contractor Research Documentation Form included in file: (x) File 1

8. Summarize (a) review background (type of business, etc.), (b) major review issues, (c) conciliation efforts and (d) overall compliance assessment and recommendation.

9.		COMPLIANCE OFFICER	ASST. DIST. DIRECTOR	DISTRICT DIRECTOR
	SIGNATURE			
	DATE			

[   ] = Continued
SCRR CC-50

-1-

488

PART A: PREPARATION

PAST PROBLEMS/KNOWN COMPLAINTS

. Past Problems. If there were no prior OFCCP compliance reviews or investigations, check here and go on to Part II below. ( )

f any problems were identified in any past OFCCP compliance review or complaint investigations, indicate yes or no as pplicable for part (a) below and list dates of the review/investigation and any major problems identified. At the point in this eview when you determine whether a problem has recurred, complete part (b) below.

ast Problems? Yes/No. Explain if yes.

b) Recurrence? Yes/No. Explain if yes.

I. Known Complaints. If no complaints were filed with other agencies, check here and go on to the next page.
   ( )

f a complaint(s) was/were filed with other agencies, list the agency with which it was filed, the basis, issue, current status and he area of the contractor's workforce it appears to concern. If at any point in the review there is a potential systemic problem n the complaint area, complete part (b) below.

a) Complaints filed.

Agency	Basis	Issue	Status	Job Group/Department

b) Potential Systemic Discrimination? Yes/No. Explain if yes.

-2-

PART A: PREPARATION
INITIAL REVIEW OF AAP AND SUPPORT DATA SUBMISSIONS
EXECUTIVE ORDER: AAP RECEIVED ON TIME [ ] YES [ ] NO
AAP DATES: RECEIVED:

	INDICATE		Y/N	
	INCLUDED ?	REASONABLE ?	ACCEPTABLE ? (TEXT ONLY)	IF NO PAGE #5
Workforce Analysis				
Utilization Analysis				
Job Group Analysis				
Availability Analysis				
Identification of Underutilization				
Current Goals				
EEO Policy Statement				
Dissemination of Policy				
Responsibility for Implementation				
Identification of Problem Areas				
Development of Action Programs				
Internal Audit and Reporting Systems				
Support of Community Action Programs				
Consideration of Minorities/Women Not Currently in the Workforce				
Sex Discrimination Guidelines				

SUPPORT DATA

Report on Goals				
Applicant Flow				
Hires				
Promotions				
Terminations				

DISABILITY/VETERANS AAP RECEIVED [ ] YES [ ] NO

	INDICATE		Y/N	
	INCLUDED ?	REASONABLE ?	ACCEPTABLE ? (TEXT ONLY)	IF NO PAGE #5
Policy Statement				
Review of Personnel Policies for Proper Consideration of Qualifications				
Review of Physical and Mental Job Requirements				
Reasonable Accommodation to Physical and Mental Limitations				
No Reduction in Compensation				
Outreach, Positive Recruitment and External Dissemination of Policy				

-4-

PART A: PREPARATION

EEO TREND ANALYSIS   ( ) EEO-1   ( ) EEO-6

Trends. Examine long term and short term trends of minority and female representation in: (a) the total workforce, (b) white collar EEO categories, (c) blue collar EEO categories. If there were negative trends, discuss below. Check here it there were no negative trends and go on to number 2. ( )

Category Patterns. Determine if there were any negative trends of minority or female representation by EEO category patterns. If there were negative trends, discuss below. If there were no negative trends, check here and go to number 3. ( )

Particular Group. Determine if there were any substantial disparities in the trends of a particular minority group or of men or women of any particular minority group. If so, explain below. If there were no negative trends check here and go on to the next page. ( )

Refer to the optional EEO-1/EEO-6 Trend Analysis Worksheets on pages 19 and 20 of the optional pages of the SCRR for guidance in assessing net changes in minority and female representation.

review of the EEO-1 statistics show the following:

4

PART B: AFFIRMATIVE ACTION

AAP and Support Data Submissions   [   ] Executive Order   [   ] Disabled/Veterans

#	AAP AND SUPPORT DATA PROBLEMS	ACTION TAKEN AND/OR PLAN TO RESOLVE	On-site ?
a	b	C	d

PART B: AFFIRMATIVE ACTION

AAP AND SUPPORT DATA SUBMISSIONS [ ] EXECUTIVE ORDER [ ] DISABLED/VETERANS

#	FINDINGS/CONCLUSIONS	Resolved	RESOLUTION? (If yes, how resolved. If no, recommended resolution)	AAP or other referenced pages	Included	Para. #
e	F	g	H	I	j	k
.						
.						
.						
.						
.						

5a

PART B: AFFIRMATIVE ACTION
EVALUATION OF GOOD FAITH EFFORT

Identify any goal areas where additional information is needed to evaluate good faith effort.						
QUESTIONS CONCERNING GOOD FAITH EFFORT						
#	GOAL AREA	MIN/ FEM	PR/ CUR YEAR	POSSIBLE CAUSES/PERTINENT AAP COMMITMENTS	ADDITIONAL INFORMATION NEEDED	ON-SITE ( )
A	b	c	D	e		g

[ ] Continued

PART B: AFFIRMATIVE ACTION
EVALUATION OF GOOD FAITH EFFORT

				CLOSEOUT DOCUMENT	
	(Continued)			Inc. ? ( )	Para. #
#	FINDINGS	GFE (Y/N)	IF NO, SUPPLEMENTARY INFORMATION, CONTRACTOR POSITION, EVALUAITON		
h	I	k	l	l	m
			.		

GFE = GOOD FAITH EFFORT
[ ] Continued

-6a-

PART B: AFFIRMATIVE ACTION

IMPLEMENTATION OF GUIDELINES ON RELIGION AND NATIONAL ORIGIN AND SEX DISCRIMINATION GUIDELINES		
Verify the contractor's implementation of the guidelines on religion and national origin and the sex discrimination guidelines, specifically including maternity leave policy. If not, explain: and, if you identify a potential discrimination problem, include the issue on page 14, "Summary of Potential Discrimination Problems."		
RELIGION/NATIONAL ORIGIN VIOLATION **YES/NO** **IF YES, EXPLAIN**		**Pot. Disc.**
SEX DISCRIMINATION VIOLATION **YES/NO** **IF YES, EXPLAIN**		**Pot. Disc.**

] = Continued
Working Paper Page(s) ___

-8-

PART B: AFFIRMATIVE ACTION
I. IMPLEMENTATION OF DISABILITY/VETERANS REQUIREMENTS

REFERENCE 41 CFR 60-741 AND 60-250	DID THE CONTRACTOR TAKE THE REQUIRED ACTION (YES/NO)? IF NO, EXPLAIN. SECTION 503 (DISABILITY) AND SECTION 402 (VETERANS)	PROBLEM [D/V]	RESOLVED	CLOSE-OUT DOC. INCL.	CLOSE OUT PARA #
HAS THE CONTRACTOR INVITED EMPLOYEES AND APPLICANTS TO IDENTIFY THEMSELVES AS INDIVIDUALS WITH DISABILITIES AND COVERED VETERANS? [741.5(c) (1); 60-250.(d)]					
HAS THE CONTRACTOR POSTED THE LOCATION AND HOURS DURING WHICH THE AAP MAY BE REVIEWED BY EMPLOY-EES AND APPLICANTS? [741.5(d); 250.5 (c)]					
HAS THE CONTRACTOR REVIEWED ALL PHYSICAL AND MENTAL JOB REQUIREMENTS? [.6 (c)]					
DID THE CONTRACTOR LIST ALL SUITABLE EMPLOYMENT OPENINGS WITH THE STATE EMPLOYMENT SERVICE? [250.4 only]					
DID THE CONTRACTOR UNDERTAKE APPROPRIATE OUTREACH, RECRUITMENT, DISSEMINATION OF POLICY AND OTHER AFFIRMATIVE ACTION? [.6(f)]					
HAS THE CONTRACTOR REASONABLY ACCOMMO-DATED THE PHYSICAL AND MENTAL LIMITATIONS OF QUALIFIED EMPLOYEES AND APPLICANTS WHO ARE INDIVIDUALS WITH DISABILI-TIES OR SPECIAL DISABLED VETERANS? [.6(d)]					

9

PART B: AFFIRMATIVE ACTION

II. IMPLEMENTATION OF DISABILITY/VETERANS REQUIREMENTS
[SECTION 503 (DISABILITY) AND SECTION 4212 (VETERANS)]

HAVE PERSONNEL PRACTICES A OR JOB REQUIREMENTS SCREENED OUT QUALIFIED INDIVIDUALS WITH DISABILITIES OF SPECIAL DISABLED VETERANS?

EVALUATE AT LEAST THE FACTORS BELOW. IF THE ANSWER TO ANY QUESTION IS YES, DISCUSS (A) THE PARTICULAR POLICY OR PRACTICE; (B) THE MEDICAL STANDARD INVOLVED AND THE JOB(S) TO WHICH IT APPLIES; (C) WHETHER THE CONTRACTOR CAN DEMONSTRATE THAT THE MEDICAL JOB REQUIREMENT INVOLVED IS JOB RELATED, CONSISTENT WITH BUSINESS NECESSITY AND WITH THE SAFE PERFORMANCE OF THE JOB; AND, (D) IF THE CONTRACTOR CANNOT SO DEMONSTRATE, IDENTIFY ANY QUALIFIED INDIVIDUALS WITH DISABILITIES OR SPECIAL DISABLED VETERANS WHO, AS A RESULT, HAVE BEEN REJECTED BECAUSE OF THEIR DISABILITY FOR JOBS WHICH THEY COULD HAVE PERFORMED, WITH OR WITHOUT REASONABLE ACCOMMODATION.

REFERENCE 41 CFR 60-741 AND 250	EVALUATION FACTORS	PRO- BLEM D/V	RE- SOLVED	CLOSE OUT INCL.?	CLOSE OUT PARA#
7. DO APPLICATION FORMS REQUEST INFORMATION ON MEDICAL CONDITIONS OR TYPE OF MILITARY DISCHARGE? (Y/N) [.6(d)]					
8. DOES THE CONTRACTOR HAVE A POLICY MANUAL FOR PERSONNEL (Y/N)? IF SO, ARE THERE ANY MEDICAL RESTRICTIONS GENERALLY OR FOR SPECIFIC JOBS? (Y/N) [.6(c)]					
9. DO POSITION DESCRIPTIONS/ QUALIFICATION STANDARDS CONTAIN ANY MEDICAL RESTRICTIONS? (Y/N) [.6(d)]					
10. DOES THE CONTRACTOR REQUIRE PRE-EMPLOYMENT PHYSICAL EXAMINATIONS OR PHYSICAL EXAMINATIONS FOR PROMOTIONS OR OTHER CHANGES IN STATUS? (Y/N) [.6(e)(c)]					
11. IS THERE ANY EVIDENCE FROM OTHER SOURCES (E..G., A COMPLAINT, INTER-VIEWS) OF BLANKET MEDICAL RESTRICTIONS OR RESTRIC- TIONS FOR PARTICULAR JOBS? (Y/N) [.6(d)]					

-9a-

PART C: POTENTIAL DISCRIMINATION
RESULTS OF REVIEW OF WORKFORCE ANALYSIS
Identify potential problems in minority and female representation, as applicable within departments/units, possible lines of progression (within departments or across department lines), grade or salary levels, supervisory positions vs. those supervised, etc.

WERE ANY PROBLEMS IDENTIFIED IN THE FOLLOWING:

Departments/Units?   YES/NO   If yes, explain

Lines of progression?   YES/NO   If yes, explain

Grade or salary level?   YES/NO   If yes, explain

Supervisory positions?   YES/NO   If yes, explain

Other problems?   YES/NO   If yes, explain

-10-

PART C: POTENTIAL DISCRIMINATION		
COMPENSATION/OTHER ANALYSES		
1. Compensation. Are there any indicators of compensation problems of minorities or women vs. non-minorities or men in the following areas:	**YES/NO Explain below if Yes**	**Violation # in LOC/CA**
[a] minorities or women in the same jobs as non-minorities or men, but clustered lower in the pay range for the jobs;		
[b] minorities or women concentrated in jobs that appear similar to those held by non-minorities or men but pay less, and;		
[c] any problems with broad compensation systems		
2. Other. Have any other analyses of potential discrimination issues identified problems?		

-12-

	PART C: POTENTIAL DISCRIMINATION			
	SUMMARY OF POTENTIAL DISCRIMINATION PROBLEMS			
#	TYPE (IRA, WFA, $, COMP., OTHER)	POTENTIAL PROBLEM	INVESTIGATIOVE PLAN/ ACTION TAKEN	On-Site
a	b	C	d	e
				Y

			PART C: POTENTIAL DISCRIMINATION			
#	D I S C F O U N D	R E S O L V E D ?	SUMMARY OF POTENTIAL DISCRIMINATION PROBLEMS	W O R K S H E E T S U S E D	I N C L U D E D	P A R A G R A P H #
F	g	h		I	j	k

-13a

Active Case Management Directive

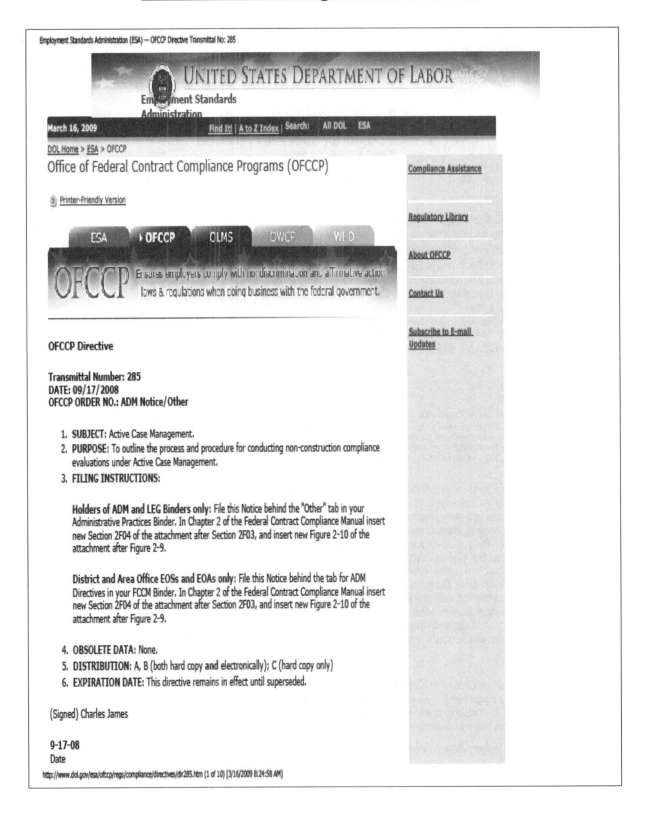

Employment Standards Administration (ESA) — OFCCP Directive Transmittal No: 285

Charles E. James
Deputy Assistant Secretary for
Federal Contract Compliance

EMPLOYMENT STANDARDS ADMINISTRATION
U.S. DEPARTMENT OF LABOR
OFFICE OF FEDERAL CONTRACT COMPLIANCE PROGRAMS
WASHINGTON, DC 20210

ADM NOTICE/OTHER

1. **SUBJECT:** Active Case Management.
2. **PURPOSE:** To outline the process and procedure for conducting non-construction compliance evaluations under Active Case Management.
3. **BACKGROUND:** On August 19, 1997, OFCCP revised its regulations at 41 CFR Part 60-1 and introduced a new approach for conducting supply and service (non-construction) compliance reviews of federal contractors. [1] Specifically, the regulation at 41 CFR 60 1.20 (a) (1) authorized the use of a "tiered" compliance review process. Under the tiered review system, a compliance review begins with a desk audit and may include an on-site review and an off-site analysis, if necessary. The regulations implementing VEVRAA and Section 503 contain parallel provisions. See 41 CFR 60 250.60, 60 300.60, and 60 741.60.

---

[1]/In addition, the 1997 revisions to the regulations at 41 CFR Part 60-1 authorized the use of "compliance evaluations" to examine contractor compliance with requirements of Executive Order 11246. The term "compliance evaluation" refers to any one or any combination of the following four investigative procedures: Compliance Review, Off-site Review of Records, Compliance Check, and Focused Review. The compliance evaluation approach was adopted in the VEVRAA regulations in November 1998, and incorporated in the Section 503 regulations in June 2005.

The chief purpose of Active Case Management (ACM) is to concentrate Agency resources on identifying and remedying cases of systemic discrimination, thereby enabling the Agency to use its resources in a more effective and efficient manner. ACM also aims to quickly and efficiently close out reviews where there are no indicators of systemic discrimination present. As most compliance reviews will require only an abbreviated desk audit, as opposed to the full desk audit and on-site, the ACM approach necessitates specific desk audit procedures and closure letters. ACM was put in place by Memorandum from the DAS dated July 25, 2003, and amended by Memorandum dated December 11, 2006. This Directive supersedes those memoranda, institutionalizes the ACM process, and incorporates it into the Directive System. The focus on systemic discrimination under ACM has led OFCCP to have record enforcement results (in terms of back pay and annualized salary and benefits and of number of workers recompensed who had been subjected to unlawful employment discrimination) for three consecutive years, FY 2005-2007.

4. **ACM PROCESS AND PROCEDURES:** All compliance reviews begin with a standard desk audit, which is a major component of a compliance review (41 CFR 60-1.20). By careful and systematic review of the documents and materials provided by covered contractors and subcontractors, OFCCP can begin to determine whether these establishments are: 1) complying with relevant

provisions of 41 CFR Chapter 60, and 2) providing equal employment opportunity on the basis of race, color, religion, national origin, sex, or status as a qualified individual with a disability or protected veteran. Under ACM procedures, only cases producing indicators of potential systemic discrimination (defined as potential affected classes of 10 or more applicants/workers) are to proceed beyond the desk audit phase with the exception of paragraph 5 ("Quality Control") below. [2]

2/The procedures set forth in this Directive differ from those specified in Federal Contract Compliance Manual (FCCM) Section 2U01, revised January 1999. In particular, 2U01 directs that "[i]n order to close the compliance review after the desk audit, the CO must ensure that no outstanding substantive issues exist." In order to accomplish this, Section 2U01 states that the CO may need to request additional materials for review during the desk audit, and also suggests areas for further inquiry. However, under the ACM process, the CO will pursue a case beyond the abbreviated desk audit stage only when indicators of possible systemic discrimination are found, except as described in paragraph 5. To the extent that there is a conflict between FCCM guidance and the ACM procedures contained in this Directive, the ACM procedures contained herein take precedence over FCCM instructions.

The following are the specific procedures for ACM:

a. Upon receipt of the contractor's Affirmative Action Program (AAP) and supporting personnel activity and compensation data, the Compliance Officer (CO) will determine if the personnel activity and compensation data requested in the scheduling letter have been received.[3] If so, the contractor's personnel activity and compensation data will be analyzed for possible systemic discrimination indicators (i.e., a potential affected class of 10 or more applicants/workers). If the data has not been received within the required time period (30 days from contractor's receipt of scheduling letter), the CO will contact the contractor establishment and follow regular show cause notice options.

b. Following these analyses, if there are **no indicators of systemic discrimination, no further action is to be taken and the contractor is to be issued the attached ACM closure letter** and the compliance evaluation closed as an off-site review of records. The closure letter notes that the closure should not be interpreted as a finding of compliance or of noncompliance.

3/Follow the procedures outlined in the FCCM 2D through 2F.

c. If **systemic discrimination indicators are found, a full desk audit is to be conducted.**[4] The desk audit results will determine whether the contractor should be asked to submit additional information regarding Executive Order 11246 compliance to the district/area office, and/or whether an on-site review is necessary. As part of the full desk audit, the CO will also evaluate the contractor's compliance with its obligations under Section 503 of the Rehabilitation Act, the Vietnam Era Veterans' Readjustment Assistance Act (VEVRAA), and Executive Order 13201.[5]If the CO does a full desk audit under Executive Order 11246, the CO is to do a full desk audit under Section 503 and VEVRAA. If the CO does an on-site review under Executive Order 11246, the CO is to also do an on-site review under Section 503 and VEVRAA. If the full desk audit or on-site review indicates that there is no systemic discrimination or apparent non-compliance with Section 503 or VEVRAA, one of the closure letters at Figure 2-8 or at new figure 2-10 in the FCCM (attached) is to be issued, and the compliance evaluation may close as an off-site review of records, a focused review, or a compliance review depending upon the circumstances. For all on-site reviews, the CO will document the contractor's compliance with Executive Order 13201 as provided in Directive Transmittal No. 269 (June 8, 2005). Closure information will be entered in CMS in the appropriate status codes. **At no time may a Notice of Violation that alleges discrimination be issued without an on-site review.**

4/Follow FCCM 2G through 2R.

5/Follow FCCM 2I as amended by the July 10, 2008 Directive entitled "Federal Contractor's Online Application Selection System."

    d. **If the AAP is not compliant and indicators of a possible systemic violation are absent, the CO should try to remedy the deficiencies during the desk audit.** If the AAP or supporting data deficiency is a major violation that cannot be resolved during the desk audit (e.g., summary personnel data is not maintained, but records are available for inspection on-site), the CO may conduct a focused on-site inspection. Based on the desk audit or on-site results, the appropriate closure letter at Figure 2-8 or 2-9 of the FCCM for technical or substantive AAP violation determinations would be issued and the appropriate CMS status closing codes entered.

5. **QUALITY CONTROL:** As a quality control measure, to ensure that contractors are developing and implementing AAPs and that they are maintaining the required supporting data, a full desk audit of the materials submitted is to be conducted on every 25th contractor listed in the Federal Contractor Selection System (FCSS), even in the absence of systemic discrimination indicators. In addition, a full compliance review - including an on-site review - is to be conducted on every 50th contractor listed in the FCSS, even in the absence of systemic discrimination indicators. These contractor establishments will be identified by the FCSS in the National Office. [6]

The desk audit results (in the every 25th review) will lead the CO to conclude whether additional information should be requested and/or whether an on-site inspection is required for unresolved problem areas. Included in the full desk audit will be an evaluation of the contractor's compliance with its obligations under Section 503 of the Rehabilitation Act, VEVRAA, and Executive Order 13201. Based on the desk audit and evaluation results for this group of contractors, Figure 2-8 or 2-9 of the FCCM will be issued to the contractor, and the case closed as an off-site review of records, a focused review, or a compliance review, as appropriate. For all on-site reviews, the CO will document the contractor's compliance with Executive Order 13201 as provided in Directive Transmittal No. 269. CMS status codes will be entered based on the type of review closure.

6. **REVIEW PERIOD:** As with other compliance reviews, contractor establishments that are evaluated using the ACM abbreviated desk audit process, as outlined in paragraph 4, above, will be exempted from a compliance evaluation for 24-months from the date of case closure.

6/The use of ACM procedures does not waive the right of OFCCP to conduct a full compliance review in accordance with 41 CFR Part 60-1 to determine compliance with any of the laws under its purview. Nor does it limit in any way OFCCP's authority to pursue an individual complaint of discrimination.

Employment Standards Administration (ESA) — OFCCP Directive Transmittal No: 285

(Signed) Charles James

Charles E. James
Deputy Assistant Secretary for
Federal Contract Compliance

Sept. 17, 2008
Date

Attachment: Revised FCCM Chapter 2 inserts.
New Figure 2-10
Current Figures 2-8 and 2-9

U.S. Department of Labor
Employment Standards Administration
Office of Federal Contract Compliance Programs

Federal Contract Compliance Manual (FCCM)
Chapter II-Desk Audit

2F04 ACM PROCESS AND PROCEDURES

All compliance reviews begin with a standard desk audit, which is a major component of a compliance review (41 CFR 60-1.20). By careful and systematic review of the documents and materials provided by covered contractors and subcontractors, OFCCP can begin to determine whether these establishments are: 1) complying with relevant provisions of 41 CFR Chapter 60, and 2) providing equal employment opportunity on the basis of race, color, religion, national origin, sex, or status as a qualified individual with a disability or protected veteran. Under ACM procedures, only cases producing indicators of potential systemic discrimination (defined as potential affected classes of 10 or more applicants/workers) are to proceed beyond the desk audit phase with the exception of the Quality Control provision below.[1]

The following are the specific procedures for ACM:

a. Upon receipt of the contractor's Affirmative Action Program (AAP) and supporting personnel activity and compensation data, the Compliance Officer (CO) will determine if the personnel activity and compensation data requested in the scheduling letter have been received.[2] If so, the contractor's personnel activity and compensation data will be analyzed for possible systemic discrimination indicators (i.e., a potential affected class of 10 or more applicants/workers). If the data has not been received within the required time period (30 days from contractor's receipt of scheduling letter), the CO will contact the contractor establishment and follow regular show cause notice options.

b. Following these analyses, **if there are no indicators of systemic discrimination, no further action is to be taken and the contractor is to be issued the ACM closure letter** (Figure 2-10) and the compliance evaluation closed as an off-site review of records. The closure letter notes that the closure should not be interpreted as a finding of compliance or of noncompliance.

1/The procedures set forth in this section differ from those specified in Federal Contract Compliance Manual (FCCM) Section 2U01, revised December 1998. In particular, 2U01 directs that "[i]n order to close the compliance review after the desk audit, the CO must ensure that no outstanding substantive issues exist." In order to accomplish this, Section 2U01 states that the CO may need to request additional materials for review during the desk audit, and also suggests areas for further inquiry. However, under the ACM process in this section, the CO will pursue a case beyond the abbreviated desk audit stage only when indicators of possible systemic discrimination are found, except as described in paragraph 5. **To the extent that there is a conflict between other FCCM guidance and the ACM procedures contained in this section, the ACM procedures contained herein take precedence.**

2/Follow the procedures outlined in the FCCM 2D through 2F.

c. **If systemic discrimination indicators are found, a full desk audit is to be conducted.**[3] The desk audit results will determine whether the contractor should be asked to submit additional information regarding Executive Order 11246 compliance to the district/area office, and/or whether an on-site review is necessary. As part of the full desk audit, the CO will also evaluate the contractor's compliance with its obligations under Section 503 of the Rehabilitation Act, the Vietnam Era Veterans' Readjustment Assistance Act (VEVRAA), and Executive Order 13201.[4] If the CO does a full desk audit under Executive Order 11246, the CO is to do a full desk audit under Section 503 and VEVRAA. If the CO does an on-site review under Executive Order 11246, the CO is to also do an on-site review under Section 503 and VEVRAA. If the full desk audit or on-site review indicates that there is no systemic discrimination or apparent non-compliance with Section 503 or VEVRAA, one of the closure letters at Figure 2-8 or 2-10 is to be issued, and the compliance evaluation may close as an off-site review of records, a focused review, or a compliance review depending upon the circumstances. For all on-site reviews, the CO will document the contractor's compliance with Executive Order 13201 as provided in Directive Transmittal No. 269. Closure information will be entered in CMS in the appropriate status codes. **At no time may a Notice of Violation that alleges discrimination be issued without an onsite review.**

3/Follow FCCM 2G through 2R.

4/Follow FCCM 2I as amended by the July 10, 2008 Directive entitled "Federal Contractor's Online Application Selection System."

d. **If the AAP is not compliant and indicators of a possible systemic violation are absent, the CO should try to remedy the deficiencies during the desk audit.** If the AAP or supporting data deficiency is a major violation that cannot be resolved during the desk audit (e.g., summary personnel data is not maintained, but records are available for inspection on-site), the CO may conduct a focused on-site inspection. Based on the desk audit or on-site results, the appropriate closure letter at Figure 2-4 or 2-6 of the FCCM for technical or substantive AAP violation determinations would be issued and the appropriate CMS status closing codes entered.

QUALITY CONTROL: As a quality control measure, to ensure that contractors are developing and implementing AAPs and that they are maintaining the required supporting data, a full desk audit of the materials submitted is to be conducted on every 25th contractor listed in the Federal Contractor Selection System (FCSS), even in the absence of systemic discrimination indicators. In addition, a full compliance review - including an onsite review - is to be conducted on every 50th contractor listed in the FCSS, even in the absence of systemic discrimination indicators. These contractor establishments will be identified by the FCSS in the National Office. [5]

Employment Standards Administration (ESA) — OFCCP Directive Transmittal No: 285

The desk audit results (in the every 25th review) will lead the CO to conclude whether additional information should be requested and/or whether an on-site inspection is required for unresolved problem areas. Included in the full desk audit will be an evaluation of the contractor's compliance with its obligations under Section 503 of the Rehabilitation Act, VEVRAA, and Executive Order 13201. Based on the desk audit and evaluation results for this group of contractors, Figure 2-8 or 2-9 of the FCCM will be issued to the contractor, and the case closed as an off-site review of records, a focused review, or a compliance review, as appropriate. For all on-site reviews, the CO will document the contractor's compliance with Executive Order 13201 as provided in Directive Transmittal No. 269. CMS status codes will be entered based on the type of review closure.

REVIEW PERIOD: As with other compliance reviews, contractor establishments that are evaluated using the ACM abbreviated desk audit process, as outlined in paragraph 4, above, will be exempted from a compliance evaluation for 24-months from the date of case closure.

5/The use of ACM procedures does not waive the right of OFCCP to conduct a full compliance review in accordance with 41 CFR Part 60-1 to determine compliance with any of the laws under its purview. Nor does it limit in any way OFCCP's authority to pursue an individual complaint of discrimination.

Figure 2-10:

ACM Abbreviated Desk Audit Closure Letter

Certified Mail
Return Receipt Requested

Date

Name of Establishment CEO
Title of CEO
Establishment Name
Street Address
City, State, Zip

Dear [Name of CEO]:

We recently scheduled a compliance review of the equal employment opportunity policies and practices at your establishment located at [address]. Based on the findings made during the desk audit, we have determined not to proceed further with the compliance review.

This letter is to notify you that the compliance review of your establishment has been closed. Please be aware that this did not constitute a comprehensive evaluation of your employment practices and policies. Accordingly, this closure should not be interpreted as either a finding of compliance, or of noncompliance. We encourage you to continue your efforts toward equal employment opportunity, and your vigorous self-monitoring of both your efforts and results.

We appreciate the cooperation and courtesies extended by you and your staff.

Sincerely,
[District Director]

cc: [Name of Corporate CEO]
[Name of properly designated representative]

Figure 2-8:

CLOSURE LETTER FOR NO APPARENT VIOLATIONS OR TECHNICAL VIOLATIONS

(Name of CEO)
(Title of CEO)
(Establishment Name)
(Street Address)
(City, State, Zip Code)

Dear (Name of CEO):

Our recent evaluation of your equal employment opportunity policies and practices at (Name and Location of the Establishment reviewed) has been completed.

[Select either Paragraph 2 or Paragraph 3 and 4]

(2)

During the compliance review process we found no apparent violations of Executive Order 11246, as amended, Section 503 of the Rehabilitation Act of 1973, as amended, or the Vietnam Era Veterans' Readjustment Assistance Act of 1974, as amended (38 U.S.C. 4212). This determination may be modified by the Regional Director, or by the Deputy Assistant Secretary for Federal Contract Compliance, within 45 days of the issuance of this letter.

[OR]

(3) or (4)

During the compliance review process, we identified and resolved the following violation(s): [identify the technical violation(s) resolved during the compliance evaluation, including the appropriate regulatory citation and specific remedy]. It is understood that this/these problem area(s) will not recur.

We found no additional apparent violations of Executive Order 11246, as amended, Section 503 of the Rehabilitation Act of 1973, as amended, or the Vietnam Era Veterans' Readjustment Assistance Act of 1974, as amended (38 U.S.C. 4212). This determination may be modified by the Regional Director, or by the Deputy Assistant Secretary for Federal Contract Compliance, within 45 days of the issuance of this letter..

[Option]

The Office of Federal Contract Compliance Programs sincerely appreciates the cooperation and courtesies extended by you and your staff during the conduct of the compliance review.

Sincerely,

(Name of District Director)
[District Director]

cc: (as appropriate)

Figure 2-9:

CLOSURE LETTER FOR SUBSTANTIVE VIOLATIONS

(Name of CEO
(Title of CEO)
(Establishment Name)
(Street Address)
(City, State, Zip Code)

Dear (Name of CEO):

Our recent evaluation of your equal employment opportunity policies and practices at (Name and Location of the Establishment reviewed) has been completed.

Subject to the implementation of commitments detailed in our Conciliation Agreement dated (date), it is the determination of this office that there are no further apparent violations of the requirements of our regulations. This determination may be modified by the Regional Director, or by the Deputy Assistant Secretary for Federal Contract Compliance. However, if neither the Regional Director nor the Deputy Assistant Secretary for Federal Contract Compliance takes action on it within 45 days of my signature on this Agreement, it shall be deemed approved

This determination does not preclude a future determination of noncompliance based on a finding that the commitments are not sufficient to achieve compliance.

[Option]

The Office of Federal Contract Compliance Programs sincerely appreciates the cooperation and courtesies extended by you and your staff during the conduct of the compliance review.

Sincerely,

(Name of District Director)
District Director

cc: (as appropriate)

🔺 Back to Top   www.dol.gov/esa

Frequently Asked Questions | Freedom of Information Act | Privacy & Security Statement | Disclaimers
Customer Survey | E-mail This Page | Important Notices

U.S. Department of Labor, Frances Perkins Building, 200 Constitution Ave., NW, Washington, DC 20210
www.dol.gov | Telephone: 1-866-4-USA-DOL (1-866-487-2365) | TTY: 1-877-889-5627 Contact Us

INDEX

ABOUT THE AUTHOR

William H. Truesdell

Currently, Mr. Truesdell is President of The Management Advantage, Inc., a personnel management consulting firm located in Walnut Creek, California. Prior to beginning this business in 1987, Mr. Truesdell spent over twenty years in management with American Telephone & Telegraph. More than half of that time was in human resources and the balance in operations management. He has managed both union-represented and non-represented work groups.

He is an expert in the subjects of personnel practices, employee handbooks, equal opportunity, and performance management programs. He was director of equal opportunity and affirmative action for AT&T's thirteen western states, and as such, was responsible for investigation of employee complaints and the negotiation of settlement agreements with federal and state enforcement agencies.

His firm has developed affirmative action plans for clients such as the State Bar of California, Perot Systems, Research Libraries Group, Textron, Magellan, First Consulting Group and many others. He is sought after as a speaker and trainer on the subject of Affirmative Action planning and implementation. Through his company, Mr. Truesdell is a member of the Better Business Bureau. He has also earned the designation as Academy Certified Diplomat (ACD) by the American Academy of Certified Consultants and Experts. Over the years he has been honored by various organizations for his community support and involvement. Those honors come from such organizations as the YMCA, Junior Achievement and the Private Industry Council. He has held leadership positions in employer groups such as the Northern California Employer's Round Table and the Northern California Industry Liaison Group. He holds a Bachelor of Science degree in Business Administration from the California State University at Fresno. He was an Extension Instructor for nine years at the University of California at Berkeley, Teaching human resource management courses, and he is certified as Senior Professional in Human Resources (SPHR) by the Society for Human Resource Management.

He is the author of several books including, *Secrets of Affirmative Action Compliance, Secrets of Investigating Discrimination Complaints, Secrets of Hiring and Firing, Easy Employee Supervision, Before Diversity* and *Your Entrepreneurial Success Story.*

Why Call Us
for Your Affirmative Action Plan Support?

16 Reasons

❑ You don't have time to do the work.

❑ You have never done AAP development before.

❑ You have never seen 41 CFR 60 regulations before.

❑ You want to keep revenues flowing from federal contracts.

❑ Your contract revenue is more than $50,000.

❑ You have more than 50 employees.

❑ You can't explain the difference between EEO and AA.

❑ You have just received a letter from the Department of Labor saying you are scheduled for an audit and you have no AAP ready.

❑ You want an expert in EEO and AAPs to teach, counsel, guide or support you in your work.

❑ You need someone to tell you what to expect in an audit.

❑ You have never been through a compliance review before.

❑ You don't want to say, "I'll take the risk," without knowing what that risk really is.

❑ You want someone who has taught these subjects to thousands of human resource managers across the country and at the University of California at Berkeley.

❑ You want to save the huge expense of hiring a recognized expert on a full-time basis.

❑ You know you need help from experts for other compliance requirements such as income taxes, law suits and medical issues. Affirmative Action compliance is no different.

❑ You want to do things right.

\aapbroc4.pub

Get Government Agreement on Your Affirmative Action Plan

Our Services Include:

Affirmative Action Plan Development

- ❑ Narrative Sections
- ❑ Statistical Analysis Reports Including:
  - ◆ Job Group Analysis
  - ◆ Availability Analysis (2-factor)
  - ◆ Utilization Analysis
  - ◆ Goals

Affirmative Action Plan Implementation

- ❑ Executive, Management and Employee Training
- ❑ Disparate Impact Testing (Impact Ratio Analysis)
- ❑ Job Description Development and Review
- ❑ Interviewer Training
- ❑ Policy Review and Revision Recommendations
- ❑ Development of Recruiting Sources
- ❑ Employee Surveys
- ❑ Discrimination Complaint Investigations
- ❑ Documentation Systems Supporting "Good Faith Effort"
- ❑ Basic EEO Training for all Personnel

Compliance Review Support

- ❑ Training for Managers in Compliance Review Process
- ❑ Advice & Counsel for HR Professionals
- ❑ Communication with OFCCP

\aapbroc2.pub

Notes

Notes

Notes